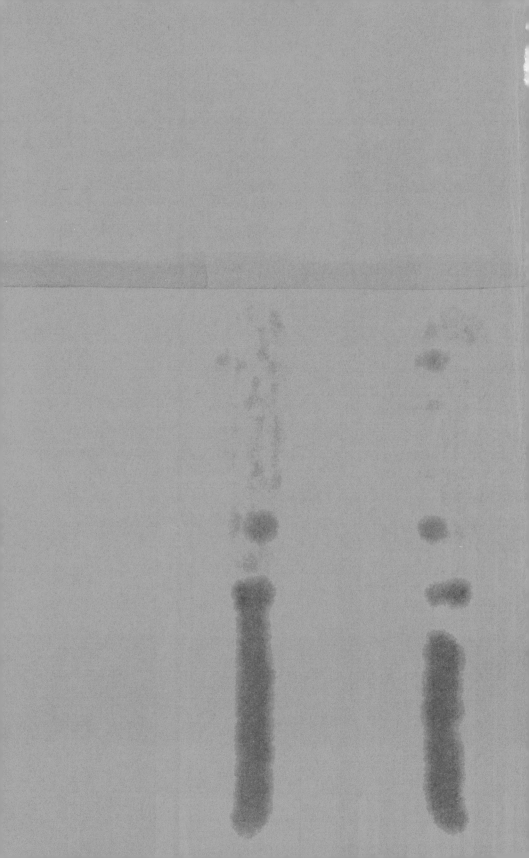

BUSINESS AND THE MEDIA

Edited by
Craig E. Aronoff
Georgia State University

Goodyear Publishing Company, Inc.
Santa Monica, California

Library of Congress Cataloging in Publication Data

Main entry under title:

Business and the media.

    Essays from a symposium sponsored by
the Chair of Private Enterprise, College of
Business Administration, Georgia State University, and held in Atlanta, Sept. 7–9, 1977.
    Includes index.
    1. Mass media and business—Con-
gresses I. Aronoff, Craig E. II. Georgia
State University. College of Business Administration.
HD59.B868   659.2   78-10394
ISBN 0-87620-104-4

Published by
Goodyear Publishing Company, Inc.
Santa Monica, California 90401

Y-1044-0

Current Printing (last digit):
10 9 8 7 6 5 4 3 2 1

Cover Design: Matt Pomaski

Printed in the United States of America

To Marvin and Pat Aronoff, my parents, who are at last discovering what they've wrought.

PREFACE

As an occasional journalist, a sometimes public relations practitioner, and a full-time business professor with considerable interaction with members of the business community, I have been aware for several years that all was not right between the various worlds that I professionally inhabit. Nor was this observation unique to me. More and more journalists and business people have spoken and written in public forums on the subject of their mutually troublesome relationships.

To bring form to this ongoing debate, I was able to bring together over two dozen prominent and articulate individuals representing the news media, business, labor, public relations, the consumer movement, and academia for "Business and the Media: A National Symposium." Sponsored by the Chair of Private Enterprise, College of Business Administration, Georgia State University, the symposium was held in Atlanta, Georgia on September 7–9, 1977. Abbreviated versions of the original essays collected in this volume were first presented at the symposium.

Many questions are raised in this book:
- How is business pictured by the media?
- Are the media biased in relation to business?
- Do the media emphasize the negative aspects of industrial and commercial enterprise?
- Does the media's pursuit of profit influence the pursuit of truth?
- Do the media serve as "watchdogs" of business behavior?
- Can the media motivate business to behave in a socially responsible manner?
- To what extent do the media facilitate public understanding of the American economic system and economic issues?
- How does business seek to influence the media?
- How do others seek to influence the media in opposition to business?
- How can the image of business be improved?
- How is labor pictured by the media?
- Are the media biased in relation to labor?
- How do labor relations in media industries influence reportage of labor?
- How can the media do a better job of reporting on business and economics?
- How can business help the media present a clearer and more accurate picture of business and economics?

Each of these questions is answered in not one, but many ways.

The book is organized into six sections. "Overviews" offers a variety of perspectives on the business/media relationship and establishes issues which will be alluded to throughout the volume. The authors in this section include a media critic, a business critic, two noted journalism educators, and the nation's leading public-service advertiser.

Sections 2 through 4 present the major parties in the debate—"Business Views" and "Media Views"—and the people who are frequently in the middle—"Public Relations Views." That these entities are not monolithic will become readily apparent to the reader since as many disagreements will be found within these sections as between them.

Sections 5 and 6 are rather special in that they look at two specific issues: "Organized Labor and the Media" and "The Business of the Media," and examine media industries and institutions as businesses. A thorough consideration of the business/media relationship requires insights into each of these subjects.

Special thanks for assistance in making this book possible are owed to Dr. Michael H. Mescon, holder of the Chair of Private Enterprise, and to my long-suffering friend and colleague, Dr. Francis W. Rushing. In the planning and administration of the Symposium, I am greatly indebted to my associate director, Dr. T. Kay Beck, and to my assistant, Ms. Gwen Owen, as well as to Ms. Barbara Burton, assistant to the Chair of Private Enterprise. Mrs. Colleen Martin and Ms. Diane Peacock withstood tremendous pressures in the preparation of the manuscript and have my admiration as well as gratitude. And finally, I thank Ms. Kathy Houser, who did for me a thousand small things which no one else could do.

Craig Aronoff
Georgia State University

CONTRIBUTORS

Burge, W. Lee
Crown, John A.
Cutlip, Scott M.
Davis, Harold E.
Efron, Edith
Ellis, Elmo
Evans, M. Stanton
Finn, David
Fox, Muriel
Green, Mark
Hurleigh, Robert F.
Johnson, Nicholas
Joyce, Tom
Keim, Robert P.
Lawrence, John F.
MacDougall, Curtis D.
Malabre, Alfred L., Jr.
Melody, William H.
Raskin, A. H.
Rutherford, William T.
Stoddart, Richard S.
Udell, Jon G.
Zack, Albert J.

CONTENTS

INTRODUCTION

The American republic has prospered because of two interdependent marketplaces which to a greater extent than in any other nation have been maintained as free in their operation. These are, of course, the marketplace of ideas and the marketplace of goods and services. The relatively unrestricted operation of the marketplace of ideas is maintained through freedoms of press and speech as guaranteed by the First Amendment to the Constitution of the United States. The marketplace of goods and services, more regulated than in the past but still characterized by broad individual discretion, is described as a system of free or private enterprise not guaranteed in law but deeply ingrained in the American ethos and American institutions.

In the course of two centuries the meaning of terms like "free enterprise" and "the free press" have changed with social, cultural, economic, and (particularly) technological changes. The technology and economics of "mass," as in "mass production" and "mass media," have restricted access in both the marketplace of ideas and the marketplace of goods and services. As access has become restricted, freedom of the press and freedom of enterprise, once provinces of the many, have become privileges of the few. Competition, which once supposedly assured that from the babble of many voices truth would emerge and that resources would be optimally allocated in relation to societal needs and values, has become less effective as a source of regulation as fewer entities have had the ability to compete.

The fundamental processes of press freedom and private enterprise have been concentrated and centralized. Today we see these processes not as characteristic of all the participants of our socioeconomic system, but as the venue of institutionalized segments of society called "the media" on one hand and "business" on the other. This is not to say that either business or the media is a monolithic entity speaking with one voice, but simply to suggest that this is the context in which the relationship between these institutions must be considered.

In many ways business and the media are kindred spirits. At the most obvious level the mass media in the United States are with very few exceptions profit-seeking organizations offering information as a commodity in the marketplace of goods and services. The mass media are part of the corporate world, replete with accounting, marketing, and labor problems. Editors and publishers of newspapers and magazines, owners and managers of television and radio stations are prominent members of the Chambers of Commerce, the Rotary Clubs, and the United Ways—in short, the business community—in virtually every city and town in America. These groups have been called "conservative" in this country, and rightly so, for they have a vested interest in the status quo.

Another area in which business and the media share common experience is that each has been the object of devil theories—that is, both are easy targets for blame in whatever evils and ills are experienced by individuals or society. Where once people held the devil responsible for societal difficulties, we've now seen them blamed successively and cumulatively on robber barons, Wall Street, Madison Avenue, and the mass media.

More subtly, we see business and the media responding to reduced competition in their respective marketplaces in similar ways. As the marketplace of ideas has become less self-regulating, other forms of regulation have emerged. Protected from governmental regulation by the First Amendment, the media in general and print media in particular increasingly have become characterized by the social responsibility theory of the press, a form of individual self-regulation based not on the marketplace, but on some editorial conception of the commonweal. Social responsibility has also become a key concept of the business world, where it is also a sort of self-regulation based on managerial conceptions of the public good, often used as an innoculation or antidote to governmental regulation.

Just as the media compete in the marketplace of goods and services, so business competes in the marketplace of ideas. On one level the competition is strictly commercial—the ideas are those of what to buy. This level is by no means a trivial one. Information is the stuff of free economic decision making. The greater our information, the closer we may approximate that greatest of all decision makers, *homo oeconimus,* economic man. Moreover, when the allocation of societal resources is made through numerous private economic decisions, the effectiveness of the marketplace depends on those decisions being well informed. Thus, as individuals and as a society our economic well-being depends upon a free flow of information.

On a second level business's competition in the marketplace of ideas is more profound and, in the long run, more telling in the maintenance of a predominately private enterprise economy. Since private enterprise is not guaranteed by the Constitution its ultimate arbiter is public opinion. In effect, private enterprise is an idea that competes with other ideas about the manner in which society should allocate its resources.

While it is true that America has never witnessed a completely private enterprise economy, it is also true that over the past half century individual economic decision making has been increasingly restricted. With the onslaught of consumerism, environmentalism, a revolution of rising entitlements, and initiatives flying banners of equality and health, business has been under unprecedented scrutiny and has received enormous criticism. Public opinion of business has ebbed to the extent that many in the business community claim that private enterprise is itself in jeopardy.

Since the media have often been the scrutinizers and the bearers, if not the originators, of criticism, business has been wont to blame the media for the decline of its standing in the public mind. As business once learned to deal with labor, politicians, and then regulators, it now seeks to learn how to deal with the media in its adversarial role. Businesspeople are irked by public exposure of what was once private information. They are angered by the seeming inability of reporters to understand and accurately report on business and economic issues. They are frustrated by the inadequacy of their own efforts to influence public opinion.

Recognizing the paramount importance of business and economic news in the 1970s, journalists have been forced to grapple with an area in which they have little experience or expertise. In many cases journalists claim that their job has been made more difficult by those who demand better coverage. Business executives are often described by journalists as arrogant, inaccessible, obscure, unresponsive, manipulative, and insensitive to the requirements of the media.

To progress beyond unproductive charges and countercharges, I have attempted in this volume to bring together thoughtful, experienced, and constructive voices representing the diverse parties who participate in and observe business/media interactions.

SECTION 1 OVERVIEWS

The issues growing from the relationship between business and the media are many, complex, and diverse. Thoughtful observers of the interaction of these societal institutions do not agree as to the nature and definition of the issues, much less on their causes and effects, descriptions and prescriptions. Moreover, any given observer's identity doesn't necessarily offer good clues as to the stand that individual will take. Businesspeople are almost as likely to lay blame on business as on the media when problems arise among the two.

As with all relationships as complicated as this one, social, cultural, historical, economic, moral, political, psychological, technological, even linguistic factors come into play. All of these factors are considered by various authors at various places in this book. But prior to launching into the more specialized viewpoints of journalists, public relations practitioners, and businesspeople, and before looking at the media as businesses or discussing the nature of labor/media relationships, it is necessary to step back for broader perspectives. In this first section of *Business and the Media,* five authors offer more or less generalized overviews on issues that will be addressed throughout the book.

While each of the three sections that follow this one derive continuity from what their authors are, this one is marked by what its authors are not. None of the authors is a reporter, editor, media manager, public relations practitioner, or intimately involved with major corporations. Though they are involved in the business/media relationship, each of these individuals is, in a sense, at least one step removed. For this reason they may be more able to see the forest rather than just the trees.

The authors in this section are necessarily a very mixed group: a media critic, a business critic, the head of the Advertising Council, and two of the nation's most prominent journalism educators. Collectively they describe from their own particular points of view the hows and the whys of the business/media relationship and attempt to articulate some

1

of its more pressing issues and problems. Some choose to place business and the media in the broadest of social and cultural contexts, while others bring a historical perspective to the discussion. Still others single out specific issues with which to deal.

More than anything else, however, these authors should raise questions in the reader's mind.

THE MEDIA AND THE OMNISCIENT CLASS

EDITH EFRON

In order to understand the complex relationship between business and the media, both institutions must be viewed in cultural context—especially since the media reflect cultural values. Describing this cultural context, Edith Efron sees a population baffled by modern science, technology, and industry. Like primitives worshipping their idols, today's society has seen the rise of modern idolaters who invest scientists, technologists, and industrialists with omniscience and then condemn them for not knowing the answers to all problems.

According to Efron, the media belong to this new class of primitives, a class which combines a morbid ignorance with a driving hostility for business and a lust for power over it. Most reporters, she claims, are mindless transmission belts for even the most ludicrous charges against business, the symbolic scapegoat for all ills in this society.

A "News Watch" columnist for TV Guide, *Ms. Efron has worked for the* New York Times, Time *magazine, and* Life *magazine. She has written for* Esquire, Barron's Weekly, Commentary, *and other publications and is the author of* The Newstwisters.

The press is a derivative institution. It reflects, it does not create, the culture in which it functions. One cannot, therefore, discuss press treatment of a complex subject without setting it in cultural context. This is certainly the case in the media treatment of business and industry—and particularly in the area of the mountingly frenzied charge that science, technology, and industry constitute a threat to the health and the life of the citizenry. To understand the role of the press, one must first know the cultural context of that mounting frenzy.

Paradoxically, the press's role can best be identified by removing oneself entirely from our sophisticated modern society and briefly examining a certain aspect of primitive life. Part of the entrenched lore of modern societies is the tale of the savage who, at the sight of the magic stick carried by alien intruders which hurls death across great distances, or at the sight of the giant silver bird in the sky which carries alien intruders in its belly, falls on his knees and worships those intruders as gods. This is not an apocryphal tale. As we know, the Stone Age natives of several New Guinea islands in the South Pacific, which served as U.S. bases during World War II, have turned the awesome flight of thousands of airplanes bearing unintelligible cargo into a divine manifestation and pray for their reappearance and for the permanent bounty that will accompany their return—a phenomenon known as "the cargo cults."[1]

This is usually discussed with a certain amusement, but it merits serious examination, for it embodies certain psychological truths about mankind in general. There are only a limited number of reactions to the assumption by a human being that he is in the presence of gods—beings with a superior form of consciousness—and anthropology, indeed, the history of religion, records all of them. The gods are presumed to be omniscient. The individual is filled with awe before that omniscience and with a sense of his own powerlessness. He grovels and worships and seeks to appease the Omniscient Ones. Perceiving them as responsible for his destiny, he seeks their protection by means of rituals of prayer. If that protection does not arrive, however, or if harm befalls him, he may grow angry and seek to punish the Omniscient Ones for what he then perceives as their willful malevolence—this time, in the form of ritual ceremonies of scapegoating. If the malevolence persists he will seek a yet more powerful juju—a different set of omniscient gods to pit against the first set in order to control or cancel out their power, in a search for what might be called metaphysical checks and balances. And, finally, when he is certain that he has found such an omniscient counterforce, the savage may even seek to destroy the power of the first set of Omniscient Ones.

THE MODERN SAVAGE

There is less than meets the eye in the amusement with which many moderns contemplate primitive responses when they are directed toward modern technology, for, in the most fundamental sense, millions of moderns are not significantly different in their approach to technology from the savage. There are surface differences, of course. Familiar from birth with what they unself-consciously call technological "miracles," the moderns do not fall on their knees before a new "miracle" invention or a new "miracle" drug, nor do they worship industrial innovators as gods. But they experience a sense of terrifying impotence before many forms of the new technology. The superhuman scientists who create new and evil machines, drugs, or life forms in laboratories, or the omniscient computers that take over the world, are enduring themes in popular art.[2] Such moderns understand the root source of industrial achievements no more than does the savage. The mental operations that have produced the phenomena are unknown to them. They do not understand the reasoning process, the method of deduction and induction, the disciplined formation of hypotheses and the systematic testing of those hypotheses by the law of noncontradiction, nor do they understand the trial-and-error process or the integration of new knowledge with old. In effect, they do not understand the processes of learning, of creativity, of discovery, of invention. To them, the achievements of science, technology, and industry *are* actually miracles. And the minds from which these miracles spring are perceived, in some sense, as omniscient. Indeed, to the modern primitive the entire science-technology-industry triad is perceived as an omniscient class.

It is consequently not surprising that we see in our own society the identical series of responses to the Omniscient Ones that we find in savage cultures. There is the incomprehending worship of the omniscient scientists and technologists in those segments of the population which assume that all knowledge is now available, that all problems can now be solved, and that industry has both the power and the moral obligation to solve them. The familiar religious incantation begins with the words, "If we can put a man on the moon, why can't we . . ." The modern primitive terminates this phrase with the mention of the particular bounty he desires, ranging from the abolition of all existential penalties for worker, consumer, and parental laziness, irresponsibility, and lack of foresight; through the elimination of stupidity, bigotry, and crime; to a cure for all known diseases—indeed for the prevention of death itself.

There is the anger, denunciation and scapegoating of the omniscient class when it fails, for reasons always seen as willfully malevolent, to provide the desired protection and bounty. And that anger is always accompanied by the search for an alternative juju—a counterbalancing omniscient being, the State—whose power can be pitted against industry to force it instantly to comply with the frustrated desires. The religious incantations here are, "Let's pass a law," or "Let's regulate, or nationalize, or expropriate industry" in the supposition that coercion by the State will instantly produce the demanded benefactions.

And finally, in the face of enduring evidence that industrial omniscience is not functioning as desired, or that some measure of risk or danger even accompanies some of its benefactions, there is the desire to destroy industry altogether. And here, the deadly incantation is, "Stop growth!" usually accompanied by ritual keening over the natural paradise on earth that existed before this powerful and malevolent force had appeared.

All these eminently modern responses to industry are, in psychological essence, identical to the various mental processes of the savage in the face of omniscient beings.

Who are these modern savages? Some, of course, are actual primitives. It is quite clear that a primal scream of irrationality has emerged in our society, in which virtually all intellectual discipline and content has been eviscerated from our public educational system. We are engulfed by the rise of illiteracy, by the loss of even the most minimal intellectual skills, by the very destruction of language itself—the very means of conceptualization. We are surrounded by graduates from our schools who communicate in symbolic grunts, the "now" generation which allows nothing into its consciousness but the immediate and the sensorially perceived. And, noncoincidentally, this degeneration is accompanied by a wave of such phenomena as witchcraft, fanatical religious cults, a growing belief in magical powers of consciousness, in telepathy, in ESP, and above all in psychokinesis—the power of consciousness to dominate external existence without the burdensome intervention of mind. All this is now part of our modern society.[3] Ironically, it is precisely during this period that science and technology have exploded in creativity and in increasingly specialized complexity, so that the cognitive abyss between the scientific culture and the primitive is now wider than ever in history. Under such circumstances it is not surprising to find a replication of savage responses to our complex scientific-technological-industrial institutions.

It would be an enormous error, however, to assume that we are talking here about some abandoned underclass or *lumpenproletariat.* These are also characteristics of millions in our so-called highly educated classes. A college degree is no guarantee of an absence of such characteristics. Positions of great power and influence are held today by men with the minds of primitives. Indeed, there is serious reason to believe that a primitive lack of comprehension of the world of science-technology-industry is in the cultural ascendency, that it dominates many aspects of our universities, our bureaucracies, our professions, and our media.

Several years ago Irving Kristol sent a shock wave of recognition through those who were increasingly aware that some kind of destructive lunacy had been set loose among those commonly called the "intelligentsia." He wrote a now-historic essay called "Business and the New Class," published in *The Wall Street Journal,* in which he loosely defined that "new class" as "a goodly proportion" of the academic, professional, media, bureaucratic, and foundation worlds.

"Members of the 'new class,'" he wrote, "do not 'control' the media, they *are* the media—just as they *are* our educational system, our public health and welfare system and much else. . . ." And he said:

> We have managed to create a generation of young people which, for all the education lavished on it, knows less about the world of work—even the world of their fathers' work—than any previous generation in American history. They fantasize easily, disregard common observation, appear to be radically deficient in that faculty we call common sense.
>
> Nor, it must be said, are their teachers in a much better condition. The average college professor of history, sociology, literature, political science, sometimes even economics, is just as inclined to prefer fantasy over reality.[4]

Above all, Kristol pointed out, this new class is hostile to the business community, and his explanation is as follows:

> [O]ne should understand that the members of this class are "idealistic" in the 1960's sense of that term—i.e., they are not much interested in money but are keenly interested in power. Power for what? The power to shape our civilization—a power which, in a capitalist system, is supposed to reside in the free market. This "new class" wants to see much of this power redistributed to government, where they will then have a major say in how it is exercised. . . . [They] are convinced they incarnate "the public interest" as distinct from all the private interests of a free society.[5]

Kristol, in sum, declared that the new class displays two fundamental characteristics: it combines a morbid ignorance with a driving hostility for business and a lust for power over it. He was referring, in fact, to a morbid ignorance of economics. But the same morbid ignorance prevails in the realms of science and technology, which are the hidden base of modern business.

In effect, this new class seeks to *become* the Omniscient State which forces science, technology, and industry to execute its whims and wishes. This aspiration could only emerge in people who are morbidly ignorant of the nature and genesis both of industrial innovation and production. Only such people could conceivably imagine that brute force—the only power actually possessed by the State—can generate scientific, technological, and industrial discovery. But this is precisely what the new class imagines—just as it is imagined by all compulsive interventionists, by all socialists, by all communists, by all totalitarians. This entire group of people always assumes both that the State is omniscient, and that it can force ideas, knowledge, discovery, and achievement out of producers by controls, threats, punishment, jail sentences, and ultimately by killing them. The unbroken historical record of the failure of all States to produce science, technology, and industrial wealth in this fashion—indeed, an unbroken historical record of the paralysis and destruction of innovation and productivity by the State—does not affect the new class in the slightest. A world full of evidence does not deter them. As Kristol says, they are dominated by fantasy, not fact. They believe in the Omniscient State with the full fervor of primitives—which is to say, they believe in "power," which is to say, they believe in intimidation, fear, and guns. And they aim these guns right at that creative coalition of reason, science, technology, and industry that has emerged under our privately owned, profit-oriented industrial system. They are a special twentieth-century breed of anti-capitalist primitives.

THE POLITICS OF THE NEW CLASS

It is important to understand the political nature of the new-class primitives, because their politics is actually their disguise. Anti-capitalist attitudes have a high social status in our culture, and it is precisely that high status that conceals from so many the fact that in the new class we are actually confronting ignorant, fantasy-ridden primitives. Or, to be more precise, we are confronting the persistent primitive fantasy of a world in which all will one day be protected from life's risks and pains by a class of omniscient and infallible producers who will be forced to provide the dreamed-of safety and security. That religious fantasy, often called "socialism," is widely viewed today among many in our so-called educated classes as the ultimate in social vision. And there is understandable confusion in a society where those who most loudly lay claim to being the wisest among us, with the right to speak in the name of "the people," are actually in the grip of mystical delusions.[6]

The prestigious anti-capitalist politics—actually the new "public-interest" politics—with it reputation as an expression of elite wisdom, actually serves as cultural camouflage for the primitivism. That cultural camouflage reaches its peak when scientists themselves join the anti-capitalist throngs, almost invariably moved by a desire to control science, technology, and production in fields other than their own. It is, in fact, the combination of political and scientific camouflage that protects this wave of neoprimitivism and gives it its current awesomely destructive influence in our industrial society.

This, then, is the broad context in which to consider the anti-business bias of the media. And in this paper, I will illustrate that bias with two complex examples: the nuclear-power controversy and the controversy over toxic and carcinogenic substances, and the coverage they have received in the mass media, specifically in network news.

NUCLEAR POWER: PRO AND CON

First, the controversy over nuclear power. This is an explicit battle over the *safety* of nuclear technology and is entirely focused on the state of knowledge of the nuclear scientists and nuclear engineers. It is thus important to know who are the people that constitute the two sides of the highly polarized controversy and to assess the state of their knowledge of nuclear science and technology.

The opposition to nuclear power generally comes from the largely lay public-interest groups led by Ralph Nader, the consumerist and environmentalist groups, and an associated group known as the Union of Concerned Scientists.[7] Without scientific supporters the opinions of the public-interest groups would actually be of no great significance—particularly since the majority of the public has consistently supported the building of atomic energy plants and so, until recently, has the government. Who are these "concerned scientists"? The literature of this organization includes several documents worthy of note which answer this question.[8] One is a short manifesto entitled, "Scientists' Declaration on Nuclear Power," and subtitled, "From the Declaration presented to Congress and the President of the United States on the 30th anniversary of the atomic bombing of Hiroshima and signed by more than 2,000 biologists, chemists, engineers, and other scientists."

Curiously, in the UCS's own short summary of the signers of their Declaration there is no mention of nuclear scientists or engineers. To illustrate this group they list fifty-five of the most prestigious scientific names on their list. Of the fifty-five, sixteen are biologists, five are chemists, three are M.D.'s (one of whom is a surgeon); two are mathematicians, one is a geologist; three are mechanical and electrical engineers; and two are not even identified in terms of scientific specialties, but merely as members of scientific research organizations. In addition, there are seventeen physicists, twelve of whom are *not* specialists in nuclear physics. In that entire list of fifty-five concerned scientists—offered as the cream of the antinuclear crop—only five men are identified by UCS as having had anything to do with nuclear physics in their professional lives, and one is James Bryant Conant, president emeritus of Harvard University, who was head of the Manhattan Project and later high commissioner of Germany. He was actually an administrator and statesman.

In fact, only four people on that entire list of fifty-five allegedly stellar scientists are identified as having any significant knowledge of nuclear science, and only one of the four is a nuclear scientist of resounding fame—George Kistiakowsky, professor emeritus of Harvard. Given the nature of their fellow signers, their alliance with the others can scarcely be defined in terms of a common expertise. It can only be a political alliance.

And that deduction is confirmed by the very manifesto, for the UCS literature opens with a demand that construction of nuclear power plants be blocked: "We . . . urge a drastic reduction in new nuclear power plant construction starts before major progress is achieved in the required research and in resolving present controversies about safety, waste disposal and plutonium safeguards." And it ends with a demand that no nuclear technology be exported to foreign countries. It is a political statement. The manifesto was geared to the anniversary of Hiroshima because the UCS always seeks deceptively to associate peacetime atomic energy with exploding nuclear bombs, in full awareness that light-water reactors are not bombs and cannot possibly explode. That, too, is a political propaganda statement. Finally, the UCS's list of scientists itself is a form of propaganda by men, most of whom are seeking to use their status as scientists in non-nuclear fields to make people believe that scientific figures who "know" are opposed to nuclear power. In the context of nuclear power, however, most must be considered laymen themselves and constitute a set of political clones of lawyer Ralph Nader. Some, of course, may even be followers of Barry Commoner, that other famous leader of the anti-nuclear group, a biologist who has declared himself expert in both the realms of energy and economics and has published a book explaining that only socialism can solve our energy problems.

The Union of Concerned Scientists is well aware of the humiliating shortage of bona fide nuclear scientists and engineers on its list of luminaries. To strengthen their position, they include, along with their manifesto, a reference to two other scientific allies. They report that "two present members of the UCS staff resigned from the federal government's nuclear safety program"[9] as an act of disapproval of the Atomic Energy Commission, which allegedly is indifferent to the hazards of nuclear plants. One might think that with such a shortage of experts in the field, the UCS would eagerly name these two experts. They are not named, and it's not difficult to guess at the reason. There have been three such resignations. Two of those who resigned have been exposed in *Newsweek* magazine as members of a fanatical religious cult called "Creative Initiative." That cult teaches, among other things, that God disapproves of plutonium.[10]

All this is what is meant by the concept "scientist" in the literature of the Union of Concerned Scientists, the major scientific organization dedicated to the blockage of nuclear power plants. It is not science at all, but adversary politics masquerading as science, a politics which seeks the unilateral arrest of nuclear energy in the United States while demanding as a precondition of the continuation a guarantee of a risk-free technology—namely, while demanding that nuclear science meet the standard of omniscience.

Now, where in this controversy do the actual nuclear physicists and nuclear engineers stand? The overwhelming majority stands, of course, on the side of those who desire to continue the building and development of nuclear power plants. In the state of California, when the public was given an opportunity to vote on a "Proposition 15" which, like the UCS literature and manifesto, advocated the blocking of nuclear plants if absolute guarantees of risk-free technology were not forthcoming, 5,700 nuclear scientists and engineers, including a group of Nobel laureates in nuclear physics, signed various manifestos condemning Proposition 15. Yet other such manifestos were circulated at press conferences throughout the nation, signed by such eminences as Nobel laureates Eugene Wigner, Hans Bethe, Willard F. Libby, James Rainwater, and Felix Bloch, as well as by James Van Allen, discoverer of the Van Allen radiation belts; Edward Teller, head of the Lawrence Radiation Laboratories; Norman Rasmussen, professor of nuclear physics at the Massachusetts Institute of Technology; Ernest C. Pollard, a leading authority on the effects of radiation on living cells; Luis W. Alvarez, John Bardeen, Edward M. Purcell, I. I. Rabi; Lee Du Bridge, president emeritus of the California Institute of Technology; and physicist Robert E. Marshak, head of CUNY.

In all these manifestos, the pro-nuclear-power scientists make these points: (1) that the twenty-year international record of safety in nuclear plants was higher than that in any other industry; that in two decades there has never been a radiation-related fatality; and that statistics reveal that safety in nuclear plants is far higher than that in any other energy industry; (2) that such technological problems as still require solution can only be solved in the course of practical application, and that, by definition, technology cannot be improved in an existential void; and (3) that given the finite nature of fossil fuels and the limited state of energy technology outside the fossil-fuel field, nuclear power is the only certain long-range source of energy available to the United States, whose industrial civilization, military security, and very existence depends on energy.[11]

One such document, called "Scientists' Statement on Safety of Nuclear Energy," contained an attack on the intellectual honesty of many in the anti-nuclear forces, as well as on Proposition 15 itself:

> In recent months, we have become increasingly alarmed by a shift in emphasis in the current national debate on nuclear energy. All too often, arguments have been supported by quotations taken out of context, untested assumptions, and emotional rhetoric; scientific data have been stretched far beyond their area of reliability. In defense of their preconceived stands, some participants in the debate have even raised improbable scenarios of the future which can only lead to confusion and fear.[12]

That is the other side of the nuclear-energy controversy—the side taken by the authentic experts in the field, who neither claim, nor tolerate demands for, omniscience. It is political only to the degree that one construes a desire to keep the United States and its citizens alive as a political position open to dispute.

THE MEDIA AND THE DEBATE OVER NUCLEAR ENERGY

We can now briefly examine the media performance in this context. The media, in sum, have been faced with Ralph Nader's largely ignorant legions on one side, and on the other with virtually all of the greatest nuclear scientists in the world. How have they covered this controversy? Only one formal study of this question exists. *Barron's Weekly* commissioned me to do it, and it was published in *Barron's* on June 7, 1976. The study summarizes and quotes from every network news story between the dates of February 3, 1976, and June 7, 1976, terminating the day before the first citizens' referendum on nuclear power—California's referendum on Proposition 15. The news reports covered a period of four months, during which the two conflicting groups fought to influence the voters. The detailed study should be read, of course, but its six major findings can be summarized here:

1. Not once during the four-month period was the voice of a single Nobel laureate or prominent nuclear scientist who favored atomic energy plants heard on any of the three networks. Their press conferences, their manifestos, their positions, their reasoning, their profound expertise might as well not have existed. Nor was the nation told that the 5,700 California nuclear engineers had come out in support of atomic power. With few exceptions, the voices of defenders of atomic power heard on the networks were industry executives—businessmen who were cast as defensively guarding their profits from the attacks of "idealists," who alone cared about the safety of "the people."
2. The voices and positions that dominated the network news were those of three men who had resigned from regulatory positions in a protest carefully timed to coincide with the controversy over Proposition 15. CBS's "60 Minutes" gave over one full segment of its show to such a man, who warned that nuclear technology was not risk-free, therefore acutely dangerous. The two others dominated the news for the full four-month period. They were the two members of the religious cult mentioned earlier. Though, at the height of the up-

roar, *Newsweek* broke the story of their cultist connections and reported that the group was widely described as "fanatical," not one network put this information on the air or independently pursued that story.

3. The warnings of the two cultists were ceaseless and thunderous; that a frightful nuclear catastrophe was imminent; that the intellectual complexities of nuclear science and technology were overwhelming (to them); and that the technology was not guaranteed to be eternally risk-free. The nuclear power plants were incessantly attacked for violating the standard of omniscience and infallibility. Network newsmen competed for the honor of airing reports of old accidents and problems that had occurred at nuclear plants—accidents which had not caused fatalities, and problems that had been or were being solved. The details of one particular accident, a fire at the Brown's Ferry nuclear plant, were told and retold on the air in terms of the stark horror that might have been unleashed had the safety technology failed: a cloud of deadly radioactivity, the reporters explained, would have moved over a huge area and killed hundreds of thousands, indeed millions. The fact, of course, is that the safety technology did not fail; it worked when an accident occurred; and that is the purpose of safety technology. But this was not the perspective stressed on the air by a press gripped by the standard of omniscience.

4. Not once during the four-month period was there a mention of the Rasmussen Report, the 3,000-page safety study conducted for the Atomic Energy Commission and the U.S. Nuclear Regulatory Commission by sixty nuclear scientists and engineers under the supervision of MIT's Norman Rasmussen. On the basis of twenty years of operation of nuclear plants, the scientists concluded that the chances of death to any individual as a result of a reactor accident (assuming 100 plants) was 1 in 5 billion. Nor did any network see fit to put accidental death itself into perspective by making it clear that we all continuously and inevitably live with a factor of risk: the chances of any individual's being killed in any one year by a motor vehicle is 1 in 4,000; by falls, 1 in 10,000; by fires, 1 in 25,000; by drowning, 1 in 30,000; by guns, 1 in 100,000; by air travel, 1 in 100,000; and by any type of accident at all, 1 in 1,600.[13] The only message that went out ceaselessly over the air was that risk in a nuclear plant was intolerable because in a nuclear accident "millions" of people would ultimately die, not of crushed or broken bodies, but of *cancer.* The symbolic threat of cancer replaced all thought, all context, all rational discussion of probability of danger and, above all, of benefit/risk calculations.

5. The outright myth that light-water nuclear reactors can explode like bombs was transmitted on one network—ABC—by an incredibly illiterate exchange between anchorman Harry Reasoner and science editor Jules Bergmann:

HR: How safe *is* nuclear power?
JB: Safe, but not safe enough.
HR: In a nuclear accident, you might kill a million people, right?
JB: It's possible. You might more likely kill a hundred thousand or so, if the thing blew up.[14]

"The thing," of course, cannot "blow up," and these Hiroshima-like estimates of "a million" or "a hundred thousand" deaths by explosion were lifted straight from anti-nuclear propaganda.

6. Never once in the four month period was it mentioned on any network that atomic energy was the only fully developed technological substitute, so far, for fossil fuels and was thus the only form of energy production which was guaranteed to sustain our civilization for thousands of years.

In sum, the bias favoring the anti-nuclear side of the controversy was overwhelming. With some variations—ABC being the most illiterate, NBC being somewhat more balanced than the others, and CBS being aggressively and militantly anti-atomic power—the three networks actually functioned as press agents for the Nader forces. Essentially, during that four-month period before the California election, two messages went out over the national airwaves: (1) nuclear power plants are desperately dangerous and will kill millions with cancer; and (2) if the nuclear industries cannot guarantee technological omniscience and infallibility, nuclear power production must be stopped. It was the mindless stop-growth coverage of scientific primitives.

It is finally of interest to compare this coverage, retroactively, to network coverage on three separate occasions when Communist China actually exploded nuclear bombs, and radioactive clouds drifted over the United States. The networks reported on each event disinterestedly and briefly, told us for several days in a row where the cloud was, and that was that.[15] For reasons best known to the networks and to their Naderite allies, *real* radioactive clouds from the explosions of *real* nuclear bombs that were *really* traveling over America were not big news. Clearly, to the journalists, they could not compare in stark horror with that imagined explosion which released that imagined radioactive cloud that killed those imagined millions near Brown's Ferry. As usual, new-class journalists are more impressed by fantasy than by fact.

TOXIC SUBSTANCES

Now, for the second major controversy—the one revolving around the hazards of toxic and carcinogenic substances. No one living in the United States need be told that for about ten years there has been a steady drumbeat of media reports informing us that American industry and modern technology are inducing disease and death in the American public—above all, that they are giving us cancer. The chemicals in our fertilizers are giving us cancer. The chemicals in our pesticides are giving us cancer. The chemicals in our foods are giving us cancer. The chemicals in our water, the chemicals in our drugs, the chemicals in our work places, the chemicals in our productive processes, the chemicals in packaging, the chemicals in clothing, the chemicals in our building materials—are all giving us cancer. In sum, American industry is a lethal institution engaging in mass murder for profit. The conclusion: all this deadly science and technology must be stopped cold. That, at least, has been the media message, and inevitably it has taken its most lurid form in network news.

What is wrong with this message? Aren't toxic and carcinogenic substances emerging from our laboratories and factories? And shouldn't anything be done about it? Certainly, they are. And certainly, something should be done about it. And yet, the network message has been an almost savage distortion of the problem. Those who have analyzed network coverage have largely concentrated on three documentaries produced in 1975–1976: CBS's "The American Way of Cancer," CBS's "The Politics of Cancer," and NBC's "What Is This Thing Called Food?"[16] They were chosen for analysis because they constituted autonomous units that could be readily examined, and because, presumably, they represented the networks' most serious and responsible thought on the subject. Four sets of analyses have been made by different groups and individuals, including myself, each using a somewhat different approach to the problem, and I will briefly describe all four.

I will start with my own, because it functions logically as an introduction to the others. In a series of short essays in *TV Guide*'s "News Watch" column in the past year,[17] I have concentrated almost exclusively on the missing context of the coverage, without which a sane perspective is impossible. A great many crucial issues have proven to be missing from network coverage, and the following were the most important:

1. Never, in any of these documentaries—or, for that matter, in any news program on the subject that I have ever seen in the past decade—has any scientist been interviewed to explain the misleading concept of "safety." The public has never been

taught that there is no such thing in existence as a "safe" or risk-free substance. Every substance that exists is "toxic" to someone, in some quantity. The scientific formula LD 50 represents that amount of any substance which will kill half the people who ingest it, and every substance on earth potentially has an LD 50 "rating."[18] Whether it be the purest of water, the healthiest of mother's milk, or the most beneficent sunshine, at some point, and in some amount, it will cause damage, disease, and death to some number of people. Thus, in the realm of "safety," the only rational questions one can ever ask are: (1) what is the safety level of any substance for most people? and (2) since individual response varies greatly, what are the benefits of any substance, or any combination of substances, to any given individual as opposed to the risks? However intense the demand of modern primitives for guaranteed protection from all risk, they cannot have it. That is not the nature of the universe. But the networks do not tell people so.

2. Never in any of the documentaries, or in any news program to my knowledge, has it been made clear that the safe-natural versus dangerous-chemical dichotomy is false and misleading, that natural substances are not automatically safe, and synthetic chemicals are not automatically dangerous. Never has it been made clear that there is no chemical difference between natural and man-made chemicals—in fact, never has it been made clear that everything that exists is chemical. The concept "chemicals" in network coverage is continually used by reporters as an equivalent of filth, toxicity, or poison, in contrast to the allegedly wholesome and safe substances provided by "nature."

3. Never has the public been informed of the toxic and carcinogenic potentials of natural foods.[19] For example:

Some foods contain disease-producing substances:
- bananas, pineapples, and cheese contain chemicals that raise blood pressure;
- peaches, pears, strawberries, brussels sprouts, spinach, white turnips, carrots, and cauliflower contain chemicals that cause thyroid disease.

Some foods contain substances that are virulent poisons:
- spinach, cashews, almonds, cocoa, and tea contain poisonous oxalates and free oxalic acid;
- potatoes contain the poison solanine;
- fish and shellfish contain the poison arsenic;
- lima beans break down during digestion into the poison hydrogen cyanide.

Some foods are carcinogenic:

- orange juice, flour, cabbage, turnips, sassafras, and nutmeg contain carcinogens;
- egg yolks are carcinogenic to mice;
- spinach contains nitrate which converts to nitrite when stored in the refrigerator overnight, and nitrite is converted in the stomach to nitrosamines, which are carcinogenic.

And finally, our own saliva contains nitrite, transformed in the stomach into nitrosamines, which, again, are carcinogens.

What is the significance of these facts? And why does their omission matter so desperately? Because without them there is no way to assess the new-class furor over the danger to health of industrialization. The problem becomes very clear when one knows that the cancer bans are based on certain government regulations and guidelines declaring that there are *no* tolerable safety levels for carcinogens, and that any substance that is carcinogenic at *any* level or dosage is to be removed immediately from the marketplace.[20] If this principle is rational, then it cannot only apply to synthetic carcinogens; it must apply to all carcinogens. And if that is rational, it means that the government must also immediately ban such things as this:

- the classical American breakfast composed of orange juice, bacon (nitrite-preserved) and eggs, and toast;
- the classical American lunch composed of sandwiches of cured and processed meats topped off with coleslaw and Russian dressing;
- Christmas dinners composed of turkey with stuffing, or of ham, biscuits, gravy, creamed turnips and spinach;
- New Year's Eve egg-nogs sprinkled with nutmeg;
- all breads, cakes, and cookies made of flour.

Indeed, if the regulations on carcinogens were consistent, an extraordinary part of our diet would instantly become illegal. The effects would be even more extraordinary if regulations were also consistent in the entire realm of toxic and poisonous substances. Today, the government seeks to ban lead-based house paint or glasses with lead designs on the grounds that such substances might *accidentally* be eaten. If it also sought to ban foods with toxic and poisonous chemicals that are *intended* to be eaten, most of our fruits, many of our vegetables, and all fish and shellfish would also be up for banning.

Clearly, regulations which, if consistently applied, would obliterate so much of the human diet would be irrational. And yet, if such bans are irrational for natural substances, why are they rational for synthetic substances? One must at least hypothesize that the all-or-nothing principle is invalid, and that there must be reasonable safety levels in the realm of both toxic and carcinogenic substances, natural and synthetic.[21]

THE NETWORKS: SIN BY OMISSION

Those, indeed, are the questions on the minds of serious scientists.
They are concerned today with establishing safety levels of all toxic
substances, including those bestowed upon us by nature, and with
devising reliable animal testing methods for all poisons and carcinogens (those presently in use are not reliable). They are concerned with
setting logical and consistent standards for banning substances from
the marketplace, and they are concerned with establishing rational
risk/benefit standards. But such considerations clearly expressed and
explained have not been on the air. So long as the existence of naturally toxic and carcinogenic substances is evaded, so long as natural
chemicals are portrayed as sacrosanct and only commercial synthet-
ics are portrayed as toxic or lethal, the problems can never be rationally identified or discussed.

The practical result of this omission is, of course, that the material that is circulated on the network air carries one strident message
by sheer default: "Science, technology, and industry are murderous
institutions—American industry is killing for profit." That, logically,
must be the message if one withholds information about naturally
toxic and carcinogenic substances.

The overriding message, in other words, is identical with that to
be found in the study of network coverage of nuclear power, and essentially for the same reasons: the scientists who would present the
controversial issues in full context are virtually absent from the air. In
this area, as in that of nuclear power, the information all too often is
provided by people who are not legitimate experts. In addition to
new-class scientists and regulators, who by definition are dedicated
to anti-industrial and anti-capitalist interpretations of all phenomena,
the networks offer up a dramatis personae of alleged experts from outside fields and agitated laymen: labor leaders, workers, wives, children, and politicians, all of whom speculate passionately about scientific issues of which they are entirely ignorant.

It is only fair to say that on August 28, 1977, after writing the
first draft of this paper, I discovered one network program which
partly contradicts this pattern. It was NBC's "Meet the Press," which
interviewed Dr. Arthur Upton, head of the National Cancer Institute,
who is eminently competent to discuss the issues which have generally been missing from coverage and who did so, however briefly, on
this program. The press attitudes—the interviewers on this program
emerged from the print media—were, however, unaltered. The result
was a continuously contested interview in which the reporters were
far less interested in Dr. Upton's information than in challenging
him. The dominant theme of their challenge was the alleged derelic-
tion of the National Cancer Institute in neglecting the preventive as-

pect of cancer research in the form of investigating "environmental"—meaning industrial—carcinogens, such activities receiving only 15 percent of the funds going to current cancer research,
while other types of research, such as investigations of the role
of viruses in causing cancers, were still receiving large sums of
money.

Upton managed to make these points on the air: that the causes
of cancer are still unknown, and that "viruses are still a likely cause
of cancer." He also said: "Prevention of cancer is more difficult than it
may seem. If we knew how to prevent cancer today, we would not
have moved in that direction [of virus research]." And Upton pointed
out that the risks of cancer might be related to the dosages—a challenge to the all-or-nothing theory. Finally, he summed up the reliability of laboratory tests equating animal cancers and human cancers
with a telling word: *tentative*. This was an excellent program, both in
terms of the interviewee and his statements, assuming that the viewer actually grasped them. Usually, they were stated only once and
were not elaborated upon.

This failure to elaborate on crucially important matters was not
Upton's fault. He was never invited to do so and was, in fact, prevented from doing so by the reporters, who did not appear to know or
understand the significance of his statements about the as-yet un-
learned or the unknown. None sought to learn the implications. And
certainly, it occurred to none to question the logic or justice of punitive conduct to industry, given the degree of ignorance in which
cancer research is still operating. Thus, the program, while infinitely
superior to most of what has been on the air, constituted a kind of
tokenism. The press itself treated Upton and the Cancer Institute as
defendants, culpable of indifference to industry-caused cancer.

CAST CONFRONTS THE NETWORKS

Another set of analyses of the network coverage of these issues comes
from an organization of scientists called CAST—the Council for Agricultural Science and Technology—with headquarters at Iowa State
University. CAST consists of an association of sixteen agricultural
science societies, including the American College of Veterinary Tox-
icologists,[22] and it has invited two groups of scientific specialists to
analyze two of the network documentaries.

The first CAST group consisted of Dr. Sheldon D. Murphy, associate professor of toxicology, Harvard University School of Public
Health; Dr. Ralph Fogleman, doctor of veterinary medicine, president
elect of American College of Veterinary Toxicology; Dr. W. Eugene
Lloyd, professor in the Veterinary Diagnostic Laboratory, Iowa State

University, Ames, Iowa; Dr. Keith Long, director of the Institute of Agricultural Medicine and Environmental Health, University of Iowa, Iowa City; and Dr. Wayland J. Hayes, professor, Center in Toxicology, department of biochemistry, Vanderbilt University, Nashville, Tennessee.

This CAST group analyzed CBS's "The American Way of Cancer." The thesis of this CBS documentary was quite explicit. It was that industrialization in general, and American industrialization in particular, was a major cause of cancer; and that the pre-industrial nations have far lower cancer rates by virtue of suffering from far less science, technology, and industry. The documentary focused heavily on reports of cancer-causing substances affecting workmen in American factories. The CAST group made three broad points:

1. CAST charged CBS with a sensationalized and inaccurate portrayal of the problem. The review group challenged narrator Dan Rather's statement that "America is number one in cancer," pointing out that it is in conflict with the 1973 World Health Organization Statistics Report, vol. 26, pp. 30–33, showing that the United States stands midway among the developed countries as regards the death rate from cancer. In 1970, there were ten countries with cancer death rates higher than ours.

2. CAST pointed out that the lower rates of cancer in the so-called underdeveloped countries were not due to a beneficent lack of industrialization, but quite the contrary. Because modern drugs are not available, these countries have not controlled infectious diseases, which kill off large numbers of their population. As CAST put it, "Fewer persons are in the 'cancer age.'" They simply don't live long enough.

3. And CAST, while agreeing that workers in certain stages of the manufacture of certain substances (such as benzene, asbestos, and plastics) were developing cancer at a higher rate than the rest of the population, objected to CBS's exaggeration of the phenomenon. The review group pointed out that the incidence of environmentally caused cancer associated with peoples' industrial occupations accounts for less than 1 percent of the cancer in industrialized countries, according to statistics compiled by the International Agency for Research on Cancer, a part of the World Health Organization.[23]

The scientific panel which prepared this response to CBS concluded: "CBS apparently knows full well the scare value of the word 'cancer' and has chosen to exploit that value. The report was unbalanced and in our judgment dangerously misleading and inflammatory."[24]

CAST invited yet another group of scientists to analyze NBC's documentary, "What Is This Thing Called Food?" The members of the review group were Thomas H. Jukes (chairman of the task force), professor, Space Sciences Laboratory, University of California at Berkeley; Chest B. Baker, professor, department of agricultural economics, University of Illinois; Edward E. Burns, professor, department of soil and crop sciences, Texas A & M University; Glenn Davis, attorney, Pacific Legal Foundation; Harold Hafs, professor, department of physiology and dairy science, Michigan State University; and Hardin Jones, professor, department of medical physics and physiology, University of California at Berkeley.

Since both the documentary and the CAST critique covered a great many issues, I shall confine myself here to the least technical of the CAST critiques—all pertaining to error and distortion caused by NBC's failure to include crucially necessary context.

For example: Betty Furness, the narrator, aired the speculation that "glutamate and aspartate might together cause brain damage in children, one adding to the toxic effect of the other." The CAST scientists considered this scientifically illiterate. They pointed out that glutamate and aspartate are necessary amino acids, that they are naturally generated in our bodies, and that they are food substances present in abundance in every natural protein that we eat.

The CAST group was similarly critical of NBC's out-of-context treatment of the danger of nitrite in bacon. CAST pointed out that without the small amount of nitrite used as a preservative millions would be at the mercy of botulism, a virulent poison. CAST further condemned the documentary for failing to report that "the amount of nitrite normally produced in the mouth of each of us each day, and swallowed in the saliva, is greater than the amount of nitrite contained in a pound of bacon."

The CAST review group extensively criticized that important portion of the NBC documentary devoted to warning viewers of the dangers of DES—diethylstilbestrol, a synthetic estrogen. NBC reported that this drug, given to women ten to twenty years ago to prevent miscarriages, had produced vaginal cancer in a small percentage of their daughters. Then NBC warned that this same drug was now being used in cattle feed to produce a greater proportion of lean meat. (Actually, NBC erroneously said *fat* meat.) The danger, said the network, was that DES residues in beef liver could give people cancer. The CAST group made three important contextual points—all missing from the documentary:

1. CAST observed that estrogens are naturally produced in the body, and that all estrogens, both natural and synthetic, are carcinogenic if the levels are sufficiently high.

2. The CAST group elaborated: "Each day a woman of childbearing age normally produces in her body quantities of estrogens with potency equivalent to the DES in 5,000 pounds of liver from DES-treated cattle."

3. And the review group reported that one well-documented series of women who had been given DES in pregnancy—none of whose daughters had contracted vaginal cancer—had received doses of twelve grams of DES. This, reported CAST, was "equivalent to the maximum amount present in 100,000 tons of beef liver from cattle treated with DES."

The basic scientific error made by NBC, the CAST group concluded, was the failure to grasp that it is the dosage, the amount ingested, that makes a chemical—natural or synthetic—poisonous. Clearly, the CAST scientists in this group, at least, are consistent. They are postulating safety levels for *all* toxic and carcinogenic substances; they are not evading the issue of natural carcinogens while demanding that all synthetic carcinogens be outlawed.

This CAST group, too, concluded that the coverage was hostile to industry: "By clever use of horror stories and guilt by association, NBC attempted to scare viewers into thinking we are the victims rather than the beneficiaries of our food supply."[25]

WHELAN'S ANALYSIS

Finally, there is a fourth analysis done by Dr. Elizabeth Whelan, an epidemiologist associated with the Harvard School of Public Health. Dr. Whelan criticized all three network documentaries and published her analysis in *Barron's Weekly* of November 15, 1976. Since many of the criticisms made by Dr. Whelan overlap with those already cited, I will not repeat them here but will isolate two important groups of observations made by her alone.

Dr. Whelan's principal scientific objection to all three documentaries was that in their determination to attach the responsibility for cancer to industry, they had failed to inform the public of information she considers most desperately necessary: that most cancer today is linked to cigarette smoking and to obesity traceable to overeating—both resulting from activities *voluntarily undertaken by the consumers themselves, and over which they have control.* In effect, Dr. Whelan was identifying and protesting the irrational displacement of responsibility from the individual to industry which is a characteristic of new-class thought.[26]

In addition, Dr. Whelan identified the analytical chaos of the three documentaries. There was a failure to differentiate expertise from lay opinion; a failure to differentiate between hazards to a tiny fraction of the populace and to the populace at large; and a failure to differentiate between suspicions, guesswork, and fantasies and solid scientific evidence. All were lumped together in a disorganized stew, the only common denominator of which was an insistent warning against the danger of industrial civilization.

Dr. Whelan concluded: "All three documentaries masqueraded as unbiased presentations on the topics of cancer causation and food safety, but an emotionally charged message came through loud and clear: we have a cancer epidemic in this country, and rapid, uncontrolled industrialization is to blame. 'Agribusiness,' it is not so subtly suggested, is making money at the expense of America's health. . . . And what is the networks' solution? Each of the shows was organized around the general theme voiced succinctly in 'What Is This Thing Called Food' by a chemist named Dr. Ross Hume Hall: 'The solution is to stop. To stop the technology. To hold it in abeyance until such time as we have an idea what is going on.'" Dr. Whelan ironically entitled her analysis, "Stop the Technology."

And so much for the second illustration of news bias.

ANTI-CAPITALIST PRIMITIVISM

In the realm of toxic substances, just as in the realm of atomic energy, the same pattern prevails. There was an almost frantic commitment by network journalists to the view that science, technology, and industry are death-dealing institutions. There was an almost militant refusal to include any contextual, qualifying, or critical information which might give the public a balanced perspective on the issues. And there was the same shrill cry: "Omniscience or nothing!" This was not reporting that sought to educate citizens to evolving problems and dangers within a generally beneficial context. It was the hysterical stop-growth reporting of scientific primitives.

If it were that alone, however, there would be more hope. One could organize a struggle to get scientifically competent analysts onto network staffs. Blindly resistant to criticism though the networks might be, such a goal assiduously fought for might be attained. But the problem is, as I said earlier, that the primitivism itself is not recognized. It is camouflaged and rationalized by the diffuse ideological perspective of the new class—that of anti-capitalism. This political attitude, which perceives business as eternally malignant, and which can never grasp the overpowering benefits of capitalism, simply reinforces the illiterate terrors of science and technology and endows all charges against industry, however irrational, with a moral aura. It is actually that moral aura which is impenetrable.

In a recent essay published in *The Wall Street Journal*, Rutgers sociologist Peter Berger explained the genesis of this moral rigidity. He wrote:

"If one central delusion afflicts a large portion of the American intelligentsia, it is the failure to perceive the connection between capitalism and liberty. . . . In the demonology of our intellectuals, there are two distinct sets of ogres, perceived as habitually holding hands: the torturing henchmen of dictatorial regimes and the greedy, exploitative capitalists. Yet the data indicate a rather different empirical relationship. . . . There is not a single democratic regime in the world today that does not have a capitalist economy. To put it differently, there is not a single non-capitalist democracy in the world today. Put differently again, there is not a single socialist country with a democratic form of government. And it is difficult to find a socialist country with a passable record on human rights, including the so-called economic rights of which the Left is so enamored."[27]

But this is precisely what the new class, focused on taking over State control of science, technology, and industry, does not know and apparently cannot endure to know. This blind hostility to capitalism, this demonology as Berger puts it, turns most reporters into mindless transmission belts for even the most ludicrous charges against business. To such minds, the notion that American industry can profit by exterminating its customers sounds right and reasonable. Such a view does have a good solid theological base where demons are concerned, for the dead do expand their empire. But this has nothing to do with the operations of a free market where profits are to be gained only from the living.

Nonetheless, this demonology today is a source of moral pride in sophisticated journalistic circles. And because they are proud of it, because they perceive their own hostility as righteous, it no more occurs to the average reporter that there might be valid information to be dug up in support of the pro-industry side of any controversy, than it would occur to him that there might be valid information to be dug up in support of the Hitlerian position. In this realm, there is no such thing as "investigative reporting," and ignorance reigns supreme. Consequently, anyone, however immaculate his scientific reputation, who offers information in rebuttal of the Naderite line is met by that reporter with a blind, hostile glare of suspicion. Like a Puritan housewife scenting the presence of witches, the reporter scents the presence of evil. His very righteousness dispenses him from seeking to understand the challenging information or from obeying the minimal injunctions of his profession to cover business-related controversies fairly. And when the controversies are of the kind I have been discussing, no knowledge of science sets off an alarm signal in his mind, either because he has no such knowledge, or because such information as he has cannot dent that self-esteem mechanism which informs him that the anti-business side of any controversy must be the good, the true, and the noble.

It is not difficult to see the trends ahead of us. So long as this moral set prevails, the neo-primitives in journalism will continue with their distorted coverage of business issues. Business will continue to be the symbolic scapegoat for all ills in this society. The blind demand for omniscience will continue unabated. And business will be perpetually judged guilty by that standard of omniscience; guilty of knowing everything while viciously refusing to solve problems; guilty of intellectual malignity, never of innocent error; retroactively guilty of knowing in the past that which it did not and could not know; prophetically guilty of knowing a future which it does not yet and cannot know; in sum, guilty of every cognitive crime save of the mistakes necessarily attendant on the learning process, that learning process of which the primitives are hopelessly ignorant.

THE PERVASIVENESS OF THE OMNISCIENCE PREMISE

Since the preceding analyses concentrated on network coverage alone, there is a danger that the reader of this paper might conclude that this pattern applies primarily to the more popular, and presumably more ignorant, mass media. It is consequently useful to offer an illustration of the identical mental process that recently appeared in one of the most sophisticated and scholarly publications in the land—indeed, in a publication which customarily sees through most of the new-class follies. In an essay in *The Public Interest* by Christopher Stone in the Summer 1977 issue, Stone summed up "the most critical problems we now face" in the realm of industrial hazards as follows:

> The food we will eat tonight (grown, handled, packaged, and distributed by various corporations) may contain chemicals that are slowly killing us. But while we may have misgivings in principle, we cannot know with certainty *that* we are being injured by any particular product, or *who* is injuring us. We would also have a difficult time proving *the nature and extent* of our injuries (even more so proving the extent attributable to any particular source). Finally, the evidence to be evaluated is ... perhaps [so complex and technical] that the courts or even agencies cannot realistically be expected to unravel it, especially after the fact. Worst of all, by the time we discover what is happening—for example, that teen-age girls are developing vaginal cancer because of medication their mothers took before they were born—it is often too late.[28]

Here, Mr. Stone lucidly sets forth what he himself describes as a set of unknowns and, to date, unknowable dangers. The only instance he offers of known damage is the case of DES, the drug given several decades ago to prevent miscarriage among a small fraction of women, a tiny fraction of whose daughters developed vaginal cancer a generation later. Incredibly, however, this very passage serves to illustrate Mr. Stone's thesis of the difficulty of assigning legal responsibility to what he calls "corporate misbehavior," a "misbehavior" which, according to his definition, includes the "distribution of a faulty product." Why that which was and is unknown to the best minds of science constitutes "corporate misbehavior," Mr. Stone does not say. It is his tacit assumption that industry is responsible at every moment for all knowledge, that it is to be judged both retroactively and prophetically by the standard of omniscience. His essay is entitled "Controlling Corporate Misconduct," and nowhere in it does Mr. Stone suggest that the failure to know that which at any time is unknown does not constitute "corporate misconduct"; that it cannot be "controlled" by the State; that it cannot be prevented and should not be punished; and, quite simply, that we must live with the risks entailed in an absence of omniscience and infallibility, correcting errors as knowledge grows.

This is a striking illustration of the nature of the retroactive and prophetic guilt built into the omniscience premise. That it can slide, undetected, into a sophisticated essay published by The Public Interest is evidence of the incredible pervasiveness of that omniscience premise and of its irrationally punitive implications for industry.

That, in essence, is why we are discussing the relationship between business and the media. And that is why some gentlemen hope to find ways to make the media love business more. They will be about as successful as a convocation of heretics discussing ways to make themselves more lovable to the lords of the Inquisition. The truth is, there is only one way for businessmen to appease the lords of the Inquisition: they must repent; they must confess; they must admit that they know everything and have maliciously chosen to damage and kill people for profit; they must bend their backs to the lash of the State and submit to new-class rule.

This may sound shrill and exaggerated to some ears. We live in an era where truth is reputed to be a moderate phenomenon, lying like a squashed rabbit in the middle of the road. I call your attention, therefore, to an editorial cartoon that appeared in the August 21, 1977 issue of the New York Times.[29] (See opposite.) The cartoon shows precisely what I have described. It shows Uncle Sam—the State—lashing a yoked, blindered team of briefcase-bearing businessmen moving in lockstep, their backs bent under the crack of the whip.

Washington Is Thinking Over the Regulatory Agencies

There Must Be Something Besides Rules, Rules And More Rules

Source: © 1977 by The New York Times Company. Reprinted by permission.

Does the cartoon accompany an indignant exposé? Not in the least. On the contrary, the *Times* writer is echoing here the latest wrinkle in regulatory thought. Perhaps, he says—echoing the views of Charles Schultze, economic adviser to the president—this yoking and lashing of businessmen could be made more *efficient.* Perhaps it might be more efficient to force business to obey the whims, caprices, and orders of the presumably omniscient State by manipulating businessmen with taxation and tax credits.[30]

By contrast, imagine what the accompanying *Times* article would say if those yoked, bent, and blindered beings cringing under the lash of the State were labeled "women" or "blacks" or "homosexuals" or "communists," let alone "scholars" or "journalists." Would the *Times* use this caricature to illustrate an article describing the desirability of making the State's coercion more efficient? It would not. Indeed, the cry of moral horror over the very existence of such coercion would split the heavens with its intensity. But no such horror is felt on behalf of businessmen.

This open and unselfconscious commitment to what, were the victims from any other group, would be instantly identified as enslavement; this entrenched view that shackling and lashing the industrialist class is righteous, while shackling and lashing any other class of citizens is evil—that is what the businessmen are up against today. One cannot appease such a psychology. One can only fight it.

There is a vast and expanding public relations lore in the business world about ways to fight this battle, but none of it, as far as I know, even remotely approaches the essence of the problem, which is the problem of omniscience—the status of *mind* in the industrial world. Stated in a different way, the American industrialists are being denied basic First Amendment rights. That constitutional right, which protects freedom of thought, opinion, and expression, is well understood as applied to the press. It states that Congress may make no laws abridging its intellectual freedom. It does *not* state that the press must be accurate, fair, or even truthful, for freedom includes the right to be ignorant, to learn, to make mistakes in the course of learning, to be wrong. Today, American citizens in science, technology, and industry are being denied that right. By assuming a nonexistent omniscience and infallibility in these groups, those who do not understand either the discovery process or the production process are effectively behaving as if business alone may not be accorded the freedom of thought—which includes the freedom to be ignorant, to learn and make errors—that is constitutionally accorded to all.

That is the most fundamental problem faced by business today. It cannot be solved by public relations gimmickry. It requires something far more difficult, an educational and philosophical crusade that penetrates into every aspect of our educational system and political life, and that attacks the very root of the error: the primitive terror in the face of that complexity of consciousness which is not understood, and the primitive demand to be protected from the risks and hazards of life and of the universe itself.[31]

NOTES

1. Glynn Cochran, *Big Men in Cargo Cults* (Oxford: Clarendon Press, 1970).

2. For example, *Frankenstein, Dr. Jekyll and Mr. Hyde, Dr. Strangelove, 2001*, etc.

3. In view of the current attempts to attribute declining literacy (and declining SAT scores) to television and to recent political events, the reader might find it helpful to be reminded that in the fifties, Rudolf Flesch called the nation's attention to the problem with a best-seller called *Why Johnny Can't Read*; in the sixties President John F. Kennedy discovered that the percentage of students seeking careers in the rationally demanding sciences and technology had dropped sharply; in 1975 a *Time* magazine essay—"Can't Anyone Here Speak English?"—documented illiteracy among both college students and professors; and by the late seventies the liberal journal, *The Humanist*, was launching a crusade against a nationwide acceptance of super-

stition, magic, and witchcraft and its exploitation by ostensibly educated groups, including the media.

4. Irving Kristol, "Business and the New Class," *The Wall Street Journal,* May 19, 1975, p. 8.

5. Ibid., p. 8.

6. The fact that the "new class" shares many fundamental political attitudes with the intellectual left is scarcely coincidental. The "new left" of the sixties has been absorbed into the liberal establishment, works within the system, and now determines the orientation of the new class. It is explicitly anti-capitalist, and many of its leading intellectuals are self-proclaimed "new socialists." For two analyses of the fantasy-ridden nature of socialist thought, see "The Poverty of Socialist Thought," by Stephen Miller of the National Endowment for the Humanities, *Commentary,* August 1976; and "The Socialist Myth," by Peter Berger, professor of sociology at Rutgers University, *The Public Interest,* August 1976.

7. It is impossible to provide a complete list of all the anti-nuclear groups, which are constantly proliferating. In February 1976, the Rockefeller Foundation sponsored a task force of the major environmentalist groups opposing, among other things, nuclear power. Its representatives were: the Friends of the Earth, Sierra Club, Environmental Defense Fund, the Audubon Society, Natural Resources Defense Council, Zero Population Growth, and others. Similarly, there are a number of purely scientific groups which take the anti-nuclear-power position. In this paper I cite the Union of Concerned Scientists alone because it is the largest and apparently the most prestigious.

8. The most recent mailing of the Union of Concerned Scientists, which I received during the month of August 1977 while working on this paper, identifies its membership and goals in two documents called "Scientists' Declaration on Nuclear Power" and "What You Should Know about the Hazards of Nuclear Power." The latter document presents an endorsement by Ralph Nader (who is not a scientist): "They [the Union of Concerned Scientists] have performed a public service which will go down in history." Nader's statement was made, says the UCS document, on ABC-TV's "Dick Cavett Show." All UCS documents referred to in this paper can be obtained at the Union of Concerned Scientists, 1208 Massachusetts Avenue, Cambridge, Massachusetts 02138.

9. From a letter addressed to "Dear Fellow Citizen" and signed by Daniel F. Ford, Executive Director, Union of Concerned Scientists. Intended to be used in multiple mailings, the letter bears no date (see above).

10. Religion Section, *Newsweek,* March 15, 1976. The information on the divine view of plutonium as expressed in the teachings of this cult comes from Reed Irvine, executive director of Accuracy in Media. It is of interest to note that in *Commentary,* September 1977, in an essay called "The War Against the Atom," which identifies the opponents of nuclear power as gripped by "ignorant terror" and identifies their position as "nuclear Luddism," the author, Samuel McCracken, assistant to the president of Boston University, writes: "Recently a funny thing happened at the National Council of Churches, a division of which has declared plutonium morally dubious and called for a moratorium on its use. Defenders of this bizarre intrusion of theology into science, which awoke echoes of Galileo's encounter with the

Inquisition, explained that because the scientific community was split down the middle on plutonium, the theological community ought to have a deciding vote. Plutonium, they said, was not a technical or scientific issue, but a moral one. . . . [O]ne can hardly blame the plutonophobes for trying to get the discussion into this [moral] marsh. *The problem is that the alleged split within the scientific community finds, almost without exception, all those with the relevant expertness—the specialists in nuclear physics, health physics, and radiation medicine—for, and scientists from almost every field that does not bear on the problem, against. This is as true for nuclear energy in general as for the carefully controlled use of plutonium."* (Italics mine.)

11. All information about the nuclear scientists and Nobel laureates in nuclear physics who support nuclear power, and copies of all their statements and manifestos referred to in this paper, are obtainable from CUNY physics professor Miro Todorovich, Executive Director of University Centers for Rational Alternatives, 110 West 40th Street, New York, New York 10018. Professor Todorovich was instrumental in organizing the nationwide expressions of support for nuclear power by the Nobel laureates and other eminent scientists in this field.

12. See Todorovich, above.

13. These accident statistics are taken from the Rasmussen Report, which gathered them from a variety of official U.S. sources. The sources are identified in the Report itself.

14. ABC-TV "Evening News," February 3, 1976.

15. According to the Television Film Archives of Vanderbilt University, Nashville, Tennessee, the networks carried three bulletins each after both Chinese nuclear explosions in September and November 1976. The same cursory treatment was given to the explosion of September 1977.

16. CBS, "The American Way of Cancer," October 15, 1975; CBS, "The Politics of Cancer," June 22, 1976; NBC, "What Is This Thing Called Food?" September 8, 1976.

17. Edith Efron, "News Watch," *TV Guide:* "Biased 'Science' Reporting Scares TV Viewers," January 10, 1976; "Reader Mail Brings Clashing Views on Science Column," March 20, 1976; "Dangers of the New Food Politics Should be Reported," April 9, 1977; "The Additive Scare: What Television Isn't Telling Us," June 11, 1977.

18. In *Food and Your Well Being,* by Theodore P. Labuza, professor of food science and technology, University of Minnesota (New York: West Publishing Co., 1977), LD 50 is thus defined, as used in acute toxicity tests on animals: "The animals are given single doses of the chemical by injection into the bloodstream or by feeding at a single meal. Many dosages are tested and from statistical calculations the dose level is found which kills 50 percent of the animals within one week after injection or feeding. This dose is called the LD 50 (lethal dose for 50 percent of the animals). The LD 50 is computed in terms of milligrams of the chemical per kilogram of body weight and is compared with the effectiveness level needed in the food product. Obviously, if the LD 50 level was less than the effectiveness level of the chemical, [it] could not be utilized in the food supply. . . . The decision is based on the most sensitive of the animal species tested." (p. 371)

19. The textbook used as a source of information about the toxic and carcinogenic potentials of natural foods in this paper is *Food, Nutrition, and You*, by Fergus M. Clydesdale, professor of nutrition, University of Massachusetts (Englewood Cliffs: Prentice-Hall, 1977).

20. This is the explicit direction of the "Delaney Clause," which guides the operations of the Food and Drug Administration. The Environmental Protection Agency has also elaborated what it describes as nine "principles" of carcinogenicity. The EPA presents as a "principle" its view that "a carcinogen is any agent which increases tumor induction in man or animals," thus throwing its regulatory weight toward those who would equate tumors and cancers. And, again, the EPA describes as a "principle" the view that "the concept of a 'threshold' exposure level for a carcinogenic agent has no practical significance because there is no valid method of establishing such a level." On the basis of these two controversial and unproved postulates, the EPA has developed the equivalent of its own Delaney Clause. The Council for Agricultural Science and Technology, Iowa State University, challenges both of these hypotheses in report no. 54, entitled "The Environmental Protection Agency's Nine 'Principles' of Carcinogenicity," January 19, 1976.

21. See CAST report no. 54, above. Prepared by a task force of thirteen specialists in toxicology, pathology, pharmacology, and cancer research—including Dr. Jesse Steinfeld, former surgeon general of the United States—the Report states: "In our world, exposure to carcinogens is inescapable. Humans and animals are constantly exposed to small quantities of naturally occurring carcinogenic substances. Some carcinogens are present in the air. Others are present in foods, and some of these are essential components of the diet. Still others are absorbed from the environment in other ways. Carcinogens are produced within and by the body; some of these, such as sex hormones, are essential to the continued existence of animal and human life. If every carcinogenic substance inevitably initiated a cancer on contact with susceptible tissue, regardless of the amount of the substance, the survival of any individual beyond age 50 would be highly improbable."

The scientists in this group, who are on the staffs of such schools as UC San Francisco, UC Davis, UC Berkeley, Iowa State University, University of Missouri, and the Massachusetts Institute of Technology, postulate that safety levels for carcinogenic substances must exist and advocate increasing research to identify them—including improved animal testing methods, improved epidemiological studies among human beings, and improved benefit/risk studies.

22. The other scientific societies with membership in CAST are: the American Dairy Science Association; American Forage and Grassland Council; American Meteorological Society; American Society for Horticultural Science; American Society of Agricultural Engineers; American Society of Agronomy; American Society of Animal Science; Association of Official Seed Analysts; Council on Soil Testing and Plant Analysis; Crop Science Society of America; Poultry Science Association; Rural Sociological Society; Society of Nematologists; Soil Science Society of America; Southern Weed Science Society; and the Weed Science Society of America.

23. In the March 24, 1977 issue of the *New York Times*, David Burnham

cites the findings of an independent government study which estimates that "100,000 deaths and 390,000 illnesses ... occur each year as a result of worker exposures to thousands of toxic substances, about 1,500 of which are suspected of causing cancer." Assuming the absolute accuracy of such statistics (an unlikely assumption), the percentage of the population so affected would be .005 percent for *all* occupational illnesses *including* cancer. This is not a number to ignore, but it bears little or no relationship to CBS's projection of an industrial society that is ravaging its citizenry with cancer.

24. See CAST release, October 16, 1975.

25. See CAST release, September 9, 1976.

26. Dr. Whelan does not explore the area of psychogenic influences on cancer, which, again, cannot be attributed to industry. In *The Broken Heart: The Medical Consequences of Loneliness*, (New York: Basic Books, 1977), the author, James J. Lynch, reports on some of the medical consequences of emotional strain. One example: at all ages, the divorced are twice as likely as the married to develop lung cancer.

27. Peter Berger, "The Link Between Capitalism and Democracy," *The Wall Street Journal*, August 1, 1976. /

28. Christopher D. Stone, "Controlling Corporate Misconduct," *The Public Interest*, Summer 1977, pp. 55–71.

29. Philip Shabecoff, "There Must Be Something Besides Rules, Rules, and More Rules," the *New York Times*, Review of the Week ("The Nation"), August 21, 1977, p. 4.

30. Ibid. Shabecoff writes: "Increasingly ... economists, both conservative and liberal, and politicians of both parties have been questioning whether the regulatory process as is now applied is really the most efficient and most economic way of reaching the goals of, say, worker safety or clean air or fair prices.... The Administration wants to supplement or reinforce regulation with marketplace incentives [sic] that will reward industry for achieving desired goals or penalize them economically for failure to meet them.... Shortly before he became chairman of the Council of Economic Advisers, Charles L. Schultze laid out the theoretical underpinnings of the Administration's carrot and stick approach to regulation in a series of lectures at Harvard University...."

31. Readers who are interested in pursuing the religious implications of the analysis would do well to read "Faith, Fad, Fear and Food" by Richard L. Hall, *Chemical Technology*, vol. 3, no. 7, July 1973. It is a detailed analysis of the destructive impact on the intellectual operations of the food industry generated by the religious need for "deities and devils," the need "for absolutes, for daily ritual, for escape, for objects ... to worship and abhor." It reports in detail on the evolution of a "priestly" caste of regulators and a group of regulatory "sacraments" which grow increasingly irrelevant to the scientific problems requiring solution, and, in fact, are hampering their solution. Dr. Hall, who has three degrees in chemistry from Harvard University, and who is a member of the New York Academy of Science as well as vice-president in charge of research and development at McCormick Company, writes: "All available evidence indicates that [we have done] ... an effective job of protecting people against *known* hazards. What we are now asked to do is to protect people from *unknown* hazards or known hazards from unknown causes. There, the analogy with religion hardly needs belaboring."

CONFLICT, CONSENSUS, AND THE PROPAGANDA OF THE DEED; OR ONE SURE WAY TO MANIPULATE THE MEDIA

HAROLD E. DAVIS

Despite the fact that journalists are among the most intelligent and highly motivated people in society, according to Harold E. Davis they are routinely manipulated. This manipulation occurs when two processes interact. Davis identifies these two processes as the conflict orientation of news and the propaganda of the deed. Exploring these processes, Davis shows how they have often been used to manipulate the media in opposition to business—sometimes by business itself.

Professor and chairman of Georgia State University's department of journalism, Dr. Davis is a former Washington correspondent and city editor for the Atlanta Journal. *He was public relations director and vice-president of Georgia State. He recently published* The Fledgling Province.

We all know that there are irrational people who see conspiracies everywhere, and some of them profess to believe that the media are part of a plot to damage the nation. Others believe that the media exist to promote liberal causes while proclaiming their own objectivity. Others see newspeople as individuals who use their profession to promote whatever priorities they elect to recognize. A few persons see the media as bastions of the status quo. I do not believe any of these things. Nevertheless, I am positive that the media are manipulated.

The men and women who do the news and editorial work of the nation are, in my opinion, among the most intelligent and highly motivated people in society. They take it unkindly when anyone attempts to use them, and they bristle when anyone points out that they have been used. Thus, I can say in advance that many of them will positively dislike this essay.

THE TWO "BLADES"

Manipulation of the media in America commonly occurs as a result of a process that is almost mechanical. While there sometimes might be villains in the woodwork, this is not necessarily so. The same result is produced whether the individuals involved are scoundrels or pure in heart. The process is almost as impersonal as the operation of a pair of scissors. It takes two blades to cut, and when the blades come together the result is predictable. The manipulation of the media occurs when two concepts—each so powerful that it has the strength of an independent force—meet, much in the fashion of the scissors' blades.

To grasp this, one must examine the two "blades" separately, and then together. To understand the first, please turn your minds back to the now-distant year of 1913. Students at Columbia University then enjoyed in their classrooms a collection of teachers and scholars, some of whose names are celebrated to the present hour. Not the least of them was a lean, red-haired young man, a son of the American Midwest, the offspring of the leading citizen of Knightstown, Indiana. His name was Charles Beard. It has been said that no one at Columbia in the second decade of this century could match Beard as an orator. In 1913, he had just completed a book with a modest title but a remarkable thesis. It was called *An Economic Interpretation of the Constitution of the United States,* and so focused was its power that three-quarters of a century later it is one of the two books which every serious student of American government and history must have read.

Before 1913, while instructing his students with wit and trenchancy in New York, Charles Beard was also engaged in a research project in the old Treasury Building in Washington. There he had found a collection of documents so long out of use that he had to dust them off with a vacuum cleaner to make them readable. On the basis of those documents and others found elsewhere, he set forth the thesis that was to bring down the wrath of ex-President William Howard Taft, of the newspaper owned by future President Warren Harding, and of a committee of the New York Bar Association, among others.

It took a considerable theory to produce such results. Before discussing it, we should say a word about the background against which Beard did his work. In 1913, the Constitution of the United States was venerated as a near-sacred document. It was widely believed that the fifty-five men who wrote it had merely gathered in Philadelphia in 1787, caught the pulse and heartbeat of the American people, and, most likely with divine assistance, fixed them for all time in the Constitution. Beard was certain that that was not what had happened.

The Constitution, he said, was not the work of disinterested men awash in a flood tide of patriotism. It was the product of economic pressure groups composed principally of men with money, holders of public securities, of manufacturers, and of the shipping interests. That much alone would have been disturbing to many persons in 1913. But on page 149 of his book, Beard made the most shocking statement of all. Of the fifty-five men who wrote the Constitution, he said, "at least five-sixths, were immediately, directly, and personally interested in the outcome of their labors." However Beard might seek to qualify that statement, and he did, he had been understood to say that five out of six of the Founding Fathers were motivated by greed.[1]

One might well inquire how this story concerns the manipulation of the media of America at all. It does concern it, but not because of Beard's conclusions. The important thing is Beard's approach. He began his career during the Progressive era, that creative time during which the most conspicuous flag bearers of reform were Theodore Roosevelt and Woodrow Wilson. Many intellectuals sympathetic to their aims were taking a new approach to interpreting events, an approach that has come to be called the "conflict" school of interpretation.

Beard did not originate the conflict school; he did not even define it. However, in *An Economic Interpretation,* he exemplified it. It is the premise of the conflict school that truth may be more clearly discerned if one analyzes events in terms of those things that are divisive, violent, and discontinuous. This involves clashes of purpose and conflicts of interest. Since many of the interpreters of earlier eras had emphasized the institutions of society and their slow unfolding, one readily sees that the conflict approach supplied a new thrust—a thrust which did indeed uncover much truth. Beard's thesis has been pored over and somewhat modified by later scholars,[2] but the fact remains that there is truth in it.

The conflict school itself has been dissected by twentieth-century scholars as has its near-opposite, the "consensus" school of interpretation. That school began to assert itself perhaps as early as the 1930s and reached full flower in the 1950s. Consensus writers believed that truth would be more clearly discerned if one analyzed events in terms of those things which are enduring, which bind people together, which are unifying and continuous. Consensus interpreters valued the stability of institutions. Among the important consensus writers were Harvard historian Louis Hartz and Daniel Boorstin. Boorstin in the 1950s was a great ornament at the University of Chicago, and today he is Librarian of Congress. Hartz and Boorstin, like others of their school, believed that their method allowed them to see things whole, whereas the conflict approach delivered up the truth in fragments.[3]

Not everybody is comfortable with the "conflict" and "consensus" labels. No methodology has been developed to determine with exact precision what is conflict and what is consensus. Still, the terms have been widely useful even if their application has sometimes seemed illusory.

Some scholars believe that the definitions and concepts have an application to the media of America. If we accept this and ask whether the media direct their principal interest, their greatest exertions, to conflict or to consensus news, the answer would be, with qualifications, to conflict news.[4]

FRONT-PAGE CONFLICT

The front pages of the great daily newspapers reflect the interest of reporters and editors in conflict. This does not mean that consensus material is ignored. Most feature writing is in that category, and all good newspapers value it. So too with most financial news, with most sports, with the entertainment sections of the newspaper, and with routine reports concerning the ongoing business of society. One might easily amend the list. However, the preponderance of consensus items is inside the newspaper. The message comes through that consensus is considered less important than conflict.

The point is sharper when we examine television news coverage. Vanderbilt University on August 5, 1968, began taping the evening news broadcasts of the major television networks—ABC, CBS, and NBC. We may look at the Vanderbilt videotapes to see what was said and shown on any broadcast, or we may consult the indices to the broadcasts which Vanderbilt issues. Applying the "conflict" and "consensus" labels loosely, we conclude that the networks emphasize conflict news. Given the total content of a network newscast as compared with the total content of a daily newspaper for the same day, the network emphasis upon conflict is the greater.

The editors of network news are apparently aware that a great many conflict items taken one after another make up a heavy and indigestible meal; one not infrequently finds that they lighten the fare. CBS editors have found a way to do so by placing reports from Charles Kuralt "On the Road" at or near the end of their broadcasts. Often they have put the unthreatening commentary of Eric Sevareid near the end. Sometimes they have done both in the same evening, as in the broadcast of March 17, 1975.[5] Television newspersons have talked frankly about the materials they deal with. When Chet Huntley said good night to David Brinkley for the last time on NBC on the evening of July 31, 1970, it went as follows: "The noise . . . the clamoring for attention . . . the divisions in our society. When you deliver it night after night you start feeling almost responsible for it. I'm not running away from things. I'm running away to think."[6]

We should ask why reporters and editors are attracted to conflict news. Persons who wish the press ill are quick to say that conflict sells newspapers. They are correct, but so does consensus. Several years ago, the editors of the New York Times selected twenty-five of their "most exciting" front pages published since 1862. Of the twenty-five, there were about as many clear consensus choices as conflict ones, along with some that would be difficult to classify to everyone's satisfaction.

We must look beyond commercialism to discover why editors and reporters value conflict. For one thing, it is in the high tradition of the media, which prescribes that news reporters shall be the watchdogs of the public interest. Without this function, society and the government would not operate as well as they do. And second, perhaps because of this, most of the famous prizes are given for conflict coverage. In 1959 John Hohenberg, secretary of the advisory board on the Pulitzer Prizes, published his careful study, The Pulitzer Prize Story. He could not analyze and include all the winners between 1917 and 1958. Instead, he organized his volume "on the basis of subjects that had figured most frequently in the award of prizes." The results show a heavy emphasis upon conflict. There is a third reason why conflict is emphasized. Given current news values, a reporter or news organization attempting to ignore a conflict story would shortly find that a competing reporter or organization had it.

However, it is not the principal purpose here to ask why newspersons pursue conflict news, or even what they do with it. The main purpose is to inquire what it does to them. It causes them to react, to respond, to report the conflict event. This orientation toward conflict is the first "blade" in our hypothetical pair of scissors, and taken by itself it is absolutely harmless. One blade of a pair of scissors never cuts much of anything, and it certainly does not cut out a pattern of media manipulation.

THE "PROPAGANDA OF THE DEED" CONCEPT

In conjunction with the second "blade," however, it does. In 1878, a French socialist, Paul Brousse, first defined a concept that in practice constitutes our second blade. He called it "The Propaganda of the Deed." The term means a provocative act committed to draw attention toward an idea or a grievance—in short, to get publicity. The act might or might not be related to the aims that its perpetrators wish to accomplish. Brousse's term was picked up by the anarchists of the late nineteenth and early twentieth centuries. To publicize their belief that there should be no bosses in society, they killed kings, empresses, and heads of state, along with more obscure citizens. Barbara Tuchman, in *The Proud Tower*, has recaptured the spirit of those days, re-creating what it was like to be afraid to go to a restaurant in Paris or for a walk in the Bois de Boulogne for fear that a bomb would go off—an explosion intended solely to secure publicity for the ideals of anarchism.[7]

There are three types of the propaganda of the deed, all of them based upon provocation. Any one of them can rivet the attention of the news media, since provocation predicates the existence of conflict or disagreement, elements to which the media are predisposed.

Type One, or violent non-civil disobedience. This type, perfected by the anarchists, involves the commission of a violent, illegal, and antisocial act. In the twenty years before 1914, anarchists assassinated six heads of state in pursuit of Type One. Then the technique fell more or less out of use. Extremist groups have now revived it. The slaughter of the Jewish athletes in Munich focused attention upon the idea of a Palestinian state, although the murders themselves were only marginally related to that idea. The hijacking of airliners, the setting off of bombs in crowded cities, whether in support of Croatian, Palestinian, Puerto Rican, or Basque nationalism or some other cause, are pure Type One—violent, illegal, and antisocial.

Very close to home, it has been said that when Patricia Hearst was kidnapped, the news media of the nation were kidnapped too. Before her seizure, the Symbionese Liberation Army was so obscure that few persons had ever heard of it. After her capture, the SLA demanded absolutely nothing for itself except one thing—publicity. It got it.[8]

Groups which use Type One of the Propaganda of the Deed usually believe that they have a great cause to which attention must be called. But Type One can be used for lesser reasons. It can even be employed to air personal grievances. *The Quill*, a magazine for journalists, was not amused at the irony of seeing "Anthony Kiritsis marching down Indianapolis streets with a hostage wired to his shotgun—and the still and film cameras tagging along behind him."[9] Kiritsis had a personal grievance and he wanted the world to know.

Thoughtful newspersons and news organizations are considering guidelines to help them get through Type-One situations better. As yet, however, the move toward guidelines has little momentum. Type One remains a sure method of securing vast news coverage.

Type Two, or nonviolent civil disobedience. Hannah Arendt credits Henry David Thoreau with putting the words "civil disobedience" into the political vocabulary. Thoreau spent one night in jail for refusing to pay a tax to a government that sanctioned slavery, then wrote powerfully of the experience. The fact that an aunt paid him out of jail the next morning did not detract from the drama of what he had done.[10] The distinguishing characteristics of Type Two are that the act is illegal but nonviolent, and that its perpetrator is prepared to accept the consequences of its commission. The concept was used by Gandhi and by Martin Luther King, Jr. King, from the time of the bus boycott in Montgomery in 1955–1956 until his death in 1968, often used Type Two and preached its virtues. Through it he called national and international attention to the aims of the civil rights movement. Scores of other civil rights leaders used the technique as a near-certain method of getting publicity. So did war resisters in the 1960s and others who sensed that Type Two would attract newspeople with their pads, microphones, and cameras.

Type Three, or the inflammatory pseudo-event. It has occurred to untold numbers of newspersons as well as to ordinary citizens that Types One and Two are staged to manipulate. Even so, media persons have not agreed on what to do about them. Even less have they decided what to do about Type Three. This type is characterized by provocative acts or language that are perfectly legal. One and two are flagrant forms of manipulation; Three is pervasive. Scarcely an issue of a newspaper goes to press, and scarcely an edition of radio or television news is aired, without being riddled by it. Boorstin has written extensively of pseudo-events—occurrences that are not spontaneous happenings at all, but are staged. He has not drawn the line sharply, however, between pseudo-events which are inflammatory in nature and those which are not. In short, he has not distinguished between consensus pseudo-events and conflict ones. A consensus pseudo-event—such as an anniversary celebration for a business or a hotel—is a harmless thing insofar as manipulation is concerned. It contains no conflict. The media can either cover it or not. However, a pseudo-event with conflict built in is not so harmless. Given the media's predilection, it can produce coverage for almost anyone clever or brazen enough to use it.

At the recent premiere of the film *MacArthur* in New York City, a group of demonstrators captured more than half the coverage and a part of the headline in one large daily newspaper far removed from that city. The demonstrators professed to believe, among other things, that the film was "designed to whip up support for a war in Africa or the Middle East."[11] They got what they wanted, although their demonstration was a passing thing and the film was less so.

An inflammatory pseudo-event such as this perfectly legal, if small, demonstration will almost always produce results provided it is done in the presence of reporters. But one need not take to the streets to stage a Type-Three event. Politicians, spokesmen for interest groups, and a few citizens representing little more than themselves have learned that there is another kind of Type Three that can also be effective. Every reporter is familiar with statements issued by persons seeking media exposure, and every reporter has noticed that statements which use strong language—which denounce some person, situation, thing, or institution—are most likely to find a market in the media. Daniel Schorr, in his book *Clearing the Air*, says that in the late 1960s, he came to realize that his own medium, television, puts a premium on the rhetoric of disagreement and violence. The thoughtful statements of Roy Wilkins and Andrew Young in those days could not compete with the barn-burning rhetoric of Stokely Carmichael and H. Rap Brown.

That is a game that many play. Individuals who are public figures, or who are not public figures but are trying to become one, can sometimes find their way into the media through the use of strong rhetoric. Many of them make the job easy for reporters by pre-packaging their anger or indignation in news releases. We might debate whether this form of Type Three is truly an "event." However, it is certainly inflammatory, or is intended to be.

Let us adapt Boorstin's definition of pseudo-events to establish a definition for Type Three.[12]

1. Type Three is not spontaneous, but contrived.
2. It is designed to include a strong element of conflict which may range from strongly worded language to provocative actions, so long as the language and actions are legal.
3. It is designed to be reported and is thus easy to report.
4. It is planned to be intelligible and is thus intelligible.
5. It is planned for the convenience of the media—i.e., at a time when the media will find it convenient to provide coverage.

There is an irony in the conclusions that this paper must reach. Often the emphasis of the media upon conflict is positively beneficial. It ferrets out some of the worst evils of government and society. Also, one concludes that many acts of the Propaganda of the Deed, especially Types Two and Three, have been committed on behalf of ends that were socially desirable, or even necessary. Thus neither conflict news nor certain forms of the Propaganda of the Deed are in themselves malignant. It is when the two come together that the media, which pride themselves on their independence, so often forfeit it. At that point, manipulation has occurred.

LEARNING TO PLAY THE GAME

What does all of this mean for business? Until recently, those who have used the Propaganda of the Deed most effectively have not been businesspeople. They have been consumer groups, environmental groups, labor unions, and civil rights groups, to name a few. But in 1977 and 1978, the process was discovered and used effectively by a group normally considered to be conservative. Dissatisfied farmers held tractor parades in support of 100 percent parity. They drove their tractors by the hundreds and the thousands in parades and rallies, and got their story onto countless front pages and into untold numbers of newscasts. Business may learn from their success. It would be an inept public relations person who could not suggest interesting ways by which corporations and institutions could play this rather cynical game to their own advantage, and with predictable results.

Those who wish the media no good are quick to say that all of this is a matter for great public concern. It is indeed a matter for public concern; but it is not a matter of public business. The First Amendment to the Constitution has seen to that. It is the proper business only of media persons themselves. Any rectification of the problem must be supplied by the ladies and gentlemen of the media with only such outside help as they wish to accept.

Quite on their own, however, they might wish to think again about what they automatically consider to be news. People do change their ways of looking at things. Among those who could see matters in different lights was Charles Beard, whose story occupies an early part of this essay. About eighteen years after he wrote *An Economic Interpretation*, Beard was visited by a friend, George S. Counts, and the two men went for an automobile ride over the hills of Connecticut in the vicinity of New Milford. Counts asked Beard how long it would take him to sum up all he had learned in a lifetime of study of the human condition. Beard thought he might do it in about a week. After a little while, he said it might take a day. Then he said he possibly could do it in a half hour. And then, bringing his hand down upon his knee, he said he could do it in three sentences, which he later expanded to four. Here they are:

> Whom the gods would destroy, they first make mad.
> The mills of the gods grind slowly, yet they grind exceedingly small.
> The bee fertilizes the flower that it robs.
> When it gets dark enough, you can see the stars.[13]

That is indeed one way of looking at things. It is entirely consensus, quite a change from Beard's earlier years. As moving as it is, no newspaper could take that approach to affairs, except perhaps on the religious page.

Yet there is more. Beard at times found a nice balance between conflict and consensus. When asked in 1941 whether he was satisfied with *An Economic Interpretation*, he said he was not. He had written it without sufficient regard to historical perspective, he said, and if he were redoing it, he would probably emphasize "not so much that the framers were not democrats as that they *were* republicans in a world where republicanism was forward-looking."[14] And he doubtless would have done so, retaining his original thesis entire.

In Beard's four summational sentences, he was as far in the direction of consensus as he earlier had been in the direction of conflict. But in the example just cited, he delivered up the truth, not in fragments, but as a whole. It is balanced between conflict and consensus. It contains elements of both; and it might well serve as a model for the media. It has character, it has guts, and it is fair. And that is what the news business should be all about.

NOTES

1. Charles A. Beard, *An Economic Interpretation of the Constitution of the United States* (New York: Macmillan, 1913); Eric F. Goldman, *Rendezvous with Destiny: A History of Modern American Reform* (New York: Knopf, 1952), pp. 149–55.

2. Robert E. Brown, *Charles Beard and the Constitution: A Critical Analysis of "An Economic Interpretation of the Constitution"* (Princeton, N.J.: Princeton University Press, 1956); Forrest McDonald, *We the People: The Economic Origins of the Constitution* (Chicago: University of Chicago Press, 1958).

3. John Higham, *Writing American History: Essays on Modern Scholarship* (Bloomington, Ind.: Indiana Univ. Press; London: 1970), pp. 73–74, 116–17, 143–46; John Higham et al., *History* (Englewood Cliffs, N.J.: Prentice-Hall, 1965), pp. 171–73, 222–23; Gene Wise, *American Historical Explanations: A Strategy for Grounded Inquiry* (Homewood, Ill.: Irwin Williams, 1973), pp. 343–50, 357–58.

4. Among the print media, scholars have applied the conflict and consensus labels most especially to weekly and community newspapers. See Gerald C. Stone and Patrick Mazza, "Impact of Consensus Theory on Community Newspaper Organization," *Journalism Quarterly*, Summer 1977, pp. 313–19; Clarice N. Olien, George A. Donohue, and Phillip J. Tichenor, "The Community Editor's Power and the Reporting of Conflict," *Journalism Quarterly*, Summer 1968, pp. 243–52. The community, weekly, and suburban press fall within the category of print media which, under ordinary circumstances, are consensus oriented. Large daily newspapers tend to emphasize conflict news, as do radio newscasts. A few daily newspapers achieve a sort of balance between conflict and consensus, but they are uncommon. In this category, one thinks of *The Wall Street Journal* and the *Christian Science Monitor*. News magazines, because they are compartmentalized and have a different format, make a different kind of impact from daily papers. Many specialty magazines and specialty newspapers are consensus oriented.

5. *Television News Index and Abstracts: A Guide to the Videotape Collection of the Network Evening News Programs in the Vanderbilt Television News Archive* (Nashville: Vanderbilt University, March 1975), p. 527.

6. "Legacy of Chet Huntley," *The Quill*, April 1974, p. 7.

7. Barbara W. Tuchman, *The Proud Tower: A Portrait of the World Before the War, 1890–1914* (New York: Macmillan, 1966).

8. *The Quill*, April 1974, pp. 17–19. Murray Olderman, "Patricia Hearst is Kidnapped and the Press, Too is Made Captive."

9. *Ibid.*, July/August 1977, p. 22. "Guidelines for the Coverage of Terrorism," Halina T. Czerniejewski.

10. Hannah Arendt, "Reflections—Civil Disobedience," *The New Yorker*, September 12, 1970, pp. 70–105.

11. The *Atlanta Journal*, June 30, 1977. "MacArthur Premieres with Protestors Outside."

12. Daniel J. Boorstin, *The Image, or What Happened to the American Dream* (New York: Atheneum, 1962), pp. 3–44.

13. Howard K. Beale, ed., *Charles A. Beard: An Appraisal* (Lexington, Ky.: University of Kentucky Press, 1954), pp. 251–52.

14. *Ibid.*, p. 250.

BUSINESS'S FRIEND, THE MEDIA

CURTIS D. MACDOUGALL

For all the charges that the media are biased against business or that the media are liberal change agents, Curtis MacDougall maintains that the journalistic media are bulwarks of the Establishment, the status quo, and the capitalistic system, because the media are a part of it. Throughout this century, he says, the media have sided with business and industry. The media sound the alarm against reform, according to MacDougall, who cites presidential politics, foreign affairs, and labor as areas in which the media demonstrate kinship with business.

The media are simply mirroring public opinion generated by negative experiences with business when critical business reporting occurs, MacDougall says. Considering this business orientation, the fairness and accuracy of the media, and especially their receptiveness to a variety of viewpoints, is a tribute to the spirit of press freedom.

Emeritus professor of journalism at Northwestern University, Dr. MacDougall is among the most honored of the nation's journalism educators and author of ten books. His Interpretative Reporting, *now in its seventh edition, has been the nation's standard reporting textbook for two generations. Active in the media and in politics for more than fifty years, he was a Democratic candidate for Congress in 1944 and 1970, and a Progressive candidate for the U.S. Senate in 1948.*

As a cub reporter for the *Fond du Lac Daily Commonwealth* near the end of World War I, I visited the three justices of the peace daily, primarily to obtain the names of those who had been fined for violating the automobile speed law, then fifteen miles per hour (a reasonable limit considering the condition of the horseshoe, nail-studded, pockmarked streets and the stamina of the horseless carriages). Usually, I returned to the office with a list of twenty-five or thirty. By the time it appeared in the paper, it had shrunk to five or ten as the result of visits to the office and telephone calls from the supposedly most substantial citizens with sufficient clout to persuade the editor not to expose their wrongdoing or that of a relative or friend. Strange as it may seem today, at that time an arrest for a traffic violation was considered a disgrace, the news of which one wanted suppressed at all costs.

Twenty years later, as a reporter for the *St. Louis Star-Times*, I was assigned to investigate the monopolistic practices of the milk industry in our milk shed. I visited the two big dairies, St. Louis and Pevely, and at the latter place had my one and only experience of being physically thrown down a flight of stairs. I also visited scores of small independent dairies, and I wrote a series of a half dozen or so articles to describe my findings. Dan Bishop, our Pulitzer Prize-winning cartoonist, illustrated them, and Irving Brant, our brilliant editorial writer, composed several editorials presumably to accompany my pieces. Only it never happened. The entire exhibit was turned over to the business office, and instead of an in-depth series of news articles, we enjoyed a considerable increase in big dairy advertising.

My files are replete with anecdotes of similar experiences involving fellow journalists, many of them former students, and I have heard of many more such tales. A recent case which attracted attention was the firing of Darrell Mack as editor of the *Beaumont Enterprise* and *Journal* because he ran a comparative grocery shopping list in the paper's family living section. Publisher Gene Cornwell called it "the most irresponsible story that had ever been run in the paper." It could, Cornwell explained, "conceivably have had a rather severe economic impact upon the business. It could have affected our ad lineage."

Despite the impression that these anecdotes might create, it is grossly untrue that the news and editorial policies of American journalistic media are dictated or directly influenced by advertisers. Favors, yes. Marriages, births, deaths, and social notes affecting any employee of a newspaper receive mention; it's one of the informal fringe benefits of the job. And the same is true of friends and relatives. Just as the soda jerker gives his girl friend an extra scoop of strawberry ice cream or the friendly merchant lets you have something at cost, so the publishers' golf cronies and their wives' bridge partners get a line or two more than is accorded the overwhelming majority of other citizens. No serious damage is done.

Suppression of legitimate news, especially if it involves lawbreaking, is something else. I once worked for a paper where we jocosely said the rule was, "Five dollars to put it in; ten dollars to keep it out." Students of mine used to be startled when they reached into their pockets to find five-dollar bills put there by appreciative company lawyers in the press rooms of Chicago's city hall, county building, police station, or criminal court building.

When it comes to really important matters of public concern, there is no bribery and little or no influence wielding. Principal reason: it is not necessary, and to attempt it is to injure pride and earn rebuff. As journalism more and more becomes big business, it would be superfluous to warn any publisher or editor, "Now, Joe, no radicalism in your rag today."

CONGLOMERATE JOURNALISM

The journalistic media are a bulwark of the Establishment, the status quo, the capitalistic system, because they are a part of it. Journalism is very much big business, and it has undergone the same economic changes that have affected any or all other big businesses during the past century. For instance, in 1910 there were 2,202 daily newspapers when the population of the United States was approximately 92 million. Today there are 1,762 daily newspapers to serve a population of almost 220 million. Whereas in grandfather's time virtually every city of 15,000 or over had rival newspapers, and the largest cities— New York, Chicago, and others—had from five to ten papers each, today only a very few of the very largest cities have second newspapers, and most of them are under the same ownership.

When I was a youth, there was widespread concern lest the sensational Hearst chain reach twenty. Today the Gannett-Spiedel chain owns seventy-three dailies. There are fifty-seven Thomson newspapers in this country and about twice that many in Canada and Great Britain. The Knight-Ridder chain has thirty-four newspapers, and Newhouse has twenty-nine. As for the value of this huge conglomerate investment, how do you measure goodwill or the power of a good subscription list? A year ago, Australian Rupert Murdoch paid a reputed $32.5 million for the limping *New York Post* with a circulation of nearly 400,000 daily. Three years earlier he paid $17.3 million for the *San Antonio Express* and *News*, each with about 80,000 daily and combined, about twice that number on Sundays.

According to Ben Bagdikian, premier critic of newspaper behavior since the passing of A. J. Liebling, 71 percent of daily newspaper circulation in the United States is controlled by 168 multiple ownerships. In 1930, chains controlled only 43 percent of the circulation and in 1960 only 46 percent. Of the 1,500 cities with daily newspapers, 97.5 percent have no local newspaper competition. In 1920, there were 700 American cities with competing newspapers. Today there are fewer than fifty.

In addition, most of the heavy investors in newspaper properties also own radio and television stations, magazines and book publishing houses. Most of them buy and sell as they would their shares in banks, insurance companies, oil enterprises, utilities, and other investment opportunities. In other words, journalism is a big business, a *very* big business. And the major interest of the owners is the profit-and-loss statement. None of the leading multiple owners has even visited all of the plants he owns; he probably couldn't recall the names of many if not most of his journalistic properties.

So, to charge that these high-powered financiers who happen to own journalistic enterprises along with all kinds of other money-makers are interested in undermining or seriously changing the political and economic system of this country is palpably absurd.

CONSERVATIVE NEWSPAPERS: A ONE-PARTY PRESS

Newspaper managements come by their conservatism honestly. They not only support the so-called Establishment, they are a huge part of that Establishment themselves. That their journalistic properties are so fair and accurate, so receptive to a variety of viewpoints on major matters is a great tribute to their belief in the spirit of the freedom-of-the-press clause of the First Amendment—a marketplace for controversial ideas so that a citizen can evaluate and choose in the process of governing himself. I am certain that conservative newspaper owners often are as pained by what they read in their publications as are the rest of us. They have it within their power to corrupt the news. Where else in our economy do you find any group with a greater sense of public responsibility and adherence to high ethical standards?

Now, none of this is to be translated as meaning there's no cause for complaint or alarm at the antiquarian viewpoint which characterizes many of these publications. The honest conservative paper, ethically presented, nevertheless does constitute what Adlai Stevenson in 1952 labeled, "a one-party press." As a result of Adlai's stinging rebuke, ever since then presidential campaigns have been reported much more fairly, not only in the space given rival candidates but, more importantly, in the impartial manner in which their activities are reported. Still, the press always has overwhelmingly supported the more conservative of the contending candidates for the presidency (except for 1964, when the entire country was frightened into voting for Lyndon Johnson to prevent Barry Goldwater from doing what LBJ went ahead and did anyway).

In 1976, 411 dailies with 20,951,798 circulation supported Gerald Ford, whereas Jimmy Carter was endorsed by only eighty dailies with a total circulation of 7,607,739. Richard Nixon in 1972 was endorsed by 753 dailies with 30,560,535 circulation and George McGovern by fifty-six dailies with 3,044,534 circulation. In 1968, Nixon was endorsed by 60.8 percent of the dailies with 69.97 percent of the total circulation, while Hubert Humphrey had support from only 14 percent of the dailies with 18.3 percent of the circulation. In 1964, for the first, last, and only time, a Democrat won endorsement by a

majority of the dailies committing themselves, but it was no overwhelming advantage. Johnson was favored by 400 papers with 42.4
percent of the circulation. Goldwater had 359 papers with 34.7 percent of the circulation.

SIDING WITH BUSINESS, NOT REFORM

The conservatism of the vast majority of American newspapers is indicated not only by their traditional endorsement of conservative
presidential candidates, but more importantly, it is reflected in editorial stands on issues. It is impossible to cite any cause or program or
movement which had the support of any appreciable proportion of the
orthodox press which we today can say with historical perspective
was liberal or progressive. Rather, the journalistic masters have sided
with those of business and industry who sounded the alarm against
reform. That meant, for instance, opposition to Woodrow Wilson's
New Freedom, which included the income tax, the federal reserve
system, women's suffrage, child labor protective laws, the Federal
Trade Commission, the Clayton Anti-Trust Act, and direct election of
United States senators.

Calvin Coolidge summed it up: "The business of America is
business." General Motors' Charles Wilson added: "What's good for
General Motors is good for America." A majority of newspapers supported the "old deal" philosophy of pump priming, which was institutionalized in Herbert Hoover's Re-Construction Finance Corporation. My first editor at least once weekly editorialized, "Good for
the Chamber of Commerce." He meant it, and most of his readers
agreed with him.

Then came the Depression and the New Deal. The press joined,
nay it led, the economic royalists who were bitter Franklin Delano
Roosevelt haters. Business interests and the journalistic media fought
the New Deal every inch of the way. The co-owner of a newspaper I
edited in the mid-thirties boasted of his ability to disobey or circum-
vent the NRA (National Recovery Administration) and other New
Deal laws. The American Liberty League placed its faith in the nine
old men of the Supreme Court, who came through declaring the first
round of New Deal measures to be unconstitutional. Then Elisha
Hanson, general counsel for the American Newspaper Publishers Association, advised all newspaper owners to disobey the National
Labor Relations Act and the Fair Labor Standards (wage-and-hour)
Act, which he was confident would be struck down by the high court.
When Charles Evans Hughes and Owen Roberts shifted to the liberal
bloc, they were called traitors by some and hated as much as Earl
Warren was to be some years later.

In its anti-FDR campaign, business interests had the nearly complete support of the nation's press, about the only dissenters being J. David Stern of the *Philadelphia Record,* his youthful editorial writer, I. F. Stone, and Josiah Gitt of the *York Gazette and Daily.*

The press opposed Harry Truman's Fair Deal, John F. Kennedy's New Frontier, and Lyndon B. Johnson's Great Society, whatever that was. In retrospect, with the evidence contained in a number of iconoclastic books which have appeared in recent years, the sincerity of these chief executives in promoting liberal measures is questionable; but the press took them at their face value and protested.

Throughout the three decades that I taught editorial writing at Northwestern University, and especially while doing research for my book, *Principles of Editorial Writing,* I tried to find a pro-labor editorial in an American newspaper—any newspaper, big or small. I examined the exchanges, patronized the out-of-town newspaper stands, wrote to fellow journalists, colleagues, friends, and former students on papers where such editorials would be most likely to appear. In vain. The closest I came was the stock Labor Day message to organized labor to count its blessings; it should be grateful to exist in the democratic United States where all are free and equal. All very true, but what I'd like to see just once is some prestigious paper siding with labor in some significant dispute, saying loudly, "Charge, boys. Your boss is a stinker. Go get him." Quite the contrary, in crisis situations the press invariably creates the impression that the unions are at fault, and that their goons disregard the public interest, often violently.

UPHOLDING AMERICAN FOREIGN POLICY

Journalism's pro-business indoctrination is demonstrated also in its unswerving, generally uncritical support of American foreign policy. The most important event of the twentieth century was the Russian Revolution of 1917. Since then the capitalistic world has been obsessed with fear and has devoted itself to preventing the spread of communism. In the early years there was armed invasion of the vast territory which became the Soviet Union. Counterrevolutionaries and exiles were supported. Then came nonrecognition, exclusion from the League of Nations, economic boycott, and intensive propaganda. The Soviets' enemies on either side, Hitler's Germany to the west and Japan to the east, were encouraged. They, of course, double-crossed. The Hearst press especially saw a Bolshevik behind every lamp post. We became paranoiac until finally sanity was restored, mostly by businessmen who awakened to the fact that rich markets were being neglected. Especially after the Soviet army turned back Hitler at

Stalingrad, quite some time before any of our lend-lease aid reached it, we became convinced that, evil or not, the Soviet Union was here to stay and we might as well learn to live with it—and profit from it. So, when what was called the Cold War gave way to détente, business supported it and the press followed suit. Richard Nixon went further, following some ping-pong players in paving the way for trade with Red China, and today we are gradually resuming normal relations with our neighbor, Cuba.

Economic, or business, relations are, as could hardly be otherwise, the main consideration of foreign diplomacy. The policy is fundamentally one to promote American business interests. And basically it has been supported wholeheartedly by the American press. The huge cost involved in maintaining the military establishment deemed necessary to protect the effort is virtually unquestioned. Specific projects or weapons may be debated but not the major premises. Nor, till the Watergate scandals blew the lid off, was the reality of the fear that persisted regarding dissenters.

THE CRUSADE AGAINST CORRUPTION

No American editor ever earned a greater reputation for crusading against corruption in government than Virgil M. ("Red") Newton, Jr., longtime editor of the *Tampa Tribune*. For years he was chairman of the Freedom of Information committee of Sigma Delta Chi, of which he also served as president. Similarly, he headed the Associate Press Managing Editors and received virtually every honor for public service that any professional journalism organization had to offer. The highlights of his career are related in his book, *Crusade for Democracy* (Iowa State Press, 1961). To mention only a few of his crusades: he exposed sweat shops in the Florida prison system, forced the legislature to pass a better reapportionment bill, defended migrant workers, exposed politics in the police department, helped the Kefauver committee expose syndicate gambling, fought pork-barrel politics, supported open-meeting laws, promoted the city-manager system, and so on.

Pertinent to our immediate topic of interest is the following bit of advice in this veteran crusader's book:

> We have done a number of crusades involving business but I would warn the journalism beginner to tread easily in this field. Experienced know-how is essential for the legal matter of privacy is involved. A safe policy is to look into business research only when the taxpayers, in the form of government itself, are directly involved and where the business affects the living of a whole community. And always stick closely to the records.

Crusades involving government are to expose corruption and in no way attack the capitalistic system itself. It is even more true of any attempts to expose wrongdoing in business. Most editors heed Red Newton's advice.

It is utterly impossible for any journalist to understand Supreme Court Justice Lewis F. Powell, Jr., when he complains that the media—especially the electronic media—allow their facilities to be used to destroy the free enterprise system. "One of the bewildering paradoxes of our time," Powell is quoted as saying, "is the extent to which the enterprise system tolerates if not participates in its own destruction."

Just as incomprehensible is Barry Goldwater's charge that the journalistic media make a determined effort "to replace 'big bad' business corporations with government-controlled corporations."

In commenting on these and similar criticisms of the press in the April 1977 *Quill*, Ralph O. Otwell, editor of the *Chicago Sun-Times* and immediate past national president of Sigma Delta Chi, wrote:

If the media are questioning with greater intensity the methods and motives of business, it is only because the readers and viewing public, out of their own needs and anxieties, are prompting the questions and prodding the newsmen to seek out the answers.

Otwell quoted Donald S. MacNaughton, chairman of the Prudential Insurance Company, who laid down some commandments for better relations between journalism and business, the most important being, "Thou shalt not lie." Otwell commented:

Nothing gets a corporation into hotter water than an obvious lie or transparent attempt to cover up. Yet, after Watergate and long after the problems of ITT and Lockheed, and the bribery of public officials and the legacy of illegal campaign contributions and other examples of foolish and damaging attempts to deceive the public, too many businessmen still find refuge in the outright lie or the evasive comment. The lie carries enormous potential for self destruction.

After confessing that he "tends instinctively to side with the viewpoint of business, capitalism, free enterprise, and the open marketplace," my good friend James J. Kilpatrick wrote in his syndicated column which the *Chicago Daily News* used May 27, 1977:

My friends in free enterprise can be maddening friends—bull-headed, bat-blind, insensitive and inconsistent. They spend millions to buy the best public relations advice that money can buy but, according to a Marketing Science Institute and Louis Harris and Associates survey, have an increasingly worse public image.

Jack quotes the survey's findings that 78 percent of those interviewed believe products "do not last as long as they used to," 6 percent believe it is "more difficult to get things repaired," and half believe that consumers today "are getting a worse deal in the market places than a decade ago." Only four of twenty-five industries were rated as doing as much as 25 percent of a good job. They were banks, stores, shopkeepers, and telephone companies. These respondents based their opinions not on journalistic accounts but upon personal experience. The press is mostly a mirror of opinion.

That is what I recently heard Ben Heinemann, former president of the Chicago and Northwestern Railway and now president of Northwest Industries, call it at a testimonial luncheon to honor John McWelty, who retired as managing editor of the Midwest edition of *The Wall Street Journal* after forty years. Heinemann told about 600 of us that business and the press are indispensable to each other. Business supplies the media with its raw material, and no form of advertising is so effective as a good news story. In the press there is an interplay of ideas between labor, business, and government, and the press's duty is to make sense out of fragmented information to give perspective to all aspects of our complex world.

Well, to provide that great service it takes high-powered men and women. At the McWelty affair, Warren H. Phillips, president and chief executive officer of *The Wall Street Journal* and Dow Jones & Co., stressed the urgency when he cited the press's two general failures of recent days: first, its failure to predict problems such as New York's financial crisis and the energy crisis; and, second, its failure to achieve standards of clarity and understanding in a complex age.

THE NEED TO REALIGN EDUCATIONAL PRIORITIES

So now it becomes time to start quoting myself. For years I have been screaming agreement with those high school dropouts who say that what they were being taught is not relevant. True. We expect eighteen-year-olds to know enough to vote, yet we protect them from debate or even knowledge of controversial issues about which they must make decisions. The overwhelming majority of high school graduates—maybe college graduates too—know almost nothing about either business or journalism or anything else. Most of them don't know the difference between a bond and a stock, and they never heard of a debenture or a tax anticipation warrant. Bank balance sheets, profit-and-loss statements, credit unions, mutual savings companies, wills, mortgages, leases—matters with which they will come into contact throughout their lives are neglected so that they can learn about how many parts Caesar found Gaul divided into or whether Hamlet was crazy.

While working for my doctorate in sociology at the University of Wisconsin, I elected courses in public value and labor problems from the great John R. Commons and Selig Perlman, but when I returned to newspaper work I found myself very deficient in matters economic and managed to take time out for a course in money and banking. I still didn't know enough. I should have had courses in public finance, taxation, economic history and theory, and more. Also some law. These were courses which I tried in vain to persuade journalism students to take. I told them they'd fall flat on their faces when their city editor assigned them to cover a city council budget hearing or to analyze the annual report of a county board. I advised them they'd better start learning some of the facts of the business world the comparatively easy way—in the classroom. But frankly, they were scared away by the introductory course, Economics A or 1 or whatever it was called, designed not for everyone—certainly not for journalists—but for future majors in the field and devoted almost entirely to theory and definitions of the terms invented by the so-called classical economists: economic man, reasonably prudent man, law of supply and demand, law of marginal utility, law of diminishing returns, and so on, all of which has about as much relation to reality as Jonathan Swift's Lilliputians who harrassed traveling Gulliver or J. R. R. Tolkien's hobbits. It is no wonder that only a negligible number of journalists want to specialize in business or finance. As high school and college students, they never had a chance to develop an interest.

Throughout my journalistic lifetime I have learned that classical economists don't know what they're talking about. From the right to the left, economic experts have been consistently wrong about absolutely everything of importance during the past half century. In the twenties they prattled about Coolidge Prosperity. They didn't anticipate the stock market crash nor the long depression, and they couldn't explain it when it happened. Herbert Hoover consulted them and announced, "Prosperity is just around the corner."

We went on a defense or war economy after war broke out in Europe, thereby temporarily ending our 14-million unemployment and our free enterprise system. Our economy was subsidized with business and labor mutually dependent on the artificial stimulation of government spending. The new economic order, which is not that described in the classical economics textbooks, began in the thirties and persists to this day.

As the end of World War II approached, the economists, from right to left, predicted widespread unemployment and possible depression as we converted from a war to a peace economy and tried to absorb 14 million servicemen. Franklin Roosevelt and Henry Wallace were called impractical idealists when they predicted 60 million jobs.

Since that time the experts have been consistently wrong in forecasting recession when boom has been imminent, getting inflation and deflation confused in their forecasts and shifting in their attitudes toward government spending depending on who the recipients of the largesse happened to be. Several years ago *Newsweek* asked, "What's wrong with the top U.S. economists?" and printed a chart on which one line showed the way the economy went, and the other showed the way the experts said it would go. It was laughable. Neither the Council of Economic Advisors, the Federal Reserve Board, nor the highly paid experts for banks, business institutions, and labor organizations have any but abominable records. Probably we should be thankful that we do not yet live in a completely deterministic society.

Even if the economists' records were good, and if the journalistic seers were thoroughly trained and literate, there still would remain the problem of the reader. Only a minority ever will have the interest or the know-how to read *The Wall Street Journal* or the business and financial sections of some leading newspapers. There is no one, however, who has *no* stake in the economy and for whom news of incidents and developments which affect him should not be played up in the press. It is not only future business editors for whom the lack of attention paid by the schools should be regretted. Since the Institute for Propaganda Analysis went out of business at the time of Pearl Harbor, there has been no consistent or systematic attempt to train young people in how to read or watch the news intelligently and critically.

Only a negligible minority ever will use the algebra, geometry, trigonometry, Latin, foreign languages, and such else that they're taught in high school. Surely they'll never again write a theme, as that sterile literary exercise fortunately has no counterpart in real life. However, every day of his life the American citizen will be affected by the free press. He should know what it is, what its opportunities and responsibilities are.

Much as I lament the poor attention paid business news, I regret much more the failure of the schools to instruct students in the nature and meaning of the First Amendment, especially the freedom-of-the-press clause, and to explain how the media of communication function.

HOW BUSINESS SWAYS THE MEDIA

MARK GREEN

It is quite logical for business to attempt to influence the media, says Mark Green, director of Public Citizen's Congress Watch. The manner and vigor with which businesses attempt their influence, however, bears the mark of paranoia.

Green lists seven established techniques used by corporations to bend media opinion, including buying media outlets, advocacy advertising, distributing canned editorials, hidden sponsorship, withdrawal of ads, and sponsorship of public television. He suggests that the surreptitious means of influence be replaced by candor as a means of influencing public opinion.

Green is often called the chief of Ralph Nader's Raiders. His books include, The Closed Enterprise System, Who Runs Congress?, Corporate Power in America, The Monopoly Makers, *and* Taming the Giant Corporation.

Does business try to influence the media? Is a moth drawn to a flame?

This business habit is less venial than inevitable. Companies seek profits; the media have the power to affect profits; therefore, logically, companies will try to influence that power. Wedded to this logic, however, is a paranoia exemplified by the not untypical business executive in Leonard Silk's *Ethics and Profits* who says, "The media are destructive and misinformed." This logic and this paranoia help explain the business sector's perennial and varied efforts to manipulate the opinion-shapers.

Years ago business efforts to influence the media were, to say the least, indelicate. Muckraker George Seldes once described the "contract of silence" which all newspapers had in the 1900s with the Proprietary Association of America: "Time after time when a city ordinance or a bill in the legislature anywhere in the country proposed limiting or even investigating the deadly [drug] industry, telegrams from the Proprietary Association immediately blackmailed the local or statewide press into defeating the general welfare of the public. The result was that all public health bills from the 1900s to the 1930s were almost universally opposed by the press."

The business community today is far more decorous, though the goal of bending media opinion to corporate benefit is similar. How does business do it? There are at least seven established techniques.

If you can't beat them, buy them. Perhaps taking too literally A. J. Liebling's axiom, "freedom of the press is reserved for those who own one," some companies seek to assure media access by trying to buy an outlet. Recall that in 1968 ITT sought to purchase ABC, and actually got approval from a supine Federal Communications Commission. The Justice Department's Antitrust Division then sued and thwarted the merger, thereby sparing the network the discomfort of having to cover the Dita Beard and Chile scandals while under Harold Geneen's stern gaze. At that time ABC president Leonard Goldenson was furious that the Department blocked the merger; today he tells visitors of his relief that his company was forced to, and did, succeed by its own effort.

Since then ARCO has bought the financially troubled *London Observer* (vowing to steer clear of all editorial control), and Mobil has considered buying the *Long Island Press* and even the *Washington Star*, without result. Which is just as well, for there is an unavoidable tension between an independent press and a profit-seeking corporation. DuPont interests, for example, run Wilmington's *Morning News* and the *Evening Journal*. In 1974, four editors at the papers either resigned or were fired, claiming that their board of directors opposed news stories that embarrassed the DuPont family.

Advertising, advocacy, and ad hominem. Beyond the $33 billion business spends annually to sell its products is the estimated $500 million to $1 billion it spends to promote its editorial and institutional point of view. John E. O'Toole, the president of the Foote, Cone and Belding ad agency, predicts that as government regulation of business increases, "advocacy advertising will be an essential part of the communications programs of many companies." The most prominent example is Mobil's $10 million campaign—especially those op-eds in twenty-five of the nation's largest newspapers which discuss energy and capital (we need more of both) and oil-industry critics (who are invariably dolts). The First Amendment may tolerate such propaganda, but that doesn't mean that Senator James Abourezk or columnist Tom Wicker have to like it. Abourezk took the Senate floor to denounce Mobil's "pious rhetoric," and Wicker unloaded on what he called "the self-serving, devious, mealymouthed, self-exculpating, holier-than-thou, positively sickening oil-company advertisements in which these international behemoths depict themselves as paragons of virtue embattled against a greedy world."

More troubling than pious advocacy advertising is *ad hominem* advertising. After Bronx Borough President Robert Abrams criticized the Dollar Savings Bank for "red-lining," the bank took out full-page ads in city papers headlined, "A Bronx Politician Wants Us to Start Taking Risks with Your Money," and went on to denounce Abrams.

Critics of the health-care industry, including Ralph Nader, have argued that the system spends too much on exotic gadgetry rather than preventative medicine. Crane Communications then took out a full-page ad in *Advertising Age* with the headline, "Is the Breakthrough that Might Save Your Life Being Fought by Ralph Nader?"

Now, it is difficult enough to reply to advocacy advertising. When I talked to the *Washington Post* about factual errors in a Chamber of Commerce ad on the Agency for Consumer Protection and the difficulty of affording a rebuttal, I was generously told, "We believe in freedom of the press—at $3.16 a line." But when companies with millions to spend on advertising campaigns smear or rebuke individuals in forums that permit no reply, the potential abuse by business of the media approaches its zenith.

Canned editorials. In 1964, Ben Bagdikian wrote in *Harper's* that, "For the past three years the National Association of Manufacturers has sent out editorials which have been picked up, usually verbatim, by six hundred daily newspapers, most often without attribution to the NAM source." Two years later the *NAM Reports* was so bold as to brag that its Industrial Press Service also sends out canned editorials to 3,500 weekly editors. The practice is still widespread, as a glance at the identical editorials against the proposed Agency for Consumer Protection in small weeklies will attest.

A new wrinkle is the canned cartoon. Mobil sends well-crafted pro-oil-industry cartoons around to 5,000 small newspapers for unattributed use. In one, for example, a man before an audience of children uses an ax to hack a hose into sections, as a woman in the foreground explains, "He's explaining how breaking up the oil companies would work." One Philadelphia daily editor who used such a cartoon without reference to Mobil as the source admitted that, "There is a tendency to discredit anything the corporations put out. Attribution would tend to weaken the point of my editorial." Chrysler has recently distributed a cartoon mocking air bags to 660 dailies and 5,500 weeklies. The executive who arranged this distribution, Frank Wylie, who is scheduled to become the president of the Public Relations Society in 1978, probably admitted more than he intended in his explanation that, "I am no more guilty than anyone who uses a mat service."

Hidden sponsorship. There are many other forms of the corporate sell which fail to be so labeled. A public relations firm for the Tobacco Institute in the late 1960s wrote pro-tobacco speeches for friendly, prominent doctors to deliver, and it paid acquiescent reporters $1,000 a week to write on preselected tobacco-related topics and publish the results, without mention of this sponsorship. Recently,

200 newspapers distributed as a supplement "Garden Time '76," which was actually a sixteen-page handout from Ortho, a manufacturer of garden supplies. Frank Schaumburg's *Judgement Reserved: A Landmark Environmental Case,* a book favorable to Reserve Mining in its defense of an epical pollution suit, had 10 percent of its stock bought prepublication by Armco Steel, which is a co-owner of Reserve. Large newspaper advertisements attacking the FDA's proposed ban on saccharin—"It's just another example of the arbitrary nature of BIG GOVERNMENT"—was signed merely by "The Calorie Control Council," with no indication that the Council was a group of manufacturers and processors of dietary products. In all these examples, it should not prove impossible for the participation of such interested parties to be disclosed. Writer John Brooks, for example, candidly acknowledged AT&T's help in his *Telephone: The First Hundred Years.*

The threat of withdrawal. When the *New York Post* began to run a series on supermarket abuses by reporter Stephen Lawrence a few years ago, supermarkets who advertised in the *Post* complained. The upshot: owner Dolly Schiff canceled the remainder of the series in the middle of a press run, and Lawrence eventually moved over to the *Daily News.* On the other hand, the *New York Times* completed a five-part series on the high cost and danger of drug overprescription and unnecessary surgery. As a result, drug firms, who felt that "you don't feed people who beat you up," pulled 200 pages of advertising worth a half million dollars from *Modern Medicine,* a *Times* subsidiary.

The prevalence of such events is no doubt exaggerated. For example, merchant marine interests in favor of "cargo preference" glibly try to explain away unanimously critical editorials by citing the advertising outlays in newspapers by major oil firms who oppose the legislation. Still, with so many papers suffering so much red ink, it takes a Joseph Pulitzer to be entirely indifferent to the economic consequences of editorial decisions.

Corporate television. Corporate funding of public television has progressed to the point that *The New Yorker* ran a cartoon within the past year in which a television screen flashed the following sign to its audience: "This program was *not* brought to you by Mobil." Corporate underwriting of public TV has reached some $14 million a year. It is a prestige investment that reaches a literate, upper-middle-class community. "We know our efforts have won us friends," says Mobil's Herbert Schmertz, "and we believe our involvement with PBS has persuaded an important segment of our society to look at Mobil in a new light, to be more open-minded when we speak out on issues."

From the corporate standpoint, it makes sense. But does it make sense from society's standpoint? The *Columbia Journalism Review* points out that, "Few, if any of these programs, have been of a documentary, public affairs, or investigative nature dealing with such issues as the economy, the environment, the defense establishment, or other so-called controversial areas."

TV executives agree that companies underwriting public-television programs are increasingly reviewing scripts, on the not irrational ground that they're paying the freight and are publicly associated with the content. Everyone wants public television to succeed as an alternate network (except for the other networks), but it should ideally be funded by the public via tax revenues, not by businesses who have a particular point of view to promote. President Carter's proposal to increase federal funding of public radio and television to $1 billion over the next five years is a good start toward this goal.

The media are businesses. This point is so obvious as to be overlooked. David J. Mahoney, chairman of Norton Simon, has recently written that journalism is big business and that, "The only free press is a profitable press, and that fact should give pause to the writer who thinks corporate profits are made at the expense of the consumer." The milieu in which media executives exist is a business one, as RCA and *Post/Newsweek*, each with multiple media holdings, are 31 and 452 respectively on *Fortune*'s top 500 list of manufacturing firms. When Robert Anderson, chairman of ARCO, visits Washington he invites the *Washington Post* editorial board over for a chat; Cesar Chavez does not so presume. When Henry Ford II in 1975 complained to Arthur Ochs Sulzberger that the auto makers were not getting their message about federal safety and pollution standards across to the American people, Sulzberger, the chairman of the *New York Times* and of a group called the Newspaper Advertising Bureau (NAB), called together publishing and reporting colleagues from around the country under the auspices of the NAB to hear Ford's complaint. The meeting was widely covered.

The business called network television has proven especially cautious in dealing with the business community. NBC recently bought *The Buffalo Creek Disaster,* a book by Gerald Stern about the negligence of the Pittston Coal Co. that led to that tragedy. A few days before production was to begin last September and after Pittston had complained to NBC about the projected docu-drama, the network shelved the project, calling it "untimely" in light of existing litigation.

"There is absolutely no business reporting on TV. None," complains George J. W. Goodman (aka "Adam Smith"). "TV's idea of covering the oil crisis was to go out and interview people waiting in line to buy gas. You'd think that TV would have a financial version of 'Sixty Minutes.'" True, there are occasional programs like CBS's study of Philips Petroleum ("The Corporation") a few years ago, but these illuminating critiques are more exception than rule.

It is indeed troubling that our largest companies, due to the sheer weight of their wealth, can misshape media, if not public opinion, by such devices. At the least, the hidden sponsors ought to be publicly disclosed, and airwaves owned by the public should provide time for counterads to advocacy ads. (A federal court, for example, has recently awarded Energy Action reply time under the Fairness Doctrine to run ads critical of oil companies.)

More generically, the we-they view by business must change. The approach of many business executives that the media are simply anti-business is overwrought, for business's problems stem from actual failings, such as admitted payoffs by 400 companies, rather than the reporting of such events. But the reflex to sway the media will no doubt remain. We would all be better off, however, if companies abandoned their small army of canned editorialists, editorial censors, advocacy advertisers, and media acquisition agents and focused instead on obeying the law and telling the truth. In the long run candor is preferable to manipulation, both ethically as well as strategically.

ECONOMIC UNDERSTANDING: A CHALLENGE TO THE MEDIA

ROBERT P. KEIM

Many businesspeople and educators have pointed with alarm at something they call "economic illiteracy," claiming that we are threatened with losing our economic system because we don't understand it. Others call the issue a red herring. Research sponsored by the Advertising Council showed that public economic understanding is indeed incomplete and fragmentary.

Robert Keim, Advertising Council president, maintains that the media must play a central role in improving economic understanding by focusing attention on the problem and acting as catalysts to encourage acquisition of economic knowledge. Keim describes the massive economic education campaign launched by the Advertising Council and reports that comparing 1977 survey data with 1976 indicates improvement. Americans display increased economic understanding and less desire for government regulation.

The Advertising Council yearly mobilizes over $500 million of advertising space and time contributed for the improvement of American society through mass communication. Mr. Keim was appointed to the President's Advisory Council on Minority Enterprise and was a participant in the 1974 Economic Summit Conference.

If we are to succeed in raising the level of economic understanding of the American people—and recent surveys have revealed that economic understanding by the public is incomplete and fragmentary—the role of the media is of indisputable importance. It may well be the overriding factor. Ours is indeed the media generation. The medium has become the message. Or, as Marshall McLuhan phrased it so aptly,

> all media work us over completely. They are so pervasive in their personal, political, economic, aesthetic, psychological, moral, ethical and social consequences that they leave no part of us untouched, unaffected, unaltered. The medium is the massage.[1]

It is not just the substance of what the media conveys; the simple fact that the media are conveying a certain message is enough to condition the public to accept it as a matter of truth and importance. Regardless of how the public eventually reacts, they now know that such and such a subject is important, with a capital *I*. We can underscore the importance of economic understanding when it is apparent that only one in seven Americans understands the interrelationships of business, labor, and government. We know that the route to changing this is through the media.

The freedom marchers learned this lesson well, as have the anti-war demonstrators, the student dissenters, the pro and antiabortionists, the women's rights groups, and the gay liberationists.

At one time, the Jesuits may have said, in effect, give me the child and I will have the man. Today one could well say, give me the media and I will have both the child *and* the man.

The entire history of the Advertising Council bears out the importance of this tenet. Starting in World War II, devoted to the communication of messages to the American people to help with the war effort, the Council quickly learned that simply selecting subjects for transmittal to the media and thence to the public suddenly gave a lift to the cause or program. The communications revolution did not begin with Marshall McLuhan; he helped to define its impact and significance after it had come into full flower, and he did so with great style and wit.

It is all too well known to the hundreds of individuals and organizations that come to us each year requesting our support. We hear the refrain over and over: the Council's accepting a campaign with the eventual assurance of media coverage is tantamount to success. Of course, it really isn't. There is a host of other factors. But one thing is clear. Tangible media support or coverage is the necessary prelude to success for any effort in promoting public-service causes like our current effort in economic education.

This puts an awesome power and responsibility in the hands of media. Some marginal practitioners may treat their responsibilities lightly, cavalierly, or worse. But I have discerned a steadily increasing sense of responsibility by the overwhelming majority of media people. This view may fly in the teeth of some people who feel that their ox has been gored by the media. But I nevertheless sense a generally rising tide of responsibility on the part of what we refer to as "the press." The media response to our American Economic System campaign, which I will describe later, bears this out.

THE SOCIALLY RESPONSIBLE PRESS

In *Four Theories of the Press*, Theodore Peterson, dean of the College of Communications, University of Illinois, describes what he and his coauthors refer to as "The Social Responsibility Theory of the Press," which "suggests a direction in which thinking about freedom of the press is heading." Describing the work of the Commission on Freedom of the Press, whose published reports were issued in 1947, and earlier reflections by editors and publishers, the authors state:

> These men realized that twentieth-century conditions demand of the mass media a new and different kind of social responsibility. This realization came about the time that people began to measure and assess the "communication revolution" through which they were passing. . . . The very fact that control of the press is so limited puts a new and uneasy power into the hands of media owners and managers. No longer is it easy for the press to be a free marketplace of ideas, as defined by [John Stuart] Mill and [Thomas] Jefferson. As the Commission on Freedom of the Press said, "protection against government is not now enough to guarantee that a man who has something to say shall have a chance to say it. The owners and managers of the press determine which persons, which facts, which versions of these facts, shall reach the public." This uneasiness is the basis of the developing Social Responsibility theory: that the power and near monopoly position of the media impose on them an obligation to be socially responsible, to see that all sides are fairly presented and that the public has enough information to decide; and that if the media do not take on themselves such responsibility, it may be necessary for some other agency of the public to enforce it.
>
> Let us say again that the Social Responsibility theory should not be thought of as an abstraction produced by a group of scholars who made up the Hutchins Commission. The theory has been so treated by some factions of the press with which the Hutchins Commission was in bad odor. But all the essentials of this theory were expressed by responsible editors and publishers long before the Commission, and have been stated by other responsible editors and publishers since and quite independently of the Commission. It is a trend, not an academic exercise.[2]

To corroborate the final sentence in this quotation, let me cite one example of what I deem to be this social responsibility theory of the press as a growing trend. On the night of November 20, 1974, the Advertising Council presented its annual public-service award to Katharine Graham, chairman of the Washington Post Company. It was a dramatic, one might say electric, evening. The Grand Ballroom of the Waldorf Astoria . . . Katharine Graham, widow of Phil Graham, one of the Advertising Council's great chairmen of an earlier date . . . daughter of Eugene and Agnes Myers, both longtime supporters of the Council. Mrs. Graham, a former member of our Public Policy Committee who relinquished that post because of the heavy burdens of running the Washington Post Company, which, as you know, includes *Newsweek*, broadcasting properties, etc. A beautiful, talented, eloquent lady who had just come through one of the most cataclysmic events in press history—Watergate. Here was an opportunity to bask in the glory of that epochal triumph. Yet how did Mrs. Graham reflect on this experience?

Many have said that Watergate was a classic demonstration of the purpose and potential of the free press. I won't quarrel with that. But I would like to suggest that the problems which have more recently come to the fore provide a broader and more subtle, and thus perhaps in some ways greater, test of the ability of the press to serve the public interest in a time of great strain and danger.

Like Watergate, these other topics have their labels too—energy, the economy, food, growth, environment. But each of these is the shorthand for a mass of facts and factors so complex that we may find Watergate was easy by comparison. Moreover, Watergate, for all its scope and gravity, was a traditional kind of story which required traditional techniques of investigative reporting which the American media have learned to provide so well.

Investigative talent, however, even combined with all the balance and dispassion and stamina the press can summon, won't be enough for coverage of the crises in food and oil and the economy which seem to be drawing near.

Those stories will demand other abilities as well. The first is the ability to comprehend a number of very arcane fields, ranging from macroeconomics to geology to corporate taxation—subjects which have usually been left to the specialists till now. It is no easy business to become conversant in such fields, especially if their practitioners devote much energy to keeping their fields obscure.

Once reporters themselves have mastered such mysteries, the next challenge is to put them in terms which the general audience can grasp. This is both easier and harder than it used to be. Just as the Advertising Council's responsibilities now have become much more complicated and challenging than the simple promotion of war bond sales, so we have outgrown the time when intricate matters could be explained in simple, geewhiz terms. The public is generally much better informed these days. Like most things, this development has the defect of its merits. We can ask more of our audience, but they, conversely, ask much more of us.

Thus, people want and need to know more than the outlines of the problem. They want to know how and why: why the cost of sugar has gone sky-high; how the latest tensions in the Mideast developed and what their effect will be; how something which used to be viewed as a regional problem, such as early snowstorms in New England or a shortage of boxcars in Nebraska, will change the price of fuel or bread. And, more and more, people want to know how the system works.[3]

That is just one example of what I see as the emerging social responsibility of the press. Just as business is responding to unforeseen and unanticipated social responsibilities thrust upon it by history, so is the press. Progress is uneven in both cases. There are errors of commission and omission by both parties. But it should be more clearly understood in both quarters that the same historical forces are affecting both business and the press. Social responsibility, like walking upright, must be learned and must be consciously and steadily pursued. And both groups have found in programs of economic education an opportunity to carry out this responsibility.

GETTING TOGETHER

The dialogue between the Fourth Estate—and may I call business the "Fifth Estate"—has been opened long before this. But this volume is an encouraging evidence of what has to be an accelerated process all over the country—in large meetings and in small ones. In face-to-face encounters, in new attitudes—open-minded attitudes—in new processes and new approaches.

As a sign in my office says, "America. It only works as well as we do." It's the slogan, by the way, of a public-service advertising campaign on productivity that we have been doing for the past five years.

May I note as an example the following item in the July 25 issue of *PR News:*

> Elimination of inaccurate reporting and misleading statements about business and economic matters may be an impossible dream; but the results are now in on an unusual and highly intelligent approach toward minimizing their occurrence. This is an experimental program recently conducted by the Graduate School of Industrial Administration at Carnegie-Mellon University, Pittsburgh, PA. It provided for five (out of 20 who applied) well established business or economics journalists to join a nine-week, intensive course (in economics and business management) designed for middle-management and senior business and government executives. Studying with the Fourth Estaters were 55 such men and women from the U.S. and foreign countries. Funding of the experiment (cost about $40,000) was provided by grants from such Pittsburgh-headquartered companies as Allegheny Ludlam, Cyclops Corp., Gulf Oil, PPG Industries and Goodyear Tire & Rubber. Plans for a similar program early next year (with some revisions) are already under way.[4]

Another development which augurs well for the improvement of economic and business reporting is the new Media Awards Competition announced by the Champion International Corporation to be administered by the Amos Tuck School of Business Administration at Dartmouth, whereby yearly awards will be made to the media in various categories for excellence in treating those "arcane" economic subjects referred to by Katharine Graham.

The triad of media, universities, and business actively promoting mutual understanding and knowledge may well be the ultimate solution to the mammoth problem of economic illiteracy that faces us.

How do we accelerate this kind of exploration of new approaches and new responses to the evident need for improved economic understanding? Out of the welter of things that concern people and institutions, how do we achieve a greater share of mind for this particular concern?

In 1974, the Advertising Council accepted just such a challenge: to use its specialized methodology of public-service advertising to encourage people to want to know more about economics, to raise their level of interest, and to motivate them to take individual and group actions to improve their own knowledge and that of others.

We were not naive enough to believe that public-service advertising could teach economics; nor did we want to tell people *what* to think. We simply wanted them to think, to balance out in their own minds the questions that have been left pretty much to the experts in years past.

Is this an audacious idea? Of course it is. The idea of a democracy that would rely on an enlightened public was an audacious idea over 200 years ago. And to us, our objective was completely consistent with the notion that a free people having access to knowledge could use it intelligently and to good purpose.

But having such a high-minded purpose and working out the details are two different things. When we accepted this challenge in 1974, I recalled the story attributed to Will Rogers, in which he offered to solve the German U-boat menace in World War I. The solution, he said, was simply to heat up the temperature of the ocean water until it became so unbearably hot that the German submarines would have to rise to the surface, where they could be quickly destroyed.

"But how can you possibly heat up the ocean water to that degree?" he was asked.

"I've given you the concept," Will replied. "It's up to you to work out the details."

With the cooperation of the media, we have succeeded in the limited period of time since then in raising the temperature of the water to an encouraging degree. We are stirring up the U-boats. We still have a long way to go, but we have made substantial progress.

WORKING OUT THE DETAILS

Our first step was to conduct a comprehensive research study to determine the degree of public awareness, knowledge, and understanding of our economic system. To accomplish this and the subsequent advertising for all media, we had the rare good fortune to be able to enlist the services of Compton Advertising as our volunteer advertising agency contributing its creative services as well as its research know-how and its marketing and communications skills.

We also appointed a volunteer coordinator for this campaign, an executive who heads up marketing, advertising, or public relations for a major corporation: William A. Bartel, vice-president of the Celanese Corporation, who fulfills that role superbly.

And then, of course, we rely on the media to provide the space and time free of charge for this as for our twenty-eight other campaigns, obtaining over $500 million worth last year.

Normally, the organizations, both public and private, that request campaigns from the Council are expected to defray the out-of-pocket costs for the production and distribution of advertising materials— films, slides, engravings, mats, posters, printing, etc.

One of the missing "details" as we began to plan the American Economic System Campaign was a qualified and interested sponsoring organization from the private sector—which gives you some idea of why we have a problem in the field of economic education.

While we did receive an initial grant from the U.S. Department of Commerce that provided us with the seed money to develop the research and the ensuing prototype advertising, the secretary of commerce had made it clear to us at the outset that subsequent funding would have to come from the private sector.

With the help of our Industries Advisory Committee and under the direction of William F. May, chairman of American Can, we embarked on a major fund-raising drive. And thanks to the response of business and foundations, we have been able to finance the communications program to date, although we still have a long way to go to achieve our overall financial objectives.

Our research study was completed by Compton Advertising in 1975. Involving almost 3,000 face-to-face interviews averaging one and a half hours each, the study was described by the New York City Council on Economic Education as "the most recent, most detailed and most thorough appraisal of the economic literacy of the average American in a generation."[5]

Among other things, the survey revealed that economic understanding by the public is incomplete and fragmentary. Few Americans are totally uninformed, but few are highly knowledgeable, even among "elite" groups. The interrelationship of business, labor, investors, and others in the economic system is understood by only one in seven Americans at large and only one in three businessmen.[6]

A substantial number of Americans see themselves as playing a passive role in the economic system, as consumers who spend money. Only one-half of employed people recognize their role as producers or providers of service.

If we did nothing else in our attempt to improve the status of economic education, this study would alone have been a substantial contribution. But to us and its many readers since then in academe, in the business and labor community—to editors and thought leaders generally—this study has provided a basis and rationale for subsequent efforts to improve economic understanding.

Convinced as we were that the advertising messages would be too limited in scope to transmit economic information in detail, we determined that a booklet should be offered that would explain as clearly, concisely, and engagingly as possible what were the basic elements and relationships characterizing our economic system. Entitled "The American Economic System ... and your part in it," the booklet was drafted and redrafted. Economists at the Department of Commerce and the Department of Labor provided the basic substantive information and economic data. Charles Schulz, creator of *Peanuts*, contributed the illustrations. It has been a success story unparalleled in Advertising Council history, for within one year of its being offered to the public, almost three million copies of the booklet were ordered and distributed.

Which brings us back to the media and to what they have done to assist us in our efforts. We have been delighted with their overall support.

Over $12 million in measurable free space and time has been provided by the media in carrying the messages for the first six months of the campaign. The advertising asked economic questions which the research revealed Americans to be hazy about. Over 3,000 daily and weekly newspapers have carried our public-service messages:

Do you really know what happens when business profits go up or down?
Does America need more government regulation? Or less?
How much change does our American economic system need? A lot? A little? None?

Over 400 business and consumer magazines have run comparable public-service advertisements. Over 3,500 outdoor posters ("Every American ought to know what it says") have been posted. Over 110,000 transit cards have been mounted in subways, commuter trains, buses, airports, railroad and bus terminals. Over 400 television stations and 1,000 radio stations have run our initial wave of public-service announcements, garnering a total of 281,526,000 TV home impressions.

Over and above the cooperation we have received from the media in running our public-service ads, we have received heartening cooperation in the use of editorial space. The *Milwaukee Journal*, the *Oklahoma City Times*, the *Lincoln Nebraska Journal & Star*, and over sixty other newspapers have reproduced the booklet in tabloid size as supplements. This has boosted the circulation of the booklet's contents by an additional 5 million, over and above the original 3 million, to a total of 8 million.

This is more than twice the number of the most popular textbook on economics. The number of booklets and reprints should reach 10 million—the largest distribution of any Advertising Council booklet offered in its campaigns in more than thirty years.

TO REACH THE PUBLIC YOU MUST FIRST REACH THE PRESS

As we say over and over, we are not educators, we are not economists, we are communicators. Our effect is catalytic. We seek to engage the interest and multiply the efforts of other organizations and individuals.

The first target audience for any Council campaign is the media itself. The media are always their own masters, as well they should be, deciding if our campaigns are important and worthy enough to achieve their support. If the media accepts our campaign, then the public becomes our audience.

We have just released our second year's wave of advertising: "How high is your E.Q.?" (Economic Quotient). People seem to enjoy being put to the test, and our print ads will each embody a mini economic quiz, along with attention-getting headlines, persuasive body copy, answers to the true/false questions printed upside down, and the offer of our free booklet for more information. Comparable ads will also be distributed to outdoor and transit advertising companies.

Our new E.Q. television public-service announcements have been filmed in two versions. One offers the booklet directly, and the other urges viewers to visit their local library for more information. The American Library Association is recommending to 10,000 libraries throughout the country that they display a counter card with a supply of booklet request forms.

A series of booklets supplementing our original one is now being prepared by Learning Management, Inc. Subjects will include productivity (already published), inflation, employment, profits, world trade, etc. A new, fully illustrated children's version of our original booklet, "The American Economic System ... and your part in it," with delightfully executed illustrations by Roy Doty, is also being completed.

Discussion-leader guides will be published for our basic booklet as well as the subsequent ones in our "Issues" series.

So, you can see what has been done not only in striving to draw people in, to challenge and to motivate them, but also in providing an array of substantive learning materials in response to any initial interest aroused by the advertising messages that are given national exposure by the media.

Is this the be-all and the end-all? Of course not. The ultimate payoff will come in the further response by educators and others, as well as ourselves, to the growing demand for economic education materials.

What other means are we using to achieve our multiplier effect? For one thing, we are publishing a bimonthly newsletter, "The Economic Communicator," now in its seventh issue and distributed free of charge to over 50,000 interested individuals such as corporate chief executive officers, school superintendents, presidents of labor unions and trade associations, members of Congress, heads of college and university economics departments, media executives, etc.

When we launched our campaign a little over a year ago, the mail, phone calls and visits almost engulfed us. We have given over 200 presentations and speeches; we have distributed over 5,000 Action Kits containing information and samples of our work and suggesting how others might get involved.

The American Advertising Federation and its 165 local advertising clubs have endorsed the campaign and have encouraged the development of economic education programs in their cities. In a competition we jointly sponsored with the American Advertising Federation, we gave awards to their chapters in three cities—Milwaukee, Tulsa, and Salt Lake City.

We are constantly asked if this widespread activity is really affecting the American public. One year ago, Compton concluded the first part of a pre/post study among 2,000 respondents to measure the effectiveness of the campaign (i.e., what Americans know and believe about the economic system, awareness of the advertising campaign, response to the booklet, etc.). The follow up study has just been completed to see what, if anything, has happened in the intervening year. This is a harsh test. I personally felt that one year was not enough time to show whether or not there had been any change. Our campaign was originally planned as a three- to five-year effort. It will take that amount of time, in my opinion, to see any substantial change, and even then the momentum must be maintained if we are to enjoy any long-lasting results. I was somewhat amazed to see in these early tabulations that in the short span of one year, we have made encouraging progress. People *are* listening; there are positive shifts in awareness, understanding, and attitudes.

Among the general adult population 46 million Americans are familiar with advertising about the economic system; 18 million Americans recall the Ad Council's campaign specifically; 4 million people received the economics booklet; and 1.3 million read the booklet.

Recognizing that the hoped-for benefits of the campaign were greater interest in the economic system and increased knowledge and understanding of how the system works, we were heartened to discern the following shifts:

- Those aware of the Ad Council's campaign indicated much greater knowledge of the system than those not aware—or the general public. They have a more positive attitude toward the system, have a more favorable attitude toward business, and think knowledge of the system is very important.

- Adult Americans, compared with last year, display an increased knowledge of the economic system, a more positive appraisal of the system, less desire for government regulation of economic activities, and greater interest in the subject.

- Upward shifts in understanding of the economic system are especially noted among working women, midwesterners and south/southwesterners, the young (under twenty-five years of age), and middle-income people ($10,000 to $14,999).

However, it should be mentioned that perceptible changes in attitude or comprehension were not noted in *all* categories of economic understanding.

So we must remember that we will continue to work in a terribly competitive marketplace of ideas and causes competing for public attention. That is why, as I said at the outset, the role of the mass media is so vitally important.

It is my hope that this book and others like it will serve to bolster the call to the media made by Katharine Graham for more in-depth treatment of the economy, for an understanding of the arcane realm of macroeconomics or corporate taxation, the cost of sugar, the price of fuel or bread. Above all, said Mrs. Graham, "People want to know how the system works."

In a sense, we are all on trial—the media, business, our schools and universities—for being accessories to the crime of economic illiteracy that we have allowed to happen. The verdict, as an old newspaper cliché would put it, is "hanging in the balance."

We have made progress in prosecuting our case against economic illiteracy, but so much more remains to be done. As Winston Churchill once said in another context, "It is not the end; nor the beginning of the end, but the end of the beginning."

If the social responsibility theory of the press—which can be extended to business and education as well—does indeed prevail, and I believe it will, we should then see more clearly the beginning of the end of economic illiteracy.

NOTES

1. Marshall McLuhan, *The Medium Is the Massage* (New York, London: Bantam Books, Inc., 1967).

2. Fred S. Siebert, Theodore Peterson, and Wilbur Schramm, *Four Theories of the Press* (Urbana, Ill.: University of Illinois Press, 1974).

3. Katharine Graham (address at the Annual Dinner of the Advertising Council, Waldorf Astoria Hotel, New York, November 20, 1974).

4. *PR News*, July 25, 1977, p. 2.

5. "Economics for Social Studies Teachers," New York City Council on Economic Education, vol. X, no. 1, Spring 1976.

6. The computerized data is summarized in a 176-page printed report entitled, "National Survey on the American Economic System." It is available from the Advertising Council at its printing cost. Highlights of the findings are available free of charge.

SECTION 2   MEDIA VIEWS

In years past, the media devoted their resources to reporting on the courts, city hall, politics, disasters, and wars. If business and economics were covered at all, such news was found on the business page, which usually served as a boundary between sports and the classified ads.

But the 1970s have seen economics raised from the occasional and arcane to what John Chancellor has called the decade's most important major story. Inflation, unemployment, taxes, energy shortages, international trade imbalances, farm production, and business behavior have jumped from the back page to the headlines. In the process, the media have been subjected to blistering criticism from businesses writhing under unaccustomed floodlights.

Indeed, working journalists echo some of the complaints registered by business against the media. Journalists frequently have insufficient education and experience to adequately cover business and economics. Sufficient time, space, and staff are rarely available to do a complete job, thus reporting tends to be episodic and conflict oriented.

But, the journalists emphasize, the media are not anti-capitalist and not out to destroy the private enterprise system. Complaining business executives, they maintain, are generally overly insulated, overly secretive, overly sensitive individuals who recognize neither the public's right to know nor the value of the media's role in exposing questionable business practices. Businessmen often engage in the ancient practice of seeking to slay the bearers of bad tidings, say journalists, who claim not to criticize but to report the criticisms of others.

Journalists see their profession as a high calling charged with the dual responsibility of providing information to the public and providing social feedback to the administrators of important public institutions. As the importance of business and economics increases in the public mind, journalists maintain that more reporting and more investigating are necessary to determine the extent to which businesses measure up to their social and moral obligations. This process, they maintain, will ultimately and positively affect consumers, businesses, and society as a whole.

In this section, three journalists offer media views: the head of the economics staff of one of the nation's leading metropolitan newspapers; a nationally recognized radio executive and commentator; and the news editor of our leading national business daily. They observe the business/media relationship from the vantage point of thoughtful, responsible working journalists involved extensively in the coverage of business and economics.

THE PRESS: TOO SOFT ON BUSINESS?

JOHN F. LAWRENCE

Rather than being anti-business or even overly critical of business and its practices, John Lawrence maintains that the media are far more guilty of being too soft on business. The media, he says, are viewed by businessmen as adversaries for several reasons. Business and the media see the same events from different perspectives. The media reflect criticisms of business by other aspects of society. Businessmen fail to recognize the importance of this negative reporting to the public and have a fetish about secrecy.

In fact, far more favorable than unfavorable stories about business appear in the media. Favorable stories are simply easier to do than unfavorable ones, and according to Lawrence reporters still tend to unquestioningly accept statements by business.

To improve business and economic reporting, Lawrence suggests more training for journalists, but not the indoctrination that businessmen would call for. Publishers must recognize the public appetite for business news and provide more space and staff for the subject. Businessmen must be more open and helpful. Media could then become a bridge between business and the public.

Assistant managing editor of economic affairs for the Los Angeles Times, *Mr. Lawrence supervises the gathering of business and economic news through his newspaper's worldwide network of correspondents. Formerly with* The Wall Street Journal *and a correspondent for London's* Economist, *he is the coauthor of* The '70s Crash and How to Survive It.

After an all-day reporting effort some fifteen years ago, a diligent young reporter broke the story that the Pennsylvania and New York Central railroads had quietly launched merger negotiations. After the story appeared, the Pennsy called a press conference to confirm it. But the public relations spokesman for the railroad, in front of a score of newsmen, opened the conference by bitterly chewing out the reporter's boss for printing a story "that might well have killed these negotiations."

More recently, a news release was hand-delivered to the *Los Angeles Times* newsroom a few minutes before deadline. It was an announcement from an oil company about a new pricing policy on unleaded gasoline. Several of us read the release and couldn't figure out what it meant. On the verge of dismissing it, I asked our energy writer to call the president of the company for some clarification.

The president's response was, "Just run it the way I sent it in, sonny." My response, relayed through the reporter, was that in that case, we would run nothing.

The oil company president chose to suffer a few questions. And it turned out his release was a significant move to stimulate the switch to lower-pollution unleaded fuel. The story made page one.

Just this summer, at a business seminar conducted at an eastern institution, a banker complained about incomplete and misleading news stories. A newsman responded that such stories often result from the failure of corporations to cooperate in talking to the press. And the banker shot back, "Yes, but why don't you send us a reporter who's had some training?"

As these examples suggest, all the talk about bad blood between the media and business is nothing new. As always, many businessmen simply don't like newsmen, consider them either biased or ill-informed, or both. A corporate chieftain sweats over a news release and then finds some long-haired radical fresh from journalism school has rewritten it, thrown out all the precise language cleared and double-cleared with the corporate counsel, and stuck it under a headline even more misleading.

With this attitude, it is not too surprising that businessmen are laying off on the news media a substantial part of the blame for the low esteem in which they think they find themselves. They see newsmen, whom they believe should be building up the free enterprise system and displaying some sympathy for its participants, instead tearing it down by dwelling on the negative.

"I can truthfully say that I almost never read or hear an accurate media account of a business subject with which I am thoroughly familiar," Donald S. MacNaughton, chairman and chief executive of Prudential Insurance Company of America, said in a much-quoted 1975 speech.

MacNaughton went on to note that the media too often oversimplify economic complexities and added:

> We see this today, as a running example, in reporting on the squabble in Congress over taxation of multinational corporations. If a popular vote were taken today for or against the very existence of such corporations on the basis of media coverage, the United States would probably go out of international business, to its long-term and disastrous disadvantage.[1]

MacNaughton was quick to note that some of the blame rests with businessmen's own lack of candor. But MacNaughton's views, even allowing for a bit of hyperbole, overstate whatever case business can make against the media. It may well be that MacNaughton suffers from the common problem of all human communication. Just as no two witnesses will describe an auto accident in precisely the same way, so a businessman reading an account of his own statements may be inclined to see error even in a story that accurately reflects the impact of what he said. In short, the problem often is vantage point, with the businessman suffering from being too close almost as much as the media from being too far away.

Similarly, the Prudential executive echoes a common misconception among business leaders that press coverage is destroying the public standing of business, when in fact the press is only reporting public criticism from places like the United States Congress. Moreover, there is little evidence that such public criticism has really weakened public support for the free enterprise system.

This is not to say that the media do not richly deserve some criticism. It certainly is possible to point to instances of hatchet-job reporting by zealots who couldn't see two sides of an issue if they had four eyes. But examining in a broad context the two main criticisms —that we are unfairly tough and that we are too often ill-informed— I would have to choose the latter as the larger problem. In short, I believe that the media are far more guilty of being too soft on business than being too hard.

Obviously, there is no way to document this view scientifically. But looking back over twenty years as a business writer and editor, the really hard-hitting stories I've read stand out mostly because they have been so few in number. In every case where a company's officials have complained to me about negative coverage, a check of the clips turned up a number of favorable pieces for every supposedly critical one. True, a company like Northrop or Lockheed slips into scandal, and for a time scandal is all you read about it. But even Lockheed or Northrop would find a preponderance of upbeat type features on them over the years.

A recent study by Louis Harris and Associates suggests that the public shares the view that media coverage leans more toward a bias in favor of business than the other way. In a survey of 1,510 individuals, the Harris pollsters found 47 percent believe the media cover consumer news in an unbiased manner. Only 8 percent see the coverage biased against business, while 25 percent thought that the coverage was pro-business. (The poll also found that nine out of ten businessmen felt the media were basically out to report bad news and wrongdoing when dealing with a business subject.)[2]

Really hard-hitting stories on business are many times more difficult to do than favorable stories. This reflects the complexity of the issues usually involved, the generally less-cooperative attitude of sources on such matters, and the need for precision, if nothing else, to avoid libel suits. Moreover, contrary to the impression left by Watergate, only a minority of financial writers is drawn to such investigative or critical efforts. As the quality of individuals interested in working in the financial section has increased—and it certainly has increased over the past decade or so—this shortage of talent has eased. But it by no means has disappeared. Most investigative talent still resides with the metropolitan staff, not the financial staff. Outside of the few biggest and most financially sound papers, the financial staff too often consists of one or two people—enough to keep up with incoming news releases, and that's about all.

BUSINESS REPORTING: TOO SHALLOW AND UNINFORMED

There is still a tendency on the part of business writers to report without much checking the statements of business leaders. Hence, when the big steel companies, on the heels of their settlement with the United Steelworkers, began announcing the need for price increases, few stories made any effort to weigh the cost of the settlement against productivity gains enjoyed by the industry. I'm not saying the steel companies were wrong, just that what they said got reported uncritically.

This tendency to accept what business is saying reached tragic proportions during the long hot stock market of the 1960s. Business writers extolled the virtues of gunslinging mutual-fund managers. Skepticism toward the conglomerate movement was limited. (In fact, the toughest attack on the conglomerate movement ultimately came from big business itself, which headed for Washington as the raiders turned their attention toward gobbling up some staid old names.) The stock market was covered for the most part like a sports page covers the home team when it's hot.

Ultimately, this coverage turned around. As the basic weakness of the accounting methods of the period began to emerge, the press started digging and gave the public a good glimpse of what had been going on. Of course, by then the public already was counting its losses.

Such experiences should make the media wary of the story about the overnight millionaire or the company doubling its profits every year. They make good reading, but the reporting should be detailed. What I'd like to see is more stories about the entrepreneurs in the middle, those who have neither made it big nor failed—in other words, the most common type. We succeeded in getting such a story on a young company recently and appropriately headlined it, "A Typical 'Success' Story: Dream Not Yet Fulfilled." But it took a very experienced reporter to handle it.

Which brings up the subject of training. It appears that an increasing amount of business criticism directed at the press focuses on lack of adequately trained reporters. "My advice to the business community is to stop worrying so much about whether or not members of the press are prejudiced one way or the other," Frederic W. West, Jr., president of Bethlehem Steel Corporation, told members of the American Newspaper Publishers Association last year. "Let's realize that some of the reporting that gets our blood up is probably more muddled than it is malicious."[3]

Similarly, Ben W. Heineman, president of Northwest Industries in Chicago, told a gathering of media and public relations people in June, "The business community has the right to expect that the reporters and editors who chronicle the business events of significance are well trained and have done their homework."[4]

Lack of training or experience in covering business clearly is a problem. One case I can report personally goes back to the run-in between the steel companies and President John F. Kennedy over a price increase the president thought he had helped head off by pushing wage restraint on the union. Just before U.S. Steel raised prices, a Bethlehem Steel official had told the company's annual meeting that foreign competition was so stiff the industry ought to be thinking about lowering prices. One reporter who hadn't covered business as a regular beat took that as a promise to keep prices down. In fact, however, the steel official was just moaning over the way things ought to have been, an attack against the recent settlement with the union.

When U.S. Steel announced the price move, Bethlehem quickly followed, and the appearance created by the story of a sudden turn-around led the Kennedy Administration to send FBI agents in droves to try to develop evidence for an anti-trust case. The FBI dutifully dragged reporters who had covered the Bethlehem meeting out of bed. My call came about 5 A.M.

IS SPECIALIZATION THE ANSWER?

Often the lack of training businessmen see in reporters stems from the pressures of the news business. The crush of events requires an editor to tap a general assignment reporter in an unfamiliar area. As financial staffs grow in size, as I believe they are, this should become less of a problem. The average reporting experience of the twenty-four-person Los Angeles Times financial staff now is over ten years. The staff is often used to help out on stories handled by other departments, such as the insurance impact of the Santa Barbara fire or the financial problems of city hall.

On the other hand, few financial writers are formally trained in business or economics. Nearly all have learned on the job. Is that bad? That is a matter for debate. Certainly, I would like to have several MBAs working for me. Unfortunately, not many MBAs take that training to become journalists. The alternative is to send good newsmen back to school. To some extent this is being done with the help of some excellent seminar programs at universities.

However, I believe businessmen generally see the importance of this training in terms of indoctrination rather than true education. They figure a student of economics or business administration will better understand the profit motive. I doubt that is the case, because I doubt there is that much misunderstanding of the importance of profits.

Why not just hire specialists, or employ them part-time? One reason is that the specialist who can write for a lay audience is a rare bird. The one big advantage a generalist brings to a subject is a fresh approach, a questioning even of basics. That kind of questioning is vital to our system, if sometimes a nuisance to the business leader being interviewed. One big-name economist complained to me earlier this year that he had just received a call from a reporter for one of the most respected financial newspapers. "The man admitted he knew nothing about the subject," the economist said. It was obvious the economist felt he had wasted his time. But I would ask whether being forced to explain a complex subject to a reporter is any different from having to explain it to the general public. And knowing this particular economist, thank God for the reporter.

Business used to regard old-time reporters who covered them regularly as part of the club. I know one reporter in particular who would get raving letters from his sources every time he wrote about the industry he'd been assigned to for many years. I pity the general reader trying to decipher what he wrote, however.

There are two other problems with the specialist system. If the specialist is too sympathetic he will insulate the industry from public reaction and leave the public ill-informed. That can encourage abuses that will cause more problems later. Moreover, if specialists are to be used, what about the specialist on such things as environment who may get too close to that subject, to the detriment of industry?

THE CASE OF THE "PROBLEM BANKS"

For the most part, businessmen fail to recognize the importance of seeing anything negative about them reported to the public. A prime case was the leaking in January of 1976 of a number of lists of so-called problem banks, those supposedly being watched more closely by federal regulators. When the first of these stories broke, it drew sharp responses from bankers. "If you have the information, you're not entitled to it," David Rockefeller was quoted as telling a *Washington Post* reporter.[5] Others actively criticized the media for obtaining and using the material—at least for spreading it across page one.

The case raises a number of interesting issues, not the least of which is the need for bank secrecy itself. Bankers have always insisted they are a special case, needing secrecy if for no other reason than to prevent runs on the bank. But it strikes me that the eye of public criticism, applied through greater disclosure, might have helped prevent some banks from doing some of the things that landed them on the problem lists in the first place.

Another issue is the coverage given the subject once the lists became known and the way the bankers reacted. Most bankers insisted their banks were not in trouble. Some went so far as to deny being on that list. One thing they wouldn't do was explain what the lists were, and perhaps by doing so make it clear the word "problem" didn't mean "nearly insolvent."

I'm sure like many papers the *Los Angeles Times* set out to get a thorough explanation. I called the president of one major California bank personally, was told he was unavailable, and later received a totally unhelpful call back from his flack. (That itself reflects an interesting view of the importance some businessmen place on contacts with the press and the public.)

John Getze, an experienced banking reporter, surveyed other banks named in the stories. Our argument was simple: clarify this matter and you will probably defuse it. Bank after bank refused to help, and I became more convinced the page-one play given the lists was the right play. Earlier, I had had some doubts, feeling the lists were already dated, and that the problems they probably referred to already had been heavily reported (loans to shoddily run real estate investment trusts, for instance).

Finally, one bank, Wells Fargo, did open its doors and, in effect, some of its books. I think the resulting story is something of a model of proper business communication and reasonable reporting. The story began:

> Like many bank presidents, Richard P. Cooley is calm, even-tempered and a good deliberate communicator. As chief executive of Wells Fargo Bank over the past few weeks, he's needed those qualities more than ever.[6]

Cooley admitted his bank was on one of the lists. He said it was because its "classified loans" rose at one point to more than 40 percent of shareholders' equity (basically, what shareholders have invested in the company). He then went on to explain what was meant by the term "classified." He said it meant loans made at above-average risk. Why had the bank made so many of these loans? Cooley explained that it had tried to help some of its clients through a bad recession, and he named one company as an example.

It turned out that over the past decade, only 7.5 percent of all classified loans had turned into a loss for the bank. Even doubling that rate of loss in the future would hardly pin Wells Fargo to the wall.

Summing up, who was wrong? The newspapers, for using confidential material leaked to them and for playing it on page one at the risk of creating some major uncertainties among the public? The banks, for not responding immediately when contacted by the media? The government, for supporting bank secrecy to the point banks can hide their failings behind it?

Secrecy is something of a fetish with businessmen. Years ago, many of them thought they would be severely damaged if they had to disclose their total sales. This is one of the most important hang-ups in the business/media relationship and one that probably does more harm to the business image than any willful act by reporters.

Undoubtedly, many businessmen see unfairness in media coverage of the international bribery issue. They contend bribery is a common practice and a necessary one. My feeling is the press *did* report that. At the *Los Angeles Times*, we used our foreign and domestic bureaus to do two broad roundups of the question. What we found supported the fact bribery is widespread abroad, but it also showed that many businessmen had successfully resisted bribery attempts and still obtained business abroad.

ARCO'S QUEST FOR ALASKAN GAS

Another set of issues is raised by a running story in 1975 and 1976 involving Atlantic Richfield Company and Southern California Gas, a part of Pacific Lighting Corp. ARCO and the gas company applied to the California Public Utilities Commission for permission to allow the gas company to charge consumers higher rates to finance the development of an Alaskan gas field. In effect, consumers would pay something in advance for this gas, and ARCO would thus avoid the burden of carrying the financing of the project. In return, the gas company and its customers would have first rights to gas from the field.

The proposal drew an immediate storm of protests from consumerists who argued economic coercion and unfairness on the part of ARCO. ARCO stood firm and refused to develop the field without the financing deal. Ultimately, the PUC approved but still called it "unfair and unreasonable."[7] Later, the Federal Power Commission acted to effectively kill it.

Towards the end of the controversy, a couple of representatives from ARCO visited me and argued our coverage had been unfairly balanced against ARCO's case. Their charge is worth considering.

If you measured column inches, we probably did carry more adverse comment than favorable. On the other hand, the stories largely reflected the preponderance of public statements at hearings and by PUC members, which were critical of the plan. It's possible we carried this criticism to the point of redundancy.

ARCO also believed our in-depth stories on the plan glossed over one or two complicated points in ARCO's favor. The reporter involved contended those points were never made clearly either to him or at the public hearings. Once ARCO's men explained them to us face to face, we carried them.

The broader question raised by the event is the role of the media in covering a public debate. To what extent is it our obligation to balance that debate even when the actual news flow is not balanced? Did ARCO misread the potential public hostility to its plan, a hostility perhaps more emotional than logical? Had the company foreseen this reaction, it might not have proposed the plan at all, Thornton Bradshaw, ARCO's president, told me later. It certainly didn't help ARCO in its efforts to gain more credibility as a public-spirited oil company. (To my mind, ARCO already has built up a good bit of credibility in this regard.)

HEATED DISCORD

Issues like these raised in our coverage of the ARCO deal are complex. But much of the heat between business and the media is not complex at all. Too frequently businessmen simply dislike the press because they remember some run-in with a reporter at some distant point in the past. In fact, I once walked into a bank in the middle of Kansas for the first time and had the assistant manager begin berating me the moment I said I was from a newspaper.

Similarly, I've had oil company executives attack the newspaper for carrying stories on big increases in oil company earnings on page one while playing down year-later reports of an earnings downturn (there's an ironic twist). Actually, we had put both stories on page one out of just that concern for fairness, knowing the industry was facing charges of profiteering. The executives had simply presumed what we had done and not bothered to keep track.

During the nuclear-initiative campaign in California, our science writer produced a long, detailed look at both sides of the nuclear power plant safety question. A more balanced story I can't imagine. It placed the safety question in proper perspective and I'm sure eased the fears of many. Yet at least one well-known nuclear proponent toured the state decrying the story in speeches.

Sometimes businessmen think they can't win. Sometimes we in the media feel that way, too.

HOW BUSINESS CAN MEET THE PRESS

Business contributes to its own problems with the media in other ways. I have the impression that many chief executives believe it is beneath them to talk to reporters. It is a job for the company flack. Moreover, company flacks sometimes think it is beneath them to talk to the press. They try to get promoted to vice-president so they can have an underling who does it. (I do not use the word "flack" to refer to all public relations representatives. Some do a fine job both in clearing the path to the front office and in convincing the front office to be forthcoming. It is the others who are properly called flacks.)

There are still a few businessmen who measure their success with the press in terms of column inches and who believe their advertising support for the newspaper is relevant to what that count should be. One big advertiser wrote me last year instructing me how to run his quarterly earnings story, complete with sample clippings to show the size headline. I'm afraid he was disappointed. My response in all such cases is that the advertiser gets his value through the readership of the paper—period.

A newer approach by major corporations is to have their chief executives initiate a meeting with us. It is a fine idea, but there are two problems. In most cases the executive is coming in to pitch something rather than truly to be questioned. And in most cases he does not become more accessible to us when we are initiating a query. In short, so far it is only half a step.

Finally, there are still some companies with a response to the press that goes something like the one our regular energy writer received when he called one of the biggest oil companies: "You don't understand, so we won't talk to you."

What can businessmen do to help improve relations with the press and with the public? First, they can make a decision to be open and helpful. Some years ago, major steel producers were charged with price-fixing in a much-heralded announcement from Washington. One steel company attorney was persuaded to give me a detailed look at the case. He did so with candor, even to the point of admitting his company had received legal advice some time earlier to halt the practice in question. Still, that interview made it clear the government's case wasn't a spectacular uncovering of wrongdoing but rather one that hinged on a close interpretation of law.

Not every time a company decides to be open will it be rewarded with a favorable story. But more often than not, the public has sympathy for the outfit willing to come clean.

Being accessible to the press usually means trusting more than one company official to speak for the organization. This is true because any one man may not be around all the time. And he also may not know all that's going on. I recall one year in which a steel company chief executive kept making glowing forecasts while his own sales department manager was telling reporters not for attribution that sales were turning soft. That went on for an embarrassingly long time.

Encouraging company officials to talk also means avoiding witch-hunts when something gets out the chief executive doesn't like. That same steel company used to wonder how reporters were getting certain pieces of information from it. It changed locks on filing cabinets and actually questioned people to try to find the source. It never did.

WHAT CAN THE PRESS DO?

Most importantly, the press can recognize the huge appetite for business news among the investing and consuming public. Polls even during the Vietnam War sometimes put the economy atop the list of major concerns. As editors and publishers take note of this, they will authorize more expenditure for staff and for news space or time. Too long have the newspaper accountants held down space in financial sections by pointing out how low the advertising content is. That low content is a reflection of the massive number of columns that must be devoted to tabular material, not any abundance of space for stories. This is bad accounting because business news sells papers and sells them to the right people—those with money to spend.

The media have a role that can be of great benefit to American business if businessmen will recognize this role. The media can be a critical (not just in the negative sense), dispassionate observer of the business community. They can be a bridge between business and the public, conveying to business a feeling for public reaction at the same time they keep the public informed.

The media should not be found guilty of giving business a bad image simply because they report negative developments. In fact, legitimate business should be able to look to the media to keep the heat on the unethical competitor. In doing so, the media will be contributing to a stronger free enterprise system. If the media have failed, they have failed by not performing this vital function actively enough.

NOTES

1. *Monday,* May 24, 1976, p. 5.

2. *Consumerism at the Crossroads,* a national opinion research survey of public, activist, business and regulator attitudes toward the consumer movement. Conducted for Sentry Insurance by Louis Harris and Associates and Marketing Science Institute (associated with Harvard Business School), pp. 53–57.

3. "Reporters Chided on Business News," *New York Times,* May 5, 1976.

4. "Business and the Press: Lovers Forever Unhappy," *Chicago Daily News,* June 23, 1977.

5. Ronald Kessler, "Chase, Citibank Reported to Be on U.S. Problem List," *Los Angeles Times,* January 11, 1976 (originally published in the *Washington Post*).

6. John Getze, "Problem Banks: Teapot Tempest or Tornado?" *Los Angeles Times,* February 15, 1976.

7. *Los Angeles Times,* October 2, 1975.

THE MEDIA: BUSINESS FRIEND OR FOE?

ELMO ELLIS

In contrast to the past, the press and public today give the business executive and his domain no special privileges. According to Elmo Ellis, commerce and industry have to earn their support and respect day to day.

By the same token, the media must earn their respect. If the media did not investigate questionable business dealings and share their suspicions and their findings with the public, says Ellis, they would be derelict in their duty and open to attacks on their own credibility.

Both business and the media are objects of the ambivalent attitudes of Americans who care less for institutions than their own pocketbooks. In any case, the people of this country are provided relatively little critical evaluation or analysis of business by professional journalists.

Is the business community seriously worried about the quality of news coverage it is getting, Ellis asks, or is it mainly indulging in the all-American habit of griping because it doesn't always receive the kind of coverage it wants?

Vice-president of Cox Broadcasting Corporation and general manager of WSB AM/FM (Atlanta), Elmo Ellis is a nationally recognized broadcaster. He has received the prestigious Peabody Award, the Freedom Foundation Gold Medal, the Abe Lincoln Award, and the Alfred P. Sloan Award. He is the author of Happiness is Worth the Effort *and* Radio Station Management.

Judging by discussions that go on in some of the classrooms and boardrooms of America, one might infer that a real war of sorts exists between the press and business. Granted, there are individual journalists and corporate executives who do not like or trust one another. But there is no justifiable reason to conclude—as some business leaders have been inclined to do—that the media represent one of the free enterprise system's biggest enemies and greatest threats.

Business news is increasing, and a certain amount of it evolves from unpleasant and unflattering circumstances. But to indict the media for bearing bad news is rather like condemning a doctor for advising a patient that he is ill. The press tells business and the public things they need to know.

Early newspapers were frequently referred to as "tattlers." It is still the job of media to tattle and to keep people informed about what is happening. Much of what is taking place is tied to business, industry, and the individual's livelihood. The urbanization of our society has made all of our lives more complicated and has intensified public demand for information that will increase understanding and enable a person to cope more effectively with his responsibilities.

Thus, the media, in reporting economic news, often try to go beyond a simple recital of the facts and attempt to explain how business decisions and deeds are likely to affect the average citizen. The various news channels of the nation also have been devoting more attention to the matter of corporate accountability, trying to determine whether or not businesses—especially those operating in controversial products and services—are measuring up to their social and moral obligations.

Most business executives believe that their companies are conducting their affairs in an affirmative and constructive manner, although definitions of what this means vary considerably, not only in dialogue between members of the business community and media representatives, but also within the business community itself. Lewis W. Foy, chairman of Bethlehem Steel Corporation, has lamented that, "In many cases we not only don't know what another company's or industry's position is on a given issue, but we don't even know how their interests are involved. . . .

"We've found that many of our own employees, even people in very responsible positions, don't have anywhere near as much accurate information about the company as we'd like them to have."[1]

This suggests a need for improved communications within the business community, as well as with outside sources, such as labor unions, educational institutions, and the media. More and better sharing of information might measurably increase areas of agreement.

Such dialogue could illuminate critical differences that exist in our society over issues and urgencies. A journalist, for example, who believes that this nation's energy problems pose an imminent threat might express sharply critical comments about a business that operates as though energy problems are long-range in nature. Representatives of business and the media, when discussing a question, need to be aware of their respective priorities. When is each seeking an answer, immediately, in ten years, or a century? How serious is the matter under discussion? How concerned should the public be?

HOW THE CAMPS ARE SPLIT

There are other circumstances that tend to aggravate business/media relationships and which must be understood if they are to be mastered. Rising education standards and economic expectations have been accompanied by an increased questioning of established institutions and the ways they operate. Business and the press have not escaped this critical reevaluation.

Environmentalists, consumerism advocates, energy conservationists, and equal-opportunity proponents have all contributed to a spirited examination of the private enterprise system, demanding respectful attention to a variety of criticisms and complaints. They are challenging the business community, often with dramatic success, to abandon old methods and adopt new, safer, and more efficient ways to operate.

It is the duty of the press to report fairly and objectively on such activities. If it has failed to carry out this assignment with consistency, the blame must be shared by incompetent reporters and uncooperative business representatives, who have too little mutual respect and too little understanding of each other's vital roles within the American system.

It may be more than an accident, however, that television news and consumer-action groups were tied at the top of the ethics scale in a survey commissioned by a congressional committee to determine public attitudes toward ten key institutions. Each received high marks from 66 percent of the respondents. Corporations were rated high on ethics by only 45 percent of the population.

Public trust in the leadership of major business concerns has been steadily declining, going from 55 percent in 1967 to 16 percent in 1977. By contrast, public trust in television news organizations has risen slightly, climbing to 28 percent, up from 25 percent ten years ago.[2]

Unfortunately, and usually unintentionally, the news media sometimes overemphasize coverage of an event, aggravating a sensitive or controversial situation. When this involves a particular business or industry, in an uncomplimentary or unpleasant manner, it understandably arouses the ire of the company's managers, who may conclude that the disclosures and the degree of exposure prove the malevolent intentions of media. Most journalists would deny that they have any anti-business inclination or that they foment trouble simply because they are on the spot reporting what occurs. There is some evidence, though, that news reporting—especially electronic journalism—does add to the excitement and relative importance of an event and may affect subsequent developments. Today the public is participating via television and radio in public hearings, demonstrations, campaigns, and protest meetings. So in a very real sense, the media and the audience are collaborating to change things, even if unwittingly, and much of this change has economic implications.

THE MEDIA CARRY THE MESSAGE

For instance, there's a revolution going on in media merchandising, with new forms of instant advertising and sophisticated appeals to hidden emotions, creating heavy demand for new products, selling items in tremendous quantities, and making products popular and obsolete virtually overnight.

Radio and television have become enormous influences on the foods we eat, the music we enjoy, the jokes we laugh at, the ideas and values we adopt and express in our homes and offices, schools and churches.

A new form of politics is even emerging in our mass-media society. The instant plebiscite is a reality. It has been reported that President Carter takes a nationwide poll following each of his radio and television appearances to get a measure of the public's opinion and his relative popularity. Thus, the telephone has become a voting booth and the computer has become a prophet, so that the American people now can know within a matter of minutes—or hours at most—what a cross section of the public thinks about almost any issue.

These profound changes have led some observers to the uneasy conclusion that the free individual is being manipulated and absorbed by our mass media. It is true that we live in an age of mass circulation, mass advertising, and mass response. But in this new electronic society the individual potentially has a much louder voice than his grandfather did. The aroused citizen can speak into a microphone and reach completely across the continent, shaking the windows in 50 million homes.

Minority groups have taken on an importance that was previously denied to them. Consumerism has become a vital force. At times a handful of protesters may claim more attention than they should. Thankfully, there is also a place for voices of reason and moderation to be seen and heard. Any newsmaker or legitimate spokesman can have his moment in front of the cameras. He cannot be hidden, nor can he be denied, where the press is free.

Alert business representatives have not failed to recognize this free "soap box" and take advantage of it. Virtually every large company has an active publicity department turning out news releases, films, and other materials designed to enhance its image and to share with the public its views on major issues. Because of their competing and divergent interests, businesses do not always follow the same line of thought. This leads at times to a confusing chorus of voices crying to be heard. It is not unusual to read one executive's opinion about government subsidies, interest rates, or foreign trade, and then see or hear a contradictory statement by another equally respected corporate spokesman. Economists often disagree. The secretary of the treasury approves of this country's huge trade deficit. Commerce Department spokesmen think the deficit is bad.

To further illustrate the puzzling situation, one oil company, Texaco, has urged motorists in a series of newspaper and magazine advertisements to drive less and conserve gasoline because of the growing energy shortage. Another petroleum producer, Mobil, has carried advertisements, often in the same publications, contending that there is no energy shortage and no lack of fuel sources for the foreseeable future. Such differences of opinion are difficult for the public to understand and can be more damaging to the credibility of the business world than many of the news stories that commercial interests assail as being harmful.

The fact that so many companies feel a need to explain what they are doing and to draw favorable attention to their civic and charitable contributions is evidence of their growing respect for the public. It is quite a change from the days when business was not concerned with what the public thought and concentrated on one objective: making a profit.

TELLING ALL: CYNICISM OR CONSCIENTIOUSNESS?

Two hundred years ago Adam Smith expressed complete disdain for the social responsibility of business: "I have never known much good done by those who affected to trade for the public good. It is an affection, indeed, not very common among merchants, and very few words need to be employed in dissuading them from it."[3]

It would be hard to find a statement that is more outdated. Few businesses would dare admit, even if they believed it, that they have no obligation to trade for the public good. Typical of current thinking are these lines from "The Conscience of a Company," issued by the Coca-Cola Company: "Life changes. Society's standards mature. Perhaps the biggest challenge is to be sensitive to these changing, improving and increasing expectations—and to keep finding the ways to respond affirmatively. It is a never-ending dynamic process."

Obviously, corporate morality has become more than a slogan. It connotes an attitude, a conscience at work in all types of businesses.

Social responsibility is especially meaningful to the broadcasting stations of America, which are required by the terms of their licenses to operate in the "public interest, conveniences and necessity," and to ascertain on a continual basis the needs of the people they reach and serve.

Although newspapers and magazines have no such legal obligation, the press has historically played a watchdog role over our society and recognizes that its mission is to keep the public informed and
alert.

Now the media are being challenged, along with the business
community, to reexamine their motives and their actions to see if
they are justifying their existence by doing a satisfactory job of serving their customers.

There are understandable reasons why so many people in this
country have been expressing concern in recent years about the honesty and ethics of business firms with which they have dealings.
Never a day goes by that we do not hear someone claiming that our
environment is being polluted, defaced, or robbed of its natural resources by selfish and shortsighted commercial interests. Critics have
accused businesses of producing inferior products, providing unsatisfactory service, charging abnormally high prices, and indulging in all
types of criminal and corrupt practices.

Some of these charges and assumptions are unfair. They contribute to a climate of cynicism and skepticism which has weakened the
morale of the business community and intensified the uncertainty of
the public. Still, it is quite obvious that a certain number of companies do engage in unethical and underhanded business practices. By
ignoring the best interests of the public, they provide ammunition for
the negative press reports that displease so many business executives.
If the media did not investigate questionable business dealings and
share their suspicions and their findings with the public, they would
be derelict in their duty and open to attacks on their own credibility.

The magnitude of media's job is suggested by a nationwide telephone survey conducted in 1975 and reported in the *Harvard Business Review*. It showed that American consumers were dissatisfied
with one of every five manufactured items they buy. Complaints
ranged from inferior materials and poor workmanship to unreliable
repair and maintenance services. If this is true, then it would indicate
that business has serious, unresolved consumer problems which may
have been underreported by the media.[4]

To counteract this prevailing mood, businesses all over the nation have been spending vast sums of money on elaborate advertising
campaigns and social-action programs designed to prove that they are
discharging their corporate responsibilities and responding with sincerity and generosity to public needs and concerns.

Is this great effort to enhance the image of the corporate conscience a result of media insistence? The answer is only a qualified yes.
Business activities provide subject matter for only a small percentage
of the nation's daily news. Relatively few reporters and commen-

tators are properly trained to deal authoritatively with economics and commerce. Experienced business editors are few. Most television and radio stations, and the majority of newspapers, have no full-time staff member assigned to write and report business news. On a daily basis, the people of this country are provided relatively little critical evaluation or analysis by professional journalists of what businesses are doing and whether or not the managers and employees of these firms are serving the public in a fair and honest manner.

But the media have been consistently and effectively utilized by outside observers, investigators, and critics of the American business community. Ralph Nader has become a nationally recognized figure through media exposure. The press, radio, and television have made Nader's Center for the Study of Responsive Law familiar to virtually every household. Its investigations and attacks on specific products and industry practices have been widely and frequently disseminated in print and on the air.

Although the motives and methods of some consumerism spokesmen have provoked a great deal of discussion and considerable controversy, there can be little doubt that such activities have made business executives more conscious of how their companies are perceived by the public and have spurred them to initiate various programs designed to improve standards of safety and performance, quality of products, and reliability of services.

THE JOURNALIST AS SOCIAL ACTIVIST

In reporting various chapters of the daily drama of economic action and reaction, the press has been to a degree a participant, but the role of the journalist as a social activist in the business arena has been slow to develop and has been overemphasized. Business journalism only began to emerge in this country as the nation moved from an agrarian to an industrial economy. For many years, writers who dealt with economic subjects considered as their main mission the glamorizing and glorifying of the merchant, industrialist, and financier.

Edwin T. Freedley, who wrote in 1856 *A Practical Treatise on Business*, expressed his desire to be of service "to those for whom I entertain a higher respect than for any other class of men in the world—I mean the active, intelligent businessmen of the country— and especially to those who are fitting themselves for business pursuits."[5]

In the intervening years, blind adoration for the nation's business leaders has changed to a more realistic appraisal. Gone are the legions of naive admirers who put implicit trust in the words and deeds of industrial giants. Today, the press and public are inclined to give the business executive and his domain no special recognition or privileges. Commerce and industry have to earn their support and respect day by day. When something significant happens in the business world, people want to know what it means. Sometimes this news is favorable, and at other times it may be unfavorable. But there is little reason to believe that a vindictive press corps rejoices when business is in trouble, or that the public has any desire to put unreasonable controls on the free enterprise system. Most Americans simply want to know how their own pocketbooks will be affected when something important occurs on the economic front. Providing satisfactory answers is media's main mission, and it is a sobering task.

HOW THE PUBLIC COPES

Long ago when the economy of this nation was far simpler, consumers generally dealt with suppliers, buying directly from the butcher, the baker, and the shoemaker. Confidence and trust in the locally owned and operated business was high because the customer and the merchant were neighbors and friends.

Today's shopper must cope with a complex, depersonalized marketing and distribution system. When customers are upset about unsatisfactory service or inferior merchandise, they may not know what to do or to whom they can turn for help. If they complain, they may be instructed to fill out a form or write a letter, and end up engaging in a debate with a computer. Consequently, numerous cases of customer dissatisfaction are never resolved properly because the procedure is too difficult and unrewarding. This tends to substantiate the contention of certain consumer advocates that American business is not properly motivated or responsive to the public's needs.

It is inevitable that numerous grievances will be referred to media to check and report on, adding to the suspicion that business and the media are implacable enemies, and that the public distrusts both.

This is far from the truth. Actually, most Americans are ambivalent in their thinking about both business and the media. Repeated studies have revealed that citizens would like to see less "government intervention," but they also want more "government regulation" of consumer products, occupational safety, and environmental standards.

This inconsistency of opinion carries over as well to the news media. The public apparently wants more inside information on government and business, but is inclined to censure the press for being too inquisitive, overly zealous, guilty of "muckraking" and of pursuing "destructive investigations."

Although public criticism of established institutions has increased markedly in the past decade, it does not necessarily follow that the American people are disenchanted with their economic and social system. It merely means that individuals and organizations are no longer afraid to voice their complaints, and their verbalizing may be more a sign of support than of renunciation.

If Americans did not trust media, they would not rely so heavily on the information that press, radio, and television deliver to them. And if the public distrusted business as much as public-opinion pollsters sometimes suggest, then our entire society would not be so involved in the ownership and operation of business, nor would people patronize the myriad of commercial enterprises that they do. It is inconceivable that Americans could have little faith in our manufacturing companies and still purchase so many washing machines and automobiles. Similarly, if distrust of bankers were rampant, Americans would not have their hard-earned billions stored away in savings and checking accounts all over the country.

BUSINESS'S REACTION TO PRESS

Business cannot expect to have the absolute confidence of the public, any more than it can ask for the unquestioning trust of media or the government. But commerce in America does enjoy a vast amount of public loyalty, and it should recognize the right of the people to monitor and evaluate the quality of service received from business.

On the other hand, the business community also has rights. These include the right to insist on freedom from harmful, destructive government regulation and freedom to reply and respond to critics in the media, in education, in the pulpit, and in the general public. Business has an impressive story of progress and service to tell, individually and collectively, and it can generally mount convincing arguments to support its actions. Unfortunately, among corporate executives who have expressed willingness to communicate with the media, one frequently hears it said that the press is uncooperative and unresponsive. "How do we communicate since we don't own the printing press?" asks the public relations director of one of the country's largest companies.

Mobil Corporation has bought nationwide advertising to state its case, which includes this claim: "Materials provided by commerce or industry in the form of news releases, speeches, white papers, special studies and other documents or even face-to-face briefings have not proved to be the answer, because of the selective use of such materials."[6]

Donald S. MacNaughton, chairman of the Prudential Insurance Company of America, has been more harsh in his criticism, announcing that he is fed up with "glib, shallow, inaccurate reporting and editing."[7]

Expressions like these—and they are numerous—make it appear that some business leaders may be more occupied with the deficiencies of the press than with their own corporate shortcomings. On the other hand, they may not be unduly worried about either. A "Survey of Business Opinion" conducted by Baruch College School of Business and Public Administration asked several hundred top executives to place in order of importance a list of national issues and problems. Housing, pollution, and equal employment ranked sixth, seventh, and eighth out of twelve.[8] Problems with media was not even offered for consideration as a present concern or as an anticipated difficulty in the future, nor was consumerism. It makes you wonder: Is the business community seriously worried about the quality of news coverage it is getting, or is it mainly indulging in the all-American habit of griping because it doesn't always receive the kind of treatment it wants?

THE PARAMETERS OF THE PRESS

Regrettably, purveyors of news create their share of mistakes. They are constantly struggling against deadlines, incomplete information, and involved situations that defy simple explanations. Add to this the inescapable fact that news reporting can never be any better, or any more accurate or meaningful, than the capability of the journalists who carry out the assignments.

Since the invention of the printing press, there have never been enough topflight communicators. Some practitioners of the reporter's art are admittedly immature, inadequately educated, and lacking in respect for the news they are supposed to handle as objectively and carefully as possible.

Even a competent and conscientious reporter is handicapped by the complexities of today's society and often baffled by the many ways news sources can become confused and distorted from the propaganda of special-interest groups, the silence of the uncooperative, and the imposition of dozens of natural and artificial restrictions, including unclear laws, inconsistent judges, and subjective juries. To these negatives, one must add such problems as public ignorance, prejudice, apathy, bad eyesight, defective hearing, and emotional imbalance.

Millions of people read poorly or not at all. Countless others get distorted impressions of what they see or hear, and then criticize the media for inflating the news and playing tricks with the truth. The American people are notorious for what they don't know about business and economics. Sad to say, many have no desire to improve their knowledge or to clarify their misconceptions.

The reporter who covers a controversial story in expert fashion may well be accused of manipulating information and exaggerating facts in the interests of sensationalism. Those who make such indictments generally overlook the basic causes of bad news.

In the arena of commerce and industry, when misdeeds and faulty actions come to light can the responsible journalist close his eyes and turn off his microphones and cameras?

Never has there been greater need for mass media to try to make sense out of all the seemingly senseless things people do—the troubles they compound, the laws they violate, the debris and ugliness they stack up in ugly piles, the inequities they tolerate, and the deficiencies they ignore. On the positive side, it can be argued that a reporter is doing his patriotic duty by informing the public about such matters. Historically, this has been the democratic way to deal with problems and to effect beneficial changes and logical improvements.

Admittedly, it is easier to theorize about the redeeming qualities of the free press than it is to document stories of its success in improving the social and economic fabric of America. Most of the time the media reflect and respond. They rarely initiate or instigate. Investigative journalism is the exception rather than the rule, and this is especially true in the way the press deals with business news.

Dr. Tim Ryles, director of the Office of Consumer Services for the State of Georgia, urges the media to become more active in probing and exposing questionable business practices, not to embarrass or indict the entire business community, but to put the public on guard against those who operate in an irresponsible manner. While there is understandable opposition among some businessmen to intensified news surveillance, not all representatives of the commercial world share this attitude. A growing number of enlightened business leaders have publicly stated that the future viability of their organizations will depend on how honestly and effectively they respond to basic consumer expectations, and they welcome the opportunity to prove their dependability.

Frederick W. West, Jr., president of Bethlehem Steel Corporation, is typical of such executives. He believes that the press can be an ally in keeping the business community sensitive and alert to the growing expectations of the public.

"To wind up this whole subject of bias," he says, "my advice to the business community is to stop worrying so much about whether or not members of the press are prejudiced one way or another. Let's work harder to earn their confidence and respect."[9]

This is an excellent suggestion, but it is by no means universally accepted or practiced. A high percentage of corporate executives continue to exhibit a profound distrust of the media, which they suspect of wanting to exaggerate and intimidate rather than inform and illuminate. Consequently, a number of executives refuse to have any contacts or communication with media representatives.

When asked if reporters should let the public know about any fraudulent business practices they uncover, corporate heads are virtually unanimous in saying, "Yes, it is the journalist's duty to disclose such information." But it is not uncommon for a business spokesman to complain bitterly about the unwarranted intrusion of the media when he or his company gets unflattering news coverage.

Herbert E. Markley, president of the Timken Company, has jokingly suggested that some business officials fear, on the one hand, that they will not be quoted right, and on the other, that they will be.

AN UNEASY RELATIONSHIP 'TWIXT BUSINESS AND MEDIA

In principle, the business community wants the truth told about how it conducts its business, but there is often a difference between agreement in principle and practice. No commercial enterprise relishes having its mistakes widely publicized, and few business leaders get any enjoyment from reading or hearing of their competitor's troubles, reasoning that adverse publicity is harmful to all business. As a result, so-called "negative" news about commerce and industry not only is widely resented by the business community, but the newspaper or broadcasting station which disseminates such information on a regular basis is almost certain to get a reputation for being unfriendly to business.

> Reporting the news has always meant telling people things they may not want to hear. In times of social conflict, this task is all the more difficult. Skepticism turns to cynicism. Detachment is too often perceived as hostility. The clamor to "tell it like it is" too often carries with it the threat to "tell it like we see it, or else." The Greeks were not alone in wanting to condemn the bearer of bad tidings. [10]

There is both irony and inconsistency in the uneasy relationship that exists between business and media. In the first place, they need one another. Billions of dollars spent for advertising by private enterprise should promote friendship and mutual respect, rather than distrust. Secondly, business leaders who complain that they are badly treated by media express dissatisfaction at times with too much news coverage and at other times with too little.

Actually, a high percentage of daily business news is favorable. Local stories about achievements, advancements and promotions, acquisitions, expansion, and profit making fall into the positive category and often occupy half or more of the space in the average newspaper's business section.

It is other news of an unflattering nature that causes so much pain in corporate councils—reports of bankruptcies, fraudulent dealings, consumer grievances and law suits, and the "gloom and doom" prophesies of energy and environmental spokesmen.

Obviously, the bad must be reported along with the good if any news medium is to properly cover business news. Corporate morality and social responsibility can only have real meaning where businesses are just as willing to talk about their failures as their successes. There must be a commitment to excellence of products and service that is convincingly and consistently demonstrated.

This can best be accomplished by impressing every employee of a business with the altruistic philosophy and principles that motivate the firm and encouraging free discussion of the company's methods and decisions, both within the organization and with the press. The individual is the key, and responsibility for any company action—favorable or unfavorable—rests with each employee, not the mystical "corporation."

The president of the Chamber of Commerce of the United States, Richard L. Lesher, believes that the vigilance of the press can do much to help employees and employers discharge their duty to the public. The role of the press, he says, is crucial in developing consensus on changing definitions of social responsibility, "which most business leaders are anxious to demonstrate, provided it is clear exactly what society expects."[11]

Lesher regrets that the media don't always provide this clarification. "If I have a complaint about the behavior of the media with respect to business," he says, "it is this: too often, media coverage of a major socioeconomic issue emphasizes the sensational and the simplistic at the expense of the balanced and the analytical. Such shallow coverage tends to encourage zealotry in dealing with complex problems."[12]

Many business leaders are especially bothered by television, where some newscasters apparently concentrate more on entertaining with "happy talk" and gimmickry than imparting useful and reliable information.

Engaging in "showmanship" to attract customers is nothing new. Years ago metropolitan newspapers carried on vicious "circulation wars," with flamboyant editors trying to be more sensational than their competitors.

The current "show biz" approach to news should not be taken too seriously. It will not last. Responsible journalists will prevail, and they are struggling to master a more serious problem: how to cope with increasingly complicated news developments, all of which impact favorably or unfavorably on the public.

There is no such thing as an isolated event, and this has particular pertinence in the business arena. Virtually any type of economic decision is destined to cause reverberations in many quarters. What might appear initially to be an innocent, innocuous statement or action by a business executive could turn out to affect millions of lives.

It is asking a great deal of even the most astute reporter to be able to grasp the significance of each fact he learns and to interpret the information properly. Relatively few business reporters can meet the challenge.

The late Chet Huntley lamented that "the degree of ignorance concerning economics in this country is incredible."[13]

Business spokesmen are correct when they complain that too few journalists understand the meaning and benefits of profits. Rare is the reporter who is prepared to deal with such intricate matters as energy supply, economic forecasting, or the inner workings of a corporation. Yet how many business executives are trying to improve this situation by willingly supplying information, putting it into context, and explaining how it is likely to affect the individual citizen?

All too often reporters and executives pursue conflicting goals. The reporter wants all the facts, whereas the executive wants to carefully and selectively release the information at his disposal. As one financial editor explains: "To a reporter, a fact has an inherent worth, in and of itself. To a businessman, a fact is an asset to be invested."[14]

Journalists are supposed to be probing, questioning, suspicious of motives. If they ask embarrassing questions, these can best be handled by business spokesmen who have facts and figures handy and are willing to interpret them as fully as necessary to minimize mistakes and confusion.

Companies should look for people "who are willing to move away from anonymity and who are willing to confront the public-information process as one of the ingredients of the business leadership of tomorrow."[15]

Even with good-faith efforts on both sides, there will be difficulties and differences of opinion. Citizens' movements will continue to grow and demand reforms. The public will increasingly view the corporation as an entity that is accountable for its decisions and deeds. Business must learn to accept greater public scrutiny.

THE KEY: MUTUAL RESPECT AND UNDERSTANDING

"From time to time we've all heard business leaders chastise the press for not being more like cheerleaders for the community. You and I know that such is not a proper role," says Robert W. Scherer, president of Georgia Power Company. "Still, it is incumbent upon all of us in business to assist the press in recognizing stories for their news value, especially when these stories serve to inform a public so that it can make a wiser decision regarding its own economic future."[16]

Scherer has been an exponent of an aggressive public-information program, which he believes has promoted understanding with both the media and the public.

In a related opinion, Louis Lundborg, former chairman of the board, Bank of America, regrets that the business community has tended to view itself as something apart, something walled off from society as a whole, creating unnecessary suspicion and hostility.

> The fact is that we are all tremendously dependent on one another. Business, government, the consumer, the media, academia—we are all interdependent. It is time to stop throwing rocks at one another; to stop using cliché epithets to describe others; to recognize that for all the special interests that divide us, there are more common interests that should unite us; and to recognize that there is much to be done, and time is running.[17]

For those business representatives who still fear that their future is endangered by the "unbridled" power of the press to inspect, investigate, and accuse, Eric Sevareid has some words of reassurance.

> The press, after all, speaks with a thousand voices, in constant dissonance. It has no power to arrest you, draft you, tax you, or even make you fill out a form—except a subscription form, if you're agreeable. It is the power of government, especially the federal government and more particularly its executive arm, that has increased in my time. Many politicians have come to power in many countries and put press people in jail. I can't think of any place where the reverse has occurred. . . .
>
> I can think of innumerable cases where the press has led authority to situations of crime and corruption. I can't think of any case where sins of commission or omission by the press have resulted in gross injustice, at least in the sense of innocent people going to jail.[18]

The corporate councils of America would be well advised to encourage the press to do its job and do it well, giving business matters all the attention they deserve. Instead of asking for less attention, business executives should insist on more and better news coverage.

As one approach to meeting the need for improved reporting of economic realities and issues, the National Association of Manufacturers has joined with the American Newspaper Publishers Association and the Association for Education in Journalism to design a program to strengthen the training and education of future journalists in business/economic reporting. Dozens of colleges and universities have responded and initiated efforts to improve their curricula and teaching methods in this field of journalism.

In addition, some of the nation's major corporations have started to underwrite fellowships in business and economics courses for journalists.

It is quite obvious that a growing number of journalists are aware of their shortcomings and are striving to raise the level of professionalism in all fields of communication, including the reporting of business news. It is a never-ending task because the difficulties of determining the truth and sharing information clearly and dispassionately seem to increase day by day.

The commercial world will surely be reported more accurately in years to come if representatives of both business and the news media strive to establish and maintain a relationship of mutual respect and understanding. Journalists have much to learn about business and its many problems, and businessmen could benefit from a better understanding of how news is gathered, processed, and delivered.

This exchange of knowledge can only take place by opening doors and encouraging a free and fair dialogue. Questions should be welcomed on both sides and answered fully in simple, candid, plain talk. The news media will never be able to report only good, pleasant, and complimentary news about business. And they should not be expected to do so. But print and broadcast journalists can and should steep themselves in economics and sharpen their ability to interpret business and financial affairs in a consistent and competent manner, helping the public understand what one occurrence means in relation to another, and providing reliable analysis and satisfying explanations of those events deemed worthy of being reported.

That is the most the corporate community can expect. It is the least it is entitled to get.

NOTES

1. Lewis W. Foy, in an address to the International Association of Business Communicators and the Business Roundtable, Chicago, January 22, 1976.

2. Ralph Ottwell, "Big Bad Business in the Hands of the Devil Press," *The Quill*, April 1977, p. 16.

3. Adam Smith, *An Inquiry into the Nature and Causes of the Wealth of Nations* (London: Methuen & Co., Ltd., 1930), p. 421.

4. "Upset Consumers Often Quiet—Poll," *Atlanta Journal,* July 10, 1977.

5. Edwin T. Freedley, *A Practical Treatise on Business* (Philadelphia: Arno, 1856), p. 5.

6. Joseph Poindexter, "The Greater Industry-Media Debate," *Saturday Review,* July 10, 1976, p. 17.

7. Donald S. MacNaughton (speech excerpted in *New York Times,* March 7, 1976).

8. OBI Interaction, Organizational Behavioral Institute, July 1, 1977.

9. Frederick W. West, Jr., "Economic and Business Reporting: Strengths and Weaknesses" (speech to American Newspaper Publishers Association, New York, May 4, 1976).

10. *A Free and Responsive Press* (Twentieth Century Fund Task Force Report for a National News Council, New York, 1973), p. 3.

11. Richard L. Lesher, personal letter to the author, May 10, 1977.

12. Ibid.

13. Chet Huntley, "Media Antipathy Toward Business," *The Wall Street Journal,* August 7, 1973.

14. Joseph Poindexter, "The Great Industry-Media Debate," *Saturday Review,* July 10, 1976, p. 22.

15. Arthur R. Taylor (address to the Financial Executives Institute, New Orleans, October 21, 1975).

16. Robert W. Scherer, personal letter to the author, June 16, 1977.

17. Louis B. Lundborg, "Making a Living in the Third Century," *Saturday Review,* July 10, 1976, p. 42.

18. Eric Sevareid (remarks on the First Amendment delivered at the National Association of Broadcasters Convention, Washington, D.C., March 28, 1977).

WATCHING THE ECONOMY: A NEWSPAPERMAN'S VIEW

ALFRED L. MALABRE, JR.

The information reported in the media can have a major influence on the attitudes and actions of policymakers in both the public and private sectors. In this article, Alfred Malabre, one of the people who reports the information, tells how he gets it and puts it together.

The most important aspects of economy watching, according to the news editor of The Wall Street Journal, *are placing things in perspective, judgment on how to play stories, and maintaining close tabs on sources of available data.*

The data are provided by governmental and private statistics. The perspective is provided by talking with experts (recognizing their biases) and by seeking out the grass-roots people in industry. Judgment must be provided by the journalist through knowledge and experience.

Mr. Malabre has covered the economy from Bonn, London, Chicago, and New York for nearly twenty years. He writes the Journal's *Monday morning "Outlook" column and has contributed to* Harper's, Saturday Review, *and the* Encyclopedia Britannica. *He is the author of* Understanding the Economy: For People Who Can't Stand Economics.

Years ago, back in the 1960s when William McChesney Martin was the chairman of the Federal Reserve Board, an item appeared on the Dow Jones Financial News Ticker that caught the eye of several *Wall Street Journal* editors, including myself, in New York.

Mr. Martin was making a speech somewhere—I forget exactly where—and in it, according to the news ticker, he expressed a "serious concern" about an apparent deterioration in the quality of credit in the country.

Good heavens, we all thought, what ghastly financial development underlies that remark? Is some major bank in trouble? Has some secret Federal Reserve study unearthed a credit time bomb deep within the country's continually mounting debt pileup?

As good and dutiful editors we grabbed the telephone and dialed our man in Washington who covered the Federal Reserve Board. What did Chairman Martin have in mind in that speech? Is financial trouble brewing somewhere that we should know about, but don't?

Well, our intrepid Washington fellow got right to work with his many sources at the Federal Reserve, and inside of an hour he was back to us. Nothing to worry about, he reported. The chairman's "serious concern" about credit, it seemed, was merely a reaction to an article he had read in, of all places, *The Wall Street Journal* several days earlier. The piece, which appeared on our front page, was essentially a summary of interviews by *Wall Street Journal* reporters in various cities with mortgage lenders, credit agencies, and the like. Among other findings, the survey uncovered some concern among these outfits over the financial sturdiness of some individual borrowers. Nothing alarming, mind you. But some concern.

Indeed, in some of the interviews, the concern expressed could reasonably be classified as "serious." Which all goes to prove, among other things I suppose, the validity of a venerable advertising slogan: People who get ahead read *The Wall Street Journal*. Witness William McChesney Martin.

It underlines a point that every newspaper person, and especially everyone writing about the economic picture, should never for one moment forget or underestimate. The point is this: what we report about and write about can have a major influence on the attitudes— and ultimately upon the actions—of policymakers. So we should be darned careful that we tell it like it is, or at least like we earnestly believe it is.

Al Sindlinger, a noted private economist and poll taker, once addressed an "open letter" to the editors of *The Wall Street Journal* and the *New York Times* in which he scolded us to be more careful in our economic reporting because, as he put it, "many of the world's most important decision and opinion makers not only read your publications regularly for the news itself, but for the insight and understanding you bring to each development."

That "open letter" appeared in Al Sindlinger's biweekly report to his clients shortly after the last presidential election. He went on to state: "It is not inconceivable that someday the candidate, who on November second was chosen president, will base a major decision on something he read in the *Journal* or in the *Times*. And our next president—Jimmy Carter—will be dealing with a Congress whose members regularly read the *Journal* or the *Times*. We know that you don't take these unique responsibilities lightly."

No, Al, we don't, and we don't imagine our colleagues at the *Times* do either.

KEEPING AN EYE ON THE ECONOMY

Let me now attempt to give you some idea of how we go about our task of watching the economy at *The Wall Street Journal*. I will try to detail along the way some of the problems that can complicate the effort. And let me also make clear that my remarks pertain only to the news pages of the paper and not to our editorial page—much admired in some circles, heartily disliked in others—which deals mainly in opinion.

Facts, I like to think, go before opinion. They are the grist out of which opinions are constructed. How do we go about gathering the economic facts?

At *The Wall Street Journal* we are blessed with a large and skillful Washington reporting staff—more than a dozen highly experienced reporters and editors. These newsmen, and particularly those in the bureau who are assigned to cover such agencies as the U.S. Treasury Department, the Commerce Department, the Labor Department and its Bureau of Labor Statistics, and the aforementioned Federal Reserve Board, continually monitor the material pouring daily from Washington's relentless statistical mills.

For example, the people who cover the Commerce Department make sure that *Wall Street Journal* readers keep abreast of that agency's monthly report on the movement of the composite index of so-called leading economic indicators. This widely followed composite index, whose dozen components range from the length of the average workweek in manufacturing industries to stock-market price trends, is compiled and published by statistical experts at the Commerce Department. Over the years, it has tended to foreshadow by several months major turning points in the overall business cycle—hence the label "leading."

In any event, an absolutely essential part of the *Journal*'s economy-watching effort is the Washington bureau's monitoring of key business statistics—barometers, if you will, of the economic climate.

The leading-indicator index, of course, is among the foremost of these, but there are dozens of others: the consumer and wholesale price indexes, the unemployment rate, the trade balance, new orders for durable goods, productivity, the rate of operations of factories, the gross national product adjusted for price changes, consumer credit, the balance of international payments, and so on and so on and so on.

Some widely followed statistics originate elsewhere than Washington, I should add. For these, the *Journal* depends on other of its news bureaus.

Reporters in New York, where I happen to work, monitor the weekly money-supply report of the Federal Reserve Board, which is actually released each Thursday afternoon at a press conference held at the Federal Reserve System's New York regional bank. Reporters in New York also handle, among other important data, a report of capital-spending plans issued by McGraw-Hill and a survey of help-wanted advertising volume in major newspapers around the country conducted by the Conference Board, a nonprofit business-research organization based in New York. Reporters in the paper's Chicago bureau monitor such important matters as farm-price trends. *Journal* reporters based in Dallas keep tab on various oil-industry statistics.

To do a decent job of economy-watching, using statistics from Washington and elsewhere, requires more than a simple parroting of press releases from particular governmental or private organizations. It is essential that the reporter handling the story try to put things into the broadest possible perspective.

Let's return for a moment to the index of leading economic indicators. Let's suppose that economic activity has been expanding briskly for, say, two years. Let's suppose that the leading-indicator index has been rising briskly for about the same length of time, or perhaps slightly longer, since the index normally moves up or down several months ahead of general business activity.

Now, let's suppose that this particular month the Commerce Department report shows, for the first time, a decline in the index. Not a steep drop, but nonetheless a decline.

How does the reporter handling the Commerce Department press release handle that? Well, the chances are that the Commerce Department release will stick pretty closely to reporting just the raw data. It won't provide much help in answering questions that may enter an enterprising reporter's mind, such as: Is this a big story? Does it mean that a recession is on the way? Is the period of economic expansion nearing an end?

The experienced economy-watching reporter should be able to place such a release into perspective for readers. It's unlikely that the press people at the Commerce Department will do so.

First, the enterprising reporter would have some idea from experience that after a couple of years of sustained economic expansion the leading-indicator index does indeed tend to wobble around, perhaps dipping for a month or two, then perhaps resuming rising for several months, then perhaps dipping once again. And so on. And the reporter would know that this wobbling can happen without a recession coming along a few months later. Indeed, he would know that a wobbly leading-indicator index is the rule, rather than the exception, after a business expansion has been under way a couple of years or so.

With such knowledge, the experienced reporter, our economy-watcher, would know to be careful not to overplay (in the jargon of our business) the story.

The news that the index had dropped for the first time in more than two years of economic expansion surely deserves bigger play (lapsing into newspaper jargon again) than a report of still further gains. But in my view it would be irresponsible journalism to blow up such a one-month drop in the index into a scare story with big black headlines proclaiming the likelihood of a recession around the corner.

A sensible approach would be simply to give the data and observe that such declines do indeed often occur without a recession shortly materializing. Of course, if the index were to drop again the following month and again the month after that, a story raising the possibility of a recession just ahead would seem entirely in order. Experience shows that when the index declines for three or four straight months during an economic expansion period, serious economic trouble frequently does develop.

Parenthetically here, let me briefly observe that a gloom-and-doom headline, especially on top of economic news, invariably seems to attract more readers. As a result, there is always a temptation for economy-watching reporters, contrary to the advice of the song, to accentuate the negative.

There doubtless are times when the negative deserves to be accentuated in a business story. But I decidedly don't believe that the situation outlined above is such a circumstance. It's the sort of situation where a reporter has a real obligation to tell it like it is and, in the telling, to employ all the good judgment that he can possibly muster. In economic journalism, as in other fields of work, there is no substitute for experience.

ARE THEY JUGGLING THE STATISTICS?

I've gone on for quite a while here about statistic-watching. Before moving along to other means of watching the economy, let me simply stress again the importance of keeping a close tab on the available data. There are things that we just don't have data about—like the number of jobs going begging in the country each month. But, all in all, it's fair to say that Uncle Sam provides fuller, more accurate economic statistics than can be obtained in any other country in the world.

The statisticians in Washington who compile the key figures are career people, deeply dedicated to their profession, with much pride in their apolitical approach to putting together the figures. Politicians, including the men over the years in the White House, have been known to put out grossly misleading statements about the economic outlook. But they don't try to juggle the figures.

I wish that were true everywhere, but the fact is that in many countries the statistics simply can't be trusted. I recall visiting Brazil about a decade ago to do an article for *The Wall Street Journal* about that South American country's painfully high rate of inflation. About the time I set out to do the story, I observed that the Brazilian consumer price index seemed to be climbing a bit less rapidly than several months earlier. I was prepared to write a piece saying that the country's military leaders appeared to be making some real headway against inflation, until I discovered that they had secretly removed housing from the items priced in the index. The price of housing happened to be about the most rapidly increasing component of the index, so its secret removal helped make Brazil's entire inflation picture appear less gloomy than in reality it was.

It's a sad story, but one that happens far too frequently around the world. Fortunately, it doesn't seem to happen in America. Let's hope I'm right about this, because if I'm wrong the whole business of economy-watching in the United States becomes an exceedingly hazardous, if not pointless and hopeless, task.

PUTTING IT IN THE KING'S ENGLISH: SEE AN ECONOMIST

Economy-watching, of course, involves more than simply monitoring and reporting for readers the latest data out of statistical mills in Washington and elsewhere. The data must be explained and assessed in language that reasonably intelligent persons who aren't economists or even in business can understand.

For aid in interpreting the raw data, a prudent business reporter can turn, fortunately, to an impressive stable of experts. For there is assuredly no shortage of economic analysts in the United States.

Fortunately again, there is a remarkable willingness among even the most eminent of the experts to talk at length with the press, at least with my particular segment of the press. This willingness is doubly remarkable when one considers that many such economists can command enviable fees for their analyses. One business forecaster whom I've gotten to know well over the years—he happens to work for a large New York–based securities concern—collects as much as $20,000 a year from each of several large corporations. For these five-digit payments, this man tells me that he needs only to visit the respective corporations once a quarter. These visits normally consist of a pleasant lunch at corporate headquarters and then an hour's presentation of the business outlook, as seen in this fellow's particular crystal ball.

Even this well-paid and sought-after economist, however, invariably manages to find the time in a busy schedule to converse at length with me or one of my colleagues at *The Wall Street Journal* whenever we happen to need a bit of elaboration on some particular aspect of the business situation. In addition, we receive—gratis—this man's periodic written reports, for which clients of his firm generally must pay a considerable fee.

I should caution that, just as relying too heavily on the raw output of the statistical mills can be hazardous, so can relying too heavily on the comments of highly paid experts. First and foremost, one should keep squarely in mind that all these individuals have their particular prejudices; they all have axes of one sort or another to grind. Economists employed by large New York banks, for example, may not be the best experts to tap for objective comments about whether U.S. banks have taken dangerous risks in their loans to various underdeveloped countries in the Third World.

By the same token, economists working for stock-broker firms on Wall Street may not be the best fellows to provide impartial commentary about whether a major recession—and a concurrent sharp break in share prices—looms just around the corner. Or economists attached to huge multinational corporations may not provide the soundest opinions on the question of whether policies pursued by such corporations can cost American jobs.

I believe that an economic reporter should be wary even when interviewing a supposedly simon-pure academic economist. I recall the unhappy instance, many years ago, when a prominent financial publication (fortunately, not *The Wall Street Journal*) solicited the views of a famous university professor on a matter involving the economic impact of imports of such-and-such a widget. The professor straight-facedly declared that the widget's importation was a matter of little or no concern. Only later did it develop that the professor, at a fat fee, was performing economic research for the Widget Importers Trade Association.

Economists who get deeply involved in the political arena can also pose a problem for economy-watching reporters. As a general rule, I've found that commentary issued by economists in power— currently, economists closely tied to the Democratic Party—almost always are overly optimistic about the economic road ahead. Conversely, economists out of power—currently, those attached to the Republican Party—invariably seem excessively gloomy about business prospects.

For example, some of the top economists within the Nixon administration repeatedly asserted—when they were in Washington in the late 1960s and early 1970s—that inflation would soon simmer down. Instead, as we all painfully found out, inflation kept on worsening. Recently, in contrast, some of these same people have appeared extremely concerned about the possibility that inflation will soon be getting even more severe than it now is. They are saying, in effect, that their Democratic counterparts, now in the driver's seat, are running things badly and as a consequence will fail to keep inflation down—or, for that matter, the economy up.

How does a business writer cope with prejudice—intentional or unintentional—among the experts?

Unfortunately, I have no easy answer to that. You obviously must try to learn something about the predilections of the man or woman that you happen to be interviewing. And then you must be careful to present the particular expert's view in such a manner that the reader will clearly discern that it should be taken with at least a modicum of salt.

I am convinced, the hazards notwithstanding, that much can be gleaned through soliciting expert opinion. The raw statistics can go only so far. For example, it was on the advice of a senior economist at the National Bureau of Economic Research, a nonprofit organization based in New York, that I finally abandoned using a particular government statistic purporting to show the actual purchasing power of the average worker's weekly paycheck—what it could really buy in terms of goods and services.

For very sound reasons that I won't elaborate now, the purchasing-power statistic, this expert convinced me, simply wasn't reliable enough to be cited with confidence in *Journal* articles. I confess that without this advice, I wouldn't possibly have been able to make that judgment for myself. As I indicated, it helps to know something about the background of the expert you happen to be interviewing. In this case, my source was a former commissioner of the Labor Department's Bureau of Labor Statistics.

TAPPING THE GRASS ROOTS

This brings me to a third major facet of economy-watching. It is the most difficult technique, requiring considerable time and perseverance. But it can also prove to be the most rewarding.

I am talking, essentially, about the business of actually going out into the field, be it a convention hall or wherever, and through extensive buttonhole interviewing with dozens of individuals coming up with a story that can shed some new light on how the economy may be performing and where it may be heading.

As an illustration, let me recount a procedure that I've found successful in the past.

Years ago, I worked as the appliance-beat reporter for the *Journal.* As such, I regularly attended the vast get-togethers of appliance dealers from all around the country held once a year at the giant Merchandise Mart building in Chicago. During these conventions, which normally went on for the most of a week, I scurried about conducting dozens of interviews with the assorted appliance men and women assembled.

Out of these get-togethers, I would attempt to discern a broad pattern that could be pulled into shape as the basis of a major economic-trend piece for the paper. It never ceases to astound me how forthcoming most individuals are in such interviews. This is particularly so, I have found, among people in business for themselves, such as many of the appliance dealers at the Merchandise Mart.

In any event, by seeking information from these dealers on such matters as sales, inventory levels, costs, and prices, I found that I was often able to emerge with trend-spotting articles of some significance in the broader economic picture.

For example, I recall an article done in early 1960 under the headline, "Appliance Anxiety—Worried Dealers Cut Prices as Sales Lag, Inventories Pile Up." The economic softness described at length in the appliance business in that article—largely on the basis of the Merchandise Mart interviewing—soon spread to other important segments of American industry. In fact, a full-fledged recession set in during the late spring of 1960. Those Merchandise Mart interviews turned out to be an important bit of early evidence that general economic trouble was on the way.

Obviously, the article was well worth the effort of trying to buttonhole appliance dealers for the better part of a week. Eventually, of course, the evidence of softness in the appliance business would show up in industry-wide statistics compiled and issued by appliance trade organizations, and ultimately in wide-ranging Commerce Department data. But my admittedly unscientific sampling in the Merchandise Mart predated the official, industry-wide data by a goodly number of weeks.

As do other methods of economy-watching, this buttonholing technique entails hazards.

First, the reporter has to be very certain that a definite pattern is evident. If you fail to interview a very broad cross section of dealers, for example, there is a major risk. Or, if you try to fabricate a clear trend when there really isn't any—always a temptation—there is a major risk. If half the dealers interviewed say that sales are going great and half say that sales are lousy—watch out.

A second hazard involves interpreting correctly what is really being said. I have learned that businessmen—whether appliance dealers or captains of giant industrial corporations—tend to be excessively pessimistic near the end of a recession and excessively optimistic near the end of a recovery. This tendency puts a burden on the reporter to make certain, in the questioning, that the businessman really means what he is saying.

If an appliance dealer tells you that his sales have been lousy, don't leave the matter there. Was last week's sales volume better or worse than the volume the week before? Even if volume is down from a year ago, how does it compare with a month ago? Two months ago?

It's vitally important for a reporter trying to keep a tab on the economy to recognize that businessmen, like individuals in all walks of life, tend to project the future from the recent past. The buttonholing approach to economy-watching can prove exceedingly valuable. But, as with other economy-watching approaches, one must be aware of the hazards.

AS CYCLES GO, SO GOES THE ECONOMY

I've said a good deal here about other people's prejudices—the possible prejudices of economic analysts, the prejudices, if you will, of businessmen who believe that bad times or good times in the recent past will automatically translate into bad times or good times in the near future.

Let me now say something about a prejudice that I have developed over the years. It's a prejudice that many economy-watchers may not share. I recognize this. But I cling to my prejudice because, quite simply, it has worked for me. It has helped me keep tabs better on economic developments.

My particular prejudice, as I try to keep abreast of the economy from year to year, is to try to view business developments within a business-cycle framework.

What do I mean by a business-cycle framework?

More precisely, I have grown convinced that the economy moves in a cyclical pattern of expansion and contraction phases—the business cycle, if you will. And I have become further convinced that a reporter attempting to assess the state of the economy at a particular time can benefit greatly by recognizing where within the business cycle things stand.

Take the case of a reporter writing an article about the outlook for capital spending. Capital spending, business-cycle experience teaches us, tends to lag the ups and downs of such broader facets of the economy as consumer spending by several months. It often keeps on rising for a while after a recession sets in, and it can be slow to resume rising after a recession ends.

Armed with a knowledge of this tendency, a reporter writing an article about the outlook for capital spending is likely to do a better job of it than one with no familiarity with business-cycle history, no perspective. For example, I would be very wary of optimism expressed by capital-goods executives if such yardsticks as consumer spending were indicating that a recession might be developing. And I would be equally skeptical of capital-goods pessimism if other economic gauges suggested that a business recovery was beginning to get under way.

Some analysts from time to time have argued that the business cycle is some sort of an anachronism which may have been highly significant in the past but is no longer relevant to serious economic analysis. I disagree. I believe that the economy will continue to experience clearly identifiable ups and downs—expansion and contraction phases. Perhaps the day will arrive when policymakers in Washington and business planners in corporate boardrooms across the nation will be sufficiently wise to keep the economy moving smoothly ever upward.

But that wisdom, in my opinion, is certainly not yet in evidence. Political leaders will continue to make policy blunders. Industrial chieftains will continue to overproduce or underproduce or produce things that people don't need or want. The upshot is that times of economic trouble—inflation and shortages, recessions and gluts—will persist. There will continue to be prosperous periods and slumps.

If this were not so, as a business writer who makes a living following economic trends, I would be in very deep trouble. I would have to think about switching to something dull, like covering baseball or horseracing. Because it is precisely the ups and downs of the economy—the never-ending movements of the business cycle—that provide all the challenge and the interest of the present job.

Economy-watching is intriguing, and it can be done with the use of common sense, patience, and a modicum of effort. And, most fortunately, you don't have to know the difference between a diffusion index and a regression series.

Let's leave that to the economists.

SECTION 3 PUBLIC RELATIONS VIEWS

In the relationship of business and the media, public relations practitioners play many roles. Some see them as catalysts; to others they are barriers or manipulators. Often they are caught in the middle between journalistic and business institutions trying to explain each to the other—no easy task when one's livelihood may depend on the reactions of either or both.

Public relations deals with public attitudes and knowledge and has traditionally worked through the media to influence and educate various publics. Understanding that actions speak louder than words, professional public relations counsel, in either in-house or consulting relationships with businesses, advise corporate management not only about what to say, but in many cases what to do as well. Some have gone so far as to describe public relations counselors as the conscience of a company or the ombudsmen who represent the public in corporate decision making.

The deterioration of public attitudes toward business over the past decade has presented new challenges to the public relations profession. "In 1965 we warned corporate clients it was time to head off a negative public reaction to industry," says Hugh Hoffman, Opinion Research chairman. As the media have assumed a more aggressive stance toward business, public relations practitioners' roles have changed; new demands have been made on their knowledge and expertise. Public relations has been charged with the responsibility of explaining not only specific businesses and industries, but the American economic system as a whole. The profession has been called upon to combat and counteract critics of the system and to cope with a new breed of investigative reporter. Moreover, these difficult responsibilities have been adopted against a background of revelations of corporate misconduct which further erode business's credibility, already tenuous from the perspectives of journalists and the public.

While called "flacks" by newspeople and faced with corporate attitudes which blame problems on failure to communicate effectively, public relations professionals have preached openness, honesty, candor, social responsibility, initiation of positive change, increased sensitivity to societal trends, cleaning of houses, and emphasized doing good as well as talking good.

Because of their position between business and media, public relations professionals have unique insights into each institution and the relationship between the two. In this section, the head of one of the world's largest public relations firms explores trends and problems in media/business relations; "the top-ranking woman in public relations" (according to *Business Week*) looks at ways in which business influences the media; and the author of the world's best-selling public relations textbook makes recommendations to both business and the media as to how they might improve their relations with each other.

THE MEDIA AS MONITOR OF CORPORATE BEHAVIOR

DAVID FINN

Business must conduct itself today with the awareness that all of its activities may be subjected to public scrutiny at any time—and that's a good thing, according to David Finn, chairman of the board and co-founder of Ruder & Finn, Inc. The media have played a major role in bringing about changes in the nature of corporate activity and thus have improved society. Nonetheless, he says that the job of public relations has changed from promoting positive publicity to dealing with negative criticism.

Finn identifies three problems that make the media/business relationship more difficult. One such problem is the contradictory advice received by business executives from public relations and legal counsel. The former typically advise openness while the latter usually advise executives to say nothing. According to Finn, business executives prefer openness and candor, but when facing potential litigation they listen to their lawyers—often at the expense of public opinion.

The author of The Corporate Oligarch *and* Public Relations and Management, *Finn has guided the development of a two-man public relations firm into one of the largest in the world. He is also a noted painter, sculptor, and photographer.*

If there is a striking difference in the way public relations was practiced a generation ago and the way it is practiced today, it may be found in the way the business community perceives the media.

As I recall it, twenty-five years ago the media were viewed by public relations practitioners primarily as targets for positive publicity about their clients. Reporters shared that view and considered it one measure of their importance in our economic system. Occasionally they had an exaggerated notion of their power and believed they could provide enormously valuable benefits to corporations if they published editorial features on commercial products or corporate developments. A page in *Life* magazine was believed by some (although rarely by clients) to be worth tens of thousands of dollars. Because editorial comments were thought to have a higher credibility than advertisements, there was speculation that the value of a page of publicity might be determined by multiplying the advertising cost of an equivalent amount of space by a factor of three. Thus, if an advertising page cost $20,000, it was considered to be worth $60,000. Because reporters felt this enormous prize could be awarded at their discretion, they sometimes resented the money public relations people seemed to be making in the process. After all, it was the reporter who was providing the value, and his meager financial rewards did not reflect the true source of the benefit.

Although some of these feelings and perceptions still remain, it has become apparent that they were based on incorrect assumptions. Editorial features on products and corporate activities are a distinct public relations benefit to corporations, but we know today there is no way that editorial coverage can realistically be compared to advertising campaigns. Publicity can be one element of a marketing program, while advertising is another and quite different element. To develop an effective advertising campaign, selling messages must be tested, media selection must be made with great care, timing is crucial, the advertising campaign must be incorporated in material used by salesmen in sales promotion materials for customers, as well as in the development of special in-store events, and so forth. Publicity can also be part of such a strategy, coordinated with the other factors of a marketing program. But editorial coverage differs radically from advertising in that timing, media selection, and message are almost completely uncontrollable. Editors publish stories that will appeal to readers, not sell products, and they do so when there is a legitimate news peg, not necessarily when salesmen are calling on their customers. Publicity may have greater credibility than advertising, but it may also have less salability. Any effort to compare the worth of equivalent space is therefore fruitless.

To imagine that a feature in *Life* magazine—or anywhere else— was worth tens of thousands of dollars to the client and would provide instant success for the sale of the product was an illusion that grew largely out of a misunderstanding of how products are sold. I am sure that there were many public relations people who encouraged this illusion as a means of inflating their self-importance and the financial value of their services. Moreover, there were many executives who were so starry-eyed about the prospect of obtaining important publicity for their products or their companies that they were ready to believe that public relations might be a magical way of achieving immediate success.

In any case, I do believe that this kind of thinking was quite prevalent in the 1950s, and that it is much less so in the 1970s. Today, one reason for this change is that *Life* magazine is gone, as are many other prime media targets of the public relations community. There are other magazines that have appeared on the scene, and there is the excitement of television, the resurgence of radio, and even the development of new media—videotape, cassettes, video records, closed-circuit television—all of which might be considered important targets for any broad-scale public relations effort. But the approach taken by the media has changed so markedly in relation to business that editorial opportunities seem to be of a different character. While media with enormous audiences such as *Reader's Digest, Parade, Family Weekly, TV Guide,* and the "Today Show" are still in the consciousness of public relations people, the publicity opportunities are far more limited than they were and the benefits of such publicity much less sought after.

Today, concern about a critical article in *The Wall Street Journal* or even the *Village Voice* is of far greater concern to the business community. The rising trend of criticism of business by the media has created a widespread impression that reporters and editors have the power to bring a giant corporation to its knees if they do an effective job of investigative reporting. Dealing with those investigations or reports of unethical or harmful or illegal behavior has become a major public relations assignment.

THE NEW MUCKRAKERS

Media attacks against business are by no means a new phenomenon. The muckrakers of the early 1900s produced major changes in American industry. In succeeding decades media attacks against the business "merchants of death," against the ruthlessness of industry during the years of depression, the monopolistic tendencies of large corporations in the years after World War II—all played a part in the shaping of twentieth-century society.

Yet, it is possible to identify the beginning of a new trend in the 1960s—perhaps with the publication of Rachel Carson's *Silent Spring* and Ralph Nader's *Unsafe at Any Speed* (although neither of them was a journalist)—when specific industries, specific companies, specific products, and specific business practices started to be attacked by what eventually became a veritable army of critical reporters.

There is hardly an industry or a product that has not had to face up to some severe criticism from the press during this period. Automobiles, oil, telephones, airlines, utilities, appliances, pharmaceutical products, paint manufacturers, food products, clothing, cosmetics, pesticides, funeral parlors, building contractors, multinational companies, advertising agencies, public relations firms—the list of business enterprises that have been vigorously attacked by the media is almost endless. Nothing like this has happened before in American history. Even the age of muckrakers was relatively short-lived, lasting perhaps only three or four years. At that time the spurt of attacks against the meat industry, the patent-medicine industry, and a handful of others burst forth in the early 1900s and then rather mysteriously subsided a few years later. The current wave of investigative reporting, however, has lasted almost two decades, and there is no doubt that its intensity is greater today than ever before.

The public relations man now is far less of an ingenious producer of marvelous editorial gifts for his clients, and far more of an experienced counselor in relating to potential or actual media attacks. Reporters see themselves as prime movers in the reform of business practices. This has led to a decided increase in the self-esteem of the press, for journalists can function as monitors of business behavior rather than beneficiaries (perhaps reluctant) of commercial interests. Unfortunately, the reputation of public relations advisors may have suffered as a result of their new role, for they are sometimes looked upon as impediments to getting at the truth, a curtain between the corporation and the probing eye of the investigative reporter. The public relations practitioner naturally has a different view of the whole process. He knows that reporters have the right to inquire about suspicious or questionable behavior on the part of corporations, and he feels that executives can do themselves the most good by telling the truth. A public relations man considers himself a window rather than a curtain and is often frustrated because his role is misunderstood—both by his client and the media.

There is no doubt that the media have played a major role in bringing about changes in the nature of corporate activity as a result of this concentrated interest in the affairs of business. There is also no doubt, at least in my mind, that this has helped to improve the nature of our society. I believe this is true despite the obvious fact that the experience has often been painful from the point of view of business interests, and that there have been many unfortunate and unnecessary casualties due to inaccurate or oversensational reporting. The latter point is particularly worthy of note, for the purpose of this paper is not to highlight the well-documented benefits of investigative reporting, but to try to identify some of the factors which lead to abuses. Hopefully, a discussion of these factors might help to remove—or at least lessen the impact of—some of the counterproductive aspects of the media/business relationship and point to a more constructive and rewarding functioning of the process.

It seems to me that there are three major elements in the process which are causing trouble. These are:

1. The role played by legal counsel in regard to corporate disclosure. This is, perhaps, the least-known aspect of corporate

communications, yet, it is in all probability the most troublesome in achieving an open, constructive communications between business and the media.

2. The critical way that reporters look at business, which leads
   many businessmen to believe that reporters have an anti-
   business bias or simply do not understand how business
   works.

3. The protective or defensive way in which business tries to
   handle itself in relation to the media, which leads many reporters to believe that business has no notion of what a free press
   is all about.

Each of these problem areas needs to be examined separately.

LEGAL COUNSEL VS. PR COUNSEL

First, the problem of business/media relations which arises from legal
considerations stems from the traditional—and quite understandable—advice given by lawyers to avoid making any public statements
which could prove to be troublesome in future legal actions. In its
most extreme form, this prompts lawyers to tell their clients to say
nothing about anything.

Perhaps the most dramatic example of this in my own experience
took place when the chief executive officer of a large public corporation committed suicide. He had entered his office about eight o'clock
in the morning and soon after jumped to his death many stories below. I received a telephone call about fifteen minutes later and was on
the scene almost immediately. By the time I arrived a crowd of reporters was outside the front door of the company offices. The recep-
tionist had been instructed by the chief corporate counsel to tell reporters only that the CEO had "died suddenly." No further information was to be provided, and the press was to be refused entry into the
offices. The reporters were furious. There was an important story to
be written, and they had to get some information from somebody. I
was incredulous about the attitude of corporate counsel and explained
that since this was going to be front-page news it would be terrible if
the coverage were to be based on hearsay rather than facts. The
lawyer insisted that there were all kinds of legal considerations that
made it impossible for anything further to be said to the press. We
argued for a while until I made the point that a no-comment policy
was unfair to the executive's wife and children. The lawyer finally
agreed that he would go along with whatever the widow wished. I
was able to get the executive's wife on the telephone, and she agreed
immediately that I should come to her house and prepare as full a
statement as possible for the press. As it turned out, the information

we were able to supply resulted in a sympathetic treatment of the tragedy, and both the corporate counsel and the family agreed in retrospect that I had been right.

This was not the first and certainly not the last confrontation between legal and public relations counsel in my personal experience, but because of the crisis atmosphere and the extreme position taken by the two participants it highlights the legal concerns about disclosure.

For the most part, I find that business executives would like to be open and candid about their affairs. They repeatedly make the point that they want the truth to be known, and that they would like to cooperate with the press as much as possible. Naturally, they decry distortions that occur in the press and worry that reporters will not get the story straight. This is particularly true when they are interviewed by a young and clearly inexperienced reporter about a complex issue involving weighty matters and possibly millions of dollars. When public relations advisors tell their clients that the only way to avoid distortions is to answer all questions as fully as possible, the instinct of most businessmen is to do so. But when there are critical issues involved, legal counsel usually has a greater influence on business executives by making it clear that speaking too freely about matters that may have to be litigated can cause a great deal of trouble for the corporation and even for the executives personally.

For obvious reasons, it is difficult for me to give specific examples. Perhaps this difficulty in itself illustrates the problem of making full disclosures about business matters. I can give, however, some prototype examples which might be helpful.

Example number one. A major public corporation faced with a health problem that later became front-page news was determined at the outset to make the right moves in regard to the public interest. Public relations counsel advised the chairman of the board to be frank about his genuine concern for public health and his intentions to assume full responsibility for any problems which might arise from company operations. Management agreed that this was the correct approach, but lawyers were not present at the first meeting between the CEO and public relations counsel. Subsequently, however, lawyers pointed out that in all probability there would be millions of dollars involved in lawsuits against the company, and that everything management said in public could be held against the company. These legal considerations were real, and as a result, the initial impulse to follow the public relations advice was curbed. Instead of being open, concerned, and outgoing in the face of a crisis, management was forced to be unresponsive and to give the unfortunate impression of being unconcerned about the human tragedies which were the subject of major press coverage. This reinforced the low opinion which many observers had of the credibility and concern of large corporations, and the incident was cited in the press as an example of irresponsible behavior on the part of business interests.

The fact was that subsequently the company was sued for millions of dollars, and it may well be true that public statements in the early days of the crisis would have resulted in more severe judgments by the courts. But this, if anything, emphasizes the basic point provided by this example: that the inhibition created by legal considerations can prevent businessmen from being completely candid in times of crisis and thereby make it more difficult for the press to get at what it believes is the truth.

Example number two. This has to do with an entire industry in which the main product has long been reported in the press as a public health hazard. The industry's reaction has been a classic of business response to criticism. First, management says that a cause-and-effect relationship between the product and the disease in question has not been proven—a statement that has been made by business leaders of every industry faced with a similar attack. Second, management says that the industry is doing more than anyone else to try to find the answer. This, too, is a true statement, and one that is always made by other industries. What is never said, however, is that industry leaders are deeply concerned about the disease and feel a genuine responsibility about any possible harm their products might do. Many reporters (and their readers) believe this apparent lack of concern to be reprehensible, and this perception probably serves to inflame the attacks against the industry. What has never been said publicly is that once again it is a legal consideration which forces management to be silent on this crucial point.

It so happens that many of the senior executives in this industry are outstanding examples of public-spirited business leaders, and their companies have been responsible for a number of landmark public-service and cultural programs in this country which have made impressive contributions to the enrichment of contemporary life. These executives would like nothing better than to deal straightforwardly and positively with any issue which arises regarding the quality and safety of their product. And, yet, for years they have been unable to say anything in public about this concern, because their lawyers have pointed out that the industry could literally be destroyed by enormous lawsuits if any potential fault were to be admitted publicly.

Again, the result has been a significant loss of respect and credibility for business in general.

Example number three. This example has to do with a multinational company that was involved in certain transactions and activities that became the subjects of critical editorial investigation. The company was one of the leaders in its industry and was recognized as a highly responsible and public-spirited corporation. It would have been in keeping with company tradition for management to speak out forthrightly about any matter which could become the subject of public interest and public concern. The notion of covering up in any way was abhorrent. (I might add, parenthetically, that ever since Watergate all business executives have been extremely sensitive to the dangers of trying to cover up information that is a subject of interest to the press.)

Here again public relations counsel urged full disclosure in connection with a series of questions that were raised in the course of a press investigation. Then came the lawyers with their concern about the possibility of stockholder suits and other forms of litigation which could be damaging to the executives involved as well as to the company itself. And the overriding objective to which all agreed was to say as little as possible in order to minimize the legal vulnerability of those who might have had some responsibility for those transactions.

In this example the difficulty in determining what the truth was about the matters being investigated was especially great since to discover the facts in a legal sense is always much more complicated than it is to discover enough information to make a good news story. As a result, management's response that nothing could be said until "all the facts were known" seemed defensive and lacked credibility.

Reporters probably do not realize what goes on in the privacy of corporate offices when the press focuses attention on one or another sensitive matter. They know, of course, that corporate executives are concerned, and that the public relations staff—and sometimes the legal staff—is involved in trying to figure out how to answer questions. What they probably don't know is that enormous amounts of time are spent by top executives and their various advisors trying to figure out how to deal with press inquiries. At critical junctures a large public corporation can tie up as many as a dozen lawyers and perhaps as many public relations executives trying to figure out how to handle an inquiry from a single reporter, and these deliberations can go on for several days or even weeks or months if the story takes that long to germinate.

Having been through a number of these sessions myself I must make it clear that I have no simple answers as to how the differences between lawyers and public relations people can be resolved. The concerns of each are real. Both are interested in helping their clients. Both can justify their position on the basis of possible consequences. If a lawyer's advice is not heeded a company can lose millions of dollars in lawsuits. If the public relations counsel is not heeded the company's reputation can be badly damaged, the price of its stock can decline, and management can become vulnerable to a takeover. Lawyers want their clients to say nothing. Public relations specialists want their clients to tell all. Ultimately, the executive must decide for himself whether a compromise is possible.

The most hopeful element in the process is the press, which is, after all, the indispensable key to the effective working of our society. Without the probing eye of the press, legal considerations would have to be paramount. If business could conduct its affairs in a society that had a controlled press, the only news that would be made public would be that presently found in house organs, annual reports, company brochures, and speeches by executives. Management could comfortably go about its business without revealing anything that might in any way be legally damaging. But the qualities of our society and the protection of public interest which all of us—business executives as well as reporters—hold especially dear would be jeopardized.

Thus, whoever wins the argument about disclosure—lawyer or public relations specialist—business knows that the free press of our country is committed to use all of its ingenuity to find out what is going on. Even if a curtain of "no comment" is raised, some reporter will probably find a way to get through.

So much for the struggle between lawyers and public relations people in regard to investigative reporting.

THE NEED TO REEDUCATE BUSINESS AND THE MEDIA

The second element of the business/media relationship which causes trouble has to do with what businessmen consider to be lack of business education on the part of the media.

There is no doubt that a great many reporters write articles about business matters without really understanding how business operates. Naturally, this leads to poor reporting and misleading, untruthful, or distorted coverage of business matters in the press.

Many businessmen believe that this can only be solved by making sure that reporters have covered business news and get a good training in the theories and practice of our system of free enterprise. There have been a number of efforts to encourage this kind of training—most recently, an excellent program sponsored by Champion International at Dartmouth College's Amos Tuck School of

Business, which will give $105,000 in cash prizes for outstanding economic reporting directed to the average reader or viewer in America.

All this is to the good. However, we in the public relations business have some additional insights to offer which might be helpful. We find, for instance, that often when an experienced journalist goes into the public relations business he has a problem adjusting to his new role. His effectiveness as a public relations practitioner may be inhibited by his highly trained instinct to be skeptical about what anybody tells him. A good reporter keeps his suspicions very much in mind when he interviews a business executive about some matter which could lead to a good story. But a public relations man can't do his job very well if he is inclined to disbelieve what his client tells him. This doesn't mean that he has to be uncritical of everything he hears, but he must have a basic confidence in his client, a genuine interest in what his client wishes to communicate, and a sympathy for his client's point of view. One of his strengths must be to maintain his own independence and objectivity and thereby help his client understand public perceptions that may be critical, but he can't do his job well if he doesn't believe in his client's integrity or identify with his goals.

All of this is foreign to a good reporter whose loyalty is to whatever he deems to be the truth. If he asks nasty questions, it is not because he is anti-business or ignorant of business; he is just being a good reporter. A wise executive will respect that reportorial style and try to be as cooperative as possible. He will know that the reporter's aggressiveness does not manifest an anti-business attitude or a lack of education in the theory and practice of business, but rather a good nose for news. Executives who don't understand this characteristic of journalism will always feel there is a chasm between the press and business that cannot be bridged. This belief serves to exacerbate the problem, for such executives can become very tense when interviewed about a sensitive matter, and the tension can arouse a journalist's suspicion that there is something to hide. As a result, a story can be blown up out of proportion to the facts, and the businessman is confronted by what he angrily describes as a distorted picture of what happened.

RECOGNIZING MEDIA AS A BUSINESS

The third element in the business/media relationship which causes trouble has to do with what journalists consider to be the businessman's lack of respect for the prerogatives and responsibilities of a free press.

For one thing, publishing and broadcasting executives can't understand why businessmen don't recognize that the media themselves are a business. Too many businessmen don't understand why a negative story is better than a positive one. They are frustrated because attacks against industry always get headlines while the good things that happen in business are either ignored or given short shrift. But the media have a product to sell just as any other business does. News and feature reporting must be interesting if people are going to read newspapers and magazines, watch television and listen to the radio. It appears to be a part of human nature that negative news is more exciting and sensational than positive news. And some degree of excitement or sensationalism is an essential ingredient in the media business just as packaging is to consumer products and promotion is to the retailing business. If there are no readers or viewers, advertisers will not advertise and the whole structure will disintegrate.

No doubt, more education on both sides would help. Just as business thinks reporters need to learn more about business, journalists would like businesses to learn more about the press. Publishers would, I'm sure, feel that much could be gained if all top executives of large corporations could be given a short course in the media business and thereby learn how to deal more intelligently and knowledgeably with the problems of communicating with the press.

We in the public relations business agree with all this. But we also share the despair of industry leaders who feel that a one-sided view of business behavior seems to result from much of the investigative reporting presently being done. It can't be true, for instance, that top executives of utility companies advocating the building of nuclear power plants don't care about the welfare of future generations, don't care about survival of life on earth, and don't care about protecting the environment. And yet the way the subject is reported in the press, a large number of people could easily believe that such is the case.

SENSATIONAL PRESS AND PUBLICITY

We see this problem not only in relation to media coverage of business news but coverage of other subjects. For instance, can there be any doubt that the problem of crime in our cities is aggravated by the sensational coverage of the media given to this subject? No wonder people are afraid to walk the streets of our big cities when so many of our media are filled with reports of crimes. After all, these crimes are a miniscule part of our lives, and it is misleading to devote such a disproportionate attention to these incidents. Certainly, news about murders, rapes, muggings, and all the rest builds audience interest and sells newspapers, but it also helps to create an atmosphere of fear which causes people to move away from the city and thereby weaken its economic and social structure. This leads to more crime, more publicity about crime, more fear, and more deterioration. Is this the proper role for the media to play? Doesn't the press have some responsibility toward the health of our society? If business in general is being called upon to demonstrate its sense of responsibility, how about the media business doing the same? What investigative reporter will investigate investigative reporting and force it to act in a way that is more consistent with public interest?

This topic, of course, has been debated at great length and still deserves further exploration. However, the point being made here is that management's antagonism to the media works. There is some justification for their frustration in the way business is portrayed. The media tend to portray many aspects of contemporary society in overly dark colors, and this is a harmful, if not destructive, tendency which should be curbed by some form of countervailing pressure.

To be sure, there are some who believe that businessmen overreact to press criticism. Living in fear of media exposure can lead to a sort of paranoia. We in the public relations business recognize that this is a danger to be avoided. Sensational articles will not necessarily destroy a business or even do damage to its reputation. They may even do some good. Businessmen are nervous when they see their names in print in connection with any kind of unfavorable comment.

One amusing example of this is the publicity our own firm, Ruder & Finn, received when we were representing the government of Iran. With Mrs. Jacob Javits as our consultant, we were extremely upset by the implications in some of the articles that appeared that Mrs. Javits's association with us represented an impropriety because her husband was the senior member of the Senate Foreign Relations Committee. The truth was that there was no impropriety. But the press nevertheless played a constructive role. Although it did not give the correct impression about the facts, it did force us to realize that there was an appearance of impropriety which was just as serious as if there had actually been an impropriety. As a result, Mrs. Javits resigned from Ruder & Finn, and Ruder & Finn resigned the Iran account. When the whole matter was behind us we realized that our business had not suffered, nor had Mrs. Javits's career, nor had the public relations of the government of Iran. It had been an uncomfortable incident, but we all learned from the experience.

It is therefore important to reaffirm the positive benefits which result from the way the press monitors business behavior—despite the many problems which beset the business/media relationship. Business conducts itself today with the awareness that all of its activities may be subjected to public scrutiny at any time. This is a healthy and positive characteristic of our society. The fruitful results of this process are reflected in positive modifications of corporate behavior in almost every industry that has been subjected to criticism. Some companies have stepped up affirmative-action programs because of public criticism. Other corporations have developed extensive public-service programs to provide support for specific segments of the community because articles in the press have suggested a corporate bias. There are many examples of companies which have improved their management structure or established needed quality-control procedures or improved the design of their products because of critical articles in the media. In still other instances, senior executives who were not performing their functions effectively have been replaced because of critical articles in the press.

For the most part, these are not examples of heroic steps taken by selfless leaders or of noble members of the press bent on reforming contemporary society. They are the result of a process in which business and the press are serving a public good by pursuing their own self-interest and thereby manifesting one of the unique strengths of our society.

THE MEDIA AND THE CORPORATION: A MATTER OF PERCEPTION AND PERFORMANCE

SCOTT M. CUTLIP

The essence of improving the business image rests not in trying to conjure up a good story when performance fails, but in sharpening corporate perceptions of emerging social and political trends, explains Scott M. Cutlip, dean of the University of Georgia's Henry W. Grady School of Journalism and Mass Communication. The role of public relations, then, goes beyond effective communication with the media to continuous monitoring of public attitudes and providing professional guidance through today's turbulent public opinion seas.

Dr. Cutlip is the coauthor of Effective Public Relations, *the all-time best-seller in the field. Recipient of the First Annual Public Relations Society of America Distinguished Service in Public Relations Teaching Award, he also has written* Public Opinion and Public Administration *and* A Public Relations Bibliography.

The continued well-being of our self-governing society depends on a *free* flow of *reliable information* on which citizens can rely for their political, economic, social, and cultural decisions. In the Miltonian concept which undergirds our society all ideas regardless of merit are entitled to a full and fair hearing in the free marketplace, where their validity is determined by their ability to win public acceptance. More than 125 years ago John Stuart Mill insisted that freedom of expression and full and frank debate of every imaginable issue were at the heart of human freedom itself.

Today, however, there are questions concerning the equal access of all ideas to the marketplace of opinion and whether TV's freeze-dried news and print media's abbreviated coverage adequately serve the "full and frank debate of every imaginable issue."

The frustrating problem that confronts all public institutions and their leaders today is that of being *heard, understood,* and *believed* in the public marketplace of ideas. This problem is not unique to the business world but is common to groups in all sectors of society. This common problem has been well summed up by an able

Canadian communicator, Eric Miller, formerly deputy director of Information Canada:

> We used to trust our institutions; they made us feel secure. But, each of
> them has seemed, gradually, to have acquired a territory and an identity
> alien to our experience and understanding. They won't tell us what they're
> doing. They won't tell us why they're doing it. They won't explain in ways
> we can get hold of, why things are the way they are. They all seem to be
> conspiring to keep us in the dark and, for all we know, in their thrall. . . .
> That frustration, which used to just make us feel jumpy, has begun to
> make us feel suspicious and even angry. The feeling has been growing for a
> decade or two.

The news media are the common carriers for the two-way flow of
information and ideas which is essential to the functioning of a
democratic society. The media are the only means we have in a large
nation to disseminate political, economic, and social information
quickly and universally. Thus, if Truth and Falsehood are to grapple
fairly in the public opinion arena—a no-holds-barred match—all
points of view must have access to the idea marketplace. The
dialogue between and among the competing ideas and institutions of
our nation is filtered through the nation's news machine. This filtering
inevitably produces oversimplification and distortion, including the
distortion of omission.

Oswald Spengler wrote in *The Decline of the West:*

> It is permitted to everyone to say what he pleases, but the Press is free to
> take notice of what he says or not. It can condemn "truth" to death simply
> by not undertaking its communication to the world—a terrible censorship
> of silence, which is all the more potent in that masses of newspaper read-
> ers are absolutely unaware that it exists. On the other hand, we recognize
> that news gatekeepers must be selective in what they print or air because
> of time and space limitations. Our media cannot possibly report "all the
> news that is fit to print." Consequently the "truth" of many causes goes
> unheeded and the actions of many institutions go unpublicized and thus
> unrewarded in the idea market.[1]

The decision of what goes on the public agenda and what does
not is made not on the basis of "truth," but on the basis of "news" as
this commodity is defined by media gatekeepers. In a busy city room
or broadcast house, such judgment calls are made thousands of times
a day. News is what the editor says it is. Far more "news" winds up in
wastebaskets than in print or on the air. Some of current events' best
scenes wind up on the cutting room floor.

In his seminal *Public Opinion*, Walter Lippmann evaluated the
modern news service as working effectively in reporting those matters where there is "a good machinery of public record," but deficient

in reporting those events not "scored," data not publicly recorded or else hidden at the source. These kinds of events—the substantial tides of change that move unreported below the surface of frothy whitecaps that the media report as "news"—do not get reported, Lippmann observed, "until somebody makes an *issue* of them." For example, our growing environmental crisis did not become "news" until Rachel Carson wrote her series of jolting articles in *The New Yorker* headed, "Silent Spring," in 1962. Journalists tend to cover that which moves. It was much easier and more salable for the news media to report a President Ford putting English muffins in a toaster than it was to probe the internecine struggle between Nixon and Ford men in the new Ford White House.

Too often the fleeting attention the busy citizen has to give to public affairs goes not necessarily to those most deserving of attention, but to causes and ideas served by public relations specialists skilled in gaining access to the media. Too often the citizen's daily intelligence comes in the form of fragmented, distorted snippets of what is "news" but passes for information. The democratic marketplace too often is tilted by the defaults and derelictions of the news media on one hand, and by the news management of government, business, colleges, churches, and other public institutions on the other. Ways in which our governmental machinery can be misused are laid out in David Wise's book, *The Politics of Lying*. Similar evidence is available on business endeavors to suppress or slant news of the corporate world. Too often public relations practitioners heavily involved in the public dialogue fail to honestly inform the public. When honesty is neglected, public relations practitioners debase not only the cause they serve, but our self-governing society as well. They corrode the channels of communication upon which all of us depend.

SHAPING THE DAILY NEWS

Given the growing power of public opinion and the constraints it imposes on all institutions, news sources have become sophisticated about the power of news and skilled in its management.

A typical example: some years ago the media whipped up a news story over the fact that an Army general had spent several thousand dollars to put silk wallpaper in his bathroom and carpet over the tile floor. While the media were having a field day with this GAO-released story, the U.S. Army softly announced it was "realigning" Mobility Command headquarters in Warren, Michigan, and moving much of the operations from the headquarters on which it had just spent $245,800 for remodeling. The more substantial story got short shrift from the media. The Army had released the somewhat embarrassing story while the reporters were covering the bathroom.

This example becomes important when you realize that the news media govern the way men and women deal with each other and with the distant world. A community fluoridates its water supply without public notice. Nothing happens. Then this fact becomes known. A community row ensues.

The mass media constitute the nation's public information system—a system in which corporate public relations men and women play an important role. This public information system embraces a nation's government, staffed by political leaders, bureaucrats, and information peddlers; its political parties, manned by agents, active workers, and public relations experts; all public institutions and the pressure groups staffed by executives and public relations personnel; and the media, manned by reporters and gatekeepers. Each of these elements performs an important, integral function in the democratic process of the public's being able to arrive at a consensus after issues are debated. One element works in relation to other elements, thus all may be lumped together under the rubric of "public information system." The struggle to shape and manage the news has escalated in intensity as the media's power and the political stakes have increased. The competition for access to these media is spirited and becoming more so. It is in this context that the business publicist works to insert his messages into the "system."

Today's communicator must cope with the fact that the news media have not adjusted their values to society's need for new information. Max Ways asserts:

> Conditioned by its own past, journalism often acts as if its main task were still to report the exceptional and dramatically different against a background of what everybody knows. News today can concentrate with tremendous impact on a few great stories. . . . But, meanwhile, outside the spotlight, other great advances in science and technology, other international tensions, other causes of social unrest are in motion.[2]

Nonetheless, it must be acknowledged that the task of our news systems is difficult. Ben Bagdikian reminds us: "The total potential information from all places is incalculable. To observe everything everywhere is impossible. Even if possible, to transmit it all would be unimaginable. And even if all that somehow could be done, no individual could ever absorb the results."

This struggle between the media's definition of "news" and an institution's definition of "truth" creates tension between news gatherer and news source. In business, for example,

Corporations make public a great deal of truth about themselves these days; in lavish brochures and reports to stockholders. . . . But the journalist wouldn't be much of a journalist if he found the reports sufficient to his purpose. He conceives of himself, inevitably, as the agent for the *buyer's* truth . . . he wants to get past the self-serving rhapsodies and get to . . . the hard truth.[3]

Roots of the differing perspectives between news source and news media can be seen in this exaggerated view of journalists held by Gay Talese, former *New York Times* reporter:

Most journalists are restless voyeurs who see warts on the world, the imperfections in people and places. The same scene that is much of life, the great portion of the planet unmarked by madness, does not lure them like riots and raids, crumbling countries and sinking ships, bankers banished to Rio, and burning Buddhist nuns—gloom is their game, the spectacle their passion, normality their nemesis.[4]

Most journalists are competent and fair-minded in reporting the day's news within the limitations imposed on them—limitations of space or time, the pressures for speed, and demands for content that excites. The practitioner must learn to live with the fact that the wheel that drives the press drives it too hard, too fast. Robert J. McCloskey, reflecting on many years as public affairs officer of the State Department, counsels, "Neither side has a corner on the market of infallibility or of being more sinned against than sinning. . . . What must be avoided at all costs are disputes which run the risk of putting the interests of the people last."

Business and the media lambaste each other with gripes and accusations which sometimes threaten to place the public interest last. To accurately evaluate the relation of these institutions, it is necessary to assess the *perceptions* and the *performances* of each.

Unfortunately, too many businessmen see this tension as stemming from the faults of journalists. As Lee Smith wrote in *Dun's Review*, "Executives are generally reluctant to go on record, but at small meetings and luncheons they have repeatedly charged the media with being slipshod, sensational, neglectful, ignorant and biased in their business coverage."[5] Typical is William C. Cates of the Argyle Research Corporation, a merger and acquisitions firm: "There's always a subliminal tone. That's because every cub newscaster knows that business is evil. . . ."

The basic conflict lies in the media's never-ending quest for exciting news, in their efforts to keep the news stream uncontaminated, and the need to deliver an audience to advertisers. On the other side are individuals, institutions, and industries that find it imperative to have their stories told to the public with accuracy and fairness. Much of the public relations expertise goes into trying to put news about an institution into a complete mosaic that provides perspective. Too often the news media are only interested in colorful, controversial fragments. Essentially, news coverage depends on the occasional and selective interest of the newsgatherers and gatekeepers.[6]

The media's definition of "news" is at the heart of this problem. To illustrate: An archbishop criticizes, with reason, the two major wire services when they base their nationally circulated story on seven lines of a twenty-page document issued after prolonged deliberation by America's Roman Catholic bishops. The former chairman of the President's Council of Economic Advisers, Herbert Stein, echoes this complaint: "Not only do the media concentrate on the short-term aspects of the economy, they also dramatize them in ways that further exaggerate their importance. Prices do not rise, they *soar.*"[7]

The media's news values are not the only source of conflict. The media's lack of manpower in numbers and in expertise required to cover today's broad spectrum of complex news is part of the problem.[8] The limitations of time and news space—either print or electronic— also result in a condensation that often distorts a complex story. Another important ingredient in this conflict is the frequent charge of denial of access to the news media altogether.

TV NEWS SHOWS: GOOD FOR A LAUGH?

All of these factors are evident to a disturbing extent in the case of television, today's most powerful news and entertainment medium. It is a truly shocking fact that today the majority of citizens depend primarily on national and local TV shows for most of their information about what's going on in the world. Responsible TV news staffers are as upset about this reliance on TV for daily intelligence as you and I are. In TV critic Ron Powers's view, "By the 1970s, an extravagant proportion of television news—local news in particular— answered less to the description of 'journalism' than to that of 'show business.'" He adds, in a provocative book, *The Newscasters*, "This transformation, carried out by sales-oriented station managers in an unbounded quest for profits, bore the profoundest implications in a way Americans were to receive information and perceive political choices." Under these circumstances, it is not surprising that Americans hold a fragmented, distorted picture of the business world.

We have a glaring example of the consultant-designed "news show"—with emphasis on *show*—in Atlanta. A show in which a sportscaster wrestles a bear and in which a bird lands on a reporter's shoulder; the type of newscast a competing TV station executive called "bubble-gum comic-strip reporting." The *Columbia Journalism Review* called it "eye-witless news." As Powers maintains,

Until local television news ceases to exploit the entertainment bias that is conditioned by its host medium, and shares some of the profit with its "market," in the form of comprehensive, compact newscasts, it is engaging in a pollution of the worst sort: a pollution of ideas. Its options should be the same as those of any polluter: clean up the mess or pay the consequences.

The able diplomat, George Kennan, asserts in his new book that our communications system communicates mostly junk. Of course, one man's junk is another man's treasure. There are many dealers in junk in our public information system. Each component in our nation's public information system has some serious soul-searching to do.

It ought to start with television, especially at the network level, because that is where the power is. The impact of television on our lives, on our values, on our politics, and on our economic system is awesome. Its reach and impact are plainly visible, although efforts to ascertain cause and effect—such as violence on the screen translated into violence of our children—are not wholly satisfactory. David Halberstam, in two perceptive articles in the *Atlantic*, sees network TV as the shaper and creature of politics, both a maker and a prisoner of public tastes.[9] Television network news, which must cover the wide, wide world in a scant 4,000 words and twenty-two minutes each night, has become, for ill or good, our most popular and credible source of news—despite the distortions imposed by its format. Its importance is made larger in the United States than in other Western democracies because we have no national daily newspaper.

Listen to Dan Rather of CBS on network news's inadequacy in reporting all the information a citizen needs in today's confusing world:

> Walter Cronkite has said that the Evening News is at best a headline service. We have tried over a long period of years to make it more, but, in the final analysis, a headline service is what we are. Television tends to be two-dimensional. Anyone who depends on it entirely for his news is not doing his job as a citizen.[10]

Television news, because of its power and the money at stake, is more and more confined to the simplistic, hard-news, page-one format style of our two major press services—the AP and UPI, the major sources of information for most Americans, whether they get their news on the car radio, from the nightly news show, or from their newspaper. TV is not equipped for investigative reporting save for the rare documentary, and these are getting rarer. Despite the lessons taught by the Vietnam War and by Watergate, TV news goes on its bland way as though these traumatic events never happened.

IN THE INTERESTS OF FAIR PLAY

Even when reporters strive to be fair, as the vast majority do, accuracy does not always result in fairness. This George Beveridge, the *Washington Star* ombudsman, admits: "In the complex, instant nature of the news business, accuracy doesn't always equal fairness." He cites this example involving Amoco and a front-page, last-edition UPI story in the *Star* bearing the banner headline, "FEA Charges Oil Firms with Price Gouging." Amoco complained that the story was one-sided, and Beveridge admitted the "one-sidedness was indisputable." The press's fetish for speed and market was at fault, not reporter villainy. "The first wire-service accounts of the FEA's allegations hit the *Star's* news desk shortly before the last-edition deadline. Awaiting the oil-company reactions at that point would have meant missing the story for the entire day. The next day's *New York Times* had the time to get both sides of the story. I think newsmen and newswomen greatly overestimate the public's appetite for hot news, a hangover from Hildy Johnson's days of many newspapers and many editions."

Responsible news executives recognize and admit the press's weakness in reporting the news of business. Charles Seib, the *Washington Post* ombudsman, admits this "is an area in which the press has always been weak." He adds: "Although what happens in corporate boardrooms can have more impact on our lives than many of the official acts traditionally scrutinized in the press, business coverage at least in the general circulation media has been both inexpert and lackadaisical. But there's new enthusiasm today, although the expertise is still lagging." Arthur Taylor, former CBS president, has made the same admission: "Journalists . . . also bear the responsibility for some of the hostility toward business. Reporters can be sloppy and irresponsible and overworked, just like anybody else. . . . Reporters tend to be by nature probing, cynical, and often anti-establishment. Many are young and have grown up in the past decade, which seemed to suggest that those in power were corrupt and selfish."

The news media cover business and economics in the same manner they cover all other public matters—in an episodic and often superficial fashion. This includes the media's failure to report the sins of business as well as its virtues. For example, when the giant retailer Sears was tried before a Federal Trade Commission administrative law judge in Chicago on charges of systematically engaging in bait-and-switch tactics, the Sears public relations staff, obviously, did nothing to publicize the testimony. This was not Sears' reponsibility. The press did little to cover the trial until it ended when Sears abandoned its emphatic denial and sought a consent order. The Sears public relations officer shrugged this off: "The story wasn't a big ticket item around here."[11] The failure here was typical of the press's inability to put a cat at every rat hole. With public relations assistance the press will cover with reams of copy the National Chicken Cooking Contest or the Pillsbury Bakeoff or the Indianapolis Memorial Day Race. Such stories provide the popcorn and cotton candy for the crowd.

Businessmen can justly quarrel with the superficiality of much of today's news coverage of the corporate and economic life of the nation. So can every other public institution—the college, the church, the voluntary agency, and government. Representative David Obey, a bright young member of Congress, recently took the Washington press corps to task for its "cheap shot" journalism which focuses more on congressional sex scandals and congressional perquisites than on "major national problems like the quality of our air and water, education, and health programs." Obey said many Washington reporters are "susceptible to the same temptation as politicians—the temptation to overdramatize, to overreach for stories and headlines, and to pander to popular prejudices." We in higher education are painfully aware of the media's superficial and episodic coverage of higher education's continuing and complex story.

The common frustration of the news source seeking to convey hard information to the public and of the viewer seeking hard information from a TV newscast can be clearly seen in this admission from Richard Kaplan, producer for the "CBS Evening News": "We just can't handle issues the way a newspaper can. A writer can go into all kinds of detail to explain things. We have to have something on film. And you've got ninety seconds to tell it." In critic Karl Meyer's phrase, conveying information over TV is "like squeezing an orange so that only the pulp remains while the juice is poured down the drain."

Most journalists I know agree that too often the ideal of objective, fair reporting has gone out the window since the saga of Woodward and Bernstein. Another reason for lack of objectivity often found in today's news reports is a misunderstanding of the need for interpretation of today's complex news. Norman J. Isaacs, formerly an editor on one of the nation's great newspapers, the *Louisville Courier-Journal,* and now a journalism teacher, has observed:

> I have long been for more and more background and interpretation. But this has never meant editorializing in the news columns. We have been seriously damaged all over the country by three types of journalist: one, the lax in ethical responsibility; two, the newspapermen with a cause and determined to jam it down the readers' throats; and three, those so poorly trained and so lacking in skills they simply seem unable to know the difference between a factual statement and an opinion.

Also at work in biased reporting is the vaunted news value of conflict. In the candid words of Martin Nolan, able Washington reporter, "The reporter has a vested interest in chaos."

In March, April, and May back a few years ago, a Senate sub-committee held hearings which were vital to the oil industry and the nation's oil import program. For seven days the committee heard what a Texaco spokesman termed "anti-industry" witnesses. These witnesses were extensively covered by the *Post*. After April 3, the pro-industry witnesses were heard. Not a single line of their testimony was reported. The score for the *Washington Post* was: anti-industry days, 300 lines; pro-industry days, 0. The business newspaper, *The Wall Street Journal*, ran only one story on the entire hearing, which covered thirteen days.

This represents the news system at work, not an effort "to get business." If business wants the full story told it will have to provide the means and manpower to report it. The oversimplified fact is that news of business and economics gets reported in episodic fashion on the nation's front pages when corporate leaders sin or oppose needed public regulation, and regularly in the business pages at the back of the newspaper or in brief commentary on the TV networks. Somehow, I am not impressed with business's oft-made claim of "business efficiency" when I read a *Chicago Tribune* banner head: "$1.5 Billion Wasted on Alaskan Pipeline." Never mind what the facts are. This fragmented news coverage ultimately crystallizes in public attitudes.

Based on a national survey on the American economic system for the Advertising Council, researchers came to this conclusion about how public attitudes are linked to their level of knowledge about economic events:

> Although Americans value the fundamental system for their personal freedoms and potential for personal growth they see in it, their description of their role in the system has a passive character. The passive role Americans cast for themselves, combined with their fragmentary economic understanding, in large measure, probably underlies their frustrations over current economic conditions and issues.

The pertinence of this finding to the nation's continued well-being is reflected in this question asked by John De Butts, chairman of AT&T: "Are the American people—through their press—sufficiently informed about business to provide a sound basis for the political decisions about the future that they will be called upon to make?"[12]

BUSINESS: SULKING AND SUSPICIOUS

Now that we have set down the weaknesses and shortcomings of the news media in fully reporting news of public institutions, including business, we must in justice record that today's news reporting is generally balanced, factual, and fair, far more balanced than the perceptions businessmen hold. America's journalism is the freest and most professional journalism on the face of the globe.

Granted, there are wide gaps and unfortunate goofs in the coverage of business, but I think it high time that business leaders quit whining about the media and face up to the realities of why business gets so much unfavorable coverage. As Justice Oliver Wendell Holmes put it, "The first step toward improvement is to look the facts in the face."

For some three decades I have been a practitioner, student, and teacher of public relations. Over these three decades, I have grown utterly weary of the complaints from the nation's corporate executives that all their problems are the result of not communicating effectively or because of the way media report their activities.

When I began teaching public relations in 1946 I studied the strident National Association of Manufacturers' campaign to explain free enterprise to the "economic illiterates" NAM saw "out there." William Whyte, then a *Fortune* editor, analyzed the effects of this campaign and concluded that "it wasn't worth a damn." That campaign of expensive newspaper ads, like many since, was shrugged off by the public as irrelevant and self-serving. The message was aimed at an audience that didn't exist about an issue that didn't exist. Yet, the consumers paid for this unwanted message. Neither NAM nor the business leaders who support it has learned much from that day to this. NAM was born at the turn of the century to fight decent hours, wages, and working conditions for laborers. It has been *against* things ever since. Consequently, any message from the NAM has little credibility with influential citizens who count in public decision making.

Some years ago an executive of the American Petroleum Institute, beating the drum of business's failure to tell its story, asserted that American industry, though a powerful giant, suffered from the defect of being "tongue-tied." The sheerest of nonsense from one of the most powerful and articulate lobbies in Washington. It is difficult for a thoughtful person to visualize industry being tongue-tied when an R. J. Reynolds Tobacco Company can spend no less than $50 million in advertising promoting its unreal, unnatural cigarette, Real, "the natural cigarette."

Business's litany of complaint continues unabated. In 1975, M. A. Wright, chairman and chief executive officer of the mighty Exxon Corporation, banged the tired drum with this assertion:

> Let me start with what I believe to be a fundamental reason for business's current low standing. In the past, businessmen have often been too preoccupied with managing their businesses to see the necessity of explaining and reaffirming to the public the benefits of the private enterprise system.

The situation has been aggravated by the tendency of businessmen to be less than open with the public regarding the operation of their businesses. As a result, many Americans not only remain uninformed about the practical economic realities of business, but have come to believe that businessmen are involved to a high degree in clandestine operations.[13]

Why wouldn't the public come to believe that "businessmen are involved to a high degree in clandestine operations" when they learn that:

- Twenty-nine of the nation's largest electrical companies admit rigging their prices in a collusion which spanned *seven years.* (During those seven years the chief culprit, General Electric Co., was spending large sums to preach the gospel of free enterprise while its top executives were price-fixing in the Moonlight Motel.) As one writer said, "the electrical conspiracy is but one instance in a disheartening pattern of hundreds of similar antitrust violations in many industries."[14]

- General Motors was far less concerned about the safety "message" than it was in destroying the safety "messenger," Ralph Nader, by its clandestine efforts to trail him and discredit him. GM's heavy-handed way of dealing with Nader brought the national auto safety legislation GM was trying to block and crystallized the consumer movement led by the charismatic Nader into a national force.

- The clandestine efforts of International Telephone & Telegraph which became a part of the stained Watergate mosaic—its dealings with the Nixon White House, Department of Justice, CIA, and other government agencies, dealings designed to block anti-trust litigation and to subvert the Allende government in Chile. Harold Geneen, now stepping down as head of ITT, is typical of businessmen who refuse to face reality. After the exposure of ITT's many efforts to corrupt our government as though the United States were but another banana republic, Geneen complains to the Senate Judiciary Committee: "As a businessman . . . I am surprised to find a company such as ours—and there are others—without much chance of stating its case, put in the category of a nonconstructive and fearsome force within our society."

- The clandestine efforts of corporations to buy the reelection of Richard Nixon in 1972 and to bribe governments overseas to sell their goods. What do you think the public believes when it learns that such large American companies as American Airlines, Braniff International, Gulf Oil, Minnesota Mining & Manufacturing, Goodyear Tire & Rubber, Northrop, Lockheed, United Brands, and others have acknowledged paying foreign officials to win contracts or have been convicted of making illegal political contributions in the 1972 campaign?

If these weren't clandestine maneuverings, then what is? To paraphrase my grandmother, clandestine is as clandestine does.

Such examples of front-page business news could run on for pages, but businessmen will find this recital painful and perhaps think it unfair.

CORPORATE ACCOUNTABILITY: THE ANSWER?

The fault here is not in media reporting, but in corporate performance. Little wonder the public draws critical perceptions of business from the unending flow of stories of business fighting regulation that is in the public interest and of wrongdoing in business.

Yet, most of the response has to do with complaints about news coverage or self-flagellation about business's failure to tell its story effectively.

Mr. Wright of Exxon is, of course, particularly upset with public criticism of the oil industry and the demands for divestiture to bring more competition to that industry. He should surely be aware of the public impact of Gulf Oil's blatant palm greasing of politicians, foreign and domestic, over the past fifteen years. Over this period Gulf Oil Corporation illegally funneled more than $5 million to a laundry list of politicians. Subsequent SEC probes brought to light comparable overseas efforts to buy governments and legislation and sell goods.

Mr. Wright should realize that his "communications problem" is in his own industry. Also, consider this debatable matter of the oil companies arguing for the depletion allowance and higher profits in order to finance explorations for desperately needed petroleum. We heard this rationale over and over during the Arab oil embargo when our petroleum prices skyrocketed. As Joseph Nolan, now director of public affairs of Monsanto, wrote in the *Harvard Business Review*: "It would be hard to imagine a more flagrant example of a company's ignoring public opinion than the tender offer of Mobil Oil Corporation to Marcor, Inc., parent company of the Montgomery Ward chain."[15] Today's thoughtful citizen sees through such contradictions in word and deed.

I fully agree with Mr. Nolan that,

> nine times out of ten, the trouble lies not so much with the communications as with two other aspects of the broad management function of public relations, Perception and Performance. The essence of improving the business image rests not in trying to conjure up a good story when performance fails, but in sharpening corporate perceptions of emerging social and political trends and in adjusting performance so there will, in fact, be a good story to tell.

Let me put it in a nutshell: when the corporations quit basing everything on the profit bottom line and accept full corporate accountability for their impact on society, and when corporation leaders quit sulking in their boardrooms and go out and engage the public in dialogue, then, and only then, will the news coverage of business improve.

The media, large business enterprises themselves, are not biased against business, but when business men and women violate the public interest as some persist in doing, the news media are obligated to report such abuses. Let us quickly call the roll of major business stories of recent years:

- The looting of Penn Central Railroad.

- The Equity Funding insurance scandal.

- United Brands' bribery of a Honduras tax official, an act for which there has been a long tradition.

- The determined efforts of Armco and Republic steel companies, combined in Reserve Mining, to put their economic interest ahead of those persons dependent upon Lake Superior for their health.

- Allied Chemical's pouring of the ant poison, Kepone, into the James River and polluting it all the way to Chesapeake Bay.

- The rise and fall of the McDonnell-Douglas DC-10.

- The rip-offs in the fixing of prices for life-giving drugs.

- The unrelenting efforts of the tobacco industry to cloud with public relations smoke the hard evidence that cigarette smoking causes lung cancer. The Tobacco Institute continues to refer to smoking as "an alleged health hazard."

- The greed of the coal companies for profit at the expense of the only land that we'll ever have and their indifference to the plight of their miners. Examples are many—whether it is the tragedy of Buffalo Creek or the refusal of mine companies to sell land to displaced mine families in Williamson. I urge you to read *Everything in Its Path*, and then ask yourself if the press accounts of Buffalo Creek were "biased."

Or this more recent story:

- The announcement of the Federal Energy Administration that because of reports that the nation's oil companies have been overcharging consumers by "billions of dollars" the FEA would make an intensified audit of the fifteen largest refiners. This FEA audit came as a result of an SEC charge that the FEA's audit program was characterized by poor management, inadequate staffing, and corruption.

Hear the complaint of David J. Mahoney, chairman and chief executive officer of Norton Simon: "The too-promotional reporting of business a generation ago has been replaced by a too-suspicious attitude today. The wave of distrust in political life has spilled over into the world of business, and the result distorts what is happening in our economy."[16] Mahoney goes on to argue that while the relationship of the press and government should be an adversary one, the same should not hold in the case of the press and business, adding, "We're on the same side." Mahoney comes up to the media from his blind side to argue for favored treatment. Business leaders ought to reconcile themselves to the fact that it is the unique function of the press to monitor the performance of all public institutions and public leaders—including the corporate world. And, please, let's not have that old chestnut about business being "private" enterprise. In monitoring business's performance, the press serves an important public service.

Another industrial executive who feels put upon by press criticism of industry is Irving S. Shapiro of DuPont. Setting up the straw man that the public believes "the big corporation has no legitimacy," Chairman Shapiro argues, "The defense has not marshalled its arguments nearly as well as [the critics]. . . ." Mr. Shapiro confuses the question of legitimacy of a mighty DuPont Corporation with the public's questioning of DuPont's right to destroy the protective ozone of this earth by its continued manufacture of fluorocarbons.

Instead of facing some of the realities of business misfeasance and malfeasance which are properly reported, businessmen continue to charge off as so many Don Quixotes tilting their lances at windmills. They would improve their public image more rapidly by accepting the advice of a once highly successful businessman and now United States Senator, Charles Percy, who believes that, "Corporate corruption is the dry rot of capitalism." Professor Arthur Schlesinger, Jr., says it more bluntly: "If business leaders expect the reverence they seem to think is their divine right, they must deal with their own Augean stables."[17]

Thus, my candid advice to the business leaders is to step back and take a hard look at your posture and your posturings. But, I am not sanguine about business's acceptance of this advice. As Michael C. Jensen wrote in the *New York Times* recently, "In business, ethics sells slowly." If you won't listen to a college professor, then heed a respected business leader—David Rockefeller of the Chase Manhattan Bank. He sees the country's loss of confidence in business because of "corporate bribery, illegal campaign contributions, and scandal at the highest level." He suggests four fundamental cornerstones for a revised business policy:

First, honesty and candor in all activity.

Second, integrity in the use of corporate resources.

Third, avoidance of conflict of interest.

Fourth, fairness in dealings with all.[18]

A scholar, Professor Patricia Shontz of the University of Michigan, after careful study of this question of business news, made this assessment:

1. Too many businessmen want media coverage that waves the flag for free enterprise, equates business leadership with motherhood, and digests economic statistics as easily as apple pie. Business and economic education would be better served if it concentrated on obtaining news coverage that is accurate in answering "who, what, when, where, and how," and more balanced, informed, and thorough in answering "why."
2. Media coverage of business and economics suffers from malevolent neglect. There is little expert staffing, poor judgment of newsworthiness, woeful inattention to perspective. Business staffers rarely do their homework on economics, accounting, and finance, with the result that business stories are too often superficial, cliché-ridden treatments of yesterday's news.[19]

I concur in Professor Shontz's assessment.

One business leader who has taken a fresh critical look at the way business news is reported and interpreted is Mr. De Butts, chairman of AT&T, a sophisticated corporate practitioner of public relations. Among other things De Butts recognizes that the press must report the misdeeds of businessmen but asks, with justification, that the media make more effort to balance this coverage with stories of business's constructive contributions. At the same time he asks his fellow executives to "face up to some plain, blunt truths: that in some measure, maybe large measure, the erosion of business's credibility is attributable to the fact that some businesses in meting out their products and services to the public have from time to time laid too heavy a thumb on the scale." He then puts his finger on the nub of the problem we discuss here today: "But if much of the press's coverage of business is superficial—and it is—I attribute it not to some malign journalistic conspiracy but rather to what I call a *conspiracy of complexity*." (Emphasis mine.)[20]

Unlike many public figures, De Butts is not ensnared and hamstrung by a "devil theory" of the press. Given the media's audience-oriented news values and the shortages of space, time, and manpower to accurately and comprehensively report the news of a complex society, part of the solution lies with business, which is, as I pointed out earlier, an integral part of the nation's public information system. Dostoevsky taught us: "If they do not understand you, fall to your knees and beg their forgiveness."

ADVICE TO THE PRESS-WORN

Here, then, is my advice to business leaders who genuinely seek a more balanced reportage of business:

First, shuck the hair shirts you have worn so long.

Second, get off that white charger you call "economic education."

Third, develop a sound, honest public relations mechanism that enables you to understand your constituent publics and them to understand you.

In a 1976 study of American opinion as it concerns public attitudes toward business, it was found that

> there is no evidence in the study that the free enterprise system is on trial with the public, or that business must re-educate the American public on our economic system. . . . Whatever negative feelings that people have about business are related to business per se—not to the system within which it works.

This study, financed by *U.S. News & World Report,* also found that the public does not think "business profits are too high. The public may not be well informed on the actual role of profit—and perhaps some education is needed—but there is no feeling that business is getting more than it is entitled to. Thus, this is not one of the critical problems."

This far-reaching study also found that the public does not blame business most for inflation, and that it does respect business's many accomplishments.[21]

Yet, the speeches of corporate leaders decrying their belief that *profit* has become a "dirty word" and exhorting the need for "economic education" to get the public to understand the glories of free enterprise seem endless. So many corporate leaders are simply obsessed with what the president of Phillips Petroleum believes is the "public ignorance" of the virtues of private enterprise. Motivated by this fallacious notion, American businesses are spending tens of millions of dollars on "economic education," which has little to do with economics in the strict sense but rather is, in the candid words of one economic-education director, "propagandizing, selling."

Paul Weaver, writing in the June 1977 issue of *Fortune,* says:

> The real objection to economic education is that the businessmen who rely on it either don't know their own minds or aren't saying what they think. For economic education isn't a coherent defense of business. It doesn't meet the charges leveled and it isn't persuasive in arguing that business serves the public interest.[22]

The reason many business executives continue to pursue these ego-massaging "free enterprise" and "economic education" windmills is because they lack an adequate public relations or public affairs staff to carefully, continuously monitor the public opinion environment and provide the professional advice that would enable their corporations to chart a safe course through today's turbulent public opinion seas.

Business leaders are equally vulnerable to the fallacies of publicity and to the public relations gimmick. Intelligent executives understand that publicity cannot be used for any length of time as a substitute for good works or for desirable corrective action. It can only serve as a spotlight to focus attention on the positive aspects of an institution's performance and to clothe institutions with personality. The fallacy of using publicity as a substitute for a solution to a problem was demonstrated early in the presidency of Gerald Ford. Soon after taking office, President Ford, confronted with a deepening economic crisis born of inflation and high unemployment, came up with the silly WIN campaign—Whip Inflation Now. The whoop-it-up campaign, button and all, was the product of his public relations staff. The campaign was a flop.

From the turbulent environment of our contemporary post-industrial society comes a message loud and clear: the requirement for truthful communication. Irving Kristol, philosopher and co-editor of *The Public Interest*, recently discussed the decline of credibility of the corporation, and pointedly told us: "Essentially, as I see it, the problem is one of candor and credibility, not, repeat, not of 'public relations.'" He goes on: "One of the reasons the large corporations find it so difficult to persuade the public of anything is that the public always suspects them."

There's a lot of sham in corporate public relations. Public relations is used with good cause to publicize genuine efforts that serve the public information system. But it is also used to divert and mislead the public and to obfuscate public issues. Take the example of the public utility that spent $50,000 to clean up the environment and $400,000 to publicize the action. As a writer in the *Harvard Business Review* pointed out, "When a company spends more on good words than on good deeds, it is giving its critics ammunition."

There's also a lot of dissembling. For example, President Robert McCulloch of the McCulloch Oil company dies. A PR spokesman tells the press he died of an apparent heart attack. A day later we learn that he died of alcohol and an overdose of drugs. A few days before his McCulloch Properties, Inc., had pleaded guilty to nineteen misdemeanor counts of criminal fraud in a Colorado court.

Here is another example. It has taken nine years, much controversy, and billions of dollars to build the Alaskan oil pipeline. Yet, when the Associated Press was doing a story a reporter queried Sohio, one of the three companies owning the Alaskan oil, to ask what plans Sohio had for distribution of its share. The reporter was told, "I can't tell you a thing, not a thing." "What's Sohio hiding?" the reader asks. The same question arises of the Cambridge Chemical Co. When an apparent chemical spill threatened two towns in Sheboygan County, Wisconsin, the company's officials in Chicago and Niagara Falls refused to answer the press's questions about the incident.

Such strategies and tactics tend to breed corporate distrust, public cynicism, and clutter our channels of communication with debris.

Thus, I endorse this counsel from Louis Harris, who has measured business's decline in public opinion over the past decade or so. Says Harris:

> You're going to have to fight the battle in terms of learning how to make news, make it on the basis of what the facts are, learn to present your case with far less emotion and far more documentation. You are going to have to do it in probably the hardest arena that exists, the one for the free competition of ideas.

BUSINESS'S CLOUT WITH ADVERTISING

One clumsy way business has in dealing with the press is to use its advertising club—a crude and self-defeating way, to be sure. Periodically, there are nationally publicized efforts of big advertisers to put the muscle on news media—such as the time General Motors pulled its advertising from *The Wall Street Journal*—but there are more frequent attempts made at the local level. Many of these are directed at the local TV news show. TV has not developed the strong immunity of tradition that protects reputable newspapers from such blatant efforts to control the news. When the auto dealers of Oklahoma City successfully blocked a consumer story from being aired by TV station KWTV by bringing pressure on the station's management, this heavy-handed censorship brought the resignation of five news staff members from the station. The story that precipitated the resignations would have explained to viewers that about 20 percent of the auto dealers in Oklahoma City were adding to their repair bills a controversial surcharge to cover shop costs that aren't normally totalled in a customer's bill.[23] Authors of one journalistic text assert: "Advertisers exercise their greatest influence over television," but provide no more than fragmentary evidence to support the assertion.[24]

THE NEED FOR PUBLIC RELATIONS PROFESSIONALS

The Seven Sisters of the oil industry seem clumsier than most enterprises in handling their relationships with the media and the public. Perhaps this is because most of them have lawyers instead of public relations professionals directing this function. For some years now Mobil has been making a big fuss about the media's denial of access to Mobil's messages. Then it makes an ass of itself by laying a heavy hand on the Columbia University's School of Journalism—for a mere

$50,000. Mobil gave Columbia $50,000 for its Walter Bagehot Fellow-
ship program. When Columbia appointed Chris Welles to direct this
program, which brings business writers back to the campus to develop the expertise they need, Mobil terminated its gift. Welles, a respected journalist, had written a book critical of the oil industry.
Mobil foolishly denied that its action constituted interference with
the program.[25] Mobil cannot buy a self-respecting institution or a credible professor. Such actions make it appear that business wants a
patsy press, not a competent one.

Superficial public relations approaches and clumsy pressures will
not work. If taken seriously, the concept of social responsibility cannot fail to introduce new considerations in decision making and substantially modify the way business is conducted. The public relations
counselor has a key role to play in these changes—if management
accepts his counsel and if the counselor measures up to his new and
enlarged role.

The lamentable fact is that there are not enough corporate practitioners available today who are capable of grasping and implement-
ing this concept of the function. Most of today's practitioners are
preoccupied with the traditional and passive role of publicity-
getting—in a word, the work of public relations mechanics.

Equally lamentable is that there are too few corporate leaders
with the guts and imagination to employ a vice president/public who
would provide candid feedback from the public. Even today, most
executives appear to want favorable "news," not candid counsel; public relations mechanics, not counselors.

MACNAUGHTON'S MESSAGE

The most sensible balance in this debate of the press versus business
was struck in a speech by a Syracuse classmate of mine, Donald S.
MacNaughton, chairman and chief executive officer of Prudential. He
sees "business and the media, like two strange dogs, one snarling, one
sniveling, circling each other warily, suspicious of each other's intentions." One would be well advised to accept Don's advice that both
sides "are going to have to work much harder to alleviate this distrust. The public is poorly served by it in an era when matters of
economics have come to dominate not only the news, but, indeed,
mankind's very future." MacNaughton suggests that:

1. Businessmen, instead of making useless threats to curb the
   power of the press, learn to understand and accommodate to
   the unique position the free press occupies under our Constitution.

2. Businessmen should understand that adversary relationships with the press will often be normal—a series of contests. He adds, "The new vigor" on the part of the press is now being employed in its dealings with institutions other than government, including business, and we in business must face up to it.
3. Another thing that business must do is to become more open about its affairs—more free with information, more candid about its plans and problems, much readier than it has been to respond to questions and criticisms.
4. If business wants to maintain its freedom and keep selling the market system, it must meet and overcome criticism in the public arena. "And this can't be done unless we report to the millions who read and listen to—and are influenced by—popular news media."

For the news media, MacNaughton has these suggestions:

1. The media should assume responsibility for establishing sound minimum performance standards for all their practitioners. The press should not discourse on any subject, particularly complex ones, except through members with an expertise in the subject.
2. Business is fed up with glib, shallow, inaccurate reporting and editing—tired of journalistic tastes which prefer sensationalism above the fundamentals—which allows a Thespian to pose as a newsman. The impetus for more accuracy and objectivity should come from within the media.
3. In summary, the media and business each have a role to play on the American scene: and their paths must frequently cross. Considerable effort on both parts is required for them to attain tolerance, appreciation and understanding for one another.[26]

NOTES

1. For a brief discussion of the media as censor, see: Eugene McCarthy, "Sins of Omission," *Harper's*, June 1977.
2. "What's Wrong with News? It Isn't News Enough," *Fortune*, October 1969, pp. 110ff.
3. Thomas Griffith, "Must Business Fight the Press?" *Fortune*, June 1974, pp. 202ff.
4. *The Kingdom and the Power* (New York: World Publishing Co., 1969).
5. "Business and the Media," *Dun's Review*, March 1976, p. 31.

6. For examples of public relations' role in shaping the day's news, see: Paul Clancy, "The Press Barely Laid a Hand on Hoover," *The Quill*, February 1976; and David B. Sachsman, "Public Relations Influence on Coverage of Environment in San Francisco Area," *Journalism Quarterly*, Spring 1976.

7. "Media Distortions: A Former Official's View," *Columbia Journalism Review*, March/April 1975, pp. 37 ff.

8. For elaboration, see: Scott M. Cutlip, "Public Relations in Government," *Public Relations Review*, Summer 1976; Jules Witcover, "Washington: The Workhorse Wire Services," *Columbia Journalism Review*, Summer 1969; and Dwight Jensen, "The Loneliness of the Environmental Reporter," *Columbia Journalism Review*, January/February 1977.

9. Issue of January 1976.

10. Dan Rather and Mickey Herkowitz, *The Camera Never Blinks* (New York: Morrow, 1977), pp. 259–60.

11. Michael Hirsh, "The Sins of Sears Are Not News in Chicago," *Columbia Journalism Review*, July/August 1976, pp. 29ff.

12. "Business and the Press" (Speech given before the Virginia Press Association, June 28, 1975).

13. "Restoring Public Credibility of Business" (Speech given at Chicago Rotary Club, December 9, 1975).

14. For electrical price-fix story, see: John G. Fuller, *The Gentlemen Conspirators*, and John Herling, *The Great Conspiracy*.

15. "Protect Your Public Image with Performance," *Harvard Business Review*, March/April 1975.

16. "On Ending an Adversary Relationship," *New York Times*, July 7, 1977.

17. "Government, Business and Morality," *The Wall Street Journal*, June 1, 1976.

18. Roscoe Drummond, "Big Business's Worst Enemy," *Christian Science Monitor*, July 20, 1977.

19. "Is Business News Bad News?" (Talk given at the Business Roundtable Communications Seminar, Chicago, April 1–2, 1975).

20. Virginia Press Association speech.

21. 1976 Study of American Opinion concerning public attitudes toward business and government, sponsored by the marketing department, *U.S. News & World Report*.

22. "Corporations Are Defending Themselves with the Wrong Weapon," *Fortune*, June 1977.

23. Joy Hart, "Blow-Out in Oklahoma City: When Push Came to Shove at KWTV," *Media and Consumer*, May 1974, pp. 7–9. For examples of efforts to influence news by use of the advertising club, see: Freedom of Information Center Report No. 367, *Advertising Pressures on Media*, University of Missouri, School of Journalism, February 1977.

24. Peter M. Sandman, David M. Rubin, David B. Sachsman, eds., *Media Casebook* (Englewood Cliffs, N.J.: Prentice-Hall, 1977).

25. John E. Cooney, "Does Business Want a Sophisticated Press or a Favorable One?" *The Wall Street Journal*, July 21, 1977.

26. "Business and the Press—Independent or Interdependent?" (Speech, American Life Insurance Association, Chicago, November 4, 1975).

BUSINESS/MEDIA INFLUENCE: WHO DOES WHAT TO WHOM?

MURIEL FOX

The relationship between business and the media is one of mutual influence. The media influence business as managers consider potential media impact when making major decisions. Business can influence the content of the media by meeting the media's needs, according to Muriel Fox, executive vice-president of Carl Byoir & Associates, Inc. The media are not anti-business, she maintains, but must face the realities of inadequate time, space, public interest, and training. Public relations practitioners can improve business coverage by providing the media with information that is designed to get the media's attention and packaged to help the media deal with their own problems and constraints.

Fox has been called "the top-ranking woman in public relations" by Business Week. *A founder and past chairwoman of the board of the National Organization for Women, she is on the advisory committee to New York City's Economic Development Administration.*

If business executives and public relations practitioners do their jobs well, meeting the specific needs of the press and the public, then we can at times succeed in gaining media support. But every working day, conversely, the media influence our own actions and reflections. Not only communications specialists, but *all* business managers realize that none of their operations can be wholly effective unless they consider the potential media impact when making major decisions.

Today, while business communicators are diligently producing a flow of press releases, media events, "photo opportunities," background papers, and other materials that we hope will prove useful to the media, the stream of communications influence flows in both directions at the same time. The media not only make news themselves, but they often determine indirectly whether an event will take place at all—and in what form—as organizations try to guess in advance how the media will respond.

This influence is wielded through editorial decisions as to which events and trends to cover, which experts to quote, which statements to shorten drastically or omit altogether. The media didn't make a grab for this awesome power; modern technology just handed it over to them, creating a media impact that is more instantaneous, more universal, and more emotionally compelling than ever before.

In practice, the flow of influential ideas today is even more complex than a merely two-directional current. It's a noisy whirlpool fed by torrents of facts and arguments from thousands of different organizations. Many of the organizations are anti-establishment and anti-business. So industry sometimes feels that its own communications effort is needed just to stay afloat, to avoid being submerged by opponents who are increasingly sophisticated, well connected, and skillfully staffed.

Given the complexity of societal information channels, the power of the media, and the strident voices of opponents, it seems unlikely that business would be successful in influencing the media. And yet, we sometimes do succeed in getting sympathetic coverage of industry information.

Hundreds of books and booklets have been written about the subject, but I'll try to list briefly a few of the main methodologies by which we help business tell its story.

There is nothing mysterious or nefarious in business influence on the media. All one needs is a meaningful story, preferably presented in a usable, instructive, provocative and—if possible—entertaining package. We need one other thing: a fair hearing from the media. We do receive that most of the time.

Nevertheless, I think it's true that business news must be more fascinating and its spokespeople more charismatic to receive the same hearing as a noncommercial organization might expect. (We labor hard to add that extra appeal.) Actually, everybody who approaches the media has some axe to grind, some special interest, whether they're speaking out as consumers or members of a religious group or civil libertarians or parents or dog owners or automobile drivers. It sometimes seems that just about any other group can attract media attention faster than business can—all other things being equal. Because business messages reflect the profit motive, in contrast to the various motives of other interest groups, the press responds more cautiously. Now, this panel isn't the occasion for us to debate the virtues or vices of the profit motive. But we *can* question whether a business message deserves a less attentive hearing than an anti-business message.

One argument we hear is that business can afford to spend more money on communications than other special interests. Yet, we know today that expenditure of money does not guarantee media success. We've all seen expensive campaigns that failed, and other messages that won public support almost instantaneously with no money spent at all. Today, many of industry's opponents and competitors in the media arena are represented by expert attorneys, lobbyists, and public relations experts. Such resources serve government agencies, labor unions, and activists of all political persuasions. This is a healthy trend. Society benefits in the long run from getting a chance to hear a variety of competing voices loud and clear—including the voice of industries that provide our jobs, our quality of life, and our national and personal security.

The accusation is sometimes made that industry uses advertising money as a carrot or a stick to ensure editorial coverage. If such a practice did succeed in the past, it does not make a notable difference today. True, some fashion and home furnishings magazines and specialized trade publications might mention a company's name more readily if the company bought an ad in the back of the book. But those are hardly major media with a significant influence on public opinion.

More than twenty-five years ago there was a saying among publicists in one large urban area that the way to the heart of a news editor in that city was through an ad purchased from the sales manager. But that practice expired long ago in that city, and now I don't believe it exists anywhere else in the country in key media that mold public thoughts and emotions. The editors of WBZ in Boston or the *Atlanta Constitution* or *Time* magazine are interested only in a good story; they couldn't care less about what's happening in the distant offices of the sales department.

It happens that we've occasionally faced just the opposite kind of problem. Our television department recently proposed a newsworthy guest to the "Today" show, for instance, and learned that the guest could not be accepted *because* his company advertised on that program, and the overlap between commercial and editorial content was against network policy. Similarly, for our client RCA we've sometimes had more luck placing news with CBS or ABC than with NBC, which is owned by RCA, because the competing networks welcomed a good story and were not worried about the *appearance* of commercial influence.

GAINING MEDIA ATTENTION: HARD SELL OR THE SOFT-SHOE?

If advertising dollars don't influence the media, what does? Best of all, hard news. And now, at a time when publications and television and radio stations are competing fiercely with one another for audiences and advertisers, there's also a growing receptiveness to what the media call "slow news," or "soft features." Those are items with human-interest appeal, or humor, or entertainment value, or controversy, or helpful information and education. When feasible, we add entertainment to a legitimate news story. For instance, to illustrate the strength of a new thermoplastic that might replace steel in automobile bodies, we let a well-known ballerina dance on the hood as hard as she could. The news—which was legitimately important—got widespread coverage because of that captivating demonstration.

We find that educational features are especially popular in the media today, and we use that approach whenever possible. America seems to be celebrating a jubilee of self-improvement that welcomes all forms of continuing education. This includes far more than simple magazine articles on how to remodel your game room or repair your own car, though we've placed those stories, too. It also includes books and courses and lengthy discussions on subjects such as economics, nutrition, energy, law, and advanced photography. As the chairman of Macmillan, Inc., Raymond C. Hagel, commented recently in an interview, education is ceasing to be viewed as something you get over with before you start to live.[1]

WHO SAYS IT'S NEWS?

So far so good. Even though tastes may differ, few media people would disagree as to whether or not a proposed feature falls into the category of entertainment or education. But how they disagree on what is and is not *news!* Business is bothered and bewildered by what it perceives as the capriciousness of editors in deciding whether a story merits news coverage.

As public relations practitioners with extensive media experience of our own, we're rather adept at advising our clients on what stories have a good chance with specific media. Often we can help our clients add new elements to a story so it has a better chance than before. But our *bete noire* is somebody else's dull story that for some unknown reason gets a big play in the news media even though it seems devoid of news value. Each one of us has a recurrent nightmare in which a CEO's voice cries out to us, "If that story made the *New York Times,* why didn't mine?"

It's a fact of communications life that the working definition of "news" is "something that an editor *regards* as news." NBC commentator David Brinkley, whose instincts I respect highly, put it bluntly: "News is what I say it is. It is something worth knowing by my standards."[2]

Despite that arbitrary reality, skillful commentators do succeed in helping companies to make news. Also, we prevent them from approaching the media with an unworthy offering. Like the mythical boy who cried "wolf," companies impair their future access if they cry "news" when they have no story.

Fortunately for the public, the media consider business news more worthy of coverage today than in the past. This wasn't always the case. During the 1930s, for instance, when John L. Collyer, president of the B. F. Goodrich Company, waged a campaign on behalf of synthetic rubber to help make our nation less dependent on natural rubber from abroad, editors believed the public would find this story uninteresting because it was, quote, "industrial." When they did report on Mr. Collyer's crusade, they generally referred to "a rubber company executive" instead of crediting Mr. Collyer and his corporation with an idea that served our country well during World War II and the postwar recovery.

It was World War II that made front-page news of business developments—including *favorable* developments involving no malfeasance or mayhem. America's business firms as the Arsenal of Democracy helped determine the outcome of the war; they helped decide the postwar viability of large and small nations; they reconstructed our own country's "peace machine"; and they created new employment possibilities for minorities and women. They were by every standard real *N-E-W-S*.

I've often observed that publicity breeds more publicity, and the press has become increasingly accustomed to covering business. Editors realize that business is news because our future depends on it. Will we create enough jobs for the young and the old, the unskilled and the Ph.D's, women and minorities with rising motivation and expectation? Will our quality of life and our democracy—including our economic system—survive the competition from conflicting systems around the world? Apart from these global questions there is also growing interest in day-to-day issues relating to business: prices, product quality, safety, health, wages, inflation, new technology.

BUSINESS AND PRESS NEEDN'T BE ADVERSARIES

Business reporting is difficult, and there have been many problems with the expanded media coverage. A May 1977 survey of 300 members of the *Dun's Review* Presidents' Panel found business leaders "more worried today than ever before about business's poor image in the eyes of the public."[3] Some of that image decline has been attributed by business to inaccurate, incomplete, or biased coverage by the media.

One result of such concern has been a multitude of articles, workshops, and conferences on the relationship between journalism and business. A thoughtful *New York Times* op-ed feature on this subject was written recently by David J. Mahoney, chairman of Norton Simon, Inc. As perhaps the most charismatic CEO in industry today, Mahoney has received plentiful and respectful media coverage. Yet, he, too, was concerned enough about the media's attitude toward business to write feelingly "On Ending an Adversary Relationship." He insisted that journalism is big business today and "the only free press is a profitable press, and that fact should give pause to the writer who thinks corporate profits are made at the expense of the consumer."[4]

A variety of other "establishment" groups are discussing the need for improved media coverage, too. Just one example was the University of Rochester's recent two-day symposium on "Medicine and the Media: Ethical Problems in Biomedical Communications." And journalists are examining the subject seriously themselves in their own association workshops and writings.

Some observers view journalists as one segment of a larger body of authorities with growing power over public and private opinion. Irving Kristol uses the term "the new class" to describe journalists and academicians and others who are in a sense "common carriers" of information, influence, and power.[5]

Although some business leaders choose to avoid contact with the media, others are pressing for closer contact. In either case, you'll usually find public relations specialists somewhere in the middle, trying to make the relationship easier for both sides.

As professionals we service the media as meticulously as we possibly can. We fill—and try to anticipate—media needs for information, visual materials, and interviews. We recognize that it's not enough just to be honest; we also have to eliminate misleading or distracting materials—what Professor Curtis D. MacDougall assailed as "puffery."

We make sure the writers receive enough information to formulate their own conclusions. We don't insult them by limiting our presentation to the "last paragraph" only—the opinion we want them to reach.

On the other hand, we do furnish—often at the front of a kit of fuller materials—a summary sheet containing newsworthy facts, brief case histories, and pithy quotations. These quotations, bearing a specific person's name for attribution, must be incisive enough to carry the business message on a freestanding basis without needing additional clarification. And they're compressed enough so they will not need to be shortened and/or paraphrased.

We recognize that many influential journalists want to speak directly with senior management. We encourage that. It makes for accurate, up-to-date answers. And it gives management a chance to convey the "feeling tone" of their own aspirations in a personal interchange. Within our clients' time limitations, we urge them to view this kind of interchange as an opportunity instead of a hazard.

A number of companies now offer intensive courses that teach business executives—as well as community leaders and government representatives—how to express themselves through the spoken word. Our own agency has been conducting this training for more than twenty-five years. Some of today's courses stress television and speech-making. Byoir's course, which is called "MediaCom," teaches executives, among other skills, how to organize their facts and arguments and how to answer questions from reporters in all media clearly and succinctly.

In an executive's spoken words—to one reporter on the phone, to a large press conference, or to a nationwide television audience—the most important element, without a doubt, is credibility. That results mainly from telling the truth, but credibility also depends on *how* you tell the truth.

Many times it's helpful to explain not only what's in it for the public but also what's in it for the corporation. Hypocrisy never persuades anybody. When a business executive points out that his company benefits most from a specific program if the public benefits too, that's credibility. As Winston Churchill is quoted as saying: "Interests don't lie."

WHY BUSINESS BACKS OFF FROM SPEAKING OUT

I'm sometimes asked whether we ever advise a client executive *not* to talk to a reporter in a specific instance. Yes, we occasionally do, and I'm not embarrassed to say so. This advice is given infrequently, but there is little alternative if one or more of the following problems prevails:

1. If secrecy of confidentiality is necessary—not merely desirable, but really necessary—then it's better to avoid an interview altogether than to tell a white lie or a half-truth. Privacy is especially valuable, at times, during industrial or diplomatic negotiations. General Motors chairman Alfred P. Sloan, Jr., credited the absence of press exposure for the success of his company's difficult negotiations with the United Auto Workers in 1948:

> We had reached an agreement with the UAW that negotiations would be conducted in relative privacy. In previous years, our collective bargaining had come to resemble a public political forum in which the union fed a stream of provocative statements to the press, and we felt obliged to answer publicly. The privacy of the 1948 negotiations made their tone more realistic from the start.[6]

2. If we know that an interview (most especially a television or radio interrogation) will use just a brief valueless excerpt of the

executive's comments instead of permitting him to state his position fully but concisely, sometimes it might be preferable to decline the interview altogether. A satisfactory statement need not be a five-minute speech. In fact, we urge our clients *not* to make long statements. They get a better result if they edit down their statements beforehand, instead of forcing the editor to do it afterwards.

Often the most we can expect—and it's sufficient—is a half-minute to one-minute-or-so comment making the most important points. That's fine! What is *not* fine is the "equal-time charade" of a few seconds that serves no purpose except to give a false impression of balanced coverage.

If five or ten minutes of a documentary is sure to include opponents' statements accusing an industry of operating against the public interest, then it serves no purpose if the industry spokesperson's reply will be edited down to five words: "No, we didn't do it." The final edited feature should at least allocate the necessary time for explaining briefly what the industry does and doesn't do and why, and how and why the opposition's charges are misleading. The more complex the subject, the more important it is to have a fair chance to set the record straight. "Equal time" and "equitable time" are not the same, and both are complicated concepts.

Some executives absolutely refuse to permit an interview on certain well-known television programs—period. I don't believe a rejection should be that automatic. Most journalists truly want to be fair and objective, whatever their personal opinions might be. In our experience we have often sat down with a program producer or writer, presented a brief written summary of a client's position on the subject at hand, and furnished written evidence supporting that position. Many programs will agree to film a concise statement and carry it *intact* on the air if it's interesting and seems to make sense. Of course, no producers can make an absolute commitment in the early stages of putting a program together; they never know what will need to be edited out because of time problems. Nevertheless, it's sometimes possible for an industry spokesperson to obtain an agreement that his/her concise "minimum" statement must be used intact or not at all.

The editing-down problem we confront in television is less severe but equally serious in the print media. Often "lack of space" explains why industry's reply to damaging charges ends up in the unused overset. The havoc may be compounded by an editor who deletes a paragraph the original reporter would have known enough to leave intact. And then, perhaps, a headline writer invents a clever headline that compounds the confusion still further. I would never guarantee to a client that such a distortion will not be committed—perhaps by writers and editors with the best of intentions. But, we can minimize the chances if we help our client to explain the situation distinctly and succinctly.

3. Another type of pitfall is the media situation where a company or industry could suffer from guilt by association if it's included in a roundup feature with other industries that really mistreat the public. Sometimes, it's advisable to avoid such a roundup situation if possible.

Let's take a specific example. I recall an important documentary that appeared on the public television network about fifteen years ago. This documentary depicted, on film, how unscrupulous businesses exploit poor and ignorant people. There were bait-and-switch merchants, fraudulent vocational schools, shoddy furniture stores that sell faulty merchandise for exorbitant credit terms, and so on. In the midst of these shocking exposés was the report of a young researcher. She had visited several stores of one retail chain and had found that certain prices in a couple of its ghetto stores were higher than the prices for those same items in a couple of its stores in middle-class neighborhoods. I happened to examine the situation rather thoroughly myself, and I'm convinced that any discrepancies were due to human error in failing over the weekend to change the price stamps on all loss-leader items that had just gone on sale for the week ahead. I believe the same researcher might have found certain other items *underpriced* in the ghetto stores through the same kind of human error. Be that as it may, the juxtaposition of this (in my opinion) minor transgression among other televised incidents of fraud and deceit was unfavorable and (again in my opinion) unfair.

The retail chain was asked to permit television camera crews into one of its ghetto stores and also to present a statement explaining the price discrepancies. As I recall, they did make the statement, which was carried briefly on the program, but did not let camera crews do any filming inside their store. Uncooperative? Perhaps. But in-store filmings would have made this visual essay even longer, more dramatic, and more damaging in association with the more flagrant abuses by other businesses shown on the program.

The fear of guilt by association should not be exaggerated, but it can't be discounted entirely. Each media proposal involving this problem must be weighed carefully on an individual basis. We're dealing here not only with facts, but also with emotional impact upon the public.

THE ALLURE OF MASS-APPEAL IN MEDIA

I will not debate at this point whether or not most journalists today are inherently anti-business. My personal opinion is that they are not, although many young reporters with liberal leanings may tend to suspect *all* establishment institutions. (Since my own personal leanings are liberal, too, with enough credentials to prove it, I don't feel apologetic about using that last subordinate clause.)

More serious a problem than personal bias is the problem of media oversimplification of extremely complex public issues, aggravated because there is inadequate space (or air time) to cover those issues fully; inadequate public interest in the kind of detail necessary for fair and balanced coverage; inadequate training on the part of most writers who happen to cover business news in the midst of their other assignments; inadequate time to verify facts and opinions before a deadline; and (sometimes) inadequate help from company employees, especially at an upper-junior or lower-middle management level, who fail to process reporters' inquiries fast enough for industry's side of a story to be included. Because of all these inadequacies, the media too often present stories with simplistic conclusions. Or the stories might focus on only one facet of a multifaceted situation.

Then, there's the question of the commercialization of news. The media in America, with few exceptions, are profit-making businesses themselves. News must be packaged and marketed as alluringly as other commercial products in order to attract customers (readers, viewers, listeners). As happens sometimes with some other products, the consumer of news is occasionally presented with merchandise that has been oversold or carelessly produced. In scrutinizing the media, we're not only evaluating a vitally necessary product—news about our world—but we're also evaluating that product's designers, manufacturers, quality testers, distributors, and marketers.

From the standpoint of the business world, which is sometimes asked to supply the raw informational material that will be fashioned and distributed by the news industry, there is one troublesome problem: to attract customers, news must be exciting and controversial and, whenever possible, negative. To reprhase the old saying, "Good news is no news." The media thrive on reprehensible happenings, not happy happenings.

CBS news commentator Bruce Morton summarized this marketing approach: "A lot of good news isn't news. And I think that's because really we still think the country works pretty well. If everybody goes home, has a nice dinner and doesn't beat his wife, that is not news. I don't come out and report it the next morning."[7]

A social psychologist who might be termed a "consumer advocate" vis-à-vis the news industry stated the dilemma even more critically. Professor Stanley Milgram of the City University of New York decried the commercialization of this essential product:

News under such circumstances tends toward decadent use. It no longer serves first the classic function of giving us information on which to act, or even to help us construct a mental model of the larger world. It serves

mainly as entertainment. .... Happily, we are able to indulge our taste for
thriller, romance or murder mystery under the guise of a patently respectable pursuit. All enlightened people are supposed to know what is going on
in the world. If what is going on also happens to be thrilling and exciting,
so much the better.[8]

Where does that leave other industries? Sometimes pleading for
media attention with a story that may change the future of our society but somehow lacks mass appeal. Sometimes praying that the
media will *not* seize upon a complex story that could be made attractive to the news consumer only through oversimplification and sen-
sationalization. Sometimes frustrated because the television lights go
quickly dark, and reporters' pads snap shut when a business official
begins to testify in reply to the testimony of a media superstar like
Ralph Nader.

Business is learning now how to summarize and dramatize its
own messages more effectively for the news media. Chief executives
are facing up to their own responsibility for dialogue with the many
publics they serve. Any person who becomes president of the United
States recognizes the importance of his role as "America's Com-
municator-in-Chief," a phrase coined by columnist Max Lerner. Now
the heads of corporations have come to realize, too, that first-rate
professional communications is not an expendable luxury but an essential function, as basic as research or production or distribution.

THE WEDDING OF TRUTH AND NEWS

The public relations profession is thriving today. The challenges are
difficult, since we must make both business and the media aware of
our commitment to presenting the full and unaltered truth. This is
even greater than our responsibility for helping our clients attract attention in order to convey an industry message. Fortunately, it is
possible—with expertise and effort—to combine full truth with news
appeal much of the time.

One technique we sometimes use is to develop negative stories,
since the media usually prefer these to positive stories. For example,
one of Byoir's clients is the Road Information Program. The media are
only moderately interested in the God-and-motherhood fact that
America needs safe roads in good repair. So instead, we've assisted the
media in identifying and deploring unsafe old roads and bridges. The
research is intensive and thorough, and it helps the media use a
newsworthy "isn't-it-a-shame" negative story to achieve positive results in public safety and convenience. One element in our road campaign, for instance, was an accurate, in-depth study of traffic growth
potential in the state of Missouri indicating that 86 percent of the

state's roads will wear out within ten years unless the effort to repair and improve those roads is stepped up soon.

Closely linked with the heightened appeal of negative stories is the growing trend to investigative reporting. That kind of reporting builds newspaper circulation and television audiences. I won't dwell on the importance of maintaining responsible standards in this field, since media executives are fully aware themselves that they can destroy a lifetime reputation in one newspaper paragraph or a thirty-second interview with a person's adversary.

Wes Gallagher, president of the Associated Press, summarized the problem himself in an Investigative Reporting Seminar at which he warned:

> We must be most careful when we go after somebody or something. Young writers often go into it with a conviction they try to uphold. . . . A great danger in investigative reporting is a lapse in fairness. The reporter may get so wrapped up in trying to prove his case he overemphasizes damning evidence and ignores the facts that show the opposite.[9]

Gallagher correctly pointed out that journalistic omission and one-sided presentation of accurate facts are more common sins than outright inaccuracy.

Mr. Gallagher and most of his associates in the media understand their own power for good and mischief. They are intensifying their efforts toward greater self-scrutiny and self-education within the media family. They also are increasing their business and economics training for reporters who cover the business beat. As you know, there has been a significant increase recently in fellowships, seminars, and awards competitions for business reporters. This is a healthy trend, and I hope the business world will continue to support such programs—with no corporate strings attached.

A more informed, more understanding press *must* be good for business. I was disappointed recently to learn that a thought I have harbored personally for years is not original with me but is actually an old cliché and an "often-repeated complaint," according to *Fortune* magazine. The complaint goes: "Any time the press covers something I know about personally, they get it wrong."[10] *Fortune* says journalists find that complaint "infuriating," yet it's depressingly well founded. In an age of deadlines and competition, most reporters try hard and do surprisingly well; but even if their facts are correct, they are sometimes incomplete and their interpretations misleading.

The word *misleading* is a crucial one, because it means that the media sometimes *lead* the public to baseless, emotional conclusions that are incorrect. I don't mean the conclusions are incorrect by the standards of an interested party who is biased against them, but they're misleading by the objective standards of *any* expert who knows about the subject.

Part of the problem is that reporters sometimes aren't expert enough themselves to select the experts they interview for their stories. They end up giving equal weight to advocates who know virtually nothing, very little, or virtually everything about a topic, with no guidance to the public as to which person's comments are better informed. Television is especially guilty of this nondifferentiation among expert and nonexpert advocates; and some of my dearest friends in the television world—documentary producers whose integrity I respect totally—have unintentionally misled the public by making this mistake.

In the old days when most journalism covered only exciting or sensational events, this problem was not so acute. But today, when the media are giving more attention to serious topics like science, economics, and business, there is more chance of making errors of inclusion, exclusion, and interpretation. We should applaud the media for paying attention to such stories at long last, even if we sometimes criticize them for knowing too little about a specific subject. David Hendin, science editor of the Newspaper Enterprise Association, summarized the problem: "Mistakes have nothing to do with irresponsibility," he pointed out. "We often just don't know any better."[11]

I do believe the business world can be helpful to the media world in this period when the knowledge of many reporters hasn't fully caught up with their recently expanded subject matter. We can give financial support to business education projects for journalists. That assists *some* reporters. But in addition, when we're working with a journalist on a specific story we can help the educational process by providing *all* the background material he/she can use—not only material that directly supports our own position. We can also provide expert analyses in addition to the facts themselves, since more and more of today's journalism involves telling not only what happened, but also what it means. Of course, we must be impeccable in revealing what is interpretation and what is fact. And we shouldn't be upset if the journalist's interpretation ultimately disagrees with our own.

THE STRATEGY BEHIND REVEALING BAD NEWS

There's another point that should be covered, and that's the question of how business communicators handle bad news. I submit that it's not only honest, reliable, and all those noble things when you reveal your bad news fully and promptly, but it's also smart communications strategy. Tell the story fast, and it will probably die down fast. The media love a scandalous story that slips out a little at a time, especially if it enables them to do some investigative reporting along the way. On the other hand, they consider nothing less newsworthy than yesterday's story if all the facts have already been revealed.

When business reveals the story it should be done candidly and completely. It should be made absolutely clear that management regrets the circumstances themselves, not the mere fact that the media found out about them. On that subject I'd like to quote without comment a "Corrections" item from the July 28 *New York Times:*

> In a United Press International Dispatch in The Times on July 6, John T. Connor, chairman of the Allied Chemical Corporation, was incorrectly quoted as saying that the disclosure of improper corporate payments could destroy a company's business and ruin the persons involved. In fact, Mr. Connor said that such payments could themselves be destructive and ruinous, not merely their disclosure.[12]

Of course, when we do release news about a bad situation we try to include—if decisions can be reached fast enough—positive news about what's being done to correct the situation in the future.

Frequently, business can take actions in the public interest that are so positive they will turn around a negative media climate decisively. This requires not just reassuring words but effective actions that produce results.

I recall one campaign undertaken by the salt industry at a time when environmentalists charged that salt used for melting ice on winter roads was damaging to autos, vegetation, water supplies, and wildlife. A few New England towns stopped using road salt altogether, and others were considering such an action.

Some of the charges against road salting were accurate, but many were not. However, instead of merely saying, "It ain't true," the industry took positive action. With our organization's help, the Salt Institute launched a public-service campaign to educate communities on the correct use of salt, including the avoidance of overuse. We helped local citizens' groups, including the League of Women Voters, among others, to organize committees that studied all the local factors related to the use of salt in their own communities—factors such as topography, water and road conditions, where and how the salt was stored, weather, traffic problems, and so on.

Dozens of salt salesmen and executives were trained in assisting these committees, even though they knew the end result would usually be less use of salt by their customers in public works departments. We produced brochures, films, and other materials to help public officials use salt correctly without harming the environment.

As a result of that public-service program, continued every year since, hundreds of snow-belt communities have reduced harmful environmental side effects of road salting. (Just about everyone agreed that salt is the most effective ingredient for melting road ice to prevent traffic accidents. It was merely a question of *correct* use—as opposed to overuse and improper storage—of road salt.) The towns that had banned salt rescinded their bans, which had resulted in serious auto accidents and road tie-ups. And, incidentally, the media in snow-belt communities have saluted the program as a business service very much in the public interest.

INFLUENTIAL FORCES IN TODAY'S COMMUNICATIONS

I've given a few examples of successful programs that helped business to influence the media in some degree, but I wouldn't imply that even the most skillful communications program has much effect on public opinion unless you're *doing* good as well as talking good. The expectations of the media influence business as much as business influences the media. It's a circle that is sometimes vicious, sometimes adversarial, but often mutually supportive.

Actually, even the leading news editors would be unrealistic if they let themselves be convinced that *they* are majority shareholders in public opinion. There are thousands of different publics today, and the members of each group are influenced most by their own peers. The old authority figures—including not only politicians and schoolteachers and doctors, but also newspaper writers—have been replaced by peer opinion. Women prefer to listen to other women, young people to other young people, blacks to blacks, auto mechanics to other auto mechanics, and so on. As business communicators we must not only speak the language of all the different publics, but we must help them to speak for themselves—to each other and for each other—furnishing them with as many facts as they need to reach their own decisions.

Another influential force in today's communications is entertainment. People's opinions are formed by the movies and television shows they watch, by the songs they sing. Even if they hum some of the words, the emotional gist of the song will affect people's attitudes and aspirations.

Advertisements and commercials are another influence, not only in their basic message, which might be, "buy this product," but also in the underlying social messages they convey, such as daddy cooking dinner more often when mommy comes home late from work; or bankers trying harder to please their customers; or today's high school kids making faster and funnier quips than their teachers and school principals.

I'm disturbed about one message being conveyed in entertainment vehicles these days. That's the exhilaration and respectability of ripping off the establishment. If thievery was such fun for charming middle-class Dick and Jane, why shouldn't ghetto folks get some kicks too by looting appliance stores during the New York City blackout?

No American believes in censorship. But maybe it's time for a "good behavior" pressure group that protests whenever movie crime is made so attractive that the audience cheers, or whenever a radio disc jockey says during a snowstorm, "You kids will be glad to learn you don't have to go to school today." People are busy today working for causes that affect them personally, but I wish somebody would found an organization that helps to promote respect for virtue and authority. Many businesspeople should help to start such a group; it's a thought.

Getting back to the subject of advertising, we sometimes advise business to run institutional ads when they want to reach the public with a message of special importance. The technique should be used sparingly and skillfully, but it does work when the message is in the public interest. For example, Johnson Wax ran full-page ads in 1975 when Samuel Johnson wanted to tell the public quickly that his company would eliminate fluorocarbon propellants in its aerosol spray products. This announcement was accompanied by a press conference, educational brochures, and a variety of other communications techniques. The company received a whole roomful of letters from the public applauding its decision.

Perhaps the most famous institutional ad ever run was written by Carl Byoir on behalf of A&P Food Stores back in the late 1930s, when Congress was considering a punitive and discriminatory tax bill frankly designed to put chain stores out of business. The A&P ad explained why the abolition of chain stores would threaten the interests of consumers, farmers, labor, and A&P's 85,600 employees. The statement included a straightforward announcement of what the company planned to do:

> Since the task we have set before us is one involving the widest dissemination of complete information to all of the American people, and since this is a profession in which we are not expert, we have engaged Carl Byoir & Associates, public relations counsel, to do this work. We realize that our views are seldom news. We know, therefore, that we must be prepared to spend a substantial sum of money in telling our story to all of the American people.

The A&P ads ran in hundreds of newspapers. The public responded with an outpouring of supportive letters, and numerous consumer groups and others endorsed the company's position. The chain-store bill died in committee after overwhelming opposition at the hearings. In addition, sales actually increased at A&P stores as the public suddenly realized the significance of its low food prices.

That campaign was an early textbook classic, and thousands of companies have conducted successful communications campaigns on a variety of topics since then. But business is not the only segment of society with communications clout and know-how today. The Nader organizations are brilliant communicators, with a virtually guaranteed audience of many millions every time they make a major statement. Consumer groups, civil rights organizations, environmentalists, and others have learned how to utilize the media for optimum success. Now, a number of backlash groups have adopted the media techniques of the liberals; and with heavy financial backing and masterful communications they have been winning battles on issues such as laetrile, child abuse laws, and the Equal Rights Amendment.

Government units, of course, from the White House down to local town halls, have learned how to plead their case effectively through the media. So business hardly has a franchise on expert public relations. In fact, business executives sometimes think they are the last group to receive a fair hearing through the media—an opinion not everyone shares with them.

CONCLUSION

In conclusion, the media have grown powerful and persuasive and extremely complex. They are far from perfect. But business is learning that well-planned cooperation with the media makes more sense than hasty avoidance. If one forum doesn't work we have to keep trying other forums until enough people hear our message enough times. As Walter Lippmann once reassured us: "The theory of a free press is that the truth will emerge from free reporting and free discussion, not that it will be presented perfectly in any one account."[13]

NOTES

1. *B.P. Report on the Business of Book Publishing,* July 18, 1977, p. 3.

2. Richard M. Detwiler, "The CEO and the Reporter," *Across the Board,* May 1977, pp. 4ff.

3. *Management Review,* July 1977, p. 6.

4. D. J. Mahoney, "On Ending an Adversary Relationship," *New York Times,* July 7, 1977.

5. Irving Kristol, "Business and the New Class," *The Wall Street Journal,* May 19, 1975, p. 8.

6. A. P. Sloan, *My Life with General Motors* (New York: Doubleday & Co., 1963), p. 398.

7. *Proceedings of the 1976 Vansant Dugdale Symposium on Communications and Community Life* (presented under the auspices of the Johns Hopkins University Evening College, Baltimore), p. 16.

8. Stanley Milgram, "Confessions of a News Addict," *Antioch Review,* Spring/Summer 1977, pp. 167ff.

9. "One-Sided Reporting Hit by Associates Press Chief," *Editor and Publisher,* January 25, 1975, p. 10.

10. Thomas Griffith, "Must Business Fight the Press?" *Fortune,* June 1974.

11. "Medicine and the Media: Ethical Problems in Biomedical Communications," *Medical Tribune,* December 3, 1975.

12. *New York Times,* July 28, 1977.

13. Detwiler, "The CEO and the Reporter," p. 4.

SECTION 4 — BUSINESS VIEWS

It was a long time ago when Commodore Vanderbilt supposedly spouted his infamous phrase, "The public be damned." While a few businessmen may still hold such attitudes, the vast majority now recognize that public opinion toward specific businesses and industries, and public understanding of business in general, substantially influences the ability of businesses to operate successfully. Today's business attitudes are accurately represented by Gulf Oil's O. J. McGill. "Our managers are asking not just is it legal," he says, "but how will it look if it hits the newspapers?"

Business values the media as conduits through which the public can be informed. This fact is amply substantiated by the billions of dollars spent annually on advertising in print and broadcast media. Moreover, business cherishes positive media treatment in news and editorial columns. But, as public opinion toward business has deteriorated over the past decade, business has tended to blame the media, going so far as to claim that the media are knowingly—or unknowingly—undermining the private enterprise system.

Among the accusations that business hurls at the media include excesses in the reportage of business failures, errors, and improprieties, coupled with blindness to business successes in building a society unparalleled in both freedom and material wealth. Sensationalism, failure to sufficiently explain events, oversimplification, taking events out of context, and even alleged anti-business bias contribute to the unbalanced reporting which results in a lack of public confidence in business. According to some businesspeople, while journalists are most skeptical when dealing with business, they seem to accept the statements of government or so-called public-interest groups without question.

Part of the erosion of public opinion is attributed to the public's ignorance of business and economic matters. From the business perspective, media coverage is both a cause and a symptom of this phenomenon. Media, they say, have failed in a responsibility to educate the public so that it can make knowledgeable decisions on matters relating to business and economics. This failure is due in large part to the ignorance of reporters themselves, who understand little about specific businesses or industries, the practice of business in general, or the behavior and function of the business system as a whole.

Businesspeople do not claim to be without fault in their dealings with the media. Business itself has been guilty of oversimplification, exaggeration, understatement, and obstruction of reporters' quests to obtain information. As a consequence, businesses sometimes damage their own credibility.

While recognizing problems and often seeing media as their cause, businesspeople feel a sense of kinship with the media. The media, after all, are businesses. And freedom of expression, so cherished by the media, is seen as inextricably connected with the economic freedoms which are fundamental to a system of private enterprise. Businesspeople call upon the media to recognize the similarities and common purpose of the two institutions and seek to dispel the notion that business and media are monolithic adversaries locked in some great ideological battle.

In this section, three individuals offer business views: the chief executive officer of a controversial company whose business is to collect information about individuals for business and industry; the vice-president/communications of a corporation noted for its generally positive relations with the media; and the former president of a radio network now serving as a communications consultant for a major business association. They describe the business/media relationship from their vantage points as high corporate officials intimately involved with the media, discussing the effects of business and economic coverage as currently practiced, pointing at problems, and suggesting solutions to those problems.

FAIR INFORMATION PRACTICES: SOME IMPERATIVES FOR THE MEDIA AND BUSINESS

W. LEE BURGE

W. Lee Burge, chairman and president of Equifax, Inc., looks at the responsibilities of both business and the media as they process and provide the information that is used by individuals in a free society to make decisions. He is primarily concerned, of course, with information concerning business as it is practiced in the United States and blames the media's handling of such information for the public's attitude toward business and the tendency to depend on government as society's problem solver. Burge speaks from the background of his own company's experience with the CBS television program "60 Minutes," noting the irony of televised inaccuracies, omissions, and exaggerations in a report that questioned the reliability and fairness of the ways in which Equifax carries out its business. Ultimately, Burge makes recommendations for the media, for business, and for both which will improve media coverage and public understanding of business.

Mr. Burge began his career as a mail clerk with the company he now heads. Long concerned with fair information practices, he is a member of The Conference Board and the National Chamber of Commerce's Panel on Privacy. He was formerly chairman of the University System of Georgia's Board of Regents.

Nearly twenty years ago, prominent British scientist and author C. P. Snow delivered a lecture in which he introduced the concept of "two cultures" to describe the gulf in communication and understanding which exists between the scientist and the nonscientist.[1] Later, Lord Snow took a "Second Look at the Two Cultures" and said the issue of greater importance was the gulf between rich and poor countries of the world, advancing the opinion that the only way the chasm could be bridged was by capital—and men.[2]

Since then a number of sociologists have adopted the term "culture" to describe and define special areas of interest and knowledge. So, perhaps today we have in our world—and in our country—many "cultures" with gulfs that need to be bridged. Certainly that is the case between the business community and the news media which interpret business to the public.

As I read, view, and listen to the media today it seems to me that business can find some solace in the fact that it is not alone in feeling that a gulf exists between it and the media. The Cincinnati Reds have been feuding with the press: Johnny Bench describes them as "cheapshot artists"; George Foster speaks of "negative writers." But the question at issue here is not the media and sports, but the media and business.

At the outset, I must publicly disclose my Fair Information Policy position, which is: I believe in the free flow of truthful information! I suggest that similarities exist between the business of Equifax and the business of the news media. We are both a part of the information industry—with the news media reporting to the general public and Equifax reporting to business and industry—and we both rely on information as our basic resource.

Like most people, a large share of my education has been gained from the press. Two journalists whom I read religiously through the years were *Atlanta Constitution* editor Ralph McGill and columnist Walter Lippmann. A guiding principle for Lippmann was his assertion that, "The function of communication in society is to make a picture of reality on which men can act." At Equifax, our experience has taught us the responsibilities a business must assume when communicating information on which important decisions are based. The greatest of these responsibilities, we have learned, is to present facts in such a way that decisions can be reached with adequate intelligence.

I feel sure that this responsibility also ranks near the top of the list of imperatives for professional journalists. Yet, I also feel that principles which should guide the press are not always pursued as consistently as they should be. Among the most important of these principles is to report the news as accurately and completely as possible and to report it objectively with the balance necessary for informed, intelligent public participation in contemporary issues.

A national opinion poll taken recently reaffirmed a lack of public confidence in business institutions which has grown worse in America in recent years.[3] An interesting aspect of the poll was its indication that the respondents' main sources of information regarding business were television news (83 percent) and newspapers (81 percent). It seems safe to say, then, that public impressions of business are attributable, at least in part, to the treatment given business news by the daily press and television.

There are other contributing factors, of course. Price fixing, illegal campaign contributions, questionable payments to foreign governments, and other instances of business mismanagement leave their own bad taste on the intellectual palates of Americans.

The periodic failure of businessmen to protect their own credibility also contributes. Frequently, we are silent when our positions on public issues should be heard, and when we do communicate, we often do so vaguely. It has even been suggested by *New York Times* cultural correspondent John Leonard that public malevolence toward business is rooted at a mythic level:

> The deerslayer, the whaling captain, the river pilot . . . these are the materials of our mythic compost heap. . . . Even as we stumped across a continent, business was an activity of shysters who needed civilizing by schoolmarms.[4]

Most of us grew up, Leonard concludes, wanting to be train robbers.

So my thoughts are not predicated on the false assumption that the news media are on a quixotic mission to "get" the business community. The source of problems existing in our relationship are too complex, and the components of public opinion too diverse, to rely on such simplistic premises.

If I were to assess proportionate blame I would say business is at least 50 percent at fault. And the media are at least 50 percent at fault for the public's misunderstanding of business. Likewise, both are equally responsible for seeking ways to improve the relationship.

THE MEDIA AS A BUSINESS

Irony of ironies, the media are businesses. Media industries are really a very successful business—twice as profitable, on the average, as the average of all business on profit per dollar of sales. Nevertheless, it often seems that the media purposefully set out to undermine the economic system of which they are a part and on which they prosper.

In what areas have the media failed to communicate fairly the real business picture to the public?

First of all, in the area of profits—or rather "excessive" profits. Public ideas about corporate profit margins are incorrect, largely because businessmen have been characterized by the media as profit mongers through bottom-line reporting. Whoever invented the term "bottom line" and then popularized the malapropism did business no service, since it seems to validate the idea that there is one single bottom line to each issue or enterprise, including profits. In reality there is no single computation—profit or loss, earnings per share, return on investment, or percentage increase over prior year—that simplistically reflects a final answer.

Our business "culture" and the "cultures" within the economic arena complicate understanding of corporate profit margins. Anyone who misleads the reader or listener that issues are simple, clear cut, black and white fails in his communication effort to picture reality. (More about that later.)

A second area in which the media have failed to communicate adequately the real business picture to the public is in their reporting about inflation in the economic "mix": its causes, its effects, its insidious undermining of quality, and its distortion of statistical comparisons.

On the same day recently, General Motors Corporation chairman Thomas A. Murphy and Ford Motor Corporation chairman Henry Ford announced their companies' quarterly earnings. Both executives took great pains to explain that the financial results were inflated. Both took great pains to point to price increases coming on new models. They might as well have been whistling in the wind from the standpoint of most news coverage. The headlines blazed, "GM First Manufacturer to Top $1 Billion Profits in Quarter." TV newscasts covered none of Murphy's or Ford's inflation concerns.

This raises a peripheral point about separate "cultures." Headline writers and news writers are frequently miles apart in emphasis and message. To paraphrase an old adage for newspaper readers, "Don't go near the headlines."

Periodically, the media have also been guilty of excesses in news reporting about product hazards and failures, which frequently alarm consumers unnecessarily. As a result, the public has grown more prone to turn to government to intercede in its behalf to redress unsupported grievances.

James L. Ferguson, chairman and chief executive of General Foods Corporation, has correctly identified this area as one in which the media must more adequately determine *when* news is news.[5] Referring to news reports about the safety of certain food products, Ferguson explains that public alarm has often been promoted simply because preliminary research data—incompletely evaluated—has been spread across the news media. In a majority of instances, he says, further examination has shown that alarm was not justified.

Perhaps the greatest area in which the media have failed to accurately picture business to the public is their portrayal of business as a defendant on trial. Frequently, the media convict business on the basis of unfounded accusations by government, advocacy groups, and business critics. Such matters as environmental concerns, employee safety matters, and legal and ethical problems are often portrayed by the media as being given short shrift by business. Treatment of business by the press demands closer adherence to the principle of being innocent until proven guilty.

PUBLIC MISIMPRESSIONS ABOUT BUSINESS

It is not my purpose to parade Equifax's media misunderstandings, but I will cite two for illustrative purposes. In early 1977, a major television network aired a report concerning my company's work in preparing consumer reports used by insurance companies to evaluate the risk characteristics of insurance applicants. The report, which was seen by approximately 16 million viewers, contained several serious inaccuracies, omissions, and exaggerations.

For instance, the program employed a college student who was represented as having been an employee of Equifax. Actually, he never worked for our firm. The program also stated that a quarter of a million people have contacted Equifax in the past five years about adverse reports on themselves. But it did not say that the great majority of these people agreed that our reports were accurate, that these people were notified that the reports had been made and invited to discuss them if they had questions, or that 250,000 inquiries represent only a minute percentage of the total number of reports we make.

We were also assured by the program that safeguards consumers are afforded by law and by our own Fair Information Practices would be explained for the public's benefit, yet they were not mentioned.

It is ironic that a program which questioned the reliability and fairness of Equifax's reporting procedures could have been both unreliable and unfair in its own reporting. The impressions it left were especially unfortunate because this was an opportunity to accurately inform the public about an important process—business information reporting—which directly affects millions of Americans each year.

Why were items of such vital importance disregarded by the program? A partial explanation might be that the time limitations inherent in a broadcast news report require the omission of details that might otherwise be included. News sometimes treats the most complex events simplistically, as prominent public relations consultant Richard M. Detwiler points out:

> The initial selection of what news editors choose to consider news gravitates toward the simple things that adapt to structural limitations of the media. The reporting of the selected simple events further simplifies. The rewriting and editing of simple material reported—to fit into limited space and time—further compresses and oversimplifies.[6]

The subjects selected by journalists to become news, however, are often not as simple as they are made to appear to be.

In selecting news stories about business, the media often receive yeoman service from business critics. I am, for instance, somewhat baffled by what appears to be an inordinate acceptance of information handed to the media by government agencies. Not long ago, for example, the Federal Trade Commission leveled a serious charge against my industry. It alleged that it had received 20,000 complaints relating to the way in which the consumer reporting industry conducts its business. Again and again, the press made headlines of the allegation, which was later proven to be unfounded.

Under the Freedom of Information Act a trade association requested documentation of the FTC's claim. Analysis of the FTC's response to the request revealed that more than 11,000 of the alleged complaints were actually telephone inquiries whose nature was undetermined. Further analysis revealed that only 682 bona fide written complaints had actually been received by the FTC. A far cry from 20,000 complaints, particularly since during the period in which the so-called complaints were received more than 600 million consumer reports were completed by consumer reporting companies.

Of course, Equifax is not alone in its feeling that fair treatment of its business is not always afforded by the news media. Mobil Oil Corporation, for instance, is spending approximately $20 million each year on communications efforts designed to counterbalance what it considers to be unfair reporting about issues in which it is involved.[7]

In one instance, Mobil filed a complaint with the National News Council after the American Broadcasting Company televised nationally a program titled, "Oil: The Policy Crisis."[8] The program was billed as "basically a primer on oil, designed to help Americans understand a highly charged and difficult problem," and ABC contended that it had been "researched and executed from every conceivable point of view." Expecting a program that was well balanced, Mobil found instead that it was misleading and one-sided.

Reviewing Mobil's complaint, the National News Council's Grievance Committee found that ABC

> did select certain facts that pointed in one direction and omit others that pointed elsewhere. Its organization of the facts presented, moreover, created one specific editorial impression: namely that government policy on oil has been manipulated over the years by the oil industry itself, to the detriment of the public's interest and for its own private profit.[9]

Equifax applauds efforts such as those made by the Mobil Corporation to rectify public misimpressions of business which are fostered through unobjective reporting. It is regrettable, however, that such efforts can almost never fully correct misunderstandings caused by a news medium's failure to live up to the journalistic ethic.

SOME IMPERATIVES FOR THE MEDIA

Walter Lippmann's theory of a free press was that, "The truth will emerge from free reporting and free discussion, not that it will be presented perfectly in any one account."[10]

In general, I accept that theory. However, I don't think it eliminates the necessity for journalists to diligently pursue objectivity, accuracy, balance, and completeness in reporting—even in the single article.

The problem of objectivity will always be the crucial one, according to Temple University journalism professor John DeMott. DeMott says that the respect which any journalist earns should be earned as a result of "the superior objectivity which he or she brings to bear in giving the public its intelligence of current events."[11]

The news media's cultivation of more complete objectivity toward business can be achieved in several ways, all of which, taken together, can help journalists "to see life steady and see it whole," as C. P. Scott, former editor of the *Manchester Guardian,* said the function of a good journalist is.

College and university schools of journalism—the training ground for most aspiring journalists—are the logical places to begin. This year, 64,000 college and university students are majoring in journalism or communications subjects.[12] Many of them will become outstanding newsmen and newswomen, a credit to their profession and our society. Others will come to "perpetuate the worst vices of journalism—ignorance and prejudice."[13]

Ben Bagdikian, former reporter and newspaper editor and now a lecturer in journalism at the University of California, writes that the appropriate justification for journalism training in higher education is

> to impart to the potential journalist a knowledge of the proper role of journalism in society, the ethics implied by his role, and encouragement of empathy with people they will study for the rest of their career, and some advice on what academic programs will provide lasting insight into society.[14]

Among journalists—sometimes veterans, sometimes newcomers to the profession—empathy with businessmen is lacking. Business appears to be viewed by too many journalists as an abstract process separated from people and ordinary life. Yet, most of what individuals seek in our society is either produced by business, serviced by business, protected by business, or provided by financial resources people earn through business.

College and university schools of journalism, by encouraging students to pursue academic programs which provide better understanding of the business community's philosophical and practical foundations, can provide a base of knowledge on which greater empathy with businessmen can be built.

An incredibly large number of Americans are poorly informed about economic subjects and, unfortunately, this includes many journalists. When a journalist does not have the background needed to handle a business story, sketchy reporting usually results.

Of course, few news reporters will ever be business experts, and I don't mean to suggest that it is necessary that they become so. There are many knowledgeable business writers and editors, however, whose expertise is underutilized. Greater use of such skilled business reporters to cover general news stories which involve business, and greater use of them as monitors of what is to be reported, can increase accuracy and objectivity.

I also feel that many of the excesses in reporting about business can be curbed if business—along with other sources—is looked upon by all journalists as a legitimate and credible interpreter of objective reality. The point is, journalists should be as skeptical as they feel they need to be with businessmen. But, they should be equally skeptical of governmental and "advocacy" groups. They are not one whit better than we—perhaps as good, but not a bit more truthful with their information.

Journalism, it has been said, is a report of material after it has been stylized. In stylizing their material, however, journalists sometimes forget that their central function is simply to report what happened.

A reporter's viewpoints about subjects he or she covers must be screened as rigidly as possible to prevent personal bias from entering; commentary must be clearly separated from news reporting. In today's complex world, however, journalists often feel obligated to interpret news events to provide understanding where facts do not seem to speak for themselves. The thin line between interpretive journalism and advocacy journalism is often crossed, though, when journalists fail to distinguish clearly for themselves where one leaves off and the other picks up.

SOME IMPERATIVES FOR BUSINESS

The source of much media and public antipathy toward business can be traced to business's lack of success in protecting its own credibility. Very little that businessmen say about themselves and their products and services is believed by the media or the general public, and much of what is believed is incorrect.

To facilitate media presentations, business has fallen into the entrapment of simplistic approaches when communicating information about profits. We use indices—for example, earnings per share—to oversimplify our profit results, and we glowingly report phenomenal percentages of increase over previous financial periods even when it is relatively poor performance. This contributes to poor public understanding of corporate profit performance and helps to explain why college students estimate corporate profit at 45 percent of sales, when in reality it is about 5 percent.[15]

Exaggeration has cost business a great deal in terms of believability. Its credibility has been more seriously compromised, however, by its penchant for understatement in situations that call for forceful communication.

In an era in which institutional communication has become synonymous with "stonewalling" in the public's vocabulary, it is imperative that business speak up publicly and without excuse when it finds itself guilty of questionable practices. "No one believes," as General Motors chairman Thomas Murphy has pointed out, "that business is blameless in every respect. For us to try to make it seem to be is worse than ineffectual: it only deepens disbelief. It suggests that we in business no longer distinguish between what is right and fair and honest, and what is not."[16]

I believe that businessmen can distinguish between right and wrong, and that, for the most part, businessmen adhere to ethical standards which should preempt public and media distrust of our actions. Where we have erred, however, is suggested by *Fortune* writer Max Ways, who has attacked us on a vulnerable point. He accuses us of engaging in "reverse hypocrisy." If the average businessman is caught in an act of kindness, according to Ways, he will apologize for acting decently and mumble something about "what he did was good for profits."[17] Business must get away from its "bottom-line scoring" of morality if it is ever to convince the news media and the general public of its adherence to ethical codes of behavior.

SOME MUTUAL IMPERATIVES

Arnold Toynbee once said, "It is a perennial human infirmity to ascribe our failures to forces beyond our control." Both the news media and business have been guilty of ascribing the tensions existing in our relationship to each other. To improve our relationship, we both must focus greater attention on our mutual imperatives. Among these are:

- Becoming more expert in communicating a true picture of reality on which the public can act, for we all have too much at stake for our society to be as anti-business as it now is.

- Constantly improving in performance in order to enhance the credibility on which public confidence in us rests.

- Avoiding over-simplifying complex, intricate issues by taking the time, and absorbing the costs, to better educate our publics.

- Adopting a philosophy that "truth will emerge from free reporting and free discussion."

If business has problems, weaknesses, shortcomings, it is the news media's job to inform the public—objectively. If business has a rebuttal, or if it feels the media need more data to weigh the factors involved, it is its responsibility to step forth. Such interchanges can only impel each of us to improve our performance. For despite differences in thinking which may exist between us, we both have an important common denominator: we are integral parts of a free system of government and enterprise, and we are both obligated to help preserve it. Fully recognizing our similarities and our common purpose may, ultimately, be our greatest imperative of all.

NOTES

1. C. P. Snow, *The Two Cultures and a Second Look* (Cambridge: Cambridge University Press, 1969), pp. 1–51.

2. Ibid., pp. 53–100.

3. William Macfarlane, "Who's Telling the Story?" *The National Underwriter* (Life and Health edition), November 13, 1976, p. 10.

4. John Leonard, "What Have American Writers Got Against Businessmen?" *Forbes*, May 15, 1977, pp. 120, 124.

5. James L. Ferguson, a published statement adapted from remarks before the Association of National Advertisers, Colorado Springs, Colorado, October 14, 1976.

6. Richard M. Detwiler, "The CEO and the Reporter," *Across the Board*, May 1977, p. 7.

7. Irwin Ross, "Public Relations Isn't Kid-Glove Stuff at Mobil," *Fortune*, September 1976, p. 110.

8. Herbert Schmertz, "The Energy Crisis and the Media" (a paper prepared by the vice-president/public affairs for the Mobile Corporation), p. 4.

9. Ibid., p. 28.

10. Detwiler, "The CEO and the Reporter," p. 6.

11. John DeMott, "The News Media's Quest for Objectivity," *Vital Speeches of the Day*, October 1, 1976, p. 747.

12. Ben H. Bagdikian, "Woodstein U: Notes on the Mass Production and Questionable Education of Journalists," *Atlantic Monthly*, March 1977, p. 82.

13. Ibid., p. 82.

14. Ibid., p. 92.

15. Robert F. Dee, "Polls, Pendulums, Paradoxes, and People" (a published address before the Economic Club of Detroit), September 29, 1975, p. 5.

16. Thomas A. Murphy, "The Corporation and Public Opinion: Economic Freedom or Government Control?" *Vital Speeches of the Day*, November 1, 1976, p. 57.

17. Max Ways, "Business Faces Growing Pressures to Behave Better," *Fortune*, May 1974, pp. 191–195, 314–320.

A LOOK FROM THE CORPORATE SIDE

RICHARD S. STODDART

Richard S. Stoddart, Eaton Corporation's vice-president/communications, maintains that business and the media are indispensable to each other but need to know one another better. A top priority, according to Stoddart, is the need for media to do a more extensive job of covering economic news. Economic news is the stepchild of the newspaper and virtually nonexistent on television. As a means by which operating media and business personnel can get to know each other better, Stoddart offers to begin an exchange program between Eaton's public relations department and a newspaper, magazine, or television station in which a business journalist and a corporate communicator would exchange jobs for at least a month.

Mr. Stoddart has served as executive director of the Cleveland Commission on Health and Social Services and was a Cleveland Heights city councilman. He is secretary of the Board of Trustees of the Educational Television Association for Metropolitan Cleveland and directs COMM/PRO, Eaton Corporation's ongoing employee economic education program.

I get a little uneasy every time I hear a speech or attend a seminar entitled "Business and the Media." My apprehension is based on the distorted picture that the title itself suggests. "Business and the Media" as a subject for discussion immediately brings to mind an image of two giant monoliths of our complex society engaged in some kind of a continuing struggle for supremacy. Each of these forces, it would seem, is a unified entity with a single goal, method of operation, and leadership.

Before we can begin to criticize the handling of economic news and information; before we can construct better working relationships between the company communicator and the business reporter, we need a fresh look at the subject and perhaps some new perspectives.

One of the best ways to dispel the perilous assumptions about "Business and the Media" is to realize first of all that the media are businesses. From the national TV network, to the daily newspaper, to trade journals, radio stations, and rural monthlies, the print and broadcast media are made up of fiercely competitive, profit-oriented business. They may inform, educate, entertain, and persuade, but they are in business to survive by making a profit.

183

To reach a happy but hackneyed "bottom line" they must have satisfied customers, lots of them. They are engaged in a continuing struggle to gain readers, subscribers, listeners, and viewers—and for the most part, advertisers. The fabulous Walters twins, Barbara and Cronkite, earn their handsome salaries as employees of profit-making companies. They earn them based on their ratings and the advertising dollars those ratings can muster. While we may admire their judgment, analytical ability, or their skill at reading, their preeminence in the broadcast journalism field depends more on charm and charisma than upon craftsmanship.

Let me interject immediately that I am all for free enterprise in the media. Most companies are willing and eager to shell out millions of dollars to the media that can deliver the goods—and the customers—through advertising. We are well aware of, and take advantage of, the awesome power and efficiency of media.

Are business and media adversaries? Far from it. We are working partners, indispensable to each other, in keeping our American economic system free and growing. Thus, rather than focusing on any struggle between business and the media, we should consider how businesspeople can work together effectively in restoring public confidence in all business.

In the first place, we've all got to get to know each other much better. If the corporate communicator looks upon the business reporter as a cynical sin seeker, and the business reporter regards the corporate communicator as the company flimflam man, we've got a long way to go. The first steps are in striving to understand and respect the problems, needs, and methods of each other's business.

Those of us on the corporate side are quick to bemoan the quality and scope of the reporting of economic news, and not without good reason. At the same time, the working press can legitimately counter that corporate officers are often evasive, defensive, and inarticulate, and that corporate news releases are filled with fluffery, puffery, and a yearning to sweep things under a variety of rugs.

The root cause of these allegations, all of which have some elements of truth, is a reluctance on the part of the press and the corporate communicator to learn enough about each other to make constructive changes in their relationships.

As a corporate officer charged with the responsibility of communicating to Eaton's many publics worldwide, I view the print and broadcast media as the most important vehicles for discharging my duties. Eaton's communications effort is concentrated on building meaningful, open, and candid channels from the corporate offices and our 124 plants to the media. Accessibility and availability of top officers, especially the chief executive officer, is the keystone of that policy. It pays off in objective, in-depth reporting of company events—even those that are "bad news." We work just as hard and thoroughly to place stories on new products and pioneering human relations practices as we did to make sure that the press has the complete details on the results of our investigation into "questionable payments." We want to earn the credibility and confidence of the press and are convinced that it can only happen by working at it—full time. We're not the first to adopt this stance, but unfortunately we're far from the last. Companies that are reluctant to open up to the press are numerous. Their fears—and they are often real fears—are based on a lack of knowledge about the press and the lack of a commitment from top management, who often view the press with alarm, dismay, and abject terror.

And why not? Newspaper and television coverage of economic news is often shallow, unbalanced, sensation oriented, and, saddest of all, ignorant of the facts—the result, once again, of having far too little knowledge of the subject.

There is plenty of expert opinion on both sides. Last year, Walter Wriston, in a speech entitled "Liberty, Leadership and License," scored the press for abuses of their freedom. A few months ago, fellow banker David Rockefeller sounded a similar message in a speech entitled "Problems, Perspectives and Responsibilities," in which he accused the press of unfairness and inaccuracy in reporting. Liberty, leadership, license . . . problems, perspectives and responsibilities— some heavy thoughts from the financial heavyweights. I might add that both Wriston and Rockefeller urged business—all business—to exhibit responsibility in communicating.

On the inevitable other hand, Katherine Graham, chairperson of the Washington Post Company, told a Conference Board audience that business leaders must display more candor in their communications. "Don't think about credibility," she counseled. "Focus instead on honesty, perspective and performance." Good advice for all of us.

Thus, while leaders in the banking business and leaders in the media business have a lot of good advice for each other, they are often unable to transmit their concern or commitment to the working levels.

MUTUAL MISUNDERSTANDINGS

The big kicker in all of the mutual ignorance between news subjects and news reporting is that the working press's lack of knowledge or concern about economics has far more impact on public opinion than what the company communications department doesn't know or understand about the press.

A case in point: A couple of weeks ago the *Cleveland Plain Dealer* ran a well-researched and thoughtful editorial on the impact of oil imports on free trade. Next to the editorial, however, was a cartoon depicting Uncle Sam unlocking a jack-in-the-box entitled "U.S.

Oil hurts free trade . . .

"The cost of imported oil plagues the free world. It's driving every free country into protectionism," said Rep. Charles A. Vanik, D-22, chairman of the House Ways and Means Committee's subcommittee on trade.

Oil from foreign countries is costing the United States $46.8 billion a year, at the rate of June imports. That huge, growing expense wiped out a trade surplus. It promises to land this country in a deficit of $25 billion by the year's end.

All industrial countries are in the same fix. So they set out to sell whatever they can to offset their deficits. They compete with each other ever more viciously. That means tariffs to keep out rival countries' steel, shoes, autos, TV sets, everything.

How else can they meet the mounting cost of oil? The Organization for Economic Cooperation and Development (OECD), which includes all the advanced countries of the free world, has a current account deficit of $35 billion it owes the members of the Organization of Petroleum Exporting Countries (OPEC).

To bring in enough cash to pay such debts, these countries push exports. Vanik points out that Japanese goods are capturing 15% of the U.S. market. Japan is accused of dumping steel, electronic products and autos.

Many West European countries give their exporting companies subsidies to make their foreign markets extra juicy. And duties are being raised like walls against outside-made goods to make them—American machinery or ball bearings, say—higher priced and less attractive.

Just the recession alone might well have caused this burst of feverish export-mindedness. For many industrial free countries the export market is 25% of the total sales area. But the oil debt has sharpened the already keen game. It encourages tariffs, duties, export subsidies and bonuses.

It drives countries into protectionism, as Vanik says. And now all the countries in the free world market must decide how to solve their trade tangles.

"I believe in trade," says Vanik. "Because if you trade with a country, you don't fight with that country." He favors a broad set of trade agreements based on global quotas in each product. And like most Americans, he is for free trade—as free as it can be kept.

But that has become less free with the crushing burden of oil cost forcing industrial countries to protect their producers, their jobs and their products in the world market.

. . . Steel rivalry keener

America's steel industry has a booming campaign going against foreign steel. Billboards say. "Foreign steel steals jobs." Steelmen demand that duties be imposed on Japanese steel, and they charge Japan with dumping steel here below cost.

Steel certainly is being imported in massive quantities. Imports are up 20% as of June 30 compared with the same six months of 1976. U.S. Steel Corp. president David M. Roderick says:

"One hundred and ten thousand jobs in steel are being lost . . . The American government should start standing up for the American worker and quit trying to coddle foreign state departments."

But the Japanese deny dumping steel. They claim they can undersell U.S. and European steelmakers because they have 30% lower labor costs, and they hold a technological lead.

How is the cost of their technological lead apportioned, though? Do exports to the United States bear a fair share of that cost?

And do publicly owned steel mills count in all employe welfare, fringes, the unpaid taxes and government subsidies in their pricing of steel for export?

U.S. Steel's Roderick claims that Italian steel, 83% government-owned, is losing $50 on every ton it sells overseas.

Japan is charged with selling steel at any price, simply because steel corporations' expense in unemployment and welfare benefits makes that nearly as attractive. Better to lose and produce than lose on idle plant and manpower.

On the other hand, American steel companies have not been blameless, Rep. Charles A. Vanik, D-22, chairman of the House Ways and Means Committee's trade subcommittee, said in an interview with The Plain Dealer:

"I was partly responsible for the first steel agreement. Wilbur Mills (former Ways and Means chairman) and I talked with the Japanese. They restrained their exports.

"But when we got the steel agreement with Japan, the steel industry here immediately jumped their price 16%."

Vanik's proposals now include "better monitoring on undue penetration of the American market. We've got to develop an early warning system on a trade assault before it gets out of control.

"We might trigger in a tariff, if the assault reaches a critical point," Vanik added. "Then if the U.S. producers raise their prices, we should call the deal off, halt that tariff, to provide more balanced control."

Keeping any vital U.S. industry alive is worth some sacrifice by Americans. But American consumers should not be forced to pay sky-high prices to maintain inefficient industries. The proper level may be hard to find, but it should stay nearer to free trade than protection in most industries.

Deficit-in-the-box.

Source: "Oil Hurts Free Trade . . . Steel Rivalry Keener," *Plain Dealer,* August 6, 1977.

Free Trade Tradition." From the box sprung out a variety of other boxes entitled "Made in Japan, Made in West Germany, Made in Italy, Made in Taiwan." The cartoon title: "Deficit-in-the-box." The cartoon, totally ignorant of the facts, implied that the trade deficit was due to our free-trade policies with these countries, when in fact, we enjoy healthy trade surpluses in almost every area of the world. Oil, of course, is the big factor in the deficit. To the reader—especially the casual reader—the message was clearly misleading. Whatever his artistic ability, the cartoonist gets a D-minus in international economics, and so does the editor, who gave the common myth of the impact of trade with other countries another boost in the public mind.

The business pages of the daily papers vary from day to day and from paper to paper as far as content and depth, but there is seldom any attempt at economic education. The business pages seem to be the stepchild of the newspaper, heavy on wire-service stories and complete with the day's transactions in the stock markets. I wonder aloud, have the major metropolitan newspapers ever given any thought as to why they must publish, every day, every transaction in the New York Stock Exchange and the American Exchange? They take up a lot of space, that's true, but is such total coverage really necessary or desirable? Could that space be put to better use with perhaps more coverage of the activities of local firms, both small and large? But, perhaps, I'm simply exhibiting some of that mutual lack of knowledge about each other's operations.

Eaton recently released the results of our investigation into our own so-called "questionable payments." The results of the investigation weren't particularly exciting. There were no slush funds, no bribes, no payoffs, and no hidden accounts. There were a few hundred dollars of illegal political contributions made by unthinking employees. There was about $125,000 paid to various people outside of the United States that could easily have been used illegally by the third parties. The biggest item in numbers was about a million dollars annually legitimately remitted to distributors and sales representatives in countries outside of their business residence. They had earned it; Eaton owed it to them. The fact that their money was sent to a country other than the one on their letterheads, however, certainly raises some questions about its eventual accounting. Still, no laws were broken.

We felt obligated to disclose the results of our investigation to the Securities and Exchange Commission and to the public via the media. Our news release carried every fact and number that we had dug up. Here's how four major newspapers covered the story:

The Wall Street Journal agreed with us that it was no big deal.

Eaton Study Shows Dubious Payments Were Relatively Small

By a WALL STREET JOURNAL *Staff Reporter*

CLEVELAND—Eaton Corp. said an investigation turned up relatively small questionable payments overseas and in the U.S.

The company said in a report filed with the Securities and Exchange Commission that between 1972 and 1976, subsidiaries outside the U.S. made payments of $2,177 to employes of government-controlled customers and payments of $25,126 to employes of nongovernmental customers in countries outside the U.S.

In addition, the company said, $91,835 was paid in commissions during the period to agents outside the U.S. "under circumstances suggesting that some portion of the payment may have been remitted by the agents to employes of government-controlled customers." The company said it didn't have any evidence that such remittances were made, however.

Eaton also said the company paid about $867,000 yearly in legitimately owed money to distributors and sales representatives in countries outside the country of their business residence.

Domestically, the company said an employe was reimbursed $100 for tickets to a political fund-raising dinner. Also, an employe got a one-week leave of absence without loss of pay while running for a state office, and two clerical employes spent some office time providing clerical assistance to a political party, the company said.

The company said the investigation, which was supervised by the audit committee of the board and now is complete, didn't turn up any evidence of political slush funds or unrecorded bank accounts.

Eaton makes capital goods, auto parts, locks and other products.

Source: "Eaton Study Shows Dubious Payments Were Relatively Small," *The Wall Street Journal,* August 8, 1977.

So, too, did the *Chicago Tribune.*

Eaton tells dubious payments of $27,000

CLEVELAND [AP]—Questionable payments overseas and in the United States have been reported by Eaton Corp. to the Securities and Exchange Commission.

The company said that from 1972 through 1976, subsidiaries outside the U.S. paid about $2,000 to employes of government-controlled customers and about $25,000 to employes of nongovernmental customers overseas.

Also, it said more than $90,000 was paid in commissions to overseas agents "under circumstances suggesting that some portion of the payment may have been remitted by the agents to employes of government-controlled customers." The company said it has no evidence the remittances were made, however.

Domestically, the company said, an employe was reimbursed $100 for tickets to a political fund-raising dinner. Also, an employe was given a paid, one-week leave of absence while running for state office, and two clerks spent office time working for a political party.

Source: "Eaton Tells Dubious Payments of $27,000," *Chicago Tribune,* August 10, 1977.

Our local papers went into a little more depth. The *Cleveland Plain Dealer* ran it this way:

Eaton probe reveals questionable payments
By John B. Harris

Foreign subsidiaries of Cleveland-based Eaton Corp. made questionable payments totaling $2,177 to employes of government-controlled firms and $25,126 to employes of non-governmental businesses between 1972-77, according to an internal investigation.

In a report filed yesterday with the Securities and Exchange Commission, the company added that an additional $91,835 was paid to sales agents in other countries, some of which may have been used for bribes.

Over the same five-year period, Eaton said that more than $4.3 million was paid to distributors and sales representatives at banks of convenience—banks in countries other than where the transaction occurred or other than the company's national origin.

These payments, usually commissions on export sales or undeducted discounts, may or may not have violated currency exchange or other laws of the foreign countries, the company said.

Eaton declined to reveal where or why the payments took place. It stressed, however, that none of the foreign payments violated U.S. law.

Domestically, the investigation also discovered several minor infractions linked to politics. One employee during the five-year period listed tickets to a $100 political fund-raiser as a job-related cost on his expense account. He has since paid it back, Eaton said.

The company also reported that one employee received a full week's salary while running for political office, and that two employes provided clerical assistance for a political party during office hours.

E. M. deWindt, Eaton chairman and chief executive, said the investigation showed "some situations where Eaton's corporate policy on ethical business conduct was not properly carried out."

He said these practices have been stopped.

Source: "Eaton Probe Reveals Questionable Payments," *The Plain Dealer,* August 6, 1977.

In the afternoon, the *Cleveland Press* ran the story like this:

Eaton reveals payments

Eaton Corp. today revealed that it made questionable payments overseas totaling $4.3 million from Jan. through Dec. 31, 1976.

The information was contained in an 8-K report filed today with the Securities and Exchange Commission.

Commenting on the voluntary investigation and the report, Chairman E. Mandell de Windt said: "The investigation revealed no political 'slush funds,' 'unrecorded bank accounts' or hidden accounts of any kind."

The report said that at the request of some distributors and sales agents, the company paid amounts that were owed to them legitimately but outside the country of their business residence. These payments averaged $867,000 yearly.

The commission payments may, or may not have been, in violation of currency exchange or other laws of the recipients countries.

The report said that payments by foreign subsidiaries did not violate U.S. laws.

Subsidiaires outside the U.S. made payments during the five-year period of $2177 to employees of government-controlled customers and payments totaling $25,126 to employees of non-government customers.

In addition, $91,835 in commission was paid to agents outside the U.S. Some portion of these payments may have been remitted by the agents to employees of government-controlled customers. Eaton said it has no evidence that such kickbacks were made.

In the U.S. Eaton's investigation discovered that an employee was reimbursed $100 in company funds for tickets to a political fund-raising dinner. The employee has made restitution, Eaton said.

Another employee was permitted a one-week leave-of-absence with pay while running for a state office. Two other employees provided clerical help to a political party. A value of $1100 was placed on this activity.

"The investigation revealed some situations where Eaton's corporate policy on ethical business conduct was not properly carried out. These practices have been stopped," de Windt said.

Source: "Eaton Reveals Payment," Cleveland Press, August, 1977.

In every case the story came from the same release. There were no interviews and only two minor requests were made for more information.

The point of reproducing these articles is not to present brownie points for the papers that were nicest to us, but to show that economic news can get pretty subjective treatment from the media. Once again, economic understanding appears to be of uneven quality.

This, by the way, is an example, not an indictment. It can easily be balanced by examples of solid objective coverage by business reporters. *Business Week,* for instance, recently did a story on Eaton's new approaches to human relations in our factories. The reporter requested, and got, free and open access to the plants involved and to individual managers and employees without taking along a corporate public relations interpreter. We knew that it was a good story, and although there are obvious pitfalls involved in such freewheeling interviews, we also had confidence in the objectivity of the publication.

The result: an objective look at Eaton's new philosophies, complete with the few warts that are inevitable in any wide-ranging program.

To understand the full impact of the story on readers, we decided to do some research. A Starch impression study found that *Business Week* readers came away from the story with a definitely improved image of Eaton. The Starch study showed that 70 percent of those readers surveyed developed positive attitudes toward Eaton. Sixty percent assessed Eaton's future outlook favorably and rated Eaton's investment appeal as good to excellent. Over 20 percent reported a change in previous conception of Eaton after reading the article. Nearly all indicated an enhancement of their views.

So, while we may sometimes be disappointed by press coverage, we are not dismayed to the point of altering our policy of access and availability. We believe that in the long run it can only serve to strengthen working relationships with the press.

TV'S COVERAGE OF THE DISMAL SCIENCE

Economics has often been cited as "the dismal science" in academic circles. Television's programming management obviously took its cue from this generality, because economics might well be considered the invisible subject on TV news.

A couple of weeks ago I asked some of the people in my department to take an in-depth view of television's finest hour—in our market, the 6 P.M. to 7 P.M. segment of local and national news. I thought that you might be interested in a breakdown of those fateful sixty minutes which, for the public, is their window to the world.

I'll admit right off that this was an unscientific random sample, but I wouldn't hesitate to wager that the format is pretty much the same from day to day and from market to market, except, of course, when unusual news occurs.

On this random evening, the local news half hour consisted of twelve minutes of national, state, and local news, four minutes of sports, three and a half minutes of weather, and a three-and-a-half-minute editorial. There were five and a half minutes of commercials and promos and twenty seconds devoted to economic news—a quick rundown on the stock market activity. This was the same amount of time as was allotted to an uplifting story and pictures of an automobile waiting for sheep to cross a road.

Of course, the national network portion devoted a lot more time to news—some nineteen and a half minutes. Eight and a half minutes were given over to commercials and network and station promos. The weather got a minute and a quarter and sports a quick ten seconds. Economic news consisted of fifteen seconds of stock market activity of the day. There were some economic elements to the news itself. A Ford Motor recall program got ten seconds, and the Alaska pipeline shutdown, twenty seconds.

I don't mean to judge the wisdom of the news editors on these programs. Their job is tough enough. My unprofessional survey just points out, once again, that economic news on a sultry summer evening has little appeal to the editors and newscasters and, in their opinion, to the public. Could it be because the powers that be in TV news don't really understand economics, or do they feel that it simply isn't interesting?

While there is obviously some criticism inherent in these remarks, I really offer them more as comments on the need for a much

---

LABOR

Where white-collar status boosts productivity

**Eaton Corp. gets results
by treating plant workers
as salaried employees**

When Arthur King III was laid off two years ago from his production job at a textile factory in Kinston, N.C., he found another job at an Eaton Corp. plant in nearby Greenville. His new job paid nearly $100 a week less than the $300 he had been making. Yet when he was recalled to the textile plant a month later, he decided to stay at Eaton. The reason: The 26-year-old King, a high school graduate, found the Eaton plant to be "a whole lot less regimented" than the factory where he had worked before.

The Greenville plant is one of 13 of Eaton's newer plants where the company has instituted a "new philosophy" of labor-management relations. Under the new arrangement, blue-collar workers are treated essentially like white-collar employees. They receive weekly salaries instead of hourly wages, participate in the corporate pension program, and get paid for sick absences. From the company's point of view, the program increases management flexibility and productivity. And while Eaton denies it as a motivation, there is little doubt that the program bolsters the company's defense against unionization. All 13 of the "new philosophy" plants are nonunion.

Most important to King and many of his fellow workers, they feel less harassed and freer to perform their work than in more conventional plants. King, for example, operates a pipebending machine as part of a 15-worker team that makes overhead guards for the lift trucks produced by the Greenville plant. Instead of indulging in harangues like the old bull-of-the-woods foreman, the team's supervisor takes a low-key approach in monitoring the team and distributing the work load. "In the other factory, I felt like someone was standing over me all the time, making me nervous," King says. "Here I can concentrate and get more done."

Finding a remedy. Eaton, a diversified manufacturer with sales of $1.8 billion last year, employs 18,000 workers in 65 plants in North America. Like many other companies, it has been experimenting with new labor relations ideas, hoping to counter the growing problem of alienation, particularly among today's younger, better-educated workers. Eaton, however, has gone further than most companies in designing a new system.

The origins of Eaton's "new philosophy" date from the late 1960s. The prospective manager of an Eaton plant being built in Kearney, Neb., wanted to avoid the kind of deterioration in employee-management relationships that had occurred in his old plant at Battle Creek. He asked employee relations manager at Eaton's Cleveland headquarters to develop a new approach that would eliminate worker distrust and regimentation on the factory floor.

"We felt that, despite the tremendous social and economic advances for the plant employee during the past few decades, the factory itself retained much of its classism and discrimination," says Donald N. Scobel, manager of employee relations research and development. Adds Scobel, who helped formulate the new system: "We wanted to see if we could create a more meaningful workplace, and secondly, we wanted a more productive organization."

Not enrichment. Eaton, however, eschewed one typical management approach in redesigning work relationships: It did not attempt to enrich jobs to make them more interesting. Nor did it assume that workers would want greater participation in decisions affecting them. Enriching jobs, Scobel says, "would have required major changes in technology in our new plants that were not practical, and we weren't sure that a lot of people wanted job enrichment."

Instead, Scobel says, the company tried to create "an enriched environment." Scobel adds: "That means that when a worker comes along who is interested in working on his equipment to learn how it works, or to get involved in total operations, he can do that. On the other hand, there are perfectly satisfactory employees who do not want a more enriched job. We are not trying to force people into more responsibility."

Productivity gains. The "new philosophy" emphasizes equal treatment between blue-collar and office workers. Thus, informal "dialogues" have replaced the formal interviews in the hiring process, probationary periods for new employees have been eliminated, and blue-collar workers no longer have to punch time clocks. No longer, as in the old days, does a foreman recite a long list of disciplinary rules to a new worker. To demonstrate management's "trust" in the worker—a key element of the new approach—no formal system of rules and penalties is applied.

The new ideas worked so well at the Kearney plant that Eaton has adopted them in all 12 of the new plants it has subsequently opened. Under the new system, production workers are allowed to repair their own equipment and to switch work stations as bottlenecks occur. They, or their representatives, are invited to attend weekly staff meetings, production planning sessions, and other discussions.

Eaton officials say the new program aids productivity growth. Hourly product output in the new plants ranges up to 35½% higher than at Eaton's older plants. Scobel cautions that these gains are attributable in part to more advanced equipment in the new plants. But data indicate that the new plants are also more efficient in other ways: Absenteeism is running at a 0.5% to 3% rate in the new plants, compared with 6% to 12% in the old plants; turnover as the result of voluntary resignations has been reduced from as high as 60% a year in the old plants to 4% in the new ones.

There are some drawbacks. Partly because of the workers' greater flexibility in performing different tasks and repairing equipment, the safety record of newer plants is poorer. And the less regimented climate sometimes reduces worker motivation. "Some employees take advantage of you," admits Rex McKinney, a supervisor at Greenville. In addition, because the new plants have fewer prescribed rules for workers, supervisors have a more difficult job than their counterparts in traditional plants. "You have to use a lot of judgement," McKinney says.

No grievance system. The "new philosophy" also omits one major feature of life in most traditional industrial plants: the formal grievance procedure. Under Eaton's system, supervisors are expected to handle workers' gripes and problems such as prolonged absences or poor performance through counseling. That is often difficult. Says supervisor Elmer Jackson at Greenville: "You try to build a spirit of pride and teamwork, but it is true that some people don't have as much ambition as others."

However, the supervisors themselves often present problems. Many supervisors up to and including plant managers find it difficult to adjust to the "new philosophy." Scobel, contending that the system can work only if management is committed to it, says Eaton has replaced several plant managers who could not throw off the rigid ways of traditional plants.

A nonunion climate. At Greenville the workers appear to enjoy an unusual level of freedom at work. And the plant provides amenities such as a recreation room. Some factory hands, who are on flexible work schedules, start work early in the morning so they can take an extended break later in the day to play table tennis or shoot pool. Ruth B. Dixon, a cable installer who formerly worked in conventional factories, sums up the attitude of many: "I enjoy not having to stand in line twice a day to punch a clock, and I like the way they leave you alone to do your job."

The 13 "new philosophy" plants are all located in rural areas of the South and Midwest, one factor that helps explain why they are nonunion. At least six union representation elections have been held at the 13 plants, and the workers—who largely come from nonunion backgrounds—have voted down the union in each case. In instituting the "new philosophy," Scobel maintains, "the objective is not to keep the union out." But obviously the combination of the nonunion tradition and improved methods in dealing with workers helps Eaton to escape unionization.

Scobel says Eaton is not pushing hard to convert its 52 existing plants to the "new philosophy," feeling that the idea will "have to grow up" in those plants rather than be imposed from above. The unions in the existing plants present an obstacle. They would oppose abolition of the grievance procedure, arguing that it is necessary to ensure that workers' complaints receive a fair hearing.

The United Auto Workers, which is generally more amenable to labor relations innovations than most unions, represents thousands of Eaton workers. It has agreed to cooperate in a trial run of a counseling program for problems such as absenteeism in two Canadian plants. "We're open-minded on the idea, but we will have to examine the effect before deciding whether it is worthwhile," says Dennis McDermott, a UAW vice president who oversees the union's Canadian units. He adds: "The counseling idea in no way supplants the grievance procedure."

Some UAW and Eaton officials privately express doubts that the new management techniques will be adopted by Eaton's older, unionized plants in the near future. "Once the we-against-them attitude builds up, it is very hard to change," says an Eaton executive.

greater effort for these two aspects of business to get together more often and more effectively so that some light might be thrown on the need for more balance and more scope in the reporting of economic news.

I would like to offer a few suggestions that, hopefully, will be implemented in the near future.

First, I am sure that there can be more productive discussions at the top level of management. It's not unusual for corporate chiefs and media top management to get together. It would be unusual for them to get together with the expressed purpose of discussing the state of economic affairs and how each of their businesses can play a hand in helping the public understand business and each other's business. Perhaps the corporate section of the Public Relations Society of America could act as a catalyst in bringing about such meetings. I know that I can readily volunteer my chairman for such a meeting.

A second suggestion involves the people working every day in communications in both of these businesses. The day has long gone that the corporate public relations function is handled by ex-newspaper people with a background and a feel for media needs. I would like to suggest a job exchange program between business journalists and company communicators. Let's swap jobs at the working level for one, two, or three months. Let's put an aspiring young public relations practitioner into the newsroom or TV studio, and put a journalistic peer into the corporate jungle.

I back that suggestion with a concrete offer to do just that in Eaton's communications department. What am I offered for one bright young corporate PR type—a business-news writer? An assistant TV news producer? A trade magazine specialist? Whatever the swap I think it will be well worth it for both sides—even if it never becomes nationwide in scope.

Finally, those of us who utilize the media to sell products can work harder to use them to sell our system. In Eaton's case, we strive to do this in two ways. First of all, we seek to sponsor TV programs that are timely and imaginative documentaries featuring in-depth, issues-oriented subjects. Presently, we are sponsoring Bill Moyers' special reports on CBS. We're not looking for numbers. We've got little to sell off the supermarket counters. We are trying to reach specific audiences who are important to our business and to this country. We've been pleased with the results.

In addition, our commercials on these programs are designed to sell not only Eaton but the American system. Several of our commercials are devoted to such subjects as the myth of planned obsolescence, in which our chairman, Del de Windt, discusses the positive benefits of open competition for consumers.

So, if the chiefs talk more—and the Indians change tribes—and we all use the media to sell our system, I believe we will have some strong beginnings and additional ideas about how to dispel that ominous cloud of ignorance surrounding these two different kinds of businesses.

We need a massive exchange of ideas before business and media can work together effectively and efficiently for improved economic understanding on the part of the public. As unashamed and unabashed free enterprisers, both business and the media business have a lot to gain.

THE SOCIAL REPONSIBILITY OF THE MEDIA IN REPORTING ON CORPORATE SOCIAL RESPONSIBILITY

ROBERT F. HURLEIGH

It is time for a reevaluation of the responsibilities of all of our societal institutions, not only of business but also of the media, according to Robert F. Hurleigh, the president of Mutual Broadcasting Company from 1957 to 1967. The media have failed to fulfill their own social responsibility because they have presented the condition and performance of American business neither fully nor fairly. This irresponsibility, he maintains, has caused serious public misconceptions about the private enterprise system which, in turn, threaten our way of life.

A reporter, commentator, and news executive in broadcasting since the mid-1930s, Mr. Hurleigh serves or has served on the boards of directors of the National Alliance of Businessmen, the Radio Advertising Bureau, and the Advertising Council. A recipient of numerous awards from such organizations as Sigma Delta Chi and the American Legion, he is currently a communications consultant for the National Association of Manufacturers.

Do the media serve as "watchdogs" on business behavior? Do the media motivate business to behave in a socially responsible manner? Both of these questions must be answered in the affirmative, without qualification. It is the media's duty to be the watchdogs of our society, thus motivating all our institutions—business included—to behave in a responsible manner.

Watchdogs, as we all know, are useful. It is their function to prevent trespassing, which they often do simply by their presence. Their barking and nipping can motivate individuals and institutions even as the attentive sheep dog motivates the flock.

We should have no trouble in agreeing on the need for watchdogs, or the fact that they function as motivators.

We may not agree, however, when I expand the subject to "The Social Responsibility of the Media in Reporting on Corporate Social

Responsibility." Surely the time is long overdue for a reevaluation of the responsibilities of all our institutions, with no exception made for the media.

The future of business in a private enterprise system is inseparable from the future of industrial democracy. Western Europe, North America, and Japan produce 65 percent of all the goods and services generated in the world. They account for 75 percent of its trade. Their profit performance drives international commerce and finance; their investments, technology, managerial genius, and agricultural productivity are the dynamic forces of prosperity everywhere. They are the world's bankers and the world's inventors. Critics of the West, in the Communist world and elsewhere, have disparaged our system for half a century, but they have not solved any of their own problems. Ironically, they now turn to the industrial democracies for the technology, the techniques of analysis, planning, and management, the industrial systems and the marketing skills which their own system seems incapable of generating.

Former secretary of state Henry Kissinger, in taking note of the strengths of private enterprise in world affairs, said:

> Whenever countries of comparable resources have run the race together—Australia and Czechoslovakia, West and East Germany, Greece and Bulgaria, South and North Korea—the economy with a significant private sector has clearly done more in fulfilling the aspirations of its people than its socialist counterpart. The world community cannot ignore the affairs of business if it is successfully to shape a new political structure that serves peace and the well-being of mankind.
>
> Private enterprise as we know it today is, in fact, an effective vehicle for the development of science and technology, for the application of new knowledge to the world's resources, for the management of the international capital markets, and for the promotion of trade and commerce among nations. No foreseeable increase in public assistance can possibly come close to meeting the needs of the developing countries. Private capital alone can close the gap, and without the conditions and restrictions that governments are likely to attach.

If the United States is to play its proper role in the world we must understand the moral basis of our national wealth. The United States earned its wealth by hard and creative work. In getting rich, we did not make anybody poor. On the contrary, the industrial development that created American wealth is playing a leading part in the process that is making it possible for the whole world to become wealthy.

In his book *The Next 200 Years*, Herman Kahn gives ten reasons why the gap between rich and poor countries actually helps the poor countries develop faster. He notes that rich countries provide markets, new technology, useful examples, and investment capital. None of this is perfect and little is provided free. But it would be much harder for the poor countries to advance if we had not gone before. The gap between the rich and poor nations is an engine pulling the rest of the world from its poor past to its rich future.

That is not to say that the United States has no responsibility to improve the world. But the responsibility it bears is the responsibility of wealth and power, not of malfeasance. We must help the Third World because we are the rich and they are poor, not because we caused their poverty.

Perhaps we shouldn't expect the less-developed countries to openly accept our perspective, since it is often to the personal advantage of ambitious leaders to blame Uncle Sam. But surely the media of this country could consider these truths and refuse to accept their arguments as to how we should behave. Surely the experienced and knowledgeable editor/journalist should know that these leaders are as self-interested and as fallible as we are—and we aren't helping them by riding the guilt wagon.

AN IRRESPONSIBLE PRESS

The essence of this tender essay is to set forth certain truths as evidence that the media have not presented fully, nor fairly, the condition and the performance of American business, and that this irresponsibility has caused serious misconceptions of the private enterprise system by the public. As public confidence hangs in the balance, so does the American way of life as we know it.

It is not strange that with the best system of communication and dissemination of information in the world we are forced to admit that "profits" and the "profit motive" are misunderstood by most Americans? Is it not strange that our media businesses—most of them publicly held and becoming multimedia in scope as they seek their own profits—seem unconcerned and unworried by the public's misconception of this factor in our economic progress which is so necessary to increase jobs?

Hopefully, there may be a reevaluation of the social responsibility of the media by its leaders, those at the top who are accountable to their stockholders and their employees and are expected to maintain a profit structure to sustain ever-increasing costs and attain the financial rewards which the investing public had reason to anticipate when they bought shares in media corporations.

Although quick to dig through banal generalities to the rock-bed specifics of other people's business, the media seldom publicize their own mistakes. This clannishness goes beyond the fraternalism of journalism to a sort of "gentlemen's agreement" to blackout any subject relating to media misfeasance, particularly if there is a shared ideology. The recent appointment of ombudsmen by a few newspapers is in recognition of the public's growing disaffection with the media. But these public defenders seldom touch on the truly important subjects but rather act as "explainers," explaining the problems of deadline or the editor's reasoning.

But as it does for most competitive businesses, the marketplace may force segments of the media to understand corporate responsibility.

Business Week magazine reported in 1976 that the financial health of the *New York Times* had seriously deteriorated. Said *Business Week*: "Editorially and politically the newspaper has slid precipitously to the left and has become stridently anti-business in tone, ignoring the fact that the *Times* itself is a business—and one with very serious problems."

In March of 1977, Arthur Ochs Sulzberger, publisher and chief executive officer of the *Times*, urged members of the Detroit Economic Club to "do some complaining . . . and fight for your rights as businesspeople." The next day, the chairman of Chase Manhattan Bank, David Rockefeller, speaking to the New York Economic Club, said he would follow Mr. Sulzberger's advice by examining a serious banking issue with which I am sure this audience is familiar.

Mr. Rockefeller asked us to recall that last year, America's newspaper headlines and nightly TV news shows were dominated by a spate of dramatic stories about banks allegedly in trouble all over the country. Understandably, these stories shook the confidence of the American public in our financial institutions at a time when confidence was badly needed.

To gain some perspective on these issues, let's look back briefly to the "problem bank" story of January 1976. It began with an article emblazoned across the front page of the Sunday *Washington Post*, which centered on Chase and Citibank. Basically, the story concerned a then eighteen-month-old confidential report of the comptroller of the currency—obtained through unnamed sources—which allegedly labeled both institutions as "problem banks" due primarily to classified loans. Reaction from the banks, the comptroller, and the chairman of the Federal Reserve Board was immediate and unified in its denunciation of the newspaper article and the implications it suggested for the soundness of the U.S. banking system. Nonetheless, the damage was done, and the media across the country joined in on what appeared to be a blockbuster story.

Two days after the *Post*'s revelations, the *New York Times* rushed to print with a one-year-old Federal Reserve Board list of thirty-five "problem" bank holding companies. Some days later, an FDIC list of

300 "problem banks" was revealed. Television anchormen warned of the "impending erosion of confidence in the banking system."

To the casual newspaper reader and TV viewer—and I should add the foreign financial markets—these stories could not help but indicate that the banking system was clearly in a shaky condition. To many, in fact, it probably appeared that the press had uncovered a scandal in financial terms which was the equivalent of Watergate.

But, far from revealing a scandal—or a group of problem banks—the facts were that the banks in question were strong and dynamic institutions supporting a strong banking and economic system. The real news was the ability of the banks to overcome losses caused by the real estate loans which had gone sour in the recession but had been covered by the prudent policy of recognizing that losses on loans do occur and setting aside funds to cover such losses should they occur. Thus, the news should have been that eighteen months earlier many of the nation's banks had been hit by heavy loan losses, but the banks in question had been able to absorb a high level of loan losses while still recording solid earnings and building a strong capital base.

Why, one might ask, was an eighteen-month-old story made to appear as reflecting a current situation? Surely the question of fairness and concern over objectivity must be considered when information a year and a half old—and taken out of context—is given bold headlines across the front pages of leading newspapers and made to appear as an accurate, balanced, and current report on the banking system.

Not one of the newspapers or television reporters noted that the banks could have set off a chain reaction by foreclosures, leading to bankruptcy and job losses that could have moved the recession into a major depression. This perspective was offered by few journalists, although financial writers and editors were aware of this fact, or certainly should have been.

Thus, we return to the need for the media's social responsibility as well as corporate social responsibility.

SWAYING THE PUBLIC WITH HEADLINES

More recently, New York City's administrators were accused of falsifying financial records to support a bond issue to gain funds to prevent municipal bankruptcy. Mayor Beame was the target of the SEC report, since he had been comptroller of the city prior to becoming mayor, although six banks and a New York brokerage firm were included in the charges as having known the city's desperate financial plight and the probability of the records being falsified even as they sold the bonds to the public. Mayor Beame, in a political pickle as he fought for reelection, attempted to shift all the blame to the banks for selling New York's municipal bonds to the public when they knew that the bonds were not supported by accurate financial information.

But anyone with half a memory knows that the media in New York were aware of the city's financial plight in 1975 and knew these facts. Yet, the media pressed the banking institutions to support the city.

It was, in a sense, a fight for the city's survival, and the media never blew the whistle, but dutifully publicized Mayor Beame's latest attempt to shift the blame and hang the evils on the horn of a "scapegoat."

There has been no reminder by the media of the perilous situation of New York City in 1975, and no reminder that the banking institutions were forced from a prudent posture by the media's support of the public's appeal to their civic duty to become involved.

Lest we forget this lack of whistle-blowing by the media on the phony financials presented by New York City's administration in 1975, we need only to note the abundance of information uncovered by the media in digging into the financial affairs of Bert Lance.

But it is ever thus. Large headlines on front pages have many of our citizens believing that corporate profits in some industries are obscene, while seldom reporting the fact that profits from media institutions are far greater on the average than the profits of other corporations.

The journalist and the editor know these facts, or should know that we have supermedia corporations through mergers and straight-out purchases of other media as well as diversification into other fields. There are corporate giants in media, and the time has come to take the blinders from some reporters who know but will not perceive, and to train, through journalism schools and workshops, those professionally engaged in reporting on the private enterprise system.

THE NEED FOR COMPETENCY IN A COMPLEX WORLD

At a moment in our nation's history when the fate of our economy and the future of our free enterprise system are among the most important stories to be covered, there are simply all too few journalists possessing the backgrounds to tell the story effectively.

Louis Banks, a former magazine editor now with Harvard Business School, says, "Reporters plunge into issues that mean life or death for management, employees, customers—even a community—without the slightest sense of business perspective. Some of them are like kids with loaded pistols, prowling through the forests of corporate complexity to play games of cowboys and indians, or good guys and bad guys. Their only interest in business is to find a negative story that will get them promoted out of business into Woodward and Bernstein."

It's no secret that businessmen and knowing journalists think newspaper coverage of business is atrocious. They feel reporters are biased against business and are incompetent to cover economic news.

The National Association of Manufacturers' educational arm, the Foundation for Economic Freedom (FEF), has a half dozen projects in the works aimed at enlightening the business editor as well as the general editor.

"We want to make these programs as wide-ranging as possible," said James N. Sites, FEF president and NAM senior vice-president for communications.

"So often the business story isn't confined to the business section. If it's unemployment or cost of living or wholesale prices . . . it's on page one," Sites said, adding that the front-page audience is less literate economically than the readers of business sections.

"What business seeks," Mr. Sites makes clear, "is simply the same kind of fair play that newsmen themselves would expect if someone were reporting on them. Not all business news is good news, and therefore business does not expect uniformly favorable treatment. What we do hope to see is a press that better understands economic realities and the gathering problems faced by the nation in this vital area."

The advisory council of FEF is made up of a cross section from the media, including William G. Mullen, executive vice-president of the National Newspaper Association; Charles Bartlett, Washington syndicated columnist; William E. Giles, editor of the *Detroit News;* Kenneth Gilmore, managing editor of *Reader's Digest;* Dr. Ray E. Hiebert, journalism dean at the University of Maryland; James Hulbert, senior vice-president of the National Association of Broadcasters; Herbert Klein, vice-president of Metromedia; Emmett Tyrrell, Jr., editor of *The Alternative;* Donald Rogers, economics editor of Hearst Newspapers; Kevin Phillips, syndicated columnist; and William Schabacker, public affairs manager of the American Newspaper Publishers Association.

Mr. Sites said he hopes such an advisory board will allay any fears that the NAM aims to manipulate journalists into reporting on business and economics the way businessmen want to be covered. And he added that "raising the competence of business-news reporting can only be good for business, for the journalism profession and, above all, for the American people, who look to the media to crystallize and make understandable the increasingly complex economic issues facing our nation."

Mr. Sites's observations are supported by a former president of CBS, Arthur R. Taylor, who has said that businessmen often complain that many reporters are biased against the profit system, but he does not believe this to be the case.

Mr. Taylor thinks that reporters simply lack an understanding of the system and therefore mistrust it, and that the public's lack of understanding and confidence toward business can be blamed on superficial press coverage. Too often, says the former president of CBS, "Reporters who are generalists are assigned to stories in which they have to explain complicated economic developments, and that too often they fail."

That, I submit, is a sad commentary on the media. The public has a right to assume that a reporter has knowledge of a subject, else the editor would not have made the assignment.

Solutions are not easily come by, but if the words "fairness" and "objectivity" can be recognized and established as goals, and competence and commitment to these goals are prime requisites to be met by both media and business, we will have made substantial progress toward reaching solutions.

It is not a question of First Amendment rights, for like Voltaire, whose remembered admonition to an antagonist that he disagreed violently with what he had said but would "defend to the death his right to say it," we hold that truth to be self-evident.

And lest we forget, Voltaire made it his business to shatter the pretensions and the hypocrisies of the social institutions of his day, leaving exposed the bitter truth. He as often ridiculed himself, once saying, "I laugh in order to keep myself from going mad."

SECTION **5**

THE BUSINESS OF THE MEDIA

There is at least one running business story which is not characterized by confrontation, which is covered continuously as opposed to episodically, but which is covered only by newspapers. That story is about the price of newsprint. Every fluctuation in the price of the paper on which newspapers are printed is duly reported to a mass public which must be fascinated with the story. Moreover, we are usually even told why the price is fluctuating.

Of all business news, why should the price of newsprint be the story most comprehensively covered? The answer is too obvious: the price of newsprint is an important factor affecting the business of the newspaper.

As many of the contributors to this volume have pointed out, the media are businesses, producing products and (hopefully) profits in competitive marketplaces. But the media are businesses with several differences: they operate in oligopolistic or monopolistic situations without threat of anti-trust action; their products are protected from governmental regulation by the First Amendment; and they claim to pursue truth, not profit, as a primary goal.

The pursuit of profit can conflict with the pursuit of truth when publishers or broadcasters attempt to attract audiences by giving people simply what they want to read, see, or hear. Considerations of profit can affect truth when information offensive to audiences or advertisers is withheld, when diversity is restricted, when funds devoted to newsgathering are restricted, when space or time devoted to news is sold for advertising, or in many other ways. Others maintain that the press cannot be truly free or independent until it is financially secure. Financial security in the form of healthy profits is the best means of assuring a press which is not subject to the influence of money.

Another economic issue confronting the media has to do with access. The First Amendment was based on the notion that from the babble of many voices truth would emerge. Everyone could participate and contribute to the marketplace of ideas. In an era of mass media and concentration the individual's freedom of expression and entry to the marketplace of ideas is economically restricted.

The authors in this section address these issues and others in their discussions of the business of the media. In a sense, these authors divide into liberal and conservative stances expressing different concerns and perspectives. Collectively, however, they demonstrate that media concerns with business and economic issues are not restricted to coverage from the sidelines. Business and business problems are as much a part of the media as of any other business.

ECONOMICS AND FREEDOM OF THE PRESS[1]

JON G. UDELL

According to Jon Udell, press freedom requires more than a constitutional guarantee. It also requires economic security and freedom. Thus, while profits may represent a conflict for the media, the pursuit of profit influences the pursuit of truth by making the pursuit of truth possible.

Udell looks at the press as an industry (a relatively large industry—the third largest employer among the nation's 451 manufacturing industries) and places profits in perspective in that context. Profits, he says, are a cost of production, a means to an end. The end, in this case, is the stimulation and maintenance of diversity and choice in media products.

Declaring that economic and intellectual freedom are inextricably linked, Udell calls for a better understanding not only of profit, but of all dimensions of our economic life in the operation of the free press and a free society.

The Irwin Maier Professor of Business at the University of Wisconsin, Dr. Udell has received the Sidney S. Goldish Award for "significant and continuing contributions to newspaper research." An economist for the American Newspaper Publishers Association, he is a director of the Wisconsin State Chamber of Commerce. He is the author of The U.S. Economy and Newspaper Growth *and* The Economics of the American Newspaper.

Freedom of the press has long been recognized as indispensable to American democracy. The First Amendment of the Constitution proclaims this freedom, and with its protection the American press probes fearlessly into areas where the media of most other nations may pry only timidly, if at all.

However, our cherished freedom of the press requires far more than its constitutional guarantee; it also requires economic security and substantial economic freedom. In other words, the free press of the United States rests primarily on two foundations: the First Amendment, or the *right* to report the news; and economic independence and security, or the *means* to report the news.

The interdependence between economic freedom and our other personal and political freedoms is not well recognized. However, in no industry is the importance of economic freedom more vivid than in the communications industry. It is, for example, highly doubtful that there would have been a timely exposure of Watergate had government owned and controlled the press of this nation. But, the free and privately owned press did investigate and expose Watergate and, in the process, initiated the democratic pressures and processes leading to the resignation of the president and commander in chief—an event which was difficult for those peoples without democracy and a free press to understand.

THE FREE MIND

Edith Efron, in an address entitled "The Free Mind and the Market," has stated, "Intellectual and political freedom and capitalism are inextricably linked. . . . If you destroy capitalism, you will destroy intellectual freedom." She documents this contention with the observation that in the free nations of the world where there has been true freedom of speech, that freedom has prevailed only so long as the nations involved have remained dominantly capitalistic.

While I do not care for the adjective "capitalistic" to describe our type of economic system, the correlation of a free press with economic freedom is not a historical accident. No government can control our right to think. There is no form of private property more absolute than our thoughts. While they can be influenced, our thoughts cannot be censored. Furthermore, government can only partially censor speech. However, a government is able to censor most of our intellectual and artistic works because they are commodities, they are products in the marketplace. As Efron observes, "The First Amendment, applied in its purest form, actually protects the marketing process of the intellectual product—starting with its inception all the way through the marketing chain, from creator to the ultimate consumer."

PROBLEMS IN EUROPE

Further insight into the role of economics in freedom of the press is provided by the problems of the remaining free presses of Europe. Unfortunately, the rapid rise of costs has produced severe economic difficulties for most European newspapers. France, Italy, and Sweden are now providing financial aid in the form of newsprint subsidies and other benefits. With governments becoming increasingly sensitive about how the press portrays them, relying on such aid is highly precarious. As Max Clos, editorial director of the financially distressed and government-subsidized *Le Figaro* of France points out, "If survival means asking for more government aid, then freedom of the press is finished."[2] A similar view has been expressed by the respected Hamburg weekly, *Die Zeit*. This German paper has asked, once journalists are dependent on proposed government aid, "will the press still dare to bite the hand that feeds it?"[3] As Ernest Meyer, director of the International Press Institute emphasizes, government aid on a continuing basis is "a very dangerous undertaking."

A CHALLENGE IN THE UNITED STATES

Thanks to a combination of circulation and advertising revenues, the majority of the privately owned media of the United States are reasonably prosperous. However, the heavy reliance on advertising, which supplies about 70 percent of newspaper revenues and almost 100 percent of broadcast revenues, creates a challenge for professional journalists. How does a free press present objective facts and news about the world and sometimes subjective promotion for an advertised product and still retain believability and respect among its readers or listeners? Perhaps even more important, will a medium's economic self-interests—its need to attract and hold advertising—be allowed to modify or otherwise bias its presentation of the news?

In 1911, a group of Chicago newspapermen felt so keenly that the press should be absolutely uncompromised by any dependence on advertising that they launched an adless newspaper, the *Chicago Day Book*. One of its moving spirits was poet and historian Carl Sandburg. The paper, a penny daily, died in 1917. Another adless newspaper, a New York City daily, the *PM*, suffered a similar fate.

Long ago, many editors derived a pragmatic solution to the need for advertising revenues while maintaining editorial independence: make every effort to keep advertising and puffery out of news columns, and keep the ad sales representatives out of the newsroom.

This solution has and undoubtedly will continue to work successfully so long as the media remain sufficiently prosperous and profitable. This brings us directly to the topic of profit.

PROFIT CONTROVERSIES

No dimension of American economic life is more misunderstood than profit. Some businesspeople believe that the basic purpose of industry is to profit, and that profits are the "engines of progress." Marxists, on the other hand, contend that profits are a great evil—the result of an exploitation of labor. Still others are persuaded that profits are primarily the product of monopoly power and the exploitation of consumers. None of these views represents an accurate vision of the great majority of profits in our nation today.

In addition to being misunderstood, most Americans grossly overestimate the profitability of industry. As you are probably aware, recent public opinion polls show that the average estimate of the profitability of American industry is 30 percent of sales revenue. Among college students the average estimate is 44 percent. This is one erroneous impression about profits which businesses wish were true. Actual data show that profits usually average around 5 percent of sales. Although 5 percent is only one-half of what the public thinks would be a reasonable profit, the really relevant issues for us to consider are encompassed by the questions: What *are* profits? What social role, for good or bad, do they play? How do profits relate to freedom of the press and our democratic way of life?

THE BLESSINGS AND EVILS OF PROFIT

First, let's recognize that profits can be a blessing or an evil, depending upon how they are derived. If huge profits are earned by exploiting labor and consumers, I doubt that any of us would consider them socially desirable, even though they might be put to good use—as were many of the profits of the robber barons in the earlier development of our nation. Our country has an extensive body of labor and anti-trust laws to prevent profits by exploitation, as well as extensive union activity and many competitive forces, in addition to tax laws, which limit the profitability of industry. In fact, in several recent years the profitability of many industries has been so low that the businesses involved would have earned more if the assets involved could have been deposited in a federally insured bank or savings and loan association. This is one of the reasons why the stock market is lower today than it was over a decade ago, even though the value of the dollar has depreciated substantially.

A reasonable profit, and in fact most profits today, are basically a *cost* of production. Modern industry, including the free press, relies heavily on technology. The technology, which is so much a source of our standard of living, requires substantial capital. That portion of the capital which is borrowed carries with it an interest obligation which is readily considered by society as a cost of doing business.

The other major source of capital is invested or equity capital. Although this capital incurs the greatest risk because borrowed capital has a prior claim on the assets of a business, we record no cost for equity capital. Certainly, those who have invested and risked their savings in a business enterprise, such as a newspaper or broadcast facility, deserve some compensation. Just as one expects a compensation for those monies deposited in the security of a federally insured bank or savings institution, a reasonable level of aftertax profit is the just compensation for and a necessary cost of invested capital.

Earlier I mentioned a dislike for the use of the label "capitalism" to describe our economic way of life. The fact is that all modern economic systems are capitalistic. Natural resources, labor, and capital are the three inevitable ingredients of modern production. All economies require capital. In fact, it would be more logical to describe Russia's economic system as capitalistic because a far larger proportion of their gross national product and income goes to capital accumulation than does our own. In turn, a smaller proportion of Soviet income goes to labor—the proletariat.

In our economy we rely heavily on private enterprise, freedom in the marketplace, the profit motive, and the forces of competition. For example, it is national policy to encourage a diversity of privately owned news "voices," and we, as consumers, have the freedom to select those "voices" which we wish to attend to. This free market system of economic organization is an integral part of our political democracy. Economics is so much a part of almost everything we do that it is difficult to envision political and personal freedom without economic freedom. As Nikolai Lenin once said, "Give me control over a man's economic actions, and hence over his means of survival, and except for a few occasional heroes, I'll promise to deliver to you men who think, write, and behave as you want them to."

From a social point of view the profit component of our American enterprise system is a means to an end. Profits stimulate and sustain a great diversity of private industry, and in so doing provide the alternatives necessary for freedom of choice to be meaningful. From a private point of view profits are the cost and compensation of equity capital. However, all capital, public or private, has a cost. Allow me to paraphrase a passage from one of Peter Drucker's books to put it in the context of a newspaper:

> If archangels instead of publishers were responsible for the management of newspapers, they would still have to be concerned with profitability, despite their total lack of personal interest in making profits. This applies with equal force to those far from angelic individuals, including the commissioners who run Soviet Russia's press and other business enterprises, and who have to run businesses on a higher profit margin than the wicked capitalists of the West.[4]

The importance of profit and prosperity to the free press does create a conflict. As media critic Ben Bagdikian puts it:

> On the one hand, the daily paper in the United States is a product of professionals whose reporting is supposed to be the result of disciplined intelligence gathering and analysis in order to present an honest and under-

standable picture of the social and political world. If this reportage is in any way influenced by concern for money-making, it is regarded as corrupt journalism. On the other hand, the American daily newspaper ... has to remain solvent and has to make a profit or else it will not survive. If it does not make money there will be no reporting of any kind, ethical or unethical. If the corporate end of the enterprise does not have an effective concern for making money it will be regarded by everyone, including journalists, as incompetent, negligent and a disservice to the community.[5]

While this "split personality" of the communications business is a constant source of potential tension between the business and editorial offices, the history of the press vividly reveals the importance of earning an adequate profit. Many a news medium has failed to earn a reasonable profit and, consequently, has ceased to serve its community in any way.

The essence of what I'm saying is this: editorial independence is essential to our democratic way of life and is protected by the First Amendment against government control. However, that constitutional guarantee is made meaningful by a diversity of news voices and the economic security of the press. As publisher John Colburn, president of Landmark Community Newspapers, has pointed out, "It is economic independence ... that provides newspapers with a strong bulwark to resist pressures from politicians, government bureaucrats, advertisers, and special interest groups."[6]

While profits are essential to editorial excellence, this is very much a two-way street. Editorial excellence contributes to profit. This is more true today than ever before because the public is increasingly better educated and more skeptical of all institutions, including business, government, the church, and the press. Editorial excellence also is increasingly important because the development of television has provided an additional mode of communication and many more competing news voices than we once had. There is evidence indicating that successful media managements are acutely aware of the interrelationship between editorial excellence and healthy financial statements. At the same time, I believe that there needs to be an even greater recognition of this interrelationship by our nation's media personnel and journalism educators. In addition, we need a better understanding not only of profit, but of all dimensions of our economic life in the operation of the free press and a free society.

PROFITABILITY OF THE AMERICAN PRESS

Prior to closing, let's take a brief look at the profitability of the American press. Fortunately, most newspapers and other communication businesses are reasonably profitable. Most are earning sufficient returns on investment to compensate equity capital and remain in business. However, some members of the communications community are in financial trouble and, over the years, quite a few have failed.

Because there is freedom of entry to the communications business, we have about as many newspapers today as there were at the end of World War II, and there are many more broadcast facilities. This is a unique phenomenon in the American economy. In most industries, economies of large scale have decreased the number of units involved.

There is much that we do not know about media profitability because many newspapers and broadcast facilities are closely held enterprises. However, there is extensive financial data for most of the publicly owned media companies. These companies, in addition to their broadcast and other operations, publish approximately 200 daily newspapers accounting for 23 percent of United States daily circulation.

John Morton, a financial analyst, calculates that in 1976 the aftertax profitability of the thirteen newspaper companies he studied averaged 10 percent of sales.[7] This was considerably higher than the 5.5 percent aftertax return of all manufacturers during the same time period. Newspapers, by the way, are classified as manufacturers by the U.S. Department of Commerce. In fact, among the nation's 451 manufacturing industry classifications, only steel mills and manufacturers of automotive parts and accessories employ more people than newspaper publishers. Therefore, in examining the profitability of the press, we are considering one of our nation's largest industries.

Profit as a percent of sales doesn't really tell us much. If profit is the cost of and reward for equity capital, then it is profit as a percent of invested capital that really counts. The absolute amount of profit is even less informative. Unfortunately, if a large corporation earns $30 million, some feel that is too much for any company to earn. Whether it is too much or too little depends upon how much has been invested. If that $30 million represents only a one percent return on equity capital, the company is probably on the verge of bankruptcy.

In 1976, the return on stockholders' equity of the thirteen media companies averaged 16 percent. The range of individual companies ran from a low of 11.9 percent to a high of 24 percent.

A 16 percent average return is fairly high. However, given the high rate of inflation, the risks associated with an equity investment, and the fact that the combination of inflation and required accounting procedures tends to lead to an overstatement of profits, the return was not unduly high. Also in most years the media do not do that well, and the average of the 13 companies may have been well above the average profitability of all newspapers, broadcasters, and magazines.

Unfortunately, the media are facing a rapid escalation of costs. For example, newsprint costs, which may constitute 30 percent or more of all costs in a large newspaper, rose 80 percent in the last three years. The escalation of postal rates has had a very detrimental effect on magazines and those newspapers using mail circulation. To remain profitable, advertising and circulation rates have been increased. These increases, combined with rigorous cost-control measures and the rebound of the economy, should allow most American newspapers to maintain their financial health. A study by Arthur D. Little predicts that the broadcast media will face greater cost increases than the print media in the years ahead.

THE ROLE OF TECHNOLOGY

To a major extent, technology is enabling most newspapers to remain profitable during a period of rapidly escalating costs. Twenty years ago newspapers were produced in ways essentially unchanged for more than half a century. But if Rip van Winkle had been a newspaperman, and had begun his twenty-year sleep in the late 1950s, he would awaken today to a technological revolution in his industry. When well managed, this advance of technology can help to insure the financial health of the news media.

EDITORIAL TRUTH AND THE BOTTOM LINE

Does the pursuit of profit influence the pursuit of truth? Obviously, the pursuit of profit should not be allowed to influence the coverage of the news or the content of the editorial page. Such an occurrence would be a gross violation of moral principles and the public trust. While of lesser significance, such a violation also would destroy a news organization's public goodwill and be bad business policy.

But, the above question also should be examined in another light. The honest pursuit of profit through good media management and the provision of a valuable public service does influence the pursuit of truth. Adequate profits enable the news media to probe deeply into the events of the day, to attract and retain high quality personnel, to withstand any pressures from government, industry, and other special-interest groups, and to meet the other responsibilities which accompany the privileges of the First Amendment.

It might also be noted that the pursuit of truth by the press also is dependent on profitable private enterprises throughout the economy. As noted earlier, approximately two-thirds of the revenues of newspapers and most of the revenues of the broadcast media are derived from advertising services. If government owned and controlled all other industry, government would hold most of the purse strings of the press.

In several significant respects, our free press does rest on two foundations: the *First Amendment*, or the right to report the truth; and *economic independence and security*, or the means to pursue and report the truth.

NOTES

1. Several components of this presentation are adapted from *The Economics of the American Newspaper* by Jon G. Udell, a book published by Hastings House in late 1977.

2. "Europe's Hard Up Newspapers," *The Wall Street Journal,* September 15, 1975, p. 10.

3. Ibid, p. 10.

4. Peter Drucker, *Management: Tasks, Responsibilities, Practices* (New York: Harper & Row, 1973, 1974), p. 60.

5. Ben H. Bagdikian, "Newspaper Economics, So What?" *Journalism Newsletter,* University of Maryland, Spring 1975, p. 1.

6. John H. Colburn, "Economics of the Press," *Proceedings: Education for Newspaper Journalists in the Seventies and Beyond,* American Newspaper Publishers Association Foundation and Association for Education in Journalism, October 31–November 2, 1973, p. 102.

7. John Morton, Newspaper Research Letter, Colin, Hochstin Co., April 18, 1977.

MASS MEDIA: THE ECONOMICS OF ACCESS TO THE MARKETPLACE OF IDEAS

WILLIAM H. MELODY

According to William H. Melody, the greatest threat to freedom of expression in the United States is not government censorship, but the possibility that private entrepreneurs will tend to monopolize the marketplace of ideas in the name of economic efficiency and private profit. Melody suggests that the mass communication process has been transformed into an economic production and marketing process responsive not to the ideas of press freedom, but to the requirements of production and sales efficiency.

If the First Amendment is to remain meaningful—in the sense of diversity in the marketplace of ideas and enhancement of individual freedom of expression—Melody advocates preserving a high degree of competition both within and between the media and establishing specific media access rights for individuals.

Professor and chairman of the department of communication studies at Simon Fraser University, Dr. Melody is a former senior economist at the Federal Communications Commission. His books include Communications Technology and Social Policy *and* Children's Television: The Economics of Exploitation.

The terms "freedom of speech" and "freedom of the press" always have been better understood as abstract principles than as practical realities. Seldom do we focus with precision on the circumstances surrounding their application. These circumstances include the substantial constraints and discriminatory barriers placed upon individuals and classes in society that make these freedoms inevitably qualified, relative, and conditional.

The important dimensions of freedom of speech as a communication process have been: (1) Who has freedom to speak? (2) about what? (3) to whom? In theory everyone has freedom to speak about matters of his or her choice to anyone or everyone willing to listen. But some people are more articulate or outspoken than others. As a result of differences in family circumstances, education, natural abilities, and other factors, some people are more widely informed and capable of speaking on a wider range of subjects. Most important, freedom to speak has meaning only when the speaker has a listener or an audience. Some speakers have very limited access to listeners; others have broad and continuous access to large audiences.

The relationships between speaker, audience, and subject matter are dynamic and interrelated. Sometimes we are recipients of the "speech" of others as individuals or as parts of small or large audiences. What we have to speak about depends heavily on what we have learned from the speech of others. Those speakers with access to the broadest network of audiences have the greatest freedom to influence the subject matter flowing through the multitude of communication networks in society. It is these privileged people that exercise primary influence over the agenda of a nation. Their freedom of speech is vastly different than that of most people.

Historically, guarantees of freedom of speech have not been positive freedoms of access to audiences. Rather, they have provided protection from the imposition of certain restrictions against freedom of speech. The First Amendment to the Constitution of the United States prevents Congress from making laws that abridge the freedom of speech and the press. Although it often is stated that the purpose of the First Amendment is to preserve an uninhibited marketplace of ideas in which truth ultimately will prevail, it simply precludes the establishment of artificial legal barriers.[1] It provides no protection to those whose freedom of speech may be denied or severely restricted by other kinds of constraints or barriers. It provides no prohibition against corporations, unions, government agencies, churches, and other institutions in society from acting to restrict the freedom of speech of individuals. It provides no guarantee that there will be a diversity of ideas in an uninhibited marketplace to which all citizens have reasonable, if not equal, access. It does not prevent the marketplace of ideas from being monopolized and barriers to entry created. It simply precludes the government from legislating government monopoly and creating the barriers.

It might be said then that the greatest threat to freedom of speech in the United States resides in the possibility that private entrepreneurs will tend to monopolize the marketplace of ideas in the name of economic efficiency and private profit. The threat is not from the political system, but from the economic system. Freedom of speech that is denied or restricted because of economic circumstances never has been protected by the Constitution or law. If, as a result of economic conditions, access to the marketplace of ideas is restricted to a privileged few, it may even be justified as necessary to achieve economic efficiency. This paper explores some of the changing economic conditions surrounding the marketplace of ideas today and the terms and conditions of access to it.

THE MASS MEDIA

In modern times, an important fourth dimension has been added to the nature of freedom of speech. In addition to the issue "Who has freedom to speak to whom about what?" must be added, "by what media?" The communications media have fundamentally changed the nature of communication processes. The development of the mass media, initially through newspapers and more recently television, created opportunities to reach vast audiences. But these vast audiences can only be reached by employing communication technology with production processes that are costly and sophisticated. Freedom to speak through the media technology is constrained by the substantial barriers of economic cost and limited production capacity. The mediated communication process is transformed into an economic production and marketing process responsive to the requirements for production and sales efficiency. The subject matter that is addressed in the mass media is influenced dominantly by the economic conditions surrounding the creation and maintenance of readership, audiences, and advertisers.

The press and television communicate information that can be selected, packaged, and sold as marketable commodities. The range in choice of subject matter available to the reporters, editors, and programming directors of the mass media is severaly restricted by the economic constraints of the marketplace. The range of choice of subject matter for readership and audiences is limited to that provided by the mass media.

The mass media add to the total number of communication processes and networks in which people may engage, but they also displace a significant portion of traditional communications. For a few select people the mass media provide a freedom of speech previously unattainable by providing access to audiences of millions. For most people they restrict their freedom of speech by denying them access to the mass media and by taking away potential listeners and readers, who now form part of a mass-media audience and receive a different set of messages. The mass media tend to make people "speak" less and spend more of their time as part of mass reading, listening, and viewing audiences. Moreover, the selected messages that are transmitted over the mass media heavily influence the content of other communication processes and networks.

But perhaps the most significant aspect of the mass media is that they have become institutions in their own right, operated primarily as profit-seeking corporations and in all circumstances subject to the constraints of economic costs. The major functions of "speaking" through the mass media—reporting, editing, program creation, advertising, etc.—have been specialized and professionalized, creating a further barrier to access for the layman. The mass media have become a standardized production and marketing process in which the messages communicated are constrained and directed in both quantity and quality to meet the economic imperatives of that process.

As an institution in its own right the press acquired special protection of its freedom of speech in the First Amendment, which states that Congress shall make no law "abridging the freedom of speech, or the press." The Constitution does not address potential conflicts between freedom of individual speech and freedom of the press as an institution. It does not define who in the press has freedom to do what. It does not examine whether freedom of speech requires access to the press by individual people. It simply precludes Congress from making any law that abridges the freedom of the press, a formal institution of speech in modern societies.

Television did not exist at the time of passage of the U.S. Constitution. It has developed under a technology and industrial structure that differs fundamentally from that of newspapers. In most respects television carries the mass media characteristics of the press several steps further. The technology and production process is more costly and sophisticated. The audiences reached are substantially larger. The capacity to supply messages is more restricted and more economically valuable. The barriers to access to "speak" over the television medium to its vast audiences are greater. Its influence over other communications processes and networks is more pervasive and dominant. By virtually all measures television is the more influential mass medium today.

If the dominant forms of communication in society are the mass media, and the marketplace of ideas has essentially become a mass-media marketplace, what does freedom of speech mean in this media environment? Are the rights of individual freedom of speech to be replaced gradually by the rights of the media organizations to constrain, swallow up, or direct the content of individual speech? Diversity in the marketplace of ideas and individual freedom of speech can be enhanced in two basic ways: (1) preserving a high degree of competition both within and between the media so as to increase the diversity of sources of information and material selected for transmission over the mass media; and (2) establishing specific access rights of individuals to the mass media under certain circumstances. This introduces difficult problems of defining operational terms and conditions of access and will still require major restrictions. Let us now turn to an examination of the conditions of competition and access in the mass media.

LAISSEZ-FAIRE AND RESTRICTIONS
ON THE MARKETPLACE OF IDEAS

The First Amendment to the Constitution was passed during an era of laissez-faire economic philosophy. The controls of government in economic affairs were being rebelled against throughout Europe. It is not surprising that freedom of speech and the press in the U.S. Constitution coincided with the publication of Adam Smith's *Wealth of Nations*, the classic work developing the case for free competition in economic affairs.

Extending from the idea of laissez-faire in domestic economic affairs, the notion of free trade among nations became fashionable, particularly among nations that would benefit from it. Free competition and free trade implied no government restrictions and free access to markets by anyone who chose to enter. But after long experience in economic affairs, it has been recognized that the freedom of entry into economic markets can be restricted by factors other than government prohibition. The monopolization of economic markets frequently has been used to establish substantial barriers to entry. The U.S. anti-trust laws have been established as policy directed toward the prevention of the accumulation of undue monopoly power and its attendant characteristics of restriction against freedom of entry to economic markets. In economic terms there has been a realization that the effective conditions of freedom of access to economic markets cannot be maintained simply by prohibiting restrictions legislated by government. It requires the active application of public policy directed to the maintenance of that freedom.

Freedom from government restrictions is a policy to follow an implicit set of rules as determined by a laissez-faire marketplace. The inherited conditions will differ among the different participants. Some will have more power, more resources, or other inherited advantages. Others will lack them and be foreclosed from effective participation. For them freedom of entry to the market means that they will have no entry or very restricted entry under severely disadvantageous conditions. Thus, nations have come to recognize that free trade will benefit some nations at the expense of others. If the international economic system is to operate to the mutual advantage of all trading nations, it may be necessary to establish certain terms of trade that to some countries will be restrictions. This has been incorporated into international economic policies for some time now.

The same issues have arisen in recent years over the free flow of information across international boundaries. Third World countries are expressing increasing concern about the meaning of an international free flow of information for them. Third World countries do not have the established media institutions with substantial resources, advanced technology, professional staff, and an inventory of vast quantities of programs, data banks, and information files. For them the free flow of information policy is one that provides access for the bombardment of Third World countries with television programs, news reporting, and other information from a few select developed countries such as the United States and the USSR. It allows other nations to interpret the world for them and to supply them with all possible sources of media production.

As such, it may prevent in these countries the development of institutions that are capable of participating effectively in the international marketplace of the free flow of information. As a result, many Third World countries now are moving to establish communication policies that will place restrictions on the free flow of information into their countries. If the free flow of information is a one-way pipeline, then diversity in the marketplace of ideas is not being promoted. The policy of laissez-faire may be a very restrictive one. Let us now turn to the nature of competition in the U.S. domestic media industries.

THE STATE OF COMPETITION IN THE MASS MEDIA

The appearance of major economic and organizational barriers to entry to the media industries has thrust into question the meaning of the First Amendment "freedoms." Do they require an affirmative dimension whereby they could be used to hold open and maintain access to the media marketplace in the face of these economic barriers? Jerome Barron argues that the First Amendment must be extended to encompass an affirmative dimension to guarantee rights of access.

> There is an anomaly in our constitutional law. While we protect expression once it has come to the fore, our law is indifferent to creating opportunities for expression. Our constitutional theory is in the grip of a romantic conception of free expression, a belief that the "marketplace of ideas" is freely accessible. But if ever there were a self-operating marketplace of ideas, it has long ceased to exist. The mass media's development of an antipathy to ideas requires legal intervention if novel and unpopular ideas are to be assured of a forum.[2]

At the time of the American Revolution only thirty-seven newspapers were published on a regular basis in the thirteen colonies. Boston, Philadelphia, and New York each had at least three competing papers.[3] But by 1790 the United States had only eight daily newspapers, although there were eighty-three weekly papers.[4] On the basis of numbers this hardly indicated an open and diversified marketplace of ideas.

In comparison, today we have what appears to be an abundance of diversity in mass communications.

In 1973, a total of 1,774 newspapers reached more than 60 million readers on a daily basis, while 9,755 periodicals of various types catered to innumerable mass and specialized audiences. Electronic mass media operating in the United States in 1973 totaled 704 television stations, 4,346 A.M. radio stations, and 2,307 F.M. stations. And to this must be added an annual flood of books: in 1969, some 1,769 publishing houses produced over 200 million textbooks and almost 900 million trade books.[5]

This basic data suggests that we have a more open marketplace than existed at the time the Constitution was written. Yet, the 1969 staff report to the Violence Commission noted:

The media today comprise institutions far different from the press of two centuries ago. The forms have changed. Circulation has increased beyond anything then dreamed of. Competitive pressures have increased and in response the media have learned from sheer necessity the art of manipulating vast audiences for economic gain. In the process of this growth and change, the ability of any single man to gain access to the "marketplace of ideas" has become all but extinct.[6]

Despite the apparent abundance of mass media today, most people experience monopoly newspapers. They receive a few television stations that show programming dominated by three networks that program homogeneously as interdependent oligopoly firms should. They receive a larger number of radio stations that broadcast a very limited diversity of programming.

The number of cities with competing newspapers has declined dramatically during the last fifty years. The percentage of cities served by more than one newspaper was down to 4 percent in 1972.[7] Where two newspapers exist, they are likely to be owned by the same person or company. In most cities, there is little competition in reporting news. There is substantial cross-ownership between local newspapers, television stations, and even radio stations in the smallest towns as well as the larger cities. Chain ownership is increasing in both the newspaper and television industries.

The Federal Communications Commission, charged with developing effective policy for the broadcast media, has adopted policies limiting the cross-media concentration through its power of licensing radio and television broadcast stations. Its one-to-a-market rule, adopted in 1971, prohibits common ownership or operation of a VHF television station and another television or radio station in the same area. In 1975, the Commission adopted rules prohibiting common ownership of daily newspapers and broadcast stations in the same service area. But these rules apply only to prospective increases in concentration, not existing concentration. Given the inherent stability of these ownership arrangements, the FCC rules are not likely to have much effect. Moreover, as a basis for developing policy limiting concentration in newspapers and access to the mass media, broadcast licensing is hardly the most appropriate basis on which to build them.

Perhaps the most significant long-term threat to freedom of access to the media is acquisition by conglomerates. The media organizations readily could be turned into the communication and public relations arms of conglomerates, serving their economic and political interests. Absorption by conglomerates might be viewed as the final stage of institutionalization of the media in an even more concentrated economic system. Individual citizens are denied effective freedom of speech through the media in order to preserve and maintain freedom of the press as an institution. The press as an institution becomes absorbed by much larger conglomerate corporations where their function is directed and constrained to serve the goals—economic, political, social, and cultural—of the company. Freedom of speech may become freedom to read, view, and listen to the media products of the national and multinational conglomerates.

As a result of increasing media concentration and centralization, Benno Schmidt has observed:

> The typical American lives in a city served by a newspaper that is a local monopoly and is owned by the same interests that control one of the local television stations. Both the newspaper and TV stations are, in turn, likely to be either part of a centrally controlled chain that holds numerous other broadcasting stations or newspapers, or part of a conglomerate corporation with numerous interests that are potentially in conflict with unbiased reporting. Moreover, the TV station is almost certain to rely on a centrally controlled network for most of its programming, including news and public affairs. Two of the existing three networks are themselves conglomerates. And most of the news conveyed by the local paper, and even more of the news that is broadcast in the area, will have emanated from one of the two national wire services. The result is that the typical American's main sources of news simply do not conform to the ideal of a wide variety of competing, locally controlled and oriented, independent organizations.[8]

PUBLIC POLICY TOWARD THE MASS MEDIA

The appropriate avenue of public policy for maintaining freedom of entry for competition in the press is the anti-trust laws. In the landmark *Associated Press* case of 1945, the Supreme Court ruled that the First Amendment does not prevent anti-trust law from being applied to the press.

> The First Amendment, far from providing an argument against application of the Sherman Act, here provides powerful reasons to the contrary. That

Amendment rests on the assumption that the widest possible dissemination of information from diverse and antagonistic sources is essential to the welfare of the public, that a free press is a condition of a free society. Surely a command that the government itself shall not impede the free flow of ideas does not afford non-governmental combinations a refuge if they impose restraints upon that constitutionally guaranteed freedom. Freedom to publish means freedom for all and not for some. Freedom to publish is guaranteed by the Constitution, but freedom to combine to keep others from publishing is not. Freedom of the press from governmental interference under the First Amendment does not sanction repression of that freedom by private interests. The First Amendment affords not the slightest support for the contention that a combination to restrain trade in news and views had any constitutional immunity.[9]

But after the policy was articulated clearly, there has been little follow-through by the anti-trust division of the Department of Justice. Concentration, centralization, and the heightening of barriers to entry has increased. In fact, the most notable action relating to competition in recent years has been the passage by Congress of the Newspaper Preservation Act[10] which permits competing newspapers exemption from the anti-trust laws under certain circumstances. This statute permits newspapers operating in the same market to enter into joint arrangements with respect to production, including printing, distribution, advertising, circulation, and other business-related functions. The papers must establish separate and independent editorial policies and maintain separate editorial and reporting staffs. A second requirement is that one of the newspapers must be under risk of financial failure if the merger is prohibited, but this test was not defined in operational terms.

Some students of the media have assessed this act by Congress as reflecting a conclusion that newspapers tend to be natural monopolies. If so, it reflects a conclusion that the inherent economic barriers to entry preclude freedom of access to the media both by individuals and by new, competitive press organizations. Whether or not the monopoly is natural, the barriers to access exist and public policy toward the press must recognize that fact.

Assuming that resolution of the problem of economic concentration in the press cannot be addressed effectively through the anti-trust laws, then the direction of public policy protecting First Amendment freedoms must be toward defining the terms and conditions of access to the press. This could mean that in future years the press may be the subject of searching analyses of alternative terms and conditions of access in a manner similar to that directed at television over the past quarter century.

There never has been freedom of entry into radio and television broadcasting. The use of the radio frequency has required licensing and regulation since inception. The terms and conditions of access rights to different groups desiring to send different kinds of messages have been a matter of continuing policy concern supported by the courts as consistent with the purpose of the First Amendment.

The first major court test of access to the press occurred in the now famous *Miami Herald* decision. The Supreme Court ruled that a Florida statute granting a right of reply to personal attacks carried in newspapers violated the First Amendment because it infringed upon the editorial function. The Court observed:

> The choice of material to go into a newspaper, and the decisions made as to limitations on the size of the paper, and content, and treatment of public issues and public officials—whether fair or unfair—constitutes the exercise of editorial control and judgment. It has yet to be demonstrated how governmental regulation of this crucial process can be exercised consistent with First Amendment guarantees of a free press as they have evolved to this time.[11]

The Court apparently equated the right of a free press to the right of editors. The right of editors to restrict limited access was determined to take precedence over the right of access to individuals. For the conflict between freedom of speech through access to the press and freedom of the institution of the press, the press won on the basis of the purported professional independence and objectivity of editorial judgment. The decision did not undertake a detailed examination of the extent of that independence and objectivity. In particular, it did not examine the economic structure within which the *Miami Herald*'s editors must operate.

The *Miami Herald* case was prompted, in substantial part, by the changing economic structure of the newspaper industry, its relationship to the other media industries, and its role in the evolving economic structure of the U.S. economy. In the future additional interpretations of the meaning of the First Amendment will be required in light of economic concentration and demands for access through existing media firms as a substitute for direct competitive entry that has been foreclosed. The day of blind faith in the inherent justice of laissez-faire in private economic markets as protecting "freedom of speech" is coming to a close. We must move on with the task of developing the spirit of the First Amendment and affirmative public policies that implement the fundamental protections built into it.

NOTES

1. See Supreme Court opinion in *Red Lion Broadcasting Co. v. FCC*, 395 U.S. 367 (1969).

2. Jerome Barron, "Access to the Press—A New Amendment Right," *Harvard Law Review,* June 1967, p. 1641ff.

3. John Tebbel, *The Media in America* (New York: T. Y. Crowell, 1974), p. 49.

4. R. K. Baker and S. J. Ball, "Violence and the Media" (Staff Report to the National Commission on the Causes and Prevention of Violence, 1969), Washington, D.C.: Government Printing Office, p. 68.

5. B. C. Schmidt, Jr., *Freedom of the Press vs. Public Access* (Palo Alto: Aspen Institute, 1976), p. 38.

6. R. K. Baker and S. J. Ball, "Violence and the Media," p. 68.

7. Robert L. Bishop, "The Rush to Chain Leadership," *Columbia Journalism Review,* November/December 1972, pp. 10ff.

8. Schmidt, *Freedom of the Press,* p. 45–46.

9. *Associated Press* v. *United States,* 326 U.S. 1, 20 (1945).

10. 15 U.S.C. §§1803 (suppl. 1971).

11. 418 U.S. 241, 258 (1974).

MANUFACTURING NEWSPAPERS

JOHN A. CROWN

The businesses that produce newspapers are like other manufacturers, says John Crown, except that most newspapers lack direct competition, and the product is protected by the First Amendment.

Associate editor of the Atlanta Journal, *a chain-owned newspaper without direct competition, Crown defends newspaper monopolies and chains. Under such conditions editorial decision making remains decentralized while economies of scale and sophisticated marketing and management skills can be utilized. These factors make newspapers more profitable and thus more secure and less susceptible to pressures other than truth.*

Mr. Crown writes staff editorials and a thrice-weekly column for the editorial page. He has been honored by the Atlanta Consular Corps for his efforts in strengthening international relations and by the North Georgia Chapter of the American Institute of Architects for his work on behalf of improving the urban environment.

The media, in providing information to the American public, are supposed to be in the business of providing true and factual information. But as businesses, the media must also pursue profit. Inevitably, the question must arise: does the pursuit of profit influence the pursuit of truth?

Despite increasing signs to the contrary, we still regard ourselves as a free enterprise society. Certainly, in comparison to other large nations we must be viewed as a free enterprise society. Although government regulation is far from minimal, private business within the United States still has the freedom to operate competitively for a profit.

Newspaper publishing is an integral part of what's left of our free enterprise system. Operating for a profit is the only way this particular industry can survive. Ergo, the answer to the question, "Does the pursuit of profit influence the pursuit of truth?" is inescapable. It must. However, it can do so in a positive and beneficial manner, or in a negative and detrimental manner.

As long as a newspaper must seek a profit in order to survive economically, it follows that the pursuit of profit is going to influence the pursuit of truth. The stronger a newspaper is in financial terms, the stronger it can be in pursuing truth. It is less vulnerable to advertisers, to political figures, to any pressure group which would bend the truth to private purposes. A financially weak newspaper is limited in its ability to stand up to those who would subvert or twist or even omit the truth.

Despite the legend and the aura that has evolved over the years regarding newspapers and their relentless search for news, we must concede that people who work on newspapers are not demigods. People who own, publish, edit, and write for newspapers are really human beings, although there are views to the contrary at both extremes. They are motivated by pressures and problems and prejudices and lofty ideals, as are other human beings. Some are weak. Some are strong. And the vast majority, I believe, are somewhere in between. I believe, however, the vast majority strive conscientiously to pursue truth at whatever cost.

THE OPERATION OF A TYPICAL NEWSPAPER

The purpose of a newspaper is to inform. It does so through the publication of news and the publication of advertisements. It throws out at the reader an enormous amount of news—all extremely perishable—on a plethora of subjects. It must be organized in some sort of comprehensive manner so that it will not overwhelm the reader and will entice the reader to be just that—a reader.

To be effective truth must be organized. Disorganized truth thrown out in a helter-skelter fashion can be dangerous. Truth in raw form is dicey in that it can help or hurt. Thus, the requirement for a newspaper is to pursue the truth and present it in orderly fashion by one set of people while another set of people just as vigorously pursues profit to enable the newspaper to disseminate that truth.

Your typical metropolitan newspaper resembles any other manufacturer who is a part of our eroding free enterprise system—hence the title of this paper. But there are two key differences.

One difference is the lack of competition from other metropolitan newspapers under separate ownership. That doesn't mean that such a metropolitan newspaper has the market of readers and advertisers as an exclusive right. What it does mean is that a metropolitan newspaper doesn't have the intense competition from one of its own kind, and I grant you that competition of this sort encourages more intensive efforts in the pursuit of both truth and profit.

But even where there is no direct competition from another newspaper, there is competition for the advertising dollar and the reader's time. There is strong competition from the electronic media, from suburban newspapers, from specialty newspapers. Anything that distracts the advertiser or the reader from newspaper pages could be construed as competition.

I recall an example given me years ago during my senior year in college. At that time Coca-Cola sold for five cents. There was a national weekly general-interest magazine, *Collier's*, which also sold for five cents. A representative of Coca-Cola visited a marketing class I was in and during the course of discussion noted that Coca-Cola looked upon *Collier's* as a competitor. He said any product that might distract the customer and divert the necessary five cents was a competitor.

That is the sort of problem newspapers face now, despite ill-conceived arguments that single ownership of metropolitan newspapers means "control" of the news. Not only are we in competition for the reader's money and the advertiser's money, but also for the reader's time. After all, there is a limit to the time the vast majority of people will spend in either reading, listening to, or watching the news.

For reasons which we shall explore later, the city with competing metropolitan newspapers under separate ownership is a true rarity and a sad commentary on the economic facts of life.

The second key difference between manufacturers of newspapers and other manufacturers is the inability of the government to interfere with the product, thanks to First Amendment guarantees.

The government can—and does—move in on newspaper manufacturers as it can on any other type of manufacturer on items pertaining to IRS, OSHA, NLRB, and all the other myriad federal and state agencies which plague and bedevil free enterprise. But at least government is restricted from issuing the kind of ruling on a newspaper's product, news, that the FDA can issue to a manufacturer of saccharine.

MERCHANDISING THE READER

In essence, a newspaper operates within the free enterprise system by buying readership. It does this by selling its product to that readership for less than it costs to produce. It then turns around and merchandises that readership to advertisers. The single-copy price or the subscription price of a newspaper could not begin to cover the costs of producing it. To print a metropolitan newspaper without advertising would be such a costly process in terms of enticing readers that it would be a self-defeating effort. The newspaper would literally price itself out of the market.

Thus, readership insures advertising. And advertising insures readership. Both combine to insure a profit for the paper. And in that way the pursuit of truth may be faithfully followed, secure in the knowledge that there will be a means of disseminating that truth.

For an example of this fact of life I turn back to the late great Ralph McGill, the editor of the *Atlanta Constitution* who made that newspaper probably the best-known of all southern newspapers. McGill was controversial, notably in his editorial columns, and I am sure that there were almost as many who hated his guts as who admired him for the courageous stands that he took. He pursued truth regardless of the consequences.

But McGill gave credit where credit was due. He had an associate named Jack Tarver who moved from the editorial and news side of the newspaper to the business side. And McGill said in later life that he would not have been able to take the stands he took—as unpopular as some were—without Tarver there to "steady the soapbox."

In other words, unless a newspaper is sufficiently sound economically it simply is not going to be able to pursue the truth or be able to disseminate any truth it may find. And it is elementary that a newspaper is going to be sound economically only if it pursues profits as well.

Even in the pursuit of profit a reputable newspaper is going to view seriously its responsibility to the reader, not just in the dissemination of news, but also in the caliber of its advertising.

Before Atlanta's notorious bathhouses were closed down by the city, Atlanta Newspapers called a halt to publishing advertisements for them—even though their advertising amounted to about $100,000 in income annually. The reason advanced by Ferguson Rood, advertising director, is that this was not regarded as desirable advertising, and there was a question of the legality of bathhouses.

A natural question would be, if you close your pages to bathhouse advertising, why not close your pages to X-rated movie advertising?

"X-rated movies raise something of a moral question," Rood says. "They may be moral to me and not to you, but at least an X-rated movie gives you what you expect. These bathhouses didn't even have water meters."

Thomas H. Wood, president of Atlanta Newspapers, puts it this way: "Unless an advertisement is illegal, libelous, or deceitful I'm going to run it. I'm not going to get involved in the business of censorship."

It is a pragmatic position. Without rigid guidelines such as these, a newspaper, particularly a newspaper without identical competition, can be placed in the position of refusing to publish advertisements that are perfectly legitimate. Those who might be offended by certain advertisements should consider the awesome and perhaps capricious power involved in censorship. And once begun, it is virtually impossible to draw a line that will apply equitably in all cases.

As an example of what the rigid guidelines mean to Atlanta Newspapers, at least $250,000 in advertising revenues is turned away annually, and one thing advertising directors do not like to do is turn away advertising. That quarter-of-a-million-dollar figure is described as very conservative by Ferguson Rood.

It follows that while the pursuit of profit is essential to the survival of a newspaper, in the case of Atlanta Newspapers there is also restraint and responsibility. It is reasonable to assume that other newspapers, equally responsible, could cite similar examples of their own.

For a newspaper that is more concerned with the pursuit of profit than the pursuit of truth, it is doubtful that prospective advertising revenues would be turned away.

It is not unusual for an advertiser, large or small, to attempt to use what he might visualize as his advertising clout to try to get something into the newspaper or to try to keep something from appearing in a newspaper. It is an attitude that apparently comes more as a reflex action than one generated by rational thought.

"We're often subjected to attempted pressures from advertisers who tell us they will place ads with us if we do this or that," Rood points out. "Our stand is that if your advertisement is connected with anything on the newspaper other than the ad itself, then there is no basis for business between us.

"We hope that our advertising people are newspaper people first and advertising people second. It doesn't always work out that way with all of them, but we make a conscious effort to make it work that way."

THE TREND TOWARD MONOPOLY

As noted earlier, the manufacturer of a metropolitan newspaper only rarely has to contend with another such manufacturer in the same city. This has given rise to a degree of concern over a newspaper monopoly. And that in turn generates concern, more imagined than real, over monopoly affecting detrimentally the relationship between the pursuit of profit and the pursuit of truth.

Why the trend toward monopoly? The most reasonable approach to an answer that I have seen was contained in a newsletter prepared by John Morton Newspaper Research at the end of 1976 for Colin, Hochstin Co., members of the New York Stock Exchange. Here is what it said, in part:

> At last count, there were 1,756 daily newspapers published in the United States. Of these, 1,038, or 59 percent, belong to a newspaper group. In 1971, by contrast, 879, or about 50 percent of the nation's then 1,748 dailies belonged to a group. The growth of group ownership is the standard usually used to measure the concentration of newspaper ownerships. What

these figures do not indicate, however, is that some of these newspaper groups are very small [and independent]. . . .

Having made the point that independent newspapers are still a large force in American journalism, we will take note of the unmistakable trend of independent newspapers and small newspaper groups to be absorbed by larger newspaper groups. There are very clear reasons why this trend has developed and why it will continue.

Daily newspapers in the United States were started as family enterprises. Typically, an independent newspaper is into the second or third generation of family ownership, and control has become fragmented; often the newer generation is uninterested in the newspaper, leaving no one to carry on the family business. Moreover, inheritance taxes often present a major problem to publishing families.

It is not surprising, then, that the owners of independent newspapers become receptive to ever escalating offers from larger newspaper groups. Larger newspaper groups, for their part, are well aware of the profit potential in operating monopoly daily newspapers. Moreover, they know they can bring economies of scale to a newly acquired newspaper, particularly in the newsprint and printing-plate purchasing that will improve profit margins; also the larger companies usually can bring more sophisticated marketing and management skills than a newspaper's former owners employed.

The continuation of a contraction of ownerships in the newspaper industry appears as inevitable as was the contraction in most other types of family-owned businesses in the past. Those who regret the eventual passing of the independent newspaper may take some solace in the fact that, so far at least, newspaper owners have seemed determined to sell out only to newspaper companies and not to a conglomerate or some other outside corporation unfamiliar with the traditions of American newspapers.

It is significant, we believe, that most of the newspapers on any list of the best newspapers in the nation are group-owned, which appears to be evidence that the groups recognize that quality in newspapers is good business as well as good journalism.

And it is elementary that a newspaper that is sound economically is going to be able to pursue truth more faithfully, more fearlessly, and more vigorously than one which is doddering financially and subject to the capriciousness of someone with an axe to grind.

As a footnote to this account of newspaper concentration, in a subsequent newsletter from Colin, Hochstin Co. the point is made—and made well—that persons such as U.S. Representative Morris K. Udall who express alarm over the trend should take a look at the inheritance and estate tax laws, created by Congress, which are instrumental in the matter.

One of the apprehensions heard from time to time regarding the concentration of newspaper ownership is that this permits management of news and editorial policies. In other words, a newspaper chain could pursue profit to the detriment of truth. There is no question that such a tactic is possible. But it is far from probable.

Atlanta Newspapers, for example, is, of course, an integral part of the Cox chain. And Thomas H. Wood, the Atlanta president, points out the fallacy of such a move.

"If the Cox organization were to undertake a unified news policy, one aimed toward pointing the news in a certain direction, the number of people who would have to be in on this centralized control would be so numerous that the secret wouldn't be kept ten days," says Wood. "When the lid was blown, and it would be, it would hurt profits. Meddling of this sort hurts the bottom line. And in the pursuit of profit the bottom line is vital."

PUBLIC VERSUS PRIVATE OWNERSHIP

There are two categories of newspaper chains insofar as ownership is concerned. There is the chain that is publicly owned, meaning that the stock is traded openly on a stock exchange, and the chain that is privately owned, in which there is no public trading of the stock.

In an April 1977 Colin, Hochstin Co. newsletter, eight publicly owned chains were examined from a financial standpoint. Advertising revenues for February 1977 were up over February 1976 for all. The range extended from as low as 1 percent to as high as 12.7 percent. It was an upward trend for January and December as well. The increase for January ranged from 7.2 percent to 31.2 percent, and for December from 11.2 percent to 24.2 percent.

In addition to advertising revenues the matter of stock data was also examined, and the picture was a healthy one in all respects. The earnings per share of the stocks of the respective newspaper groups were listed for 1976, and the price-earnings ratio for each was inviting. It wasn't surprising that the projected earnings for 1977 were higher in every case than the figures for 1976.

All of this points to the larger newspaper groups doing an effective job of pursuing profit, which should enable them to more effectively pursue truth.

The Cox organization, which includes Atlanta Newspapers, is controlled by stock that is privately owned and, therefore, no specific financial figures are available for public scrutiny. But it is logical to assume that you can get an idea of the Cox performance by studying the performance of the publicly owned newspaper groups.

"Year in and year out we don't miss the averages demonstrated by the larger newspaper groups," says Wood. "We might be a little up or a little down, but through time we have an average return on sales from a percentage point of view.

"If we found we were consistently out of line from the larger newspaper groups, we would know we were doing something wrong."

Circulation figures are, however, public knowledge. It is relatively simple, therefore, to get some idea how Cox Newspapers compares with the other newspaper groups. As of last April there were 169 different newspaper groups in the United States. Ranked by daily circulation Cox Newspapers place ninth with a daily combined circulation of 1,111,742. This does not mean, of course, that Cox ranks ninth financially. There is more involved in newspaper finances than circulation. But it should provide an indication of the general area where Cox would be found.

THE EFFECTS OF RISING COSTS ON PROFITS

In the pursuit of profit newspapers must look to their expenses. Newsprint, the paper on which newspapers are printed, was selling for $140 a ton ten years ago. Today it is selling for $305 a ton. It is simple arithmetic to see that the price has more than doubled. It is not a matter of supply and demand. The price of newsprint is set by a cartel in Canada. Ironically, while the price of newsprint was skyrocketing upward, there was a one- to two-million-ton oversupply on the world market.

Newspapers have faced this financial burden by eliminating waste and exercising frugality, as well as by increasing advertising rates and the retail price of the paper.

"Our advertisers have not felt the full impact of the rising cost of newsprint," notes Atlanta Newspapers' Wood. "We've installed automation equipment, which has meant substantial savings for us, and we used those savings to cushion the cost of advertising."

Wood notes that although newsprint and personnel costs have escalated, the actual publishing costs—by which is meant manufacturing costs—have gone down. This has been accomplished through more efficient management and control, as well as the introduction of automation equipment.

Along with these changes has come a new outlook on the part of the advertisers, which could mean a change in circulation patterns.

"In the past it was no big problem to run off additional copies of the newspaper and send them to all parts of the state," Wood explained. "Today the money paid by a subscriber in south Georgia doesn't even cover the cost of delivering the paper. It used to be that advertisers looked at gross circulation rather than the quality of circulation. But now advertisers are concerned only with the circulation that could conceivably buy their merchandise.

"With the cost of newsprint you don't run off any more papers than are actually needed. And with the cost of delivery to the far corners of the state going up, I think we're moving toward increasing the cost of the daily paper outside the retail trading zone to twenty-five cents, and the Sunday paper to seventy-five cents."

The point has been made that a newspaper that effectively pursues profit is in a better position to pursue truth. It has the resources to hire qualified talented people who can be counted on to pursue truth, to recognize truth when they find it, to organize truth in readable and understandable language, and to present it to the newspaper reader in an inviting manner. It is a continuing process.

Eight years ago I was city editor of the *Atlanta Journal,* and I had a staff of some thirty persons, including one man assigned to Washington who constituted our Washington bureau. This was in addition, of course, to the customary wire services that pour out an abundance of national and global news.

Today the city editor of the *Atlanta Journal* has a staff of forty-five persons, not including Washington coverage. That is now handled by a Cox Washington bureau composed of twelve experienced and able newsmen and newswomen.

Nor is this the ceiling in recruiting efforts to more effectively pursue truth.

"I believe we have better people in the newsrooms of both the *Journal* and the *Constitution* now than we had in the past," commented Atlanta Newspapers' Wood. "They're better educated and they're better motivated. We're making better use of them than we did in the past.

"In the interest of continuing to improve our news coverage," Wood continued, "we're planning to add six additional persons to the newsrooms of the *Journal* and *Constitution* respectively each year for the next five years. We're going to use them to better cover the local Atlanta scene and the twenty-one counties around Atlanta. We're also going to beef up our coverage of business news. And we're going to hire a graphics editor for each paper. His job will be to coordinate the art department and the picture desk to present a more inviting product.

"Some people are critical of the money used to provide color and attractive layouts. They call such moves 'frills' and seem to think they have no legitimate place in a newspaper. But what we've got to face is that unless the reader is attracted to the newspaper he's not going to read it. And if he doesn't read it, we're in trouble. The newspaper must inform. And we have to make it as attractive as possible to help the reader complete his side of the transaction."

HEALTHY PROFITS MEAN BETTER NEWS COVERAGE

Does the pursuit of profit influence the pursuit of truth? It sure does. Only a newspaper that is a healthy member of the free enterprise system can have the resources to pursue truth relentlessly, without fear or favor, and to disseminate that truth to those who want to know.

Ordinarily, when such a question is raised—whether the pursuit of profit influences the pursuit of truth—the inference is that there is something inherently bad about it. It is all too easy to jump to the conclusion that connecting profit and truth only insures the subversion of truth.

In my years at the *Atlanta Journal* I have seen people fired for cause, and I have seen disaffected persons leave voluntarily. I have also seen some of these people later make generalized charges that on occasion truth was withheld or subverted or distorted in some manner.

I can only speak from my own experience. I've held a variety of jobs on the *Journal,* but two of them would be singularly sensitive to any move to withhold or subvert or distort truth. One was the dual job of real estate editor and assistant business editor. The other was city editor. At no time have I ever experienced any attempt—overt or covert—to withhold, subvert, or distort truth for whatever reason.

There are those who view profit as a dirty six-letter word. But without profit our only option would be to work for the government, a government which owned and controlled everything and which would dictate every aspect of our lives. The free enterprise system is inextricably bound to our political freedoms, and erosion of free enterprise has a detrimental effect upon political freedoms.

It follows that a newspaper that does not pursue profit is not going to be in a position to pursue truth. A newspaper owned and controlled by government can hardly be depended upon to tell the truth about that government and the people who make up that government.

Free enterprise has its strengths and weaknesses. The people who own, publish, edit, and write for newspapers have their strengths and weaknesses. I submit that the pursuit of truth has a far better chance of success when it is backed by the pursuit of profit than if the inspiration is contained in a nonprofit government employee.

The pursuit of profit and the pursuit of truth constitute a joint undertaking which should result in mutual benefits.

FREE PRESS OR PROFITABLE PRESS?

NICHOLAS JOHNSON

According to Nicholas Johnson, the media, and especially television, are highly profitable businesses in quasi-monopolistic or monopolistic positions. Broadcasters seek to maintain minimal competition by resorting to governmental regulation. As a result the television industry's profit margins were four times those of the oil industry in 1976. However, more important than direct profit is the fact that control of mass media means societal power.

Johnson maintains that profits and power influence the marketplace of ideas in many ways, though most are covert. Access in all media, sponsorship in public and commercial broadcasting, the availability of media space or time used for news, and investment in the quality and quantity of news-gathering staff and facilities are ways in which the societal flow of ideas through mass media are adversely affected. Fortunately, Johnson says, many broadcasters and publishers want both a free and a profitable press. But the inherent conflict of interest is always present and often costly.

Mr. Johnson, a federal communications commissioner from 1966 to 1973, currently heads the National Citizens Committee for Broadcasting. A national vice-chairman of Americans for Democratic Action and a director of the National Consumers League, Johnson's regular media commentary is heard on National Public Radio's "All Things Considered," and his column appears in Access *magazine. He is the author of several books, including* How to Talk Back to Your Television Set.

Let me at the outset say how pro-business I am, lest there be any question about that. I just want to come clean. I have been a businessman myself much of my life. I worked for a corporate law firm in Washington, D.C., representing a consortium of steel companies, another group of cement companies, and an airline. Before that I was teaching law—oil and gas law, corporation law, and things like that. I ran the Maritime Administration for a couple of years. That's a $500 million-a-year business. In fact, it's more of a business than you may think it is, and I'm going to return to that point in a moment. Now I'm running a business called the National Citizens Committee for Broadcasting. It has the same kinds of problems as any other businesses. We have to make budgets and watch costs and look for profit opportunities and cut losses and be knowledgeable about the tax laws.

237

But I must say as an American businessman, committed to the business ethic as I am, that we have heard a lot of stuff about the free private enterprise system that really must be laid to rest.

The thing that has made me such a committed supporter of free private enterprise has been my experience in government. My earlier experience representing large corporations had, quite frankly, shoved me just the other direction. But the more I found out about government the less I liked it. And the more I experienced government the more I found out what it is that business really does in Washington. It has nothing whatsoever to do with the free private enterprise system, lest there be any remaining doubt in your mind about that. What business comes to Washington to do is not to cut back on government but to increase it—to have more government involvement in its business.

Business comes to Washington not to encourage private enterprise, but to encourage socialism—just as long as it can become a part of it. The largest socialist enterprise is the defense department. Others include the public highway building program. Yes, those are socialist highways that we drive on. We make a lot of profit as American business building those socialistic highways, and there is no objection whatsoever to the fact that they're socialist highways, because they make a lot of money.

Business comes to Washington asking for subsidies—systems designed to take money out of the pockets of the poor and the middle class and put it in the pockets of the rich. There's nothing wrong with that, I suppose, but it certainly isn't free private enterprise or marketplace economics.

That's what the Maritime Administration program was—$500 million a year to rich steamship companies and shipyards. Every independent economist who ever looked at that program, including economists hired by the shipping companies themselves, concluded that there was no economic basis whatsoever for that program. I mean there was no benefit that comes back to the American people. Everything that $500 million does you can do cheaper some other way. You can create jobs cheaper, you can build ships cheaper, you can move cargo cheaper, you can help the balance of payments cheaper, you can help our defense posture cheaper. But that's what those businessmen were doing in Washington. They wanted your tax dollars, and mine. Perhaps we all want other people's tax dollars. But you have to admit it's a little irrational to take the money and then say you're doing it in the name of free private enterprise.

There are restraints on foreign competition. When I was representing the steel companies and cement companies I was trying to curtail the importation of foreign-built steel and cement.

There are government-created monopolies restraining free competition. The airlines have them. The economists at the CAB threaten to bring competition into the business, and there's some considerable question as to whether the airlines really want competition.

Television stations are quasi-monopolies. Government gives them a monopoly. The broadcasting industry has fought successfully against competition from the cable-television industry for twenty years. Here you have a willing buyer and a willing seller in the marketplace. And the seller, the cable-television operator, says to the buyer, "I can bring you any television signal you want that you're willing to pay for. I can bring you the BBC by satellite. I can bring Chicago signals into Atlanta. I can bring Philadelphia signals into Washington. You tell me what you want, and I'll bring it in on my cable." And the buyer says, "That's the deal I want. I want to get all that TV." Although some folks say, "Out where we live we pay to have the garbage hauled out, not to have it hauled in." But by and large folks do want more TV for some reason that we haven't fully understood. But the broadcasters have impressed upon the FCC the notion that cable shouldn't be permitted to do that. Now, why not? Isn't that interesting? Well, because it would be competition. It would bust up their cozy little monopoly. They don't want competition; they don't want free private enterprise. They want protected markets.

Then, there's setting prices that are higher than the market would otherwise bear. It used to be, the last time I looked some years ago, to fly between San Francisco and Los Angeles cost you about four cents a mile because the CAB didn't regulate it and protect your interests. When you fly on the East Coast the same distance, between, say, New York and Washington, the CAB protects you, so instead of paying four cents a mile you pay eleven cents a mile.

The ICC has trucking rates jacked up so we're all paying some $5 billion a year more than we would have to pay if we had a free private enterprise system in trucking.

There are tax benefits galore, we all know about that.

The very creation of these agencies came about because of demands from the business community. The CAB Act was written by a lawyer I used to work for. He wrote it in the lobby of the Carlisle Hotel with some guys in the airline industry. The FCC came into existence because a bunch of broadcasters went to see Herbert Hoover. That great leader of the New Left was, at the time, secretary of commerce. They told him, "Look, this thing's gotten out of hand." He said, "What's the matter?" They said, "We have competition in broadcasting." And Hoover said, "That's a problem I can understand. You have to stomp that out." So they created the FCC, and sure enough it put 700 broadcasters off the air, and broadcasting has been a very profitable business ever since.

So let's keep all this talk about free private enterprise within reasonable bounds when we go extolling its virtues and how much we believe in it. There are a great many representatives of the business community in Washington who don't behave as if they really do believe in it.

BIG BUSINESS IS A FACT OF LIFE

Another fact of life is that we are living with big business in this country. I mean, that's the way it is. I don't pass moral judgment on it, but we have to recognize it. You have a handful of people who control most of the assets. I think some one-fifth of 1 percent of the American people own about 30 percent of all the stock. Some 200 firms control two-thirds of all the manufacturing assets. Two-thirds of American industries are shared monopolies instead of competitive. We have not been enforcing the anti-trust laws.

Ever notice how when demand goes down, the price goes up? That's not what we learned in economics about free private enterprise. That is a consequence of oligopoly, or shared monopoly where four firms or fewer control over half the business in a given industry. That is now the case in some two-thirds of all American industries.

FOOTING THE BILL FOR TV

Let's address for a moment the economic side of the TV business.

For starters, you have an add-on product cost for television every time you go into the marketplace to buy something advertised on TV. It's some $6 billion to $7 billion a year, whatever television's income was this year. Their profits were 60 percent higher than last year, and last year they were four times those of the oil industry, so no telling what they are now. But it's something like $7 billion a year of add-on cost you pay as a consumer for this stuff they call "free" TV. I once figured it up for a particular automobile that sponsored a special on TV. Everybody that went out and bought that car that year as a result of seeing that special paid $100 additional per car as its allocated cost of bringing you that TV special. So free TV does cost you something.

Then, we have to buy television's capital assets. In the newspaper business—only because they haven't figured out how to do it yet—the industry makes the capital investment. All you have to have is a front porch, and you can have the paper. There's very low capital investment on the part of the consumer. In the television business, by contrast, we have now made an investment since 1964 of some $40 billion in capital assets for the broadcasters so that they can sell us this free TV. That's for our TV receivers. The cost goes up.

These figures are probably well out of date right now because of inflation. But we were spending—in addition to the $6 billion or $7 billion a year on the added cost of the products and the $40 billion we invested in the capital (some fifty times what the industry itself invests)—$4 billion a year on new equipment and $1.6 billion a year just for the electricity to run the sets some six or seven hours a day now in the average American home. Plus whatever it is you pay for cable TV or antennas and repairs. So TV is a matter of major economic significance before you even start talking about the programs.

CONTROL OF THE MEDIA BREEDS POWER

There's been all this talk about pursuit of truth and pursuit of profits, and I just don't know where to begin with it. Control of media is power. Accept that as a given. It's true in any society, whether it's the USSR, South America, Canada, anyplace else. The way you control a society is to get control of its media.

What do revolutionaries or a military junta do? They don't go for the banks, they don't go for the factories, they don't go for the farmland; they're not trying to create job opportunity. They're going for the radio and television stations, because that's how you control the country. And whoever controls them governs. That's what the Russians discovered when they went into Czechoslovakia. They had their armies, they had their tanks running up and down the streets making a lot of noise. The Czechs kept moving their transmitters around. As long as they did, the Russians hadn't invaded Czechoslovakia. As soon as they found the transmitters it was all over.

It's the same thing in this country. Who has the power? Big business has the power. And so what do they want to control? They want to control the media. There's nothing wrong with that. If you have any sense of power that is, of course, what you'd want to control.

Boss Tweed once offered the *New York Times* $5 million to kill a single story. You don't have to edit the paper closely every day. But if you're in business, you want to have an impact on the media, and you want to try to control them every way you can. The best way to control them is to own them. But you don't have to make every editorial decision; you don't have to read every piece of copy. All you have to have is the power to kill that one $5 million story a year and the power to order your papers to endorse one candidate, because you don't happen to like the other. That's all you have to have. That's worth profit in cold economic terms, ego and power aside. And that's what we're talking about.

So we do have a problem of censorship and control of content by owners of media, and that should not come to us as any great shock. Why shouldn't an owner tell his papers that he wants them to endorse the guy he wants elected president? They're his papers. But when the owner controls the editorial side he ought to let his readers know where that judgment came from: it didn't come from an editorial writer, it came from the guy off in some other city that controls the chain. The point is he does have that power when he wants to exercise it. The ethics arise when he starts getting involved in news stories. It's a problem. Let's recognize it, not close our eyes and pretend it isn't there.

As for ownership issues, when any enterprise gets monopolistic or oligopolistic enough it thereby takes on responsibilities and obligations whether it wants to or not. And not necessarily as a matter of law. It just does so by being of a size that it was not before. If you have half a dozen, or even two, competing newspapers in a city, the responsibility of those papers is much less to accept an ad on a political issue, to run a letter to the editor in the Letters to the Editor column, to accept an article from a free-lancer off of the newspaper, or to present points of view on an op/ed page different from those of their editorial viewpoint. Those obligations are much less when you have competition. When you have a monopoly, when you own the only show in town, people are going to talk about rights of access to your news pages. And I think fairly so.

We're not talking about a bunch of long-haired hangover hippies from the 1960s trying to get into the paper. Mobil Oil could not buy time on network television to present its point of view. Mobil went to the network and said, "We will buy not one minute but two, to take care of any fairness-doctrine problem you have. We'll only use one minute. You'll get paid for both, and the other minute can be filled with the most hostile, vicious, biting criticism of Mobil Oil that any consumer group can come up with. We'll pay to produce their spot." And they couldn't get their time on the air. Ronald Reagan wanted to buy time, and he couldn't buy time on the air. The point is, watch out, because your ox may be the next one to get gored. When you start precluding access to the airwaves, when you start precluding access to monopoly papers, you have a problem that can strike at anybody.

ADVERTISING CLOUT

In respectable sections of respectable newspapers there is no tie between the advertising and the copy. There are some exceptions to that which sometimes are examined by the *Columbia Journalism Review,* and others—like real estate pages which tend not to criticize the practices of realty firms, and supermarket pages that tend to run more recipes than Jean Mayer columns about the problems of nutrition and what's being sold in the supermarkets. We even have the problem in public broadcasting when major corporations underwrite individual programs and control what gets on public broadcasting. The sponsorship practices in commercial broadcasting in the 1950s certainly were identical to that.

We're using the sponsorship/control process to what I hope you would concede is constructive advantage on the violence issue. The National Citizens Committee for Broadcasting is monitoring prime-time television. We record every instance of violence, put all that into a computer along with the commercials that appear in those programs, and then print it out at the end of the season. We rank the best advertisers in terms of quantities of violence associated with them, and the worst advertisers, and we rank the shows. Then we make that publicly available. As a result, for the first time in twenty-five years in this country, it looks like there will be a decline this fall in violence. We've had presidential task forces, the Surgeon General's Report, Senate committee inquiries, and nothing has happened. The networks promise to reduce violence, the networks lie, and the networks increase the quantities of violence. Now it looks like they may actually have to cut back. So the advertisers can be used to constructive advantage as well.

But the television business is not programming at all. It is not in the business of selling programs to the audience. The business that's being transacted is the sale of the audience, as a commodity, to the advertiser, who is the consumer. The advertiser comes to the broadcaster or publisher, who's the seller, and says, "I want to buy some people." The broadcaster says, "Well, I can give you some ordinary, run-of-the-mill folks for four dollars a thousand." The advertiser says, "I was kind of looking for women between eighteen and forty-nine. How much are they?" "They're twelve dollars a thousand. But next week on 'As the World Turns' I've got a special at eleven-fifty."

That's the way you are talked about by broadcasters. That's how they think of you—as a cost per thousand depending upon your age. They retire us all at forty-nine. Soon as you're over forty-nine, you're out.

AND NOW, THIS WORD FROM OUR SPONSORS . . .

There are other ways in which profit impacts on the pursuit of truth. We're all starting with individual perceptions. Journalists probably do as well as lawyers or doctors or anybody else in trying to describe what's going on. I don't think any of us do very well. But look at all these limits. One is how much space is available in the paper or time on the tube. The *New York Times* used to say, "All the news that's fit to print," and that's always turned on its head: "All the news that fits, we print." If you don't have the space the news doesn't get in. If somebody sells a big ad, the column's cut in half. Listen to the morning news on one of the networks. There are these little beeps before the breaks with the commercials. Sometimes if you hear the same news on a different station it doesn't have the commercial. You know what comes in that space? More news. All news that fits, we'll let you know, but if we can sell the time, you're not going to find out about it. So, that's one of the first ways in which it's cut back.

How much time is there on television for news and public affairs? Look at your local TV schedule tonight. What are there in the way of regularly scheduled public affairs shows in prime time? There's nothing. In most markets the only hour every week is on CBS with "60 Minutes." If you don't even have the time, you don't have to censor. You never put it on in the first place. And that's perhaps the predominant way in which the media's pursuit of profit affects the pursuit of truth.

Secondly, how much is the broadcaster going to spend on it? Does he have an AP and UPI wire service in the radio station? You'd be surprised how many radio stations don't. A lot of journalists in Washington read the *Washington Post,* the *New York Times, Time,* and *Newsweek.* But what about the *New England Journal of Medicine, Mother Jones,* the *Manchester Guardian,* and the hundreds of others? Does the broadcaster have anybody reading them, clipping them, and using them in bringing the news to the people of your community? There's a marvelous paper in Iowa, the *Des Moines Register,* that does. But a lot of papers don't. How many reporters are there? If you're trying to put out a newspaper without any reporters and use nothing but AP and UPI copy you're not going to be doing much investigative reporting in your town.

There's almost no newspaper that makes the simplest amenities of staff support available even to its highest-priced journalists. They don't have secretaries. They don't have research assistants. They do everything themselves. They work in a big room. They don't have private offices. That affects pursuit of truth as well, and how much they're capable of doing.

What are they assigned to? If they have to cover the police beat, if they have to cover the White House, they're not going to be covering the real story. We have thousands of journalists in Washington, maybe 10,000. But there's almost no one covering the regulatory commissions. Here's 30 percent of the gross national product of America being regulated by these commissions, and we don't even know what they're doing.

What are all these reporters doing? They're all off covering Jimmy Carter's press conference. They can do that from home, watching it on TV. They don't have to go to the White House to do that.

Finally, you have a self-selection process. What kind of reporters do you hire in the first place? It doesn't make any difference whether they leave voluntarily or whether they're fired. If they're no longer at the paper they're no longer doing the investigative stories. That's the problem in papers all across the country. If good reporters are driven off, if they're not hired in the first place, if, when a publisher accidentally gets one he drives him or her off, that is yet another way in which pursuit of profit affects the pursuit of truth.

Whenever broadcasters' and publishers' profits are threatened by some call to public responsibility we hear anguished cries of "free press." Is it free press or profitable press they truly seek? Fortunately, many want both. But it's an inherent conflict for which a democratic society pays a heavy price indeed when the pursuit of profit outdistances the pursuit of truth.

SECTION 6 ORGANIZED LABOR AND THE MEDIA

A crucial aspect of the relationship between business and the media is the way in which media observe and report the relationship between business and other societal institutions with which it interacts. Among the most potent and important of these interactions is that between business and organized labor, a relationship chronicled by the media since its stormy genesis over a century ago.

An understanding of the evolution and role of organized labor in the United States is essential to the understanding of the American economy and business system. Crucial matters of inflation, productivity, the quality of life on and off the job, and international trade are strongly influenced by the collective bargains struck by businesses and unions. Union activities in the political arena—sometimes in conjunction with business and sometimes in opposition to business—are a powerful influence on the government's role in the economy. Obviously, the media must report and explain the process of worker organization, the collective-bargaining process, and organized labor's political prowess.

The media's job in this respect is complicated by a number of factors. The episodic nature of news does not lend itself to a thorough explication of the labor movement and the ongoing relationship between business and labor. The conflict orientation of news tends to emphasize strikes and confrontation, rather than the generally cooperative and successful nature of negotiations. As a result of this there is a tendency to represent business and labor as having inevitably contradictory goals, instead of as institutions which have, in the main, come to recognize goals that transcend their differences.

Another complicating factor in the media's coverage of business and labor is the fact, emphasized many times throughout this volume, that the media are businesses. Much of the labor force in media industries is unionized, including in many cases the news gatherers, reporters, editors, broadcasters, and commentators themselves. Particularly in broadcasting, but increasingly in print media as well, union association is a condition of journalistic employment. To some this situation holds serious threats to press freedom. Others suggest that because journalists are union members, news reports will tend to favor workers over management. Still others maintain that as businesses troubled by union stands and strikes the media will tend to favor business over labor.

Labor's concerns about how it is pictured by the media are quite similar to business's concerns. Bias, lack of understanding, insufficient education, and inadequate manpower and resources devoted to coverage are themes common to the complaints of both business and labor.

This discussion of organized labor and the media brings together the nation's most respected labor commentator, organized labor's chief of public relations, a columnist and commentator who carried his fight against contractual union membership to the Supreme Court, a twenty-year veteran of labor coverage, and a lawyer and labor-relations specialist who has arbitrated labor/management disputes in media industries. Together they raise questions of how the media cover labor, how labor is pictured by the media, whether media are biased toward labor and whether any bias is negative or positive, how labor relations in media industries influences media's response to labor, and most importantly, how coverage of labor can be improved so that the American public can better understand the role of labor in the American economy and its relationship with business.

DOUBLE STANDARD OR DOUBLE-TALK?

A. H. RASKIN

A. H. Raskin, nationally syndicated labor columnist of the New York Times, *considers some of the factors that go into the composite image of labor as the public perceives it via the media. He cites the focus on strikes as a byproduct of the definition of news and suggests that this emphasis results in an "inadequate understanding on the part of the public . . . of the benefits our democratic society derives from collective bargaining." He maintains that more attention must be given to the reasons for and the results of both strikes and the vast majority of negotiations which are free of conflict. Raskin advocates opening up the bargaining process to the public, and he chides fellow journalists for abandoning interest when contracts are ratified. He also criticizes media for rewarding the most irresponsible labor leaders with the most coverage.*

Mr. Raskin has covered labor, social, governmental, and industrial affairs for more than forty years. During World War II he was chief of the labor branch of the Army's Industrial Services Division and was later the Defense Department's first director of industrial relations. Winner of many awards and coauthor of A Life with Labor, *he has been perhaps the major media source of labor information.*

Even by the skewed standards of a society in which narcissism and skepticism regularly walk hand in hand, the press and organized labor outdo all others in the capacity each has for visualizing itself as a stainless champion of truth and justice, underappreciated by the dolts and ingrates who make up the rest of the population.

On that basis it is scarcely surprising that the paladins of unionism are virtually unanimous in believing that the media are spear carriers for big business in a systematic effort to defame labor and vilify its leaders. The press, in its turn, ridicules most such complaints as the whining of excessively powerful union bosses whose cobwebbed brains are incapable of accepting the realities of an era in which idealism has drained out of the labor movement and has shifted from underdog to overdog in many vital fields.

As one who has spent close to four decades trying to acquire a little perspective in assessing these contradictory estimates, I should like to climb down from the barricades and consider some of the factors that go into the composite image of labor as the public derives it from print journalism, television, and radio.

In the first place the very definition of news as something out of the ordinary makes distortion inevitable in the overall picture of the world people find splashed across their TV screens or screaming at them from newspaper headlines. Educators, clergymen, and industrialists share labor's conviction that the aberrational and often the diseased command attention to the exclusion of the norm that is 98 percent of life. And all are just as convinced that a conspiratorial pattern often underlies the distortion.

The second basic postulate is that the press does have an institutional predisposition, in defense of the public's right to know, to be heedless of the damage it does to the rights or reputations of those on whom the spotlight is turned. Watergate, precisely because it was a high point in demonstrating the indispensability of a free and fearless press, has had the perverse aftereffect of confirming too many journalists in the misconception that the guarantees of the First Amendment are a license for excess, not a mandate for responsibility. In my own home city of New York the rights of defendants have been so atrociously mangled in some recent criminal cases that even absolutists on the freedom of the press have felt obliged to flagellate the offenders.

At the risk of convicting myself of the same self-righteousness I find so insufferable in many of my colleagues, I have to say that I have had some modest success in prodding the press to stop playing God and recognize the need for something more adequate than letters to the editor as redress for readers who felt they had been treated unfairly by a newspaper. An article I wrote ten years ago in the *New York Times Magazine* suggesting that papers appoint ombudsmen to review public complaints and act on those with merit never did take in my own paper, but it prompted Barry Bingham and Norm Isaacs at the *Louisville Courier-Journal* to create the first office of that kind, and the idea has now spread to a dozen other cities. Just last week I got a note from the newly appointed "reader's representative" at the *San Diego Union* crediting me with the inspiration for his job.

MEDIA'S COVERAGE OF LABOR ACTIVITIES

Now that I have doused myself with holy water, let me proceed to appraise the strengths and weaknesses of the media in covering labor's manifold activities, the nature of its problems, and its impact on the community. The best starting point, I think, is the coverage of strikes and collective bargaining, the area in which unions have their most direct impact on the health of the economy and the continuity of essential services.

The usual union lament in this field is two-fold. First, the media are accused of being obsessed with strikes and strike threats to the exclusion of any notice that the great majority of contracts are settled through harmonious negotiations between labor and management without the loss of an hour of work time. The second count in the indictment is that, in news about strikes or other developments affecting labor, the newspapers and TV are pushed by their own economic interests as large, monopolistic employers to tip the balance, leaving labor at a hopeless disadvantage in the struggle for public sympathy and support.

In my view this second charge is largely an anachronism, a carry-over of atavistic impressions that had considerable substance in unionism's formative years when labor coverage was considered part of the police beat. Today, with rare exceptions, publishers shun any attempt to influence the handling of labor stories, and charges of ingrained pro-employer bias are hard to sustain. Indeed, I would argue that unions locked in battles with corporations win more often than they lose in the propaganda exchange. That is not because the reporters are loading the deck in their favor, but because unions have become adept at getting their story across whenever anyone is interested enough to listen.

Union leaders are almost invariably more accessible than their industrial counterparts, who still wall themselves away behind public relations departments operating under instructions not to say anything that could possibly illuminate the situation. The other great union asset in a strike is its members and their families. When a strike turns into a siege it is standard practice for newspapers to carry sob stories detailing the hardships the strikers are suffering and proclaiming their determination to stay out until the flint-hearted bosses meet the demands of elementary justice. No matter how arbitrary the union's position in the negotiations may have been or how reckless the walkout in its implications for the company or the community, the reminder that such stories give of the human factor—little people fighting a faceless profit machine—is a plus for the union which the company's image-makers can't match.

I take more seriously the first of labor's gripes, namely that the focus on strikes makes for an inadequate understanding on the part of both the public and the union rank and file of the benefits our democratic society derives from collective bargaining as an instrument for equitable sharing of the fruits of our industry and commerce and for cooperative answers to the problems involved in keeping that productive system healthy.

But it seems to me that the important deficiency in this regard is not the one that labor centers on. I have no apology for the attention we in the media give to strikes. It is important for us to tell the public all the relevant facts about interruptions in services on which they depend. It is just as important for us to shed light on why they happen and on what comes out of them, and it is in these two crucial areas that I feel we show up least well. Needless to say, my feeling of press inadequacy on that score is even stronger in the tens of thousands of negotiations we ignore entirely because they are free of conflict, many of which have an even more profound effect on the state of the economy than those we cover.

The obstacles to our doing a better job in this area are a good deal more formidable than lack of will, and I think it might help to analyze them a bit. The first thing to recognize is that outside the realm of diplomatic negotiations between the great powers no field compares with collective bargaining in reluctance of the parties to let the public know what is really going on. The settled conviction of labor and management is that the only time the rest of the world is entitled to any useful information is when an agreement has been reached. Until then the statements issued by both sides are self-serving flapdoodle intended to mislead much more than to illuminate. Even with the current epidemic of sunshine laws aimed at stripping secrecy from governmental decision making, no parallel disposition to openness is visible around the bargaining table.

The steel industry is a perfect case in point. Much has changed in this most basic of industries since I covered my first steel strike in the turbulent period right after World War II, but one thing has remained immutable through all those three decades: the public's right to know did not exist until both sides had made their deal. That was the one thing the industry and the union could always agree on.

In the years that culminated in the 116-day strike of 1959, each bargaining round followed an unfailing ritual, with every step as predictable as if it had been programmed on a computer. The opening of talks was always preceded by a statement from the president of the United States—no matter who happened to be holding the lease on the White House—calling on the parties to be aware of their responsibility to the national interest. The country could not afford a shutdown of the steel mills; neither could it afford an inflationary settlement. That was the invariable burden of the presidential message.

The chief spokesmen for the union and the industry would solemnly respond with an affirmation of their awareness that the public occupied a third seat at the negotiating table. The nation could depend on them to put its welfare ahead of any selfish consideration. Then would follow a torrent of statistics from the union proving that every factor of profit, productivity, and living costs dictated a sizable pay increase, plus bigger pensions, more comprehensive health protection, and myriad other benefits. The industry always had at least as many figures proving just as definitively that the union's program meant higher steel prices, reduced markets, mass unemployment, and a surrender of America's supremacy in steel to foreign producers.

But the moment the parties got past this initial resort to gas warfare and settled down to serious bargaining, an iron curtain clanked down on the proceedings. Neither side would say a word to the press except that they had met and planned to meet again. At this point the reporters assigned to cover the contract talks felt obliged to set in motion their own ritualistic phase of the Kabuki dance. They would draft a sonorous statement reminding the negotiators that they had been admonished by the president to accord primacy to the national interest. A vital part of that responsibility, we were wont to say with all the fervor of Patrick Henrys, involved letting the nation know via its anointed representatives in the fourth estate how things stood at every stage of the bargaining.

The answer of the union and the industry was identical—and invariable: the one important mission for the negotiators was to arrive at a contract, and the less anybody outside knew about the specific details, the less danger there was of disruptive interference by busybodies with special axes to grind. This was a category that could embrace anyone from pensioners to steel-dependent industries. The turndown was always accompanied by assurances that, once the terms were arrived at and ratified by the appropriate bodies, the parties would be only too happy to make known what the specifics were and anything else anyone wanted to know—well, almost anything.

This left it up to the reporters to ferret out whatever they could, which was often quite a bit. But the top-level cooperation was zero, except for an occasional leak artfully engineered to serve the interests of one side or another when things got sticky. Since I stopped sweating out this farcical process of calculated obfuscation fifteen years ago, the cast of characters on the union and industry teams has undergone a total turnover, but the general approach is indistinguishable from the old. The public will be told all it needs to know after the string is knotted on the whole package. Until then the press must be content with a timetable of the official meetings, divorced from any real light on what goes on behind the sealed doors of the bargaining chamber. And even the timetable is meaningless since it calculatedly leaves out any reference to the private conferences the key negotiators hold at any hour of the day or night. Nor does it mention the secret telephone calls to influential figures in government or other positions of power and all the other arcane maneuvers behind the scenes that often figure much more prominently in the ultimate settlement than anything that happens around the green baize of the conference table.

The irony is that the impenetrability of this veil of secrecy can have disastrous results for the parties themselves, quite apart from its indefensible attributes as a conspiracy against the public. The members of the union's rank-and-file negotiating committee, whose responsibility it is to ratify whatever emerges from the inner sanctum, are as shut out of interim knowledge as the rest of the nation. When they finally do get the word on what their leaders have decided is enough, it sometimes comes as a jolt. That is exactly what did happen with the last steel negotiations in April 1977. Rebel forces in the ratifying committee voted the tentative pact down the first time it was presented. It took a second vote to get it through and that probably succeeded only because arbitration was the alternative, and no one on the union side seriously believed a neutral panel would up the ante.

I cite the steel industry in such detail not because there is anything distinctive about the padlock the companies and union put on the flow of information, but rather because it is typical of general industrial practice. The virtually unanimous view on both sides is that collective bargaining belongs to the parties, a private process to be conducted under protection of a "Do Not Enter" sign. Only when the parties have come to the end of the road, in an agreement or a hopeless deadlock, can the shade be pulled up so the rest of America can see what went right—or wrong. By that time, of course, it is a fait accompli. Wages have gone up in a manner that may cheapen the value of everybody's dollar, including the worker who is getting the raise; or a service of sufficient consequence to upset the daily life pattern of millions may be cut off without any clear advance warning to the potential sufferers that they had something serious to worry about. What's worse, nobody can do anything about either outcome at that late stage beyond wringing his hands in futile anger.

The more I watch what passes for collective bargaining in major industries the less persuaded I am that it is impractical to conduct it in a goldfish bowl. Some bargainers entrusted with power of decision in essential industries or public services are people you wouldn't trust to find their way safely across the street without a Seeing Eye dog. Why should the community have to wait until the damage has been done before registering its concern? Or why shouldn't it have some ability to put the heat on either union or management if one is being unwarrantedly stubborn? A few states have passed sunshine laws to open up the bargaining process in state and municipal contracts. The experience is still too limited to permit conclusive judgment, but thus far the need to be accountable from start to finish of the process has proved no obstruction to fruitful give-and-take in negotiations. I see no reason why the same approach is not feasible in private industry, especially since so much bargaining these days involves carbon copies of patterns already cut in the pacemaking industries, a process that could be left to computers without touch of human hand.

BETWEEN THE LINES: REPORTING THE FINE PRINT

That brings me to another point of concern in the sufficiency of our standards for covering strikes and settlements. We are much too prone to abandon interest in a negotiation the minute everybody goes back to work and even before that if the workers never go out at all. The thing we tend to forget is that the minutiae of the agreement may have a more profound impact on the general economy than the strike. In most instances we will have a big story when the handshake agreement is reached and the union orders its members to return. At that point both sides are still behind their iron curtain, holding back any announcement of the details until the members have had a chance to ratify. By the time that is done the news interest has drained out of the dispute, and the papers carry a paragraph or two giving the broad outlines of what the contract calls for. If a price boost rides along with the package the story may be a bit longer but rarely will it carry the kind of detail needed for full understanding of anything that may be tucked away in its fine print.

Just as one small example of what can slip by undetected, let me recall a "me too" situation we had among our civil service unions in New York that wound up costing the taxpayers a quarter-billion dollars in one fell swoop—a situation no one outside the inner circle of bargainers for the city and the unions knew anything about until the heist had been completed. The problem arose in the mayoral administration of John V. Lindsay when a lot of strange things had a way of happening in relations between the city and its muscular unions.

This particular aberration grew out of a parity-pay dispute involving patrolmen and sergeants in the police department. Some of the country's most prestigious arbitrators, all acting out of the purest motives, managed to sew the city into a sack from which at best it would have been difficult for the budget-makers to escape without a seemingly endless chain of pay increases to all the uniformed forces and probably everyone else on the municipal payroll as well. Then, in line with its genius for making a bad situation infinitely worse, the city secretly committed itself to a parity formula that tied together various grades in the police and fire departments in a relationship not even an Einstein could balance out. The whole thing was done in a footnote letter attached to the basic police agreement, and none of us demons of the press was attentive enough to know it was there until the policemen went to court to force the city to pay a big chunk of back pay the citizens never knew they owed. By the time every other

group had been bought off, the city had taken a long step farther down
the trail that compelled it to become a financial ward of Uncle Sam. If
the press had been as attentive as it should have been to the ingredients of the original pact, the "me too" letter would have been spot-
ted long before it became another anchor dragging down the founder-
ing civic treasury.

HOW UNION LEADERS STAY IN THE NEWS

There is one last point that disturbs me in our attitude toward what is
news and what isn't where collective bargaining is concerned. I worry
about the extent to which the labor leader is likely to disappear as a
public personality if he is not constantly outraging all right-thinking
persons by the bellicosity of his remarks at the bargaining table or by
shutting down a vital industry.

Almost the only union chiefs who get their pictures on the cover
of *Time* magazine or on a national TV network are those who are
leading big strikes or making some dire threats of political or
economic mayhem. Tie-ups with the underworld or the kind of rank-
and-file insurgency that is currently making a shambles of coal production are about the only other ways a top unionist can command
that kind of attention. Since union leaders stop being leaders if they
don't get reelected, it becomes a matter of some importance in a
million-member union for the president to make sure that his members don't forget he is around. And what better medium than national
TV, that instant uplifter, to raise his standing with the rank and file,
no matter how unfriendly the commentary that goes along with his
picture on the home screen?

We have always tended to rate national union leaders in much
the same fashion that we do top sluggers in big-league baseball, by
running batting averages on how much bacon they bring home in
each industry-wide negotiation. When the Most Valuable Player
award, as measured by press and television exposure, goes to the
unionist who has distinguished himself by outdoing all the rest of
labor's upper echelon in irresponsibility, we are certainly not contributing much to the promotion of industrial peace or to continence
in the wage-price leapfrog.

My worry about this aspect of media emphasis is heightened by
my conviction that the only hope for sanity in industrial relations lies
in getting more science into wage determination and in moving away
from the countdown tensions of deadline bargaining through such innovative devices as steel's Experimental Negotiating Agreement. Unfortunately, the civilized approach to bargaining embodied in this pact
and in the joint production committees set up in steel to meet the
import threat never have had the degree of press attention I have always believed they deserved. To be honest, the experimental agree-

ment got its maximum notice early in 1977 through the attacks leveled against it by Ed Sadlowski, the tough-talking rebel from south Chicago, when he was making his unsuccessful bid for the union presidency on a program designed to revive all the "hate the boss" militancy of the steelworkers' early years. Sadlowski became something of a media hero as a symbol of youth challenging the old guard in a giant union. His story deserved telling, but it did not deserve the overweight of coverage it got in many publications. Much less did the Experimental Negotiating Agreement deserve presentation solely through Sadlowski's negative assessment without a much greater attempt than most journalists made to explain its virtues as the most innovative attempt yet undertaken in any basic industry to substitute reason for muscle in collective bargaining.

EDITORIAL DOUBLE STANDARDS

Now seems a good time to move away from the reportorial to the editorial side of media treatment of labor. Here the favorite gripe is that editorialists apply a double standard to labor or perhaps a double-double standard. One affects their supposed gentleness to errant corporations as against the savagery with which they comment on union derelictions. Whatever truth there might once have been in that half of the double-standard complaint, I think the widespread recent excoriation of Lockheed, Gulf, and many other giant corporations for their betrayal of the ethical standards that ought to guide the conduct of socially responsible companies has largely obliterated it. Sacred cows are almost extinct in the editorial columns of most major publications.

The other double standard is harder to blink. We are accused of setting up contradictory measuring rods by which to gauge a union leader. One day we berate him for being dictatorial, arrogating too much power to himself, using the forms of democracy to stifle the rights of dissidents. The next we reproach him for spinelessness because he is not forceful enough in fighting for rank-and-file ratification of a contract negotiated in good faith between himself and his industry. I can understand why union chiefs, confronted with such criticism, feel they can't win. We will pillory them if they are strong leaders. We will do the same if they are weak leaders. For myself, I see nothing either hypocritical or wrong in the simultaneous application of both yardsticks. It is the function of an effective leader to lead, and the best leaders are those who do not bulldoze or seduce their members, but rather persuade them of the correctness of their position and of the basic integrity of their organization.

I remember a good many years ago when Jimmy Petrillo, the feisty leader of the American Federation of Musicians, ranked as labor's prime candidate for Public Enemy Number One in the eyes of most editorialists because he was striking against "canned music" in movies, radio, and everywhere else unless users paid a tax to his union. Petrillo sent a delegation to visit David Dubinsky, the widely respected president of the International Ladies Garment Workers Union, to learn why he enjoyed such a good press when the media were so clearly "anti-labor." The first thing the visitors asked to see was the garment union's publicity department. They assumed Dubinsky must have a massive organization of flacks grinding out laudatory material and peddling it to the papers. To their astonishment they learned that the whole publicity apparatus was made up of the editor of the union paper and that he rarely sent out anything to the general press. The secret of good public relations, Dubinsky confided, was to do the right thing. That remains a good maxim even in these days when many unions have taken to large-scale advertising campaigns in both newspapers and television.

As for the press, I think it is doing a vastly better job of labor coverage than it was when I started in the early New Deal days. But that is not necessarily all the improvement that is needed. It disturbs me when a conscientious official like Secretary of Labor Marshall, who came into the Carter cabinet relatively inexperienced in press relations, confessed that he was "absolutely appalled" to discover how little understanding most reporters had of labor matters. I do not write that off as demagogy on Ray Marshall's part, nor do I take much comfort from his explanation that most of the ignorance is in the smaller cities, not the metropolitan centers. Where I think Marshall stretches his point too far is in ascribing much of the misunderstanding of which he complains to a well-heeled communications system spewing anti-union material around the country. The fault lies not in any brainwashing of labor reporters, but rather in the fact that in too many papers there are no labor reporters at all. The assumption is that anyone on the general staff can handle anything that comes along in that field, and that assumption is just wrong, partly because it limits coverage to what "comes along" and partly because even that is going to be written without insight. The range of organized labor's activity in every aspect of social, economic, and political activity is too encyclopedic to permit slapdash treatment. Moreover, so much of what passes for communication in labor-management relations and in unionism generally is double-talk that experts are needed to translate it into information on which the public can rely. Only a tiny handful of publications are doing that with any measure of adequacy today. It is time to lengthen the list.

LABOR AND THE MEDIA

ALBERT J. ZACK

After noting that trade unionists tend to be quite cynical about the media, AFL-CIO public relations director Albert J. Zack considers three major topics: coverage of labor; the trend toward mergers in the newspaper industry; and the journalist as union member. He lists the "sins of the media," which include failure to acknowledge "inherent prejudices" against labor; failure to distinguish between corrupt and honest unions; the application of different standards to the AFL-CIO and the Chamber of Commerce; belief that strikes are all wrong; lack of reporting on settlements not accompanied by strikes; dependence on labels and gossip; and covering only "big names." Moreover, Zack says that while labor has fought to protect the media from infractions on press freedoms, the media have not supported labor in its efforts to utilize First Amendment rights.

Zack, a veteran member of the Newspaper Guild, led a sixteen-month strike against the Springfield, Massachusetts, newspapers in 1946–47.

Trade unionists tend to be quite cynical about the media. They expect ball scores to be accurate; retail ads calculated to encourage them to buy what they don't need; political reporting to reflect the bias of the publisher; and labor reporting to be generally skimpy and uninformed. It is a cynicism rooted, of course, in the hypocritical view the press itself takes of the First Amendment.

The free trade union movement and the free press in this country share a common breeding ground—the First Amendment to the Constitution. In drafting that very special grouping of freedoms—religion, speech, press, assembly, and petition—the Founding Fathers clearly made them interdependent, with no single freedom predominant over the others.

But the media do not see it that way. They regularly invoke their First Amendment rights to oppose or, at best, to dampen the First Amendment rights of union members. For example, no daily newspaper in America editorially supported the situs picketing bill, and most opposed it, despite the fact that the guts of that legislation was the construction worker's right to exercise free speech in the form of a picket sign.

We in the labor movement do not engage in the practice of separating out freedoms, dividing them on the basis of some "higher good," as is common practice on editorial pages across America. Freedom, to us, is indivisible—a sign to some, I'm sure, of our unsophistication.

We supported Daniel Schorr and urged the House Ethics Committee to drop its plans to seek contempt citations. AFL-CIO leaders were on the front lines in Bakersfield and elsewhere where freedom of the press was under government attack. And it wasn't because Schorr and some of the others held union membership. The Newspaper Guild even backed a reporter on a struck newspaper—a scab, if you please—fighting an anti-First Amendment court order.

Similarly, we oppose other infringements on freedoms—wiretapping, preventive detention, censorship, and obsessions with internal security that give rise to mail covers, spying on American citizens, and other gross injustices.[1] Of course, this is not a two-way street. There is no press support when it is labor's freedom that is being challenged.

Imagine the outcry against infringement on a free press if Congress were to require commercial newspapers to report the cost of editions which editorially support candidates for federal office. Yet that segment of the press which is owned by the labor movement is required to report the cost of editions supporting federal candidates.

Imagine the outrage if the federal government dictated to commercial newspapers how and what they could report about stockholders' fights within the paper itself, or overturned a board of directors' election because the publisher's wife got her picture on the society page at a Junior League fashion show while a stockholders' fight for corporate control was going on. Yet the labor press is under such government dictates.

How come? Why two standards for freedom of the press, one for commercial papers and one for labor papers? And where are the valiant defenders of freedom of the press when it is our ox that is being gored?

So, we tend to be cynical about a free press that regularly and vigorously supports constricting such freedoms as the right to strike, contending the public's convenience demands limitations on that right, while piously invoking its own freedom as the defense for unfair, biased, and wrongheaded coverage of the labor movement or for establishment of monopolies over the free flow of information so vital in a democratic society.

We are further troubled by the growing trend toward chain ownership that gave rise to Charles Seib's amendment to A. J. Liebling's maxim, to wit: "Freedom of the press belongs to the conglomerates that own it."[2]

Let me hasten to add: we do not believe the press should support our cause in lockstep. Indeed, if the editorial writers were to do a 180-degree turn and extol the virtues of unions, we would consider ourselves suspect—and with good reason. Labor should never expect support from the press for the basic and obvious fact that a newspaper publisher is merely a businessman whose business happens to be publishing a newspaper.

There is nothing wrong with this, although a good many publishers and editors seem embarrassed by public exposition of the notion that they are in business to make a profit. It damages their self-anointed "objectivity," which is a patent fraud, unattainable by mortal beings.

All we suggest is that when newspapers proclaim the commandments of labor relations—thou shalt not strike; thou shalt not be greedy; thou shalt not injure the public interest; thou shalt honor thy employer—they should acknowledge their inherent prejudice. Wouldn't it be refreshing if the editorial clobbering the union and supporting the employer in any conflict between labor and management made some note of the fact that all employers are brothers, and that in unity of management there is strength?

Having indulged in that flight of fantasy, I would like to discuss three issues: editorial and reporting coverage of the labor movement; the incessant trend toward mergers and conglomerations in the newspaper industry; and the journalist as a union member.

COVERAGE OF THE LABOR MOVEMENT

We are beginning to worry, for the newspapers' sake, about their custom of ruling, in every strike, that labor is wrong-headed, as if they were a panel of arbitrators appointed by a Higher Power. A fortune cookie is not worth buying when the strip of paper inside always carries the same legend.[3]

From the time that Joe Liebling wrote that in a 1961 column to the present, the press has not altered its coverage of the labor movement. If anything, the situation is worse today. If the fall of Richard Nixon brought any ill to the nation, it is the concept that it was journalism that was the guardian of those journalists who exposed that wicked and corrupt man.

We in the labor movement believe we played some small role in Nixon's decline and fall. After all, the AFL-CIO was the first national organization to call for his resignation or impeachment—a position that was greeted with a torrent of editorial abuse. Our integrity was impugned, and even our right to have an opinion was challenged. Scores of newspapers reprinted—without attribution—columns supplied by various right-wing organizations bent on saving Nixon, some even accusing the labor movement of treason. This is a bit of history the press now ignores as it hails this triumph of democracy as a journalistic victory, given a helping hand by a few in Congress.

Another example: in 1971 the labor movement was the sole organized segment of society warning that economic controls would not work in a free society, that controlling wages alone would not curb an inflation which was not caused by spiraling wages. We were publicly pilloried by editorialists across the country. Almost alone the labor movement battled for that article of faith of American industry—the free operation of a free market. The free press, dependent as it is upon free enterprise, could not resist the temptation of any businessman to slap down wages. Only a few editorial voices observed the truism that if the government could control wages, might not the control of profits be next?

Another example, one I find especially galling: In 1975, the labor movement brought the heroic voice of Aleksandr Solzhenitsyn to America. We wanted the world to hear his witness for human rights, and, because we did, a large number of newspapers—although by no means unanimous—charged us with threatening détente and trade with the Soviet Union. They adopted the Kissinger theory: the Soviets wouldn't like it. That fear, you will remember, resulted in the then president of the United States being "too busy" to meet the authentic voice of Russians yearning for freedom.

That event, in my opinion, was one of the major turning points in the 1976 presidential election.

Today, when the American press has deemed human rights to be worthy of being talked about again, few editorialists have reminded their readers that the American labor movement played a role in helping to restore the promotion of human rights as a cornerstone of U.S. foreign policy.

I cite these examples, not as evidence of our virtue or our foresight or our dedication to democratic principles, but as testimony to the lack of understanding by the American press of the role of labor in America—what it means, what it does, and what it is.

Some of the press is, of course, just ignorant. An awful lot of American reporters know nothing about the labor movement. On most papers the labor beat is an afterthought or a stepping stone. Trade union history and development, much less collective bargaining, are not taught in schools, including journalism schools.

If there were but one fact that I would like to impart to budding, blossoming, or already gone-to-seed reporters, it is that the AFL-CIO is *not* a union. It is a federation of unions—107 national and international unions, representing 60,000 local unions and some 14 million American workers through approximately 150,000 separate collective-bargaining agreements. It is not a monolith or a conspiracy.

George Meany cannot order any group of workers to go on strike or to sign a contract or to vote for a labor-endorsed candidate. Each union affiliated with the AFL-CIO retains autonomy over its own internal affairs, and every individual member of each union retains that very essential autonomy of saying "no" to George Meany—and any other VIP, for that matter.

But conspiracy theories sell papers.

Consider, for instance, the question of corruption. The public links the corruption in the Teamsters Union with the rest of the labor movement, because the press always headlines it as "union corruption," rarely, if ever, pointing out that the AFL-CIO expelled the Teamsters in 1957, an act many newspapers said at the time would destroy the federation.

By the same token the press refuses to call the U.S. Chamber of Commerce to task for failing to take action against the more than 200 corporations that have admitted widespread bribery, payoffs, and political corruption. In fact, the Chamber is rarely criticized in print for opposing legislation to establish a code of ethics for the conduct of U.S. business firms abroad. A double standard? You bet there is. Papers are more than willing to tell the labor movement how to run its business, but are noticeably reticent about commenting on how business runs its business.

The press is also notoriously lax in providing any substantive test for so-called public opinion polls bandied about by private interest groups. A good example is the polls which declare widespread public opposition to so-called compulsory unionism. Poll questions are frequently loaded and survey methods questionable, but a press release on a "poll" is a surefire success.

The Arkansas AFL-CIO conducted a poll last year which found nearly identical percentages opposed to so-called compulsory unionism and compulsory acceptance of freeloaders. In other words, when the question was posed, "When the workers in a plant have voted in a secret-ballot election for a union to represent all of them, should every worker pay his or her fair share of the cost of that representation?" as many said "yes" as those who opposed "compulsory unionism." I would submit that the Arkansas AFL-CIO question more accurately reflects the situation on the job than the one posed by the so-called National Right-to-Work Committee.

It is perhaps in collective bargaining where factual errors and a lack of understanding cause the most mischief. As Liebling put it in writing about the Long Island Railroad strike of 1960, "Is it possible that the public has ceased to accept the doctrine of unilateral sin in labor disputes?"[4]

For nearly a century now American newspapers have written that the public is fed up with strikes, tired of being inconvenienced, and that a wave of public indignation will soon put labor in its place. I think the American public is smarter than the editors give them credit for; the people understand, as Dwight Eisenhower said, that "there are some things worse, much worse, than strikes. One of them is the loss of freedom."[5]

First, a few facts about collective bargaining:

- The function of collective bargaining is to resolve disputes, and it is highly successful—meeting that goal in more than 98 percent of all situations.

- Union officials who conduct negotiations are elected by the workers themselves in democratic, secret-ballot elections supervised by the government, and, in many instances, the contracts themselves are voted up or down by the members.

- The right of workers to withhold their labor and to strike is just as fundamental a right as the right of freedom of the press. Those editorialists who advocate compulsory arbitration—where government sets the conditions under which workers must work and the conditions management must provide—ought to consider an equally invalid compulsion. How would they like government to have compulsory editorial power, the right to dictate what can and cannot be published? The public's convenience, in both cases, is no justification for a denial of freedom.

Despite these facts every union proposal is called a "demand" and every management proposal is called an "offer." Every strike is calculated in lost wages, never in the lost self-esteem that would result if the workers caved in to management demands and tolerated unfettered management domination of their lives. Every strike is a strike against the public interest or inflationary or pigheaded in the opinion of the press. Isn't it possible we're right every once in a while?

At the same time settlements in the absence of a strike are rarely reported, except in basic industries. Contract signings are considered non-news. The system has worked; there is no conflict. Thus, there's no story. Logic? If reported at all, settlement stories are usually loaded with company quotes about increased costs being passed on to the consumer, without any real digging to see if this is necessary. Rarely are settlements reported in terms of the increased purchasing power that will result, thus boosting sales in local businesses—a fact most local advertisers might find interesting.

Sloppy reporting of collective bargaining is symptomatic of sloppy reporting of economics generally. In most newspapers business news is depressingly superficial and reads like Chamber of Commerce handouts, which, to be sure, much of it is. As the AFL-CIO's secretary-treasurer, Lane Kirkland, put it in a discussion of economic reporting: "The dismal science is reported dismally."[6]

For example, one of the stock questions always asked of Meany at his press conferences during the AFL-CIO Executive Council's midwinter meeting is: "What percentage wage increase do you think workers should settle for in this year's collective bargaining?" Such a question reflects a gross misunderstanding of the labor movement—since the AFL-CIO conducts no collective bargaining and doesn't even consult with its affiliated unions on bargaining—and an even baser misunderstanding of the economic system, because a 5 percent raise for an airline pilot earning $70,000 a year is a helluva lot more than a 5 percent raise for a hospital worker earning three dollars an hour.

Union negotiators are rapped by the press for not being more forthcoming during negotiations. First of all, negotiators have a responsibility to the union members which takes precedent over the right of the press to know what is going on. But, more importantly, negotiators rarely have time to conduct negotiations and, at the same time, instruct a class of reporters on the mechanics and art of collective bargaining, explain costing, or make a fluid situation remain static long enough for a story to get into print.

Announcing tentative, partial, or conditional agreements or fallback positions could lead to contract rejections and thus lengthen strikes. The fact is that negotiations conducted through the media—with both labor and management posturing for public consumption rather than trying to reach agreement—generally result in the longest, most bitter strikes.

Several other issues should be raised under this section: labeling, gossip journalism, confrontation or star-system reporting, and truth in editorializing.

The press is wont to use labels—quick, easy, simplistic descriptive phrases often added for "color." For instance, George Meany is always "the cantankerous, cigar-chomping, 83-year-old curmudgeon" who speaks "gruffly" in a "heavy Bronx accent." And he is a "conservative" to boot. Because the desire for color takes precedence over substantive reporting, reporters beat a path most often to those who can be counted on to give the "best" quote, rather than those in the best position to know the subject and react seriously.

Wall Street Journal reporter David Ignatius, who put his colleagues to shame with his excellent coverage of the recent leadership elections in the Steelworkers Union, pointed out in a *Columbia Journalism Review* article that:

Meany, for example, is often characterized as "cigar-smoking," which would be a trivial detail were it not a sort of shorthand for "boss." Similarly, [Steelworkers president I. W.] Abel's name is often preceded by phrases like "$75,000-a-year steelworkers chief," which is presumably intended to mean "overpaid."[7]

Ignatius laments that business tycoons are rarely treated as the "$425,000-a-year steel company chief" Edgar B. Speer. He has placed his finger on what he calls "cultism," in respect to the romantic attachment between the press and new, supposedly more militant challengers in union elections. It is a subject worthy of more thoughtful discussion than the constraints of this paper.

As to political labeling, George Meany is called a "conservative" because he himself claims the title as the nation's number-one anticommunist. He is also the nation's number-one foe of right-wing dictators. Unless the press believe that communism is the quintessence of liberalism—a thought I find repulsive—then the rating system for George Meany is faulty. The only press yardstick for the title of "liberal labor leader" that I have been able to determine is "one who disagrees with Meany."

Gossip journalism, it seems to me, is the biggest threat to the credibility of the press since the invention of the television camera. Back when I was treading a beat the rule was two independent confirmations for each fact, but that rule no longer holds. One "source," no matter how uninformed, is all that is needed, and if it appears in a mimeographed press release, then some modern-day Diogenes carrying a Sony recorder instead of a lantern considers it gospel and never checks the fact.

Consider the following report from the August 15, 1977, issue of *U.S. News & World Report's* "Washington Whispers" column:

> George Meany's continued public pleas to Congress to raise the minimum wage from $2.30 to $3 an hour, insiders say, are just lip service to the rank and file. He has privately conceded that a Carter-backed compromise at $2.65 is the best labor can expect.

Four times—July 13, July 20, July 24, and August 1—in press releases, speeches, or testimony, Meany publicly stated the federation's support for the $2.65 compromise. "Insiders say." If the so-called "insiders" don't know enough to read the public statements of the AFL-CIO, then how can they be trusted for actual "inside" dope?

This is not the first time that totally inaccurate material has been printed in this "gossip" column—material that was not checked with my office. In fact, I have good reason to believe this piece was not even checked with the magazine's own labor reporter. He certainly knew the facts.

Confrontation reporting places the journalist in the position of creating or making news. While many examples come to mind, the best—or worst—involves the *New York Times*. In 1975, a *Times* reporter asked me if the AFL-CIO would oppose accepting the Vietnamese refugees, since unemployment in the United States was so high. When told "no," that we strongly supported giving them a haven, the reporter said: "There's no news in that." I disagreed, but his editor evidently didn't, for no story was printed.

Comparing notes with my current counterpart in the White House one afternoon, I discovered that some reporters who had been calling me for an update on the reported "feud" between George Meany and President Carter were asking the White House for similar updates. While labor and the White House disagreed on some issues, no feud existed. Our joint denials did not stop the stories from being written, including one column which stated that Meany had directed no contacts be made by any AFL-CIO staffer with the White House, at the very time we were negotiating with the president's key staff members about labor-law reform. And at the same time I was meeting with Jody Powell.

Similarly, the UPI correspondent who covers the labor beat—and quite well, I might add—told me one day that her desk had laughingly promised her a budget item and bulletin treatment any time George Meany agreed with the president. That very day Meany issued a statement supporting President Carter's proposals for Social Security financing, but the UPI desk didn't think it "newsy" enough to even merit insertion into a running story of business opposition to the president's proposal. In other words, it's not news unless there is confrontation.

The media have a fixation on the "star system," which, when they think labor, means George Meany.[8] Recently, Meany was forced to cancel out of a speaking engagement before the Coalition for a Fair Minimum Wage because he scratched his eyeball inserting a contact lens. When this was announced, the CBS crew immediately tore down their cameras, on orders from the assignment desk, because the event no longer had "news value."

The event continued. Meany's speech was delivered by his executive assistant, Tom Donahue, who among other credentials is a former assistant secretary of labor. The other members of the Coalition, composed of representatives of organizations that have 40 million members, all were present to complete their lobbying plans to pass the compromise minimum-wage bill. That bill is of major economic importance—to business as well as minimum-wage workers. But CBS deemed that, because Meany wasn't there, there was no news.

News judgment is a ticklish issue, and having been a news editor I am very sensitive to it. However, the decision whether the story merited thirty seconds on the "CBS Evening News" should not be made before the story transpired. One man, even the man who signs my paycheck, is not the news.

Rather than being complimented by the CBS action, Meany was outraged. To him, the cause of justice for working people has been his life—not vice versa.

Now, Meany is "good copy." He has earned his reputation for saying what he thinks and for representing the interests of organized labor. But George Meany is not the AFL-CIO; there are 14 million people who make up the AFL-CIO, and nobody knows that better than George Meany.

Regarding editorials, it is a source of constant amazement to me that so many newspapers demonstrate no standard of accuracy whatsoever for editorials. Scores of publications reprint, as their own editorials, columns provided by the so-called National Right-to-Work Committee. Frequently there are misrepresentations, misstatements, and downright lies in these columns. The papers use them without attribution, without checking the facts, without informing the readers whose opinion is being peddled—and obviously without shame or sensitivity.

They never inform their readers of these truths about the so-called National Right-to-Work Committee:

Fact: It is a front for anti-labor business groups (a federal judge has so ruled).

Fact: It claims a million members but is not a membership organization. All decisions on policy and personnel are made by one man, Reed Larson.

Fact: It annually raises $7 million to $10 million but makes no reports of expenditures, source of income, or other financial information to anyone.

Fact: Its name is an absolute and complete phony, since its policies guarantee no one a job. Its policies were designed, initiated, and underwritten by the National Association of Manufacturers, beginning in 1903, to bust unions.

Fact: This outfit, which vitriolicly campaigns against "compulsory unionism," recently lobbied for and got a government-subsidized mailing permit, which means that union members are compelled through their taxes to help these right-wingers raise funds.

Fact: Despite its name, it is opposing labor-law reform, which is designed to protect workers being illegally fired from their jobs because they want to join a union.

Frankly, union people are not at all surprised that this organization, which regularly uses full-page newspaper ads as a propaganda tool, should have such ready, unquestioning access to editorial pages. We believe—and we think editorial writers should believe—that a pulpit that anyone with enough money can buy speaks for financial rather than moral authority. Of course, if an editor really believes the committee's hokum, why aren't the editorials it peddles identified so that the reader knows who is the true author?

MEDIA CONCENTRATION

> There is the inevitable pressure of bigness, and the devotion to profit and
> to conformity which is the nature of the corporate beast. The good news-
> paper does things that outrage the corporate mind. It spends money it can't
> hope to recover covering the news simply because it has an obligation to
> do so; it deliberately offends good customers; it deprecates all institutions,
> including itself. Bookkeepers can't tolerate that very long, and it is the
> bookkeepers who are rising to the chief executive slots.[9]

Of the 1,500 American cities with daily newspapers, 97.5 percent
have no local competition. More than 50 percent of all daily circulation rests in the hands of twenty-five newspaper chains, and 75 percent of all circulation is controlled by multiple ownership.

It seems we've added a new "big" to the litany of big labor and big
business: "big news."

Since the parentage of public relations professionals is immediately suspect in an audience of journalists,[10] it should be left to
those who qualify as media critics to comment on whether bigness is
making any positive impact on news quality. Rather, it is for us who
worked in this business when competition was keen to recall that it
made us better reporters—and our readers were the better for it.

I never thought I would look upon the press as something which
could be stamped out with the uniformity of an auto body, yet that is
precisely what is happening. Local autonomy, and with it the indi-
viduality that brought character and humanness to the American
press, is rapidly disappearing. There is reportorial and editorial same-
ness that is saddening.

Newspaper formats, like TV news formats, will soon be syndicated, so that we can see "eyewitness news" when we pick up our
morning paper and turn on the evening news. Newspapers never
figured out how to handle the tube and hence decided to compete
with it on television's own terms—once over lightly.

I am not at all encouraged by the prospect of twenty chains owning virtually all of the papers in this country, with four sources of
news—AP, UPI, and the news services of the *Times* and the *Washington Post*—and interlocking boards of directors and television and
radio outlets. The potential for conflicts of interest is too great, with
the greatest being the conflict between profit and the public's right to
know.

In the debate over equitable postal rates for second-class publications, the voice of Barry Goldwater has been virtually alone in the
defense of smaller newspapers and greater distribution of information
to the American people through such diverse sources as the nonprofit
press and opinion journals. While I always have second thoughts
about agreeing with Senator Goldwater on any issue, I am proud that
the AFL-CIO has stood with him on this issue which is central to

freedom of the press. Senator Goldwater is concerned with maintaining a diverse press, and so are we. We recognize that freedom of the press is not free if it is restrained by a high price tag for postage.

The current proposal of the Postal Service to treat opinion matter like advertising for determining zone postal rates would be disastrous to small opinion journals. This is a real freedom-of-the-press issue, and the labor press has challenged the Postal Service on this.

There are serious anti-trust implications, however, to concentration, but I doubt whether they will ever be adequately discussed in a public forum. When Representative Morris Udall proposed a study of the monopoly trends in newspapers,[11] the industry hollered, "Freedom of the press." The fact is that media monopolies are advertising monopolies—with news content being crushed in the middle—but the press hides behind the First Amendment to guard against any discussion of its business practices.

In a column for *Publishers Auxiliary,* Udall recalled the warning of William Allen White: "The people have a keen and accurate sense that much of editorial anxiety about the freedom of the press rises out of editorial greed."[12]

In the same speech cited earlier by John McCormally, he related the following anecdote:

> I was at a meeting the other day where the featured speaker, a senior executive in a newspaper chain, lectured the assembled journalists on the value of caution. "Never get more than 10 degrees ahead of the public," he warned, "and you can be assured of a steady 10 percent profit."

Yes, Pogo, we have met the enemy and he is us.

LABOR RELATIONS IN THE MEDIA

> Guild membership shall be open to every eligible person without discrimination or penalty, nor shall any member be barred from membership or penalized, by reason of age, sex, race, national origin, religious or political conviction or anything he or she writes for publication.[13]

I am no expert on labor relations in the newspaper business. My only credentials in this field consist of having been one of the leaders of a long and unsuccessful strike at the Springfield, Massachusetts, *Daily News,* where the issue was union recognition and money in the paycheck—then about thirty dollars a week—and not the ethical question of whether a union shop for journalists would violate our First Amendment rights.

We knew then that the union shop was the way to a better life for all of us because it strengthened our bargaining position with the boss. We knew then that the so-called "open or merit shop" was nothing more than a management device to keep the union weak. We knew then that those who were promoting the "open shop" for journalists were not concerned with our First Amendment rights. As James J. Kilpatrick stated in a recent radio commentary, the First Amendment right of the free press belongs to the publisher, not the reporter or editor.[14]

But the so-called National Right-to-Work Committee seized on the unfortunate and reprehensible actions of a small group of *Washington Post* pressmen and attempted to bring the question of union shop before the Society of Professional Journalists, Sigma Delta Chi, convention. It was also raised—and rejected—in a suit brought by William F. Buckley, Jr., and M. Stanton Evans against an AFL-CIO affiliate.[15]

This was not the first time that publishers or their allied front groups have sought to use the First Amendment against media unions. The Associated Press went all the way to the Supreme Court in 1937 in an effort to get the news industry exempted from the National Labor Relations Act. Was AP interested in the First Amendment rights of its employees?[16]

Publishers have also tried to invoke the First Amendment to escape coverage under the Fair Labor Standards Act. During World War II, publishers tried to get the War Labor Board to bar maintenance of membership clauses for Newspaper Guild members. The board chairman, William H. Davis, cited the Guild's constitution and pointed out the obvious fact that only the publisher had the First Amendment right to freedom of the press.

He also noted that maintenance of membership was a voluntary agreement between the publisher and the union representing the employees. Yet what is proposed in the name of the right to work is compelling publishers *not* to sign a contract containing a maintenance of membership clause. Such a contract is a voluntary decision of the publisher. A right-to-work law for journalists, or anyone else, for that matter, is the compulsion, in a negative sense.

What was intimated in the Buckley-Evans suit and in the SPJ/SDX resolution is the specious argument used by the Lynchburg, Virginia, *News*: "When journalists can be forced to join unions, they can be forced to do—meaning write—what unions tell them."[17]

As Earl Butz would say, balderdash! Only the publisher or his agent can tell a journalist what to write. And despite claims of "objectivity," no one here is foolish enough not to recognize that every newspaper in America has what are called "policy" stories that are handled in a certain manner under strict editorial guidelines.

The Guild constitution is clear. More than 140 newspapers, magazines, and news services have Guild maintenance-of-membership contract clauses, and yet not one example has ever been cited of a union to which journalists pay dues exerting any influence on what is written.

If such coercion existed I would not be here complaining about the press, since I would be leading the "party line" and forcing newspaper reporters all over America to write how great the labor movement is.

Labor relations in the media, it seems to me, have more important issues to resolve than the long-settled question of whether a union shop infringes on the First Amendment. The technological revolution, with the inherent loss of jobs, has created a flash point in the industry. The delaying tactics used by publishers to postpone union-representation elections, along with the illegal firing of union sympathizers, constitute a threat to the workers' free choice of whether to vote for a union or not.

But what we have done is simply gone full circle. We started with publishers hiding behind the First Amendment, and that is where we must end this discussion. The root of the problem for the media— how it covers the labor movement, the increasing concentration of the power of the press in fewer and fewer hands, and the way the press treats its own employees—is the narrow view of the industry that the First Amendment only applies to them, and not to the rest of us.

The labor movement has not, does not, and will not accept that view. We think any constitutional right that's good enough for a publisher is good enough for us too.

NOTES

1. For a fuller exposition of the labor movement's view of individual freedom, see AFL-CIO president George Meany's 1973 Labor Day message.

2. Charles B. Seib, "The News Business," *Washington Post,* March 25, 1977.

3. A. J. Liebling, *The Press* (New York: Ballantine Books, 1961).

4. Ibid.

5. Proceedings of the 71st annual convention of the American Federation of Labor, September 1952.

6. Lane Kirkland, "Labor and the Press," A. J. Liebling Memorial Lecture, sponsored by the International Labor Press Association, September 29, 1975.

7. David Ignatius, "The Press in Love," *Columbia Journalism Review,* May/June 1977, p. 26.

8. Fred Allen said television was called a "medium" because it never does anything well.

9. John McCormally, editor and publisher of the Burlington, Iowa, *Hawkeye,* speaking to a University of Iowa journalism awards banquet. Reprinted in the *Congressional Record,* April 28, 1977.

10. Call girls make similar comments about streetwalkers.

11. H. R. 6098, the Competition Review Act.

12. "What's Killing Independent Newspapers? It's Time to Find Out," *Publishers Auxiliary,* April 25, 1977, p. 8.

13. Constitution of the Newspaper Guild, Article II, Section I.

14. Commentary taped December 3, 1976, for WTOP, Washington, D.C.

15. The Buckley-Evans suit was financed by the National Right-to-Work Committee's Legal Defense Foundation, which a federal judge has ruled is a business front group.

16. For a detailed discussion of this issue, see "Free Press Versus Union Membership—A False Choice," *The Newspaper Guild,* November 8, 1976.

17. Ibid.

LABOR RELATIONS IN MEDIA INDUSTRIES

WILLIAM T.
RUTHERFORD

Labor-relations problems, in the media or any other industry, cannot be understood until the basic nature of the game is explained to the spectators. William T. Rutherford explains the game and then looks at the media both in terms of how they play it and how they watch others playing it. He finds an anomaly in that media industries have been innovative and progressive in working out their own labor problems, but have been conservative and even misleading in respect to their communication to the public of labor relations in general.

An associate professor of management and business law at Georgia State University, Dr. Rutherford is a former field attorney for the National Labor Relations Board. An arbitrator, he is a member of the Industrial Relations Research Association.

Most of my friends and acquaintances who do not regularly deal with labor-relations matters tell me that some mighty strange critters seem to operate in this field. They have the impression that an inordinate number of the nation's hotheads (labor at present, management in the past) seem to be drawn to the field. They then ask me, "What attracts you to the field?" I have that strange sinking feeling in my stomach that I have just been asked a "loaded" question.

My friends' ignorance indicates that industrial-relations problems can not be understood until the basic nature of the game is explained to the spectators. Football is not a particularly enjoyable sport to watch (much less play) until you know the objectives of the opposing sides and the rules that govern the interaction of the adversaries. Thus, it is appropriate to explain the industrial-relations game to business and media newcomers before they should be asked to play or to comment creatively on the game they are watching.

I have found it helpful to the uninitiated to explain industrial relations by a rough analogy to another long-standing social-political-economic relationship—marriage. Some labor/management relationships are the product of shotgun marriages; some are marriages of convenience. A few are even love at first sight. And, as is so often true with marriages, the relationship changes and grows even though the nature of the legal ties remains the same. George Bernard Shaw has characterized marriage as an ocean of emotions entirely surrounded with expenses. At times I have heard both labor and management make such comments about their relationships. Yet it is also true that both parties have on other occasions (generally when things are going well at home) said that their relationship is mutually beneficial; in fact, they doubt if they could get along without each other.

What is the nature of the similarity between these two institutions which sheds light on how to live with and report on them? There are many similarities, but let me center on some of the most important. Both situations involve shared decision making, since decisions affect both parties. This movement from unilateral to bilateral decision making can be traumatic. Often some people, no matter what hat they are wearing—corporation president, union leader, or spectators on the sideline (for example, media people)—never get accustomed to this new way of living. If you have once called most of the shots essentially by yourself, you are reluctant to see the advantages and interpersonal challenges that flow from getting others involved. It might sound like a good, abstract ideal, but it does not live as well as it reads. So how do you make the institution work better? First, understand that each side has a legitimate role to play. Second, listen before you react. Third, realize that all marriages have their rough times. Just as it is a bit improbable to expect uninterrupted marital bliss, so is it not surprising to find that labor and management have occasional blowups. Do these occasional disruptions indicate the marriage is not working? No, not always. In fact it may be a good indicator that they are working on solving their problems rather than just sitting across the room staring silently at each other.

It is important to understand that in the labor/management marriage each party has a job to perform, and, while the jobs are different, they can be made to complement each other. It is not labor's job to manage the television station or the newspaper. It is not management's job to run the union. When both parties accept their respective roles and work together to accomplish the overall goals which perpetuate each other, then the marriage is working.

These industrial-relations marriages deserve a plug and an extra effort at understanding by all participants and bystanders, because they are consistent with and supportive of the basic political ideals upon which this country was founded. Shared decision making in matters affecting one's social and economic well-being is at the heart of the democratic form of government. Thus, it is seen that healthy collective bargaining is an integral part of our institutions which harmonizes with our national personality and governmental ideals. Yes, it might be said, as Churchill once observed, that democracy is the worst form of government except for any other form of government. But there is a recognized inherent form of good that follows from participative decision making, a truism even when the format results in a failure to reach a consensus. In a democratic society the right to agree has always encompassed the right to disagree. That right should not be compromised or castigated in one institutional relationship (collective bargaining) while generally praised in most others.

The job of living with and reporting on such a deceptively simple but subtle relationship as labor/management relations is truly a difficult one. It requires that all the parties and bystanders continually remind themselves of the basic dynamics of the relationship as they consider a particular problem that has arisen.

Within the broad description of the free collective-bargaining system and the public policy supporting it, described above, the opposing parties and bystanders will generally see two basic problems which will occasionally make news and cause frequent tensions to the parties. The earlier quote from George Bernard Shaw hints at these two basic problems. The ocean of emotions Shaw spoke of deals with the human-relations problem (for example, how can both sides keep their cool and not unnecessarily offend the other, thus shutting off effective communication?). The expenses part of the relationship Shaw spoke of involves the touchy, delicate problem of the two sides deciding just how to divide up the economic pie that brings them together.

It seems to me that much of the rhetoric in the media fails to fully educate the reader or to relate to the reader what the basic issue is, and that there is no one correct answer. Much of the writing in the media seems to imply that there is a single correct and societally proper answer to these two basic problems of economics and human relations. Well, there is not. To return to the earlier analogy of marriage: there is no single assured way to make any particular marriage work. The economic and human-relation challenges need not be handled in any one specific way in a marriage. Many authorities would say that many "modern" marriages work, not because they follow a predetermined correct pattern, but because they are specifically shaped to fit the personal and economic tastes of the two people or groups of people who are trying to stay together. Thus, reporting in the media, and analysis by the parties of their own relationship, should examine their specific personal traits and economic conditions and not someone else's "idea" of how the "perfect" couple should act.

LABOR/MANAGEMENT RELATIONS IN THE MEDIA INDUSTRY

Space will not permit an in-depth analysis of the state of labor/management relations in the media industry. However, a brief analysis of some key factors in that industry will further illustrate some of the general observations already made and some of the specific comments made in the other articles in this section. A key economic fact of life that has complicated collective bargaining in radio, TV, and the print media has been the continuous rapid change of technology in these industries. The economic upheaval brought on by these changes has presented tough problems to both labor and management. Management has argued that it must modernize its techniques to meet competition. Labor has been concerned that these changes jeopardize the job security of those it represents. Thus, both parties have struggled with how to best modernize their marriage. The problem is further complicated by the fact that within each camp there have been disagreements as to how to proceed. Thus, what the labor lawyers call jurisdictional disputes frequently crop up. Union X seeks to represent the employees in a newly emerging skill, while Union Y claims this new skill most appropriately belongs to it. Thus, these jurisdictional problems are a product of the changing technology in the industry.

Perhaps a look at the production aspect of the newspaper industry might appropriately illustrate some of the specific problems in industrial relations that technology presents. As I have learned in the few arbitrations I have been involved in which dealt with newspapers, the process of and technology in printing a newspaper is quite complex. Once the reporters and editors have done their job, somebody has to print their output, and fast. Basically, as best I can understand it, the written word first goes to a composing room where the type is set and arranged. Then this product goes to a stereotype department where the plates later to be attached to the printing presses are made. Finally, the pressroom employees actually operate and maintain the presses, which print and fold the newspaper. In each of the three areas mentioned improvements in machines and product flow are almost continuous. Employees working in these areas are concerned that these changes might eliminate their jobs. Of course, management is concerned that it continue to produce a newspaper fast enough for the breaking news and cheap enough so that consumers can afford to buy it. Various compromises to this dilemma have been worked out between the parties. Some contracts provide for layoff of employees only by attrition. Severance pay is another solution.

Another confusing aspect to labor relations in the newspaper publishing industry results from the fact that the production process is not steady. The news is delayed in transmission to the production department until the last minute so that it will be current. Then the production department must work very fast in order to get the printed word to the public while it is still current. So you have a hurry up and wait situation where fifteen people may be needed in one department at one particular period of two hours but only eight people will be needed during the remaining six hours. From the employer's point of view the most efficient way to handle the matter is to have eight regular full-time employees and seven regular part-time employees.

Unions have generally gone along with this so long as they have the ability to significantly influence the process by at least helping in determining how the full-time positions are to be filled and by whom and in regulating the number of full-time positions which in turn regulates the number of part-time positions. The union's efforts here are aimed at job security, and the employer's efforts are aimed at cost-efficient production. Is either side "wrong" in taking the particular position they take? The answer is, of course, no. Their relative positions are simply a specific example of the continuing economic problem between the parties (for example, how much of the economic pie do I get as opposed to you?).

Even when the parties have agreed on a rough percentage of the economic pie they each will get, they then must decide just what items will be split up in order to arrive at the desired result. The union may give up some job-tenure security if the wage rate of those remaining is boosted.

I have mentioned these problems in the newspaper industry to illustrate the difficulty of reporting the "news" of collective-bargaining progress. The reporter is faced with a dilemma. If he reports only about the specific squabble, the true stakes in the overall negotiations are not brought to light. Yet, if he attempts to report on the ultimate struggle (for example, how to split up the economic pie), the story just does not seem to be so newsy as before.

It seems to me that a good deal of the reporting on the right-to-work laws suffers from a similar problem. If William F. Buckley and M. Stanton Evans are compelled to join a union in order to speak over the public airwaves, as they claimed, then that is news. Yet the necessity of a union to obtain funds to pay for the services it renders is not news. And then there is the problem of just plain misleading reporting on this topic. The law on this point is clear. The National Labor Relations Act and the 1963 Supreme Court case *NLRB* v. *General Motors*, 373 U.S. 734, clearly state that a union-shop clause in a contract in a non-right-to-work state only compels payment of dues, not actual membership.

I must admit that the legal rules of which we speak are not widely known, a fact that I personally deplore. But whose fault is that? Could it be the employers are not anxious to tell their employees? If so, possibly we should be lecturing the employers, not just the unions or employees. More importantly, why has the press been so silent and/or misleading? I continue to note news reports of collective-bargaining negotiations where the media claim that the union is seeking a contract clause requiring compulsory membership of all employees. These reports do not go on to explain what compulsory membership means and most importantly what it does not mean.

Collective bargaining is an institution just about as old as this country itself. In the newspaper industry collective bargaining existed at least thirty years before the Civil War. Perhaps what is more interesting is that the bargaining in the newspaper industry has been in the forefront of innovative developments. For example, the first instances of binding-interest arbitration occurred in the newspaper industry prior to 1900. As many of you may know, interest arbitration refers to a situation where labor and management choose a third person to write their contract when they cannot reach agreement by themselves. Both labor and management have traditionally opposed this recourse fearing that their future fate is placed in the hands of an outsider not familiar with their problems who will not have to live with or explain the contract once it is handed down from on high. Yet in recent times certain industries, most notably steel, and unions and management in the public sector, have resorted to this technique when they found that collective bargaining in the old style was not working to their mutual interest or to the general public interest.

Thus, we have a strange anomaly. The press in their reporting of industrial-relations developments (other than their own) seems to me a bit conservative. Yet when it comes to matters within their own house they have been quite open-minded for a long period of time. It appears that newspapers, at least, have been leaders in collective-bargaining developments for a long time, but their reporters apparently do not know about it, or they do not fully understand the dynamics of the process going on in their own backyard.

Since I have mentioned the topic of interest arbitration in the newspaper industry, I would like to say a little more about it. It is a process that does present some problems. One of the most interesting concerns whether or not a newspaper, or for that matter any other employer, can get out of such an obligation once it is entered into. In other words, if the union and the employer once turn over the resolution of their dispute to an outsider, can either side unilaterally ever get out of the agreement? The National Labor Relations Board and the courts have recently held that they can. Of course, it has always been known that if the parties mutually agree to limit or revoke the interest-arbitration agreement then they are relieved of it. The recognized right of unilateral withdrawal was decided by the National Labor Relations Board in a case involving a Columbus, Georgia, newspaper and the Printing Pressmen's union (*The Columbus Printing Pressmen & Assistants' Union No. 252, Subordinate to IP & GCU* and the *R. W. Page Corporation,* 219 NLRB No. 54) which was sustained by the Fifth Circuit Court of Appeals (*NLRB* v. *Columbus Printing Pressmen,* 93 LRRM 3055). Once again the newspaper industry appears to have been a leader in developing an important area of public policy in labor/management relations. At least with respect to interest arbitration, it is my opinion that the media have been pretty favorable in their comments. The steel companies and the Steelworkers Union got some positive media reaction as a result of their experimental negotiating agreement, the phrase they use for interest arbitration.

MEDIA REPORTS ON THE LABOR RELATIONS OF OTHERS

How the media report on the labor problems of others is discussed by other papers in this section. However, I feel compelled to also make a few comments on the topic since in some ways it relates to the labor-relations problems within the media industry.

The results of collective bargaining in this country are very carefully crafted to meet the particular conditions that a specific employer and union face. There is no one correct solution to the differing desires of all employers and employees. Perhaps the media, being attuned to the particular problems of collective bargaining in their industry, fail to fully realize that other industries may be faced with different problems. For example, the problem of the employment and earnings impact of technological change is far less pronounced in other industries. It is true that, at high levels of generality, the problems of all employers and employees are quite similar. However, collective bargaining in this country does not deal with generalities, but the particular concerns of specific plants. The news reporter thus must become familiar with the dynamics of the industry whose collective-bargaining developments he is attempting to report.

The job of reporting the news is truly a high and demanding calling. It requires that the reporter have a vast background of knowledge about the general topic he is covering. Without such a background the reporter finds it difficult to determine just what facts are news. Thus, the reporter who covers many beats must truly be a man for all seasons. When covering international relations he must be an expert in history and political science. When covering the science beat and the development of a neutron bomb he must be an expert in the physical sciences. And, yes, when covering the industrial-relations beat, it would be quite helpful if he had a reasonably good understanding of the intricacies of that process. Since most of us cannot be expert in many fields, one solution is to develop specialists in labor-relations reporting such as is represented by A. H. Raskin and Tom Joyce. The problem with this solution is that it is economically infeasible for many newspapers, radio, and TV stations.

What then is to be done? Here are a few partial solutions. The media and those about whom the news is being written should try to at least select news gatherers who are familiar with the particular industry. Then the parties to the dispute must spend some time with that person explaining the nature of the collective-bargaining process. Yes, that is a large order, but not an impossible one. It appears that the AFL-CIO has been rather successful in this regard due to the efforts of Albert Zack. Employers should spend some time with their public relations man explaining to him the communications job necessary to accurately talk with the press and thus the public about the employer's collective-bargaining developments.

Perhaps the most frequent example of "selective reporting" involves the news accounts of strikes. Strikes do occur, and they are newsworthy and should be reported. But that should not be the end of the story, as it frequently is. The Good Book places a high value on peacemakers. Let's have some stories about the vast majority of collective-bargaining situations where a peaceful agreement is reached without any work interruption. Many local newspapers do not seem to report much about the many small and medium-sized employers in their area who regularly settle their differences without a strike. Failure to give these facts creates a misimpression among the public. They get the impression that collective bargaining generally means strikes, when in fact the opposite is the case. The fact is that more time is lost in coffee breaks each year than is lost due to strikes. You would think newspapers would know this. Newspaper strikes are relatively rare, but when they occur they sure get the coverage.

SUMMING UP

Introspection aids growth. A look at the labor-relations developments in the media industry reveals a long history of improvements and new innovations designed to fit the particular problems of that industry and the desires of its members. The media could be more effective in their news-gathering and reporting role if they could understand, translate, and apply this in-house experience to industrial-relations problems in other industries they report on.

As readers and viewers become more educated the job of the media can again concentrate on selected current events. In the meantime both labor and management representatives must be creative and cooperative in describing their squabbles to the media. If they preface their remarks by an analogy to a somewhat more familiar situation outside the industrial-relations field where disputes arise, such as marriage, then possibly this may give the uninitiated reporter a better feel for the overall situation, of which he is reporting only a part.

COMPULSORY UNIONISM AND THE MEDIA

M. STANTON EVANS

While libertarians strive to keep the media free of coercive interference, they have failed to recognize that compulsory unionism in media industries represents just such a threat, according to M. Stanton Evans. Mr. Evans, a syndicated columnist for the Los Angeles Times *and CBS Spectrum Series radio commentator, fought with William F. Buckley and against the American Federation of Television and Radio Artists (AFTRA) over this issue before the federal courts and the National Labor Relations Board. Unions, he maintains, can control the supply of newsprint, presses, ink, transportation facilities, and inhibit the process of gathering and reporting news.*

"If you want to work in the broadcast field," he says, "you have to come to terms with AFTRA."

Evans is chairman of the American Conservative Union and winner of four Freedoms Foundation George Washington medals. His books include The Liberal Establishment, The Future of Conservatives, *and* Clear and Present Danger.

In recent years there has been considerable agitation about the need to keep the American media exempt from any sort of coercive interference. Most of this discussion has focused on freedom-of-information cases, shield laws permitting the media to protect their confidential sources, and conflicts between the journalistic and legal professions on matters of pretrial publicity. From the standpoint of the working journalist, the common theme in all of these discussions is the idea that members of the press must be exempt from any form of constraint in the conduct of their duties, a theme with which I am in general and hearty agreement.

I would contend, however, that there is today an even greater problem looming before American journalists which also requires its share of attention, a problem far more serious than the question of whether I can lay my hands on a particular document, get into a courtroom, or protect my sources. The problem is that of compulsory unionism in the media, a practice long enforced in radio and television and now becoming fairly common in print communications as well. The difficulties latent in this practice are many; yet the subject has received only cursory attention in journalistic circles.

The reason that compulsory unionism poses so serious a danger to freedom of the press should be obvious on a moment's reflection: by saddling journalists with coercive obligations that can run directly counter to the ethical precepts of the profession, compulsory unionism can strangle journalistic freedom at its source. It cannot only inhibit the process of gathering and reporting the news, it can shut down that process altogether, and on numerous occasions it has done so.

Consider in this respect the sad experience of the *Washington Post*. For a span of five tempestuous years this influential newspaper was locked in combat with one of the world's most powerful politicians, the president of the United States. When the smoke had cleared, for better or worse, the *Post* emerged triumphant from this battle. It had led the charge on Watergate, as on so many other issues, and got the goods on its antagonist. It was an impressive display of media muscle, against which a supposedly power-conscious president was finally impotent. The lesson was a sweet one for many who claim to cherish the liberties of the press.

Yet strangely enough the very people who took the most alarm at President Nixon's rhetorical battles with the *Post* looked on with seeming equanimity as this important paper, a few months later, was torpedoed out of business. What the president of the United States with all his clout could never dream of doing was done with laughable ease by a striking labor union. Thanks to a walkout by its pressmen and vandalism to its presses, the *Post* was actually shut down for a day, unable to put a single edition on the streets. And for a considerable period after this shutdown it had to print its product on remote, inadequate presses, appearing as a meager shadow of its former self.

All of this, except for the destruction of the presses, was seen as perfectly normal—the usual drill of a labor-union strike. And surely this is an anomaly. It excites a tremendous outcry if a government bureau withholds some item from the press, or if a reporter's sources are demanded, or if any kind of prior restraint on publication is attempted, as in the Pentagon Papers case. But labor unions can blow a newspaper galley west, and the oracles of received opinion seem to think nothing of it.

It is worth recalling in this respect that the closest we have ever come to having a mass shutdown of newspapers in this country occurred in the fall and winter of 1973–74, when there was a serious shortage of newsprint because of a labor-union strike in Canada. As a result of this strike the size of newspapers in the Middle West was drastically reduced, which meant that numerous columns, features, and letters to the editor could not appear. Had the strike gone on much longer, and the supply of newsprint continued to dwindle, a number of newspapers might have gone out of business altogether.

Such examples might be multiplied at length. Coercive labor-union practices have taken a toll of many newspapers in recent years, delaying automation in many cases and imposing enormous economic costs through strikes in others. It is likely more American newspapers have been shut down by strikes than by any other single cause. In the decade of the Sixties alone, New York City lost four daily newspapers (the *Mirror*, the *Herald-Tribune*, the *World Telegram*, and *Journal American*), principally as a result of labor-union troubles.

The lesson of these episodes should be fairly obvious. Anyone who can control the supply of newsprint can also, if he wills, control the press. The same applies to anyone who can control access to presses, ink, transportation facilities, or the work force that puts a newspaper out. Control any one of these things—much less the whole shebang—and you have in your hands the power to control America's newspapers. The spread of compulsory unionism in the media is placing just such power in the hands of those who manipulate the coercive levers of the union movement.

UNIONISM: QUIETLY STRENGTHENING ITS GRIP ON THE MEDIA

Why is it that people who are so alert to any hint of coercion from other sources seem so oblivious of problems stemming from the power of unions? The answer, I think, is chiefly ideological. Professional journalists by and large are fairly liberal in outlook, which means not only that they have a general sympathy for the union movement, but also that they are not especially concerned about the dangers to civil liberties posed by economic controls. The normative view among liberal spokesmen is that economic liberties and political ones exist in watertight compartments, and that we may heap controls on our business system while simultaneously keeping our First Amendment liberties intact.

This exercise is impossible on the face of it, for a couple of very obvious reasons. In the first place, every newspaper, magazine, radio and TV station in America, whatever else might be said of it, is a business, at least to the extent of having to take in more money than it is paying out. And to the extent that the business system is swaddled in coercions, whether proceeding from unions or directly from the government, all these media are going to be affected. In addition, all these outlets rely on material instruments to get their product before the public—presses, cameras, transmitters, and the like. A system of coercion that can control these economic elements can in turn control the media.

The irony of the situation is deepened by the fact that compulsory unionism has been increasing its grip on the media, precisely as the fervor for augmented freedom of the press is at its height. The practice already has a total grip on major outlets of electronic communication, and it is expanding in the world of print as well. The mechanical side of most major newspapers has long since been unionized, though it is possible, as the *Post* has shown, to keep things going if the reporters and the editors show up. But the influence of the Newspaper Guild is spreading, and as it does the possibility of walkouts and overt coercion in the newsroom also increases.

A foretaste of compulsory unionism at this level is provided by the National Union of Journalists in Great Britain. There the union has demanded that editors as well as reporters be required to join and has been adamant in its desire for total say-so over editorial hiring. To make its point a couple of years ago, the NUJ called a total boycott against British papers using articles by nonunion staffers or freelancers.

"I think there is a serious danger here," said Alistair Hetherington, editor of the *Manchester Guardian.* "There are a number of people who would like to see the whole of the editorial operation brought under control. It is a fairly short step from there to a situation in which the whole policies of the paper are brought under staff direction."

Since that time the NUJ has flexed its muscles even more exuberantly and has taken to exercising powers of censorship over the British press. British journalist John Fullerton observes: "In 1974 the union expelled the editor of the *Cambridge Evening News* for trying to bring out a paper while his colleagues were on strike. . . . More recently, journalists at Barnsworth tried to get other trade unionists and local authority workers in the area to refuse to give information to colleagues who had refused to join the NUJ."

It can't happen here? Consider the case of the *Detroit News,* which has already faced demands quite similar to those advanced in England. In negotiations with the *News,* the Newspaper Guild insisted that the paper stop using material by writers who were not card-carrying union members. The management of the *News,* we are informed, "refused to shut out free-lancing, but told the union it will not increase its use of it." It may be expected that, as the influence of the Guild increases, so will requests for such control of editorial employment.

This is of course the condition now prevailing in the broadcast field, where one must go through the American Federation of Television and Radio Artists to report or comment on the networks or in the major markets. The AFTRA situation is one with which I am tolerably familiar, since I have been a compulsory member of the

union and have fought a case through the federal courts and before
the National Labor Relations Board to argue against the union-shop
requirement for journalists.

My situation with AFTRA, I suppose, is fairly typical for people
who work in the broadcast business or, for that matter, in any industry where compulsory unionism prevails. In the latter part of 1970 I
was approached by representatives of CBS radio who were putting
together a commentary series called "Spectrum." The idea was to
have a balanced format, including conservative as well as liberal
commentators, and I was to be one of the conservatives. The network
made me a financial offer, I accepted it, and for all I knew we were
ready to go.

At that point, however, I was informed by CBS that if I wanted to
go through with the deal I would have to become a member of
AFTRA, a stipulation made necessary by the AFTRA bargaining a-
greement with CBS. In this document (the standard AFTRA contract)
CBS had promised that "during the term of this agreement, we will
employ and maintain in our employment only such persons covered
by this agreement as are members of the American Federation of
Television and Radio Artists in good standing or as shall make application for membership on the thirtieth day following the beginning of
employment . . . and thereafter maintain such membership in good
standing as a condition of employment."

If I wanted the job, I really had no choice in the matter, and so I
joined up. I thus became a coerced member of AFTRA, had to tender
it my dues, and, according to its own constitutive literature, had to
submit myself to its discipline and regulations. If AFTRA had gone
out on strike against CBS, as it nearly did in 1972, I would have been
obliged to honor that strike and stop broadcasting, or else put myself
in serious jeopardy of disciplinary action from the union. How serious
that jeopardy can be may be seen from the relevant provisions of the
AFTRA constitution, which read as follows:

> Any member who shall be guilty of an act, omission, or conduct, which in
> the opinion of the [union's] board is prejudicial to the welfare of the as-
> sociation, or any of its locals, or any of its members, as such, or any
> member who shall fail to observe any requirements of the [union's] con-
> stitution, or of any by-laws, rules, regulations or others lawfully issued by
> the association, any local or any duly authorized committee or agent of
> said association or local . . . may, in the discretion of the board, be either
> fined, censured, suspended or expelled from membership. The board may
> discipline a member for each and every offense or violation. . . .

These powers of discipline, it may readily be seen, are very broad,
up to and including expulsion. And if I were expelled, according to
AFTRA's agreement with CBS, I could no longer work for CBS. Nor is

there any escape to other networks. AFTRA has the same agreement with NBC and ABC, and with most of the TV and radio stations in most of the major markets around the country. If you want to work in a substantial way in the broadcast field, you have to come to terms with AFTRA.

Quite apart from the threshold compulsion involved in this arrangement, it seems to me that some rather serious questions of press freedom (and objectivity) are raised by it. To begin with, AFTRA and the national AFL-CIO are using some portion of my dues money to promote ideological and political causes with which I happen to disagree—supporting, for example, the activities of César Chavez and the boycott against Farah Mills, getting involved in political contests (including endorsement of candidates), and so on. These are problems, of course, with compulsory unionism in any line of work, but they are especially sticky in the case of media work.

Here, for example, is an item from the winter 1974 issue of the AFTRA magazine:

> National Secretary Bud Wolff has offered AFTRA's help to the United Farmworkers Union. Noting that the United Farmworkers Union has opened a national public service advertising drive, Mr. Wolff wrote to union director César Chavez requesting "approximately 2,000 of the brochures containing transcripts of your public service radio and TV spots." Mr. Wolff has distributed this literature to all AFTRA locals advising them of the legitimate news value of the farmworkers' strike and suggesting the information be brought to the attention of members active in the news area. All AFTRANs are strongly urged to support the farmworkers' boycott and not to buy table grapes or lettuce.

As I say, I resent the fact that some portion of my dues money goes to support this kind of thing, but the larger question is otherwise: What are the implications when union members in "news areas" receive a notification from their union leaders of the "legitimate news value" of one particular faction in a dispute and are simultaneously urged by those self-same union leaders to support this faction by taking some particular action in the political or economic marketplace? What kind of news reporting can this mixture of functions and motives be expected to produce?

Even more to the point, however, is the cutting edge of coercion which the union can bring to bear to prevent broadcasters from going on the air, most notably through the strike but also, as I have indicated, through its plenipotentiary powers of "discipline." In 1967, for example, AFTRA did call a strike against the networks which resulted in the news being delivered, in generally inadequate fashion, by broadcast executives rather than professional newsmen. Certain newsmen, however, decided to broadcast anyway, with some very enlightening consequences. The *Monthly Labor Review* of the Bureau of Labor Statistics recalls the matter in a summary of a relevant court decision:

> To demonstrate the deterrent power of the union's mood in dealing with the violators of its rules, the court recalled the aftermath of AFTRA's own strike in 1967, when heavy fines were imposed on those who had crossed picket lines, including a total of $48,000 levied on only five "newest" members. A major issue in that strike was, precisely, the question of union membership for commentators and analysts. The court pointed to the attitude of those professionals as exemplified by the opposition of Chester [Chet] Huntley, a prominent commentator, who refused to go along with the union and continued his broadcasts during the strike. . . .
>
> Chet Huntley was not disciplined, as a result of a *quid pro quo* agreement between the union and the employers, but the union later regretted this precedent of exclusion: "It was a mistake not to have disciplined Mr. Huntley when he failed to honor AFTRA's picket line . . . . It may have been the biggest mistake that AFTRA ever made. . . . It should never have happened." [Poststrike statement by national president of AFTRA Mel Brandt.]

If AFTRA regretted not having "disciplined" a giant of the broadcast industry such as Chet Huntley and was determined not to make that "mistake" again, one may imagine its readiness to impose a similar discipline on a marginal figure such as myself. The more I contemplated the matter, the more it appeared to me that there were serious problems in this situation, above and beyond my personal opposition to compulsory union membership. This union could, if it called a strike, confront me with the grave decision of whether to continue with my broadcast activities, thereby incurring appropriate "discipline," or stopping my journalistic endeavor in violation of my own belief and conscience.

In 1972, as it happened, this possibility came very close to turning into a reality. A labor dispute had arisen between CBS and a technical union, and the AFTRA board decided to throw in its lot with the striking technicians. Whereupon AFTRA members in the Baltimore-Washington area received the following notification from their union:

> You and all AFTRA members are hereby ordered, pursuant to the resolution of the AFTRA National Board, to respect the picket lines of the International Brotherhood of Electrical Workers (IBEW) at CBS, or any other facility where programs or portions thereof are produced for broadcast over the facilities of CBS, and members are ordered to refrain from performing any broadcast or pre-broadcast service for CBS.
>
> This order is effective Tuesday, November 12, 1972, at 6:00 P.M. . . .
>
> You are advised that any member who violates an order of the AFTRA National Board may be found guilty of conduct unbecoming an AFTRA member and shall be subject to disciplinary action.

It will be noted that the words "order" and "ordered" appear in this brief statement four different times, a mode of address that is ordinarily not used toward free American journalists by publishers and editors, much less by coercive third parties who have assumed the power of saying who shall work, and when, and under what particular circumstances. This compulsory mode, however, is common in AFTRA statements, deployed with a fine disregard for such procedural niceties as freedom of information and the liberties of the press.

I have in my possession, for example, a more recent communique from the Washington-Baltimore local of AFTRA, addressed, not to AFTRA members, but to members of Congress. This memo informed the congressmen that AFTRA was involved in a strike against the Mutual Broadcasting System, which had had the audacity to continue operating with the help of nonunion employees. The AFTRA memo summed up the situation this way:

> Mutual has now hired non-union workers to gather radio reports from congressional hearings and news conferences. The presence of the strikebreakers has caused disruption in the hearing rooms which is likely to continue without an affirmative action by members of Congress.
>
> Your cooperation would be appreciated in reducing this disruption through exclusion of Mutual Radio strikebreakers from hearings and news conferences.
>
> The AFL-CIO, its affiliates, and the 30,000 members of AFTRA look forward to your support against this unfair employer.

In other words, because AFTRA had a dispute with Mutual, Congress was supposed to prevent Mutual from being able to cover public hearings and press conferences that all other media were entitled to attend!

Other examples in similar vein could be cited, but these are sufficient, I think, to make the point. It is clear enough that compulsory union membership introduces an element of coercion into the media that is hostile not only to the spirit of a free and unfettered press, but has on numerous occasions intruded on that freedom in very tangible fashion.

CONFRONTING THE UNION IN COURT

It was in obedience to such reflections that, in 1971, I filed a suit in federal court to challenge the power of AFTRA to embroil me in its coercions. In due course this action was consolidated with a similar case that had been brought against the union by William F. Buckley, Jr., and together our pleadings wended their way through the federal courts and finally arrived on the doorstep of the National Labor Relations Board.

I will not bore you with all the details of these proceedings, which are very complex, but will simply give a summary of the various outcomes. In federal district court, Buckley and I in essence won our case; the district judge determined that the requirement of compulsory membership was contrary to our First Amendment rights and exerted a "chilling" effect on our journalistic activities.

At the appellate level, however, the AFTRA lawyers, headed by the late Alexander Bickel, a great and very learned attorney, made a timely adjustment of their position. Under Bickel's strategy, AFTRA claimed that it did not really require that Buckley and I be "members," but only that we pay our dues. On this basis—and on the grounds that Buckley and I had failed to exhaust administrative remedies before the NLRB—the appellate court reversed.

When the Supreme Court refused certiorari, we were left with the NLRB alternative and took it. There again AFTRA argued that it did not require "membership," only payment of dues in simple recompense for the good things it had done for us. Accepting this distinction between membership and dues payment, the board declared that we did not have to maintain our memberships, but that we did have to pay over to AFTRA the dues that it required of us.

The statements of the NLRB in this decision were so astonishing that they deserve a bit of further discussion. What the board decreed, in essence, is that it is against the law, anywhere in the United States, to compel somebody to be a member of a union. Contrary to general belief, the board opined, a union can't force you to be a member to get employment where it has a contract. The most it can require of you is payment of dues. But full-fledged membership is absolutely out.

Here is the way the NLRB put the matter: "There is no dispute, and the law is absolutely clear, that a union, pursuant to a union-security clause validly authorized, can only require the payment of periodic dues and initiation fees after the statutory 30-day period and cannot, under any circumstances, require 'full-fledged membership,' or any other type of membership."

Moreover, according to the NLRB, an employer can't fire you for refusing to join a union. The board advises that "a termination of employment for reasons other than nonpayment of such dues and fees would be a violation of the [National Labor Relations] Act. Likewise, a refusal to employ an individual who refused to become a 'member' of . . . any . . . union would also be a violation of the act."

The curious thing, however, is this: though the NLRB informs us that there is no question about the illegality of compulsory membership, and even though the lawyers for AFTRA acknowledged as much, nobody seems to know this is the law. Indeed, it is common practice for workers throughout our economy to be told they "must join the union" as a condition of employment and for such requirements to be written into union contracts. So far as I know the recent utterance of the NLRB has done little to change this.

In its legal pleadings, AFTRA says that "in conformity with applicable law, [it] has stated publicly and repeatedly that the only 'membership' requirement it can impose upon petitioners as a condition of employment is payment of initiation fees and dues." Yet the standard AFTRA contract with broadcasters requires them to promise to "employ and maintain in our employment only such persons as are *members* of the American Federation of Television and Radio Artists . . . or as shall make application for *membership* . . . and thereafter maintain such *membership* in good standing as a condition of employment." (Italics added.)

Needless to remark, the word "membership" is not surrounded by quotation marks in this contract, nor does anybody tell you that all it really means is payment of dues, and that you aren't actually a "member." In other words, AFTRA has one line in the court or hearing room and quite another line out in the marketplace where jobs are sought and employment terms are actually agreed upon.

In the fall of 1975, for example, Bill Buckley asked the producers of his "Firing Line" show, RKO General, if he could drop out of AFTRA membership and still continue to broadcast. The answer was an emphatic "no."

"Unfortunately," the president of RKO told Buckley, "our own contract with AFTRA is perfectly clear in this respect; we may not broadcast anyone in 'covered employment' (which you are) unless he is a member of AFTRA 'in good standing.' AFTRA has always been very insistent on the enforcement of this provision."

All of which is standard operating procedure in the broadcast industry, well known to everyone. Thus, some months ago William A. Rusher executed a contract with NBC in New York to broadcast a series of commentaries and asked if he could avoid the requirement of union membership and still go on the air. He received the following answer from NBC:

> You will note that under the terms of paragraph 16 of this proposal you are obligated to become a member of AFTRA. I am aware of your feeling with respect to joining AFTRA, but I am afraid our labor agreement with AFTRA makes it impossible for us to accommodate you.
>
> Your employment with us falls under the terms of the current AFTRA Code of Fair Practice for New York Local Television Broadcasting; and pursuant to paragraph 84 of the agreement, you must apply for membership with AFTRA no later than the 30th day following the beginning of your employment. Should you elect not to comply with the foregoing, we will have no option except to discontinue your employment relationship with us.

So the chieftains of AFTRA are having their cake and eating it, too. Out in the job market where contracts are signed, members recruited, and dues money collected, employees are told they have to join up—with no ifs, ands, or buts. But in the rarefied atmosphere of court and hearing room, where few employees ever tread, the union concedes that compulsory unionism is legally verboten. And, on the basis of this concession, the NLRB dismisses the whole affair because "there is no justiciable issue."

YOU DON'T HAVE TO JOIN—JUST PAY YOUR DUES

It may be argued that, in financial terms, the shift from compulsory membership to compulsory dues is a distinction without a difference, and I think I have made it sufficiently clear that I object to having my dues money siphoned off by this coercive process. Nonetheless, the dividing line between dues and membership is significant in terms of discipline, going out on strike, suspension, and the like. If this is indeed the shape of the law, and the NLRB informs us it is, then obviously that fact should be made known to American workers—not just in the media but everywhere else—who are confronted daily by demands for compulsory membership. One wonders why it isn't.

In legal terms if not in practical ones, I would say that Buckley and I won roughly half our case, although the other half—the compulsory dues requirement—continues to rankle. The justification for this imposition is that the union goes in to the employer and "bargains" for us and other employees, and that we are therefore the beneficiaries of its exertions. If we didn't pay the dues, we would be "free riders" on the union, and simple justice requires us to pay up.

This line of argument, in my opinion, is an utter fraud. To begin with, there is the fact that AFTRA does not "bargain" for me and never has. The union was not involved in securing my employment and in fact has never done a blessed thing for me except send me its magazine along with periodic notices reminding me to pay my dues.

Even more to the fundamental point, however, the whole "free-rider" argument is entirely ersatz. The only reason that AFTRA claims to bargain for me—or that any union claims to bargain for all employees in an organized shop—is that the unions themselves insist on this arrangement. It is written in the National Labor Relations Law (Section 9(a)) and makes it compulsory that when a union has been certified, it shall be the "exclusive bargaining agent" for all employees in the affected unit. The actual wording of the law is as follows:

9(a) Representatives designated or selected for the purposes of collective bargaining by the majority of the employes in a unit appropriate for such purposes shall be the exclusive representatives of all the employes in such units for the purposes of collective bargaining in respect of pay, wages, hours of employment, or other conditions of employment. . . .

Now, if AFTRA is really so put upon by the necessity of bargaining for me and urgently needs my dues in compensation for its efforts, it has an easy remedy available. All it has to do is march up to Capitol Hill and ask the Congress to repeal 9(a), and let me and others like me bargain freely for ourselves. They would never do this in a million years, of course, since the "exclusive bargaining agent" privilege is in the law precisely at the insistence of the unions and forms the basis of their power.

Thus, the union compels me to accept its services as my bargaining agent, whether I want it as such or not, then forces me to pay it for the service I am coerced into accepting. First I am shanghaied, and then I am billed for transportation charges and an hourly wage for the people who have gone to all the trouble of shanghaiing me. On this analogy, the Symbionese Liberation Army should have dunned the Hearst estate for Patty's room and board.

It is this triggering action by Section 9(a) which sets in motion the whole compulsory union process and undercuts the union argument that compulsory membership (or dues) is strictly a voluntary arrangement between employers and employees. The imposition of the union as my bargaining agent is an act of government compulsion, which leads directly to the other compulsions I have detailed, so that the federal government, as well as the union, is implicated in the resulting denial of my First Amendment rights.

Compulsion, indeed, is the leitmotiv of all the matters I have discussed, and it is a problem that professional journalists, sooner or later, will have to face. Is the allegiance to freedom of the press routinely voiced by American journalists and otherwise defended from any hint of coercive intrusion, really the goal and object of our profession? Or will life-and-death power over the survival of the press be casually remanded to union organizers and officials? An answer must come soon, and if it is the latter it could sound the death knell of journalistic freedom in America.

LABOR: A STEPCHILD OF THE MEDIA*

TOM JOYCE

Because editors doubt the public's interest in labor news, and because reporters on the labor beat rarely have the education or experience, there is a tragic lack of good labor reporting. Tom Joyce, formerly chief labor correspondent for Newsweek's Washington bureau, maintains that this situation has these detrimental consequences: failure to report on "unorganized" labor; misunderstandings of the accomplishments of organized labor, its political role and power, and the contributions of the labor movement to economic problems; and a lack of awareness that the problems of today's workers are social rather than economic. Reporting on labor/management problems since the 1950s, Joyce was a Harvard Nieman Fellow specializing in labor economics.

In America today there is a work force of nearly 100 million people. By any reckoning this is a sizeable number. Consequently, one would expect that the media of this nation—probably the biggest news-gathering operation on the face of the earth—would devote considerable attention to covering developments in the labor field.

Unfortunately, this is not the case. Labor is in many ways, as the title of this paper suggests, the stepchild of the media. Indeed there is a good deal of coverage of organized labor in America today. But it more often than not deals with scandal, corruption, and confrontation. It does not deal, generally speaking, with issues behind breaking news.

A rather poignant example involves the disappearance of former Teamsters president James R. Hoffa just a couple of years ago. Hoffa's disappearance and apparent murder was reported widely and deeply. Virtually every paper in the country carried the story for days on page one. It was also a nightly event for television viewers. But very few of the stories dealt with what is happening inside the giant Teamsters

---

* At the time this paper was undertaken the author was chief labor correspondent for *Newsweek* magazine. Since that time he has become assistant director of the Council on Wage and Price Stability in the executive office of the president. The views expressed are those of the author and should not be read as an endorsement by the Council.

294

union. The stories did suggest that there is as much corruption there as ever despite twenty years of investigation. But they did not probe very deeply into conditions inside the union, such as the various political forces at work and for what purposes. And in most cases the stories failed to give the readers and viewers a very accurate description of how the union that Jimmy Hoffa once ran to his own advantage works today.

Typically the media are interested in surface labor developments like strikes, collective bargaining, and battles between organized labor and government. Typically, as well, the focus in covering labor today is on the big labor unions. There is precious little about unorganized workers and workers in low-paying jobs. One good reason for this is that there are few articulate spokesmen for these workers, unlike those who speak for workers in the UAW, the United Steelworkers, or any of those large unions that are members of the American Federation of Labor and Congress of Industrial Organizations.

IS LABOR REPORTING LACKING?

The paucity of good labor reporting in America today is tragic. The impact of working people on legislation, government decisions, wage negotiations, and all sorts of community activities is enormous. Why then is labor reporting so skimpy?

There are, to be sure, a myriad of reasons. One is that editors, probably more than the reporters covering the labor beat, do not think that labor news has very wide readership or is a very sexy subject. Certainly, on the surface, it might seem that labor news other than strikes and spectacular developments is of very little interest to the public. But don't the media have a duty to educate and not simply give the readers what it thinks they want?

When collective bargaining is coming up in a major industry, like steel, aluminum, coal, automobiles, or communications, there is a lot of attention. The media talk about the possibility of a strike. They discuss how big the demands are going to be. But, in all honesty, they deal pretty much with these matters on a surface basis. In most instances the media fail to get behind the story to tell the readers what really is happening in an industry or a union.

To be more specific, what did the media really tell the readers last time around in steel negotiations? Did the media explain that the steel industry is in a very delicate profitability situation? Did the press and television explain that it would be very difficult, given foreign competition, for the steel industry to grant large wage and fringe benefits without increasing steel prices? I don't think they did, at least not in a detailed way. Nor did the media explain to readers and viewers the background of wage and benefit increases over the past few years granted to steelworkers in several rounds of negotiations. It can hardly be denied today that the steelworkers are the elite of industrial workers. This is not to say that the United Steelworkers Union was wrong in going for the best possible settlement it could get. It is the job of a union leader to do the best he can at the bargaining table. This, perhaps, is a little beside the point. What is to the point is that very few publications, as the industry and the union got geared up for negotiations, bothered to inform readers about the background of the industry, what has been happening, and what the likely effect of a big settlement would be on the total economy.

What I am suggesting is that when the media get involved in labor reporting, homework is often either not done, or not done well. Audiences are not prepared for coming events. A good example of how the media operate is the manner in which they cover the AFL-CIO in the absence of a crisis.

Every February the AFL-CIO Executive Council goes to Bal Harbor, Florida, for its midwinter meeting. At these sessions many, many important decisions are made on a whole range of subjects: how the AFL-CIO will operate in the political arena; the way it will attempt to influence economic legislation; and in general, the way it will pursue its goals. Even though there are hundreds of big news organizations in this country, only a relative handful of reporters attend these meetings. And with some exceptions, the coverage is quite cursory. While there is plenty of opportunity for reporters to meet privately with many top officials of organized labor to develop thoughtful background, too few take advantage of the situation. Again, there are exceptions. But for the most part the press is satisfied to accept AFL-CIO press releases and position papers and then not bother to read them very carefully.

GETTING THE REPORTERS INVOLVED IN THE LABOR SCENE

The real work of the labor reporter should not be done at press conferences or in crisis situations. Obviously, a crisis situation demands coverage. A major strike, such as one in a major industry that threatens to have a serious effect on the entire economy, cannot be ignored. Neither can stories where there is serious violence or blatant corruption. This is not what I'm talking about. What I am saying is that there ought to be more reading, interviewing, and just plain old-fashioned bull sessions with labor leaders, labor economists, and industrial sources when there are no crises. This is the way that background is built—background that will allow labor reporters to write clear, meaningful, interpretive stories when they break.

One problem is that labor leaders frequently are reluctant to talk to labor reporters. Some of this is just old-fashioned suspicion. Some is because labor leaders and their assistants have been burned by the press in the past through sloppy reporting. And some is because there are constantly new faces on the labor beat. The media have a tendency to shift reporters from one beat to another much too frequently, not giving people the time to develop knowledge, insight, and contacts they need for good substantive reporting.

One who has given considerable thought to the way the media handle labor news is John Dunlop, Harvard University professor of economics and former secretary of labor, who has a deep background in labor matters.

Here are some of his thoughts on the subject:[1]

"What is the responsibility of a paper to go behind what has been headlined to the more underlying substance?

"There seems to be a feeling that people only want the headlines about strikes and things like this and do not want to hear any more.

"I think there is a big question of what kind of training people get before they undertake jobs in reporting about labor and labor/ management problems. There is certain training just to be a reporter, obviously. But I am not prepared to agree that the media can transfer people from City Hall to covering labor and economics, and that they can do it well.

"If the media took the matter of covering labor and management seriously, I think there should be some training for people paying attention to this area. There should be time to do some reading and thinking to fit new assignments with longer-range views. The media have been deficient in this area.

"There certainly ought to be some kind of arrangement for writers and reporters moving into the labor area to have a chance to learn the job. Without this there is a tendency for them to take their frustrations out on the parties.

"There is no question that this is a specialized kind of reporting. It is a vital kind of reporting as well.

"There is something else. It is important to deal with problems outside of crisis situations. If we deal with these problems only when they are at fever pitch, they cannot be handled well. At that time parties don't want to speak. It is inherent that to deal with these problems only during crises is to deal with them poorly.

"There could be a lot of good informative stories. For instance, a crisis situation could be used only as a peg to get into more substantive areas as a way of informing the public. There has not been a good story, for instance, on the iron-ore strike. This would be a good time to teach people about the fundamentals of labor relations in the iron-ore industry. This is what I mean by using a peg. That kind of story could analyze the underlying issues and tell readers a lot about incentives in the steel industry.

"The media constitute one of the very few 'artistic' areas where there are no regular critics to appraise the quality of work and the way it's being done. The drama people have critics. Professors have critics. There is something to putting people on their merits. In the media this is not being done, and people are suffering from it."

In discussing with Dunlop why he feels good reporting of labor relations is vital, he responded this way:

"It affects the political climate. Take for instance the Labor Reform bill. A lot of views here are no doubt related to how ignorant the public is about the work place. It is catastrophic that in a highly industrialized society the public knows so little about what happens in the work place."

A good number of papers pay almost no attention to developments within the labor movement or in labor/management situations. For several years now in Washington, where much labor news is generated, the *New York Times* has had only an on-again, off-again labor correspondent. For the nation's number-one newspaper of record this indeed is difficult to understand. Certainly on the national scene, in a thoughtful editorial way, Abe Raskin, my former colleague, does a very good job. But Abe is not a labor reporter. He is an editorial interpreter of labor events, a noble and necessary position. But at the same time, the *New York Times* needs and the readers of that publication need good, thorough reporting of labor developments in the nation's capital and elsewhere.

The *New York Times* is not alone. Only recently has the *Washington Post* seen fit to add a full-time labor reporter (incidentally, a very good one in Helen Dewar). For a long time the *Washington Post*, which is regarded by many as the nation's second major newspaper, had no one assigned full-time to the labor beat. This, in an editorial sense, is unconscionable. The fact is that only a handful of newspapers in this country today do have full-time labor specialists or for that matter people even covering the labor beat on a semi-regular basis. All newspapers of any size, papers in medium-sized to large American cities, should at least have people who are interested in labor, who keep abreast of developments in the labor movement, and maintain contacts with labor sources.

Journalism schools should be devoting more attention to training people on how to report labor news. Like the media itself, journalism schools generally ignore or just slide over labor news. The emphasis is on local reporting, reporting at the state-house level and reporting of national events. There can be little doubt today that most of the attention is aimed at the national level. Most young journalists aspire to go to Washington. There is glamour in covering the White House.

There is glamour in covering Capitol Hill. There is glamour in covering national politics. But sadly, it is perceived that there is precious little glamour in covering the labor beat.

This is not as it should be. The labor beat is tremendously important and interesting. What labor leaders and working people do affect the lives of virtually all Americans.

LABOR'S PUBLIC IMAGE

I don't think it can be denied that generally labor leaders in this nation today are viewed as the bad guys who drive up prices, who call strikes and disrupt the economic machinery. This is not a very complete or accurate picture of what labor leadership or the labor movement is all about. A point that should be made and is not made often enough is that what labor unions have accomplished in this decade have not been the major factor in price increases. Nevertheless, this is often the impression left in the public mind. It should be the role of the media to correct this impression. Certainly, when workers in major industries get big wage gains and benefits, prices are affected. Union settlements do raise prices. But on the whole, wage increases in recent years have not been out of line. Other factors have weighed much more heavily in inflationary pressures.

One of the major problems is that the Chamber of Commerce and other organizations who represent a particular constituency probably devote more words to what is happening in labor today than all the nation's newspapers put together.

It cannot be denied that labor is a strong political force with a lot of influence in the White House and Congress and state legislatures. For this reason alone, because of labor's clout, it deserves a lot more attention than it has been getting.

At the same time, very little is written on some of the deeper issues that involve labor. Productivity is an excellent example. To be sure, the better publications like the *New York Times* and magazines like *Business Week* and many others do report these subjects. But it is the exception and not the rule. And the audience simply is not large enough. Productivity is the sine qua non of industrial growth. Without it we cannot expect very many gains. Yet not very much attention is being paid to this subject. Oh, there are stories from time to time saying that the productivity rate did this or did that according to the Bureau of Labor Statistics. And there are scattered stories suggesting that we must do better, or that there are commissions being set up to do this and study that about productivity. But very rarely are there stories written about the root causes of low productivity. And often the impression is left out that it's the worker who is to blame. How much is written, for example, about how obsolete plants in many industries are responsible for low productivity, or that many industries because of strained capital positions cannot get adequate financing to modernize their plants?

One union that is growing by leaps and bounds and having a very deep impact on our society, especially at the state and local levels, is the American Federation of State, County, and Municipal Employees run by Jerry Wurff. But how much interpretative material is being written about that union and its goals and objectives? Certainly, we read about AFSCME when there is a garbage strike in Memphis, a police strike someplace else, or a walkout of municipal workers that disrupts local government. But what we aren't reading is what the long-range objectives of this union are, or what the long-range consequences are likely to be. Or, if you will, are we reading about the social consequences and social implications? How much discussion have we seen in the press about whether indeed a garbage worker should be earning as much as a school teacher? We have seen editorials to the contrary. But nobody, or at least very few publications are really taking the issue apart as a social problem. I am not making a recommendation one way or the other. But I do think that the question about the annual earnings of low-paid municipal workers in unattractive jobs is a legitimate subject for the media, and one where the public has a right, or indeed a need, to know more.

What I am suggesting is that Wurff's union will affect a great many American families. Let me quote from a book called *The Unions* by Haynes Johnson and Nick Kotz.

The AFSCME is capitalizing on the huge growth in public employment—an increase from 6 million to 13 million workers in 20 years—and on the general and long-time neglect of many state and local employees.

During a period when the salaries and benefits of unionized workers in the private sector rose steadily, hundreds of thousands of blue-collar employees continued to work for less than minimum wage. These hospital workers, garbage collectors, and sanitation workers were often not covered by such other basic benefits as unemployment compensation or workman's compensation, much less health care or pension benefits. Most important, public employees are not covered by the Wagner Labor Relations Act, which means that a public employer does not have to recognize or bargain with the union even though the entire work force belongs to the union.

"We've got no laws," says Wurff. "Everything is against us. We pull a strike and they take away our paychecks and send our leaders to jail, penalize our members."

Nevertheless, Wurff's union has used the strike—which is illegal for virtually all public employees—as a weapon to force a community to meet the issues being raised. Strikes or work stoppages by public employees increased from 36 in 1960 to 410 in 1970.[2]

The point is that Jerry Wurff and his associates are determined and militant. I say this in no derogatory way, because Mr. Wurff is dedicated to the welfare of the members of AFSCME. What I am saying is that the American people will be hearing a lot more about this union in the future as it continues to press for better working conditions and higher wages for state, county, and municipal employees. This is something that should not be overlooked by the media. Yet it is. The people have a right to know that this union has very ambitious goals, that it plans to move forward vigorously and strongly. The public as well has a right to know what these goals and ambitions are and what is likely to happen. And the only place the public is going to find out is through the media. And I submit that the media are not doing a very creditable job in this area.

Wurff is not happy with the quality of labor reporting today. While his reasons might be personal, they are nevertheless valid.

"I have broken in five reporters for the *New York Times* and two for the *Washington Post*," he groused. "And once they get broken in they are switched to something else. The problem is that the media sends generalists to cover labor stories when it should be sending experts. If you can believe it, I talked to one fellow from a national news magazine who did not know the difference between arbitration and mediation. The quality of labor reporting in this country is just plain lousy."[3]

I feel very strongly that ways simply must be found to encourage better labor reporting. This means developing more interest in labor news. It means encouraging young journalists to get interested in the field. It means getting editors interested as well. While the AFL-CIO is one of the best organized, most efficient labor organizations that this nation has ever seen, I am not at all sure that it is doing as much as it could be doing in developing more interest in covering labor news. Sometimes I think quite the contrary. The AFL-CIO is vitally interested in presenting its position through the media. But it may forget the fact that in order to do this there must be a better-trained cadre of labor reporters and editors and TV officials who are interested in the subject. I'm not at all certain how this can be accomplished. But I do think that with this great store of resources the AFL-CIO, which conducts all kinds of seminars and work-study programs for labor officials around the country, could be thinking more about how to develop more interest in labor reporting.

LABOR REPORTING: MORE THAN GOOD PRESS

Frequently the argument is made that less than 25 percent of the total work force is organized. What is forgotten in this argument is that what organized labor does has a tremendous impact on the unorganized. Even though there is a large differential between union members and their unorganized counterparts, the unorganized often gain from what develops among the organized. At the same time the unorganized generally are very interested in what is happening to their organized brethren.

In the context of the unorganized worker today we are hearing more and more about the minimum wage and efforts to increase it. The minimum wage is a major political issue, and there are strong voices on both sides. Yet the media, I think, have done a very cursory job in examining the issue and its implications. The media simply have not taken it apart and examined carefully the pros and cons. As a result the people remain confused—bombarded by the Chamber of Commerce and similar business-oriented groups on one side and labor on the other. What is left not understood is the fact that minimum wage is not merely an economic issue. It is a broad social issue, and it should be treated as such. Yet we hear about the minimum wage only in the economic framework.

The same thing may be said about proposed labor-reform legislation. Despite its deep importance the media generally have given the matter superficial attention. As it is presented in the media labor's efforts to reform labor laws amount to nothing more than a means of facilitating organization efforts. To a degree, this *is* a motive. But what is ignored is the fact that many workers who want to be organized today, workers who have voted to be represented by a union, are being frustrated by dilatory tactics that are allowed under present legislation. In most cases labor reporters writing about this controversial and very important subject simply give it broad-brush treatment. They're not writing about individual cases. The public is not being told about specifics; about how workers are repeatedly denied their legal right to organize because of antiquated, cumbersome machinery.

It might be interpreted that I am suggesting that labor needs more "good press." I do not mean this at all. Rather, I am saying that labor needs better coverage. I strongly believe this because I think it is essential that people in our society know more about what is happening in the field of labor and labor relations.

There can be little doubt, as noted earlier, that labor leaders frequently are chary about talking to members of the media. This is very understandable. There has indeed been too much slipshod and uninformed reporting.

In the late 1950s the AFL-CIO was meeting in Puerto Rico. At that time a reporter for a Detroit paper picked up what was nothing but pure rumor that Walter Reuther of the UAW planned to demand of GM that its contract be reopened. There was not a grain of truth in it, but the story nevertheless received top play in the Detroit paper. This is but one example of many that I could recite. The point I am trying to make is that a lot of this feeling of suspicion could be overcome by publications putting good people on the labor beat. It boils down to the media having familiar people who can be trusted and are informed.

Labor clearly has a right to be suspicious. More often than not the media have been interested in the sensational aspects of covering the labor beat. But not in the philosophical, long-range problems. The battle of the overpass at the Ford Rouge plant in 1937 is a typical example. At that time the UAW was attempting to organize the recalcitrant Ford Motor Company with little success. Frustrations bubbled over into an historic labor/management battle that attracted newsmen from all over the country. In 1936 there were the famous sit-downs in Flint, Michigan, that spread all over the country. These too were covered with great enthusiasm. There is no doubt that this was real news. It deserved coverage as did John L. Lewis's colorful confrontation with FDR in the 1930s, and many, many other dramatic incidents. But the media also have an obligation to report developments in the labor movement that are not necessarily dramatic. The fact is, however, the media certainly have not been as interested in writing thoughtful stories about the philosophy of organized labor and conditions of the work place as it has in writing about the spectacular events. The sociology of the labor beat has been left up to the scholars and historians.

With so much labor reporting concentrating on sensational events, it is not surprising that the public feels "the unions help cause unnecessary strikes, that corruption is widespread and that union leaders are more unreliable, self-interested and insensitive to the general welfare than other highly influential figures in the society."[4]

A companion, widely held view is that labor has become too powerful, both within industry and in Washington and in the nation's state houses. If labor has indeed become too powerful—and here I will make no judgment—then who is to blame? Is it possible that industry must take its share? It just might be that industry gives in too easily at the bargaining table, knowing that it can pass large wage increases along to the consumer. The notion has been developed that a strike must be avoided at virtually any cost. Might not it be better for the economy as a whole to have more strikes and perhaps a deceleration of wage increases? I am not advocating this. But some leading economists have. Yet in the press there has been almost no discussion of this idea.

It seems the media simply are not interested in dealing with discussions about how labor and management might work toward a better system of settling disputes or giving more consideration to the public interest.

There has been, of course, a good deal written about the experimental negotiating agreement between the big steel companies and the United Steelworkers of America under which unresolved issues are settled through voluntary arbitration. Since it has been working fairly well for a few years now, one would expect that the media would explore carefully what the implications are for other industries. But this has not been the case. Only superficial attention has been given to the idea, and usually not outside of stories dealing with the steel experiment.

COVERING LABOR MEANS COVERING STRIKES

Certainly, I have no exclusive rights to the notion that the media are falling down on their job of covering labor news. We have already heard from John Dunlop and Jerry Wurff, two quite disparate figures, on the topic.

One former labor writer with a much-deserved reputation for honesty, accuracy, and thoughtfulness feels the same way. He is Joe Loftus, former Washington labor correspondent for the *New York Times* and former assistant secretary for the Treasury. Let's hear what Loftus says.[5]

"The whole assignment has changed in my time. I don't think the media is covering labor and management the way it used to.

"I don't really know what covering labor really means anymore. I guess it means covering strikes, violence, corruption. Coverage is oriented this way. Certainly, politics comes into it, but only during certain periods. There is no reporting any longer of the philosophy of the labor movement or long-term goals. I suppose that most papers don't have the manpower, and editors wonder if such material is read and whether there is a readership demand.

"I can't remember a good story dealing with goals or ideology— long-range ideas—in a long time. Whatever is done in this field is done by professors or graduate students. Generally this is not seen by the public. Reporters are just not covering this kind of thing.

"It *is* important to cover the labor movement and labor/management relations on more than just a crisis basis. It is important for the readers to have a broad picture—a thinking kind of story so that they know what is motivating people. Maybe there is a feeling that no longer are there any long-range goals in the labor movement.

"It seems the rank and file motivates leaders more than they used to, but they are not given to thinking in terms of philosophy. They're limited more to catching up on wages and getting ahead of the Consumer Price Index and providing fringe benefits.

"I don't think they're [labor leaders] as concerned as they ought to be with the generation that is coming up. Neither the rank and file nor the labor leaders seem concerned about what happens in the next generation. Two examples are the auto workers and the miners.

"Speaking of the miners, this is a story that has really not been covered. Nobody is digging into it. Maybe today this is something that would be better left to a study by the Ford Foundation or an organization like this made up of people with a lot of experience. There is something going on in that union that is pretty dangerous. John L. Lewis set up the union that way. He didn't allow for any growth of leadership within the union. He didn't want to share power.

"It's important that stories like this be reported in depth with good analysis because thoughtful readers want to know everything important in our society.

"The television can't do it in an hour-long show. Nobody is really examining why miners are so restless. The pay is pretty good. There is loyalty to the union. But nobody is holding it together. But there is not any good explanation about why there is a lack of talent, and that goes right back to John L. Lewis.

"Except in coal and a few other areas from time to time, big strikes and labor violence have almost ceased. This could be one reason why labor is not getting the attention it deserves today from the media.

"There is also a problem in getting media people interested in covering what used to be called the labor beat. People want to work on Capitol Hill or in the White House. They want the glamour beats. They don't want to dig into unofficial channels of information. The *New York Times* recently has switched its labor correspondents several times. The *New York Times* is not covering labor on a full-time basis anymore. Now that the *New York Times* has abandoned its emphasis on spot news—or at least changed that policy—there is all the more reason to dig into present conditions in labor/management relations and what the future holds. Abe Raskin of the *New York Times* is doing this. But few others are."

There are, to be sure, some other views about why the media are not covering labor with much enthusiasm or in depth. Some of the fault, as was suggested earlier, might be inside organized labor itself. One who holds some very definite views on this is Sar Levitan, professor of sociology at George Washington University and a man who has observed the labor scene as a liberal intellectual for many years. He said:

"I would emphasize that labor has isolated itself. This is one reason why there isn't good reporting. There is no good contact between the intellectual community and labor. This means that there have not been good ideas generated, and therefore there is somewhat of a lack of interest in reporting the labor movement. Before World War II there was a good deal of ideology and discussion between academics and labor. This has about been wiped out. Labor has ignored the intellectuals recently and intellectuals have deserted labor.

"It is true that labor news today is not well analyzed, partly because communications, except when there is a strike, the revelation of corruption, or something like this, is badly lacking. There is very little clear and close analysis of issues involved outside of what might be considered sensational.

"I would not entirely put the blame on the media. We cannot expect a knowledgeable reporter to do basic research. If this is not done, the media have to fall down because they do not have the data. They have to rely on press releases, flamboyant moves.

"I would not entirely blame labor reporters. First of all, those of a few years ago—people like Abe Raskin and Joe Loftus—covered these things from a big reservoir of knowledge to count on. They had the help of the intellectuals who were then attracted to the labor movement. Today these intellectuals are not around.

"I would not put all the blame on the Fourth Estate, but on the principals themselves—both sides, labor and management.

"To define goals and analyze issues are the major points. Only the principals can do this, but they're torn asunder because they have no support any longer from the intellectual community.

"Most of us are workers in one form or another. We want to know what impact collective bargaining has on inflation, the work ethic, productivity in the plant, and a number of other things. This is why it is important for the people of this country to be informed about what is happening in labor/management negotiations. It is self-evident. It is important for the people to know whether pressures brought by organized labor are right or wrong. And this is a function of the media. But a function that is difficult to perform because of the things I have just said.

"It is just as important that the people understand what motivates labor's position and what the consequences of those positions might be. The trouble today is that labor leaders are caught up in institutional problems and do not have good, sound analytical advice. As a consequence, members of the media who report on labor developments do not have that kind of advice either. Why are there no longer intellectuals, or at least not as many, found in the labor movement? Society has moved in different directions. Many of the intellectuals have discovered that the money is in poverty and programs like that and went there instead of concentrating on collective bargaining. Intellectuals followed their self-interest, and labor did not make it attractive. Those who were the intellectuals in the labor movement left and were never replaced."[6]

THE EROSION OF THE WORK ETHIC

There is today a very definite change in attitudes toward work in America. A good many labor leaders will dispute this, but the evidence appears convincing. There is among many workers a feeling of frustration, a sense that the good life they see on the television is out of reach, that jobs are humdrum and repetitive, and that they're captives with no way out.

To this idea there is another part. This is that workers today do not have the attachment to their unions that they did in simpler times. The union hall used to be a center for social activity. This is no longer the case. The hard fact is that it is difficult to get union members to meetings today unless there is a burning issue. There are just too many other things to occupy their time. These changes are cited as another example of where the media are not doing their job.

The problems of workers today are social problems. Yet the media continue to treat them as economic problems—as often as not presenting stories filled with numbers and statistics and little or no social interpretation.

Once a month you will read or hear on TV the Labor Department's unemployment statistics. But how often do you see stories in newspapers or magazines or on TV about the plight of the unemployed? Who are they? Why can't they find work? In many respects these people are treated by the media as simply forgotten Americans.

All too often we hear simple explanations, such as that the composition of the work force is changing. This means, of course, that more women are at work than ever before. Then, so the argument goes, this increases the work force, and there just aren't enough jobs to go around. As a result the situation really isn't so bad because a lot of the unemployed are women, and if they were not counted among the unemployed the figures would not be so high.

This truly is a specious argument. The hard fact is that most women work for the same reasons men do—to earn a living. Twenty-three percent of the nearly 39 million women in the work force have never been married; 19 percent are widowed, divorced, or separated; 8.6 percent have husbands who earn under $5,000 a year; 6 percent have husbands who earn between $5,000 and $7,000; 11.4 percent have husbands who earn under $10,000 a year; and only 32 percent have husbands who earn over $10,000 a year.[7] It is obvious then that the notion that women are entering the work force in large numbers, displacing men, just to earn a little extra money holds no water. The point is raised here because it is yet another example of the media failing to cover the labor beat, which today is much expanded from what it was a few years ago. To be sure, some publications have delved deeply into the working-women phenomenon. But they are precious few.

In another area major changes are occurring today in organized labor. As was noted earlier, attitudes toward work are in a state of metamorphosis. Workers view their unions with less reverence. At the same time, a new breed of union leaders is emerging. They are in many cases younger, better educated, more articulate, and closer in terms of philosophy to the rank and file than some of the old-timers who are getting ready to step down. These are people like Murray Finley, president of the Amalgamated Clothing and Textile Workers of America, who, at fifty-three, looks more like a corporation official than a union leader. He's a lawyer and a deep thinker. Another is Glen Watts of the Communication Workers. The list is growing and is certain to mean changes in the way organized labor operates in the future. It would not be appropriate to go into the possibilities for change in this short paper. But these developments are tremendously important. And while there is plenty of material for good, solid, informative stories about what changes these new faces likely will bring to the labor movement, not very many stories are being written.

Why? Because labor to the media is an area to be covered, at least for the most part, only when there is conflict, violence, or scandal. To my way of thinking this is nothing short of tragic. It is not only shortchanging readers and viewers, it is creating a dangerous vacuum. The only way the public can form impressions of working people and their unions *is* through the media, and based on what the public is getting from the media today, those impressions simply cannot be very meaningful.

NOTES

1. From an interview with John Dunlop, August 26, 1977.

2. Haynes Johnson and Nick Kotz, *The Unions* (New York: Pocket Books, 1972).

3. From an interview with Jerry Wurff, August 29, 1977.

4. Derek C. Bok and John T. Dunlop, *Labor and the American Community* (New York: Simon and Schuster, 1970).

5. From an interview with Joseph Loftus in Washington, D.C., August 25, 1977.

6. From an interview with Sam Levitan in Washington, D.C., August 1977.

7. U.S. Department of Labor, Bureau of Labor Statistics, Washington, D.C.

INDEX